A Long View from the Left

Al Richmond

1973 BOSTON

A Long View from the Left

Memoirs of an American Revolutionary

HOUGHTON MIFFLIN COMPANY

FIRST PRINTING W

"Inishfallen, Fare Thee Well,"
copyright © 1949 by Sean O'Casey,
is reprinted with the permission
of The Macmillan Company.

For Genya and Nancy

Preface

INTERSPERSED AMONG THESE MEMOIRS are three essays. Given their nature, the memoirs themselves necessarily include political commentary and explication, but the essays are different. They deal with problems of American radicalism, not as they were encountered at any particular point of personal experience, but in a more comprehensive historical context.

This should forewarn the reader of the abrupt plunge from personal narrative into the essays that are Chapters II (The Generations), V (An Old Problem of American Radicalism), and VIII (Notes on Revolution and the 1930s). Indeed, the reader who is unduly put out by the break in the narrative thread may exercise the option of skipping these chapters and reverting to them later on.

But why run the risk of what may strike some readers as disconcerting intrusions? Because the essays are integral elements of the whole — and not only on the elementary premise that generalized reflections and observations are also autobiographical and that the interplay between what the narrator did and what he thinks helps to delineate what he is. More important, the essays are related to an underlying motivation for these memoirs — to make the American Communist experience comprehensible and credible to those not directly involved in it.

Anyone who ventures into autobiography, minus the fame or distinction that is the conventional credential for such an enterprise, is impelled perforce to justify it. To me an attempt to convey the Communist experience seemed important. To penetrate the inordinate obsession and mystification that shroud communism in the United States is reason enough. Beyond that the experience has intrinsic value and significance. I have tried to relate it, not as an exercise in historical research, but in personal, living, human terms. These memoirs are, therefore, intensely personal, but not purely so. They convey, I hope, what was thought, felt, and done by a vital segment of my generation — the most vital, in my opinion, because it was comprised of men and women purposefully committed to a revolutionary reconstruction of American society, to the attainment of a just, rational, human social order.

We were not the first so committed and, as attested by events and moods of the 1960s and '70s, certainly not the last. It seems to me, therefore, that we are better judged in the perspective of the long historical view than by prevalent American measures of shallow pragmatism. If, as I believe, the revolutionary impulse persists and will persist in American life, despite ebb and flow, despite recurrent celebrations of its demise, then the value and meaning of our experience can best be assayed only within this historical continuum. The abstraction — historical continuum — assumes tangible form in men and women who continue the quest and the struggle. Perhaps by better understanding what we did they will better understand what they must do. This is the hope and affirmation of these memoirs.

Among the people whose counsel, encouragement, and criticism were helpful in writing this book I am especially grateful to Dorothy Healey and Tom Van Dycke. For Nancy Richmond gratitude alone is not enough.

Contents

A Long View from the Left

I. Childhood and Revolution

BEFORE THE AGE OF NINE I had circumnavigated the globe and lived in England, the United States, Russia, and Poland. This childhood odyssey requires explanation, and here the simplicity of geography must yield to the complications of history, to war and revolution and related facets of this century's politics. My natal arrival in London, for a first instance, was the by-product of revolution; the later departure was conditioned by war.

My mother had been an active participant in the Russian revolution of 1905. She was then in her early twenties, still not rid of the innocence and parochialism of the Jewish Pale, still on the threshold of the vast universe beyond the ghetto village that was in struggling transition between the Middle Ages and the Enlightenment. She entered that universe through the narrow passage of Czarist prisons, serving six years in these after 1905, aging and maturing in them, discovering here the worldly knowledge and the range of human culture that were denied her in the *shtetl*. Upon completion of her prison term she was condemned to remain in Siberia, escaping this exile to London where her suitor (he had not been her lover) preceded her and now awaited her, having waited seven long years for their marriage and its consummation. So I was born November 17, 1913, in London Hospital in the East End, the locale being vaguely fixed in my mind by my mother's later references to such place names as Whitechapel, East India Road, Commercial Road. November is a bleak time of year in London, even in the more affluent West End where bleakness is an attribute of weather rather than an inexorable condition of life.

I was barely teething in our Bethnal Green home when the First World War began. At the end of May 1915 two other events coincided: I began to walk and the Germans began to fly over London. When a German zeppelin ushered in the era of aerial warfare, dropping the first bombs ever dropped from the sky upon a civilian population, my mother's formidable imagination leaped one war ahead of the times. In her mind's eye she envisioned the blitz that was to level the East End in World War II and concluded that London was not a fit place for an infant. Thereupon my father shipped out as a merchant seaman, running the German blockade on the hazardous transatlantic run, getting off on the U.S. side after several trips and sending us the money he had saved for our passage.

Less than two years after our arrival in the United States and only four months after my third birthday, revolution broke out in Russia. My mother's immediate response, a determination to return to her native land, precipitated a family crisis, for by then the great split in the world socialist movement had divided my parents. She wanted to complete the revolution; he wanted to finish off the Kaiser. His desire entailed no greater commitment at that moment than conscientious work in a munitions plant; he had done such work in Providence and Pittsburgh. Since the greater uncertainties and perils seemed to attend her ultimate destination it was agreed that I would remain in the United States with my father, but at the last moment my mother changed her mind. She wanted to have both the revolution and her child and she was a strong-willed woman. With the three-year-old child in tow she set out for the revolution.

The child in tow . . . it is a recurrent memory of early childhood. A robust and vigorous woman, when her mind was preoccupied she tended to walk faster and faster, as if to keep pace with her thoughts, forgetting the child, who soon was running to keep up with her, and then being startled out of her meditation by a plaintive cry, "My feet hurt . . . my feet hurt."

Freed of family my father decided to help win the war against the Kaiser as an active combatant. Rejected by the United States army because of age and infected tonsils he volunteered for the Canadian army, which was less choosy about age, and attended to his tonsils by having them cut out, a painful and troublesome operation for a man in his forties. This was the only blood he was to shed. By the time he was accepted into the Canadian army the October Revolution had rendered Russian citizens sufficiently suspect politically so that they were not shipped overseas into the war theater. He was having a run of bad luck. His courtship, thanks to the Czar's autocratic regime, had stretched out over seven long years; his active marriage had lasted less than five. And now his dreams of military combat in a righteous cause turned into the tedium of garrison duty in Canada.

His wife and son, meanwhile, had taken the long westward route to revolutionary Russia, traveling two thirds of the way around the globe, as more than five hundred Russian political exiles in the United States did that spring and summer of 1917. An invitation and passage money (estimated at $200 per head) from the Russian Provisional Government for return of the political exiles made the long trip possible. In the beginning the transpacific route was chosen to avoid the submarines that hunted in the Atlantic; in June and later there was another reason: transatlantic ship space was preempted for the armed forces of the United States. The first leg of their journey took mother and child across the United States by rail, from New York to San Francisco. There the homeward-bound revolutionaries were taken on a tour of the city, waving red flags from their automobiles and singing revolutionary songs. Their exuberance was unaffected by the character of their hosts, agents for the Southern Pacific Railroad, which had carried them across the continent, and of the Toyo Kisen Kaisha steamship line, which was to transport them across the Pacific. (Two decades later, when I settled permanently in San Francisco, my mother recalled that first visit and her enchantment with the city of tall hills and wide waters, whose Spanish name had a romantic, even exotic, ring to ears that had been attuned to the sounds of Yiddish and Russian. She insisted that even then, in 1917, she had a presentiment that she would return to this city, that it would occupy a significant place in her life.)

Sailing across the Pacific, the first stop was at Honolulu, and this chance port of call became the locale of my earliest memory, not as the remembrance of an event directly observed, but as a shadow upon a screen. A few years later I dreamed of bronzed bodies, glistening with water and sun, diving for coins in blue waters. The dream had a magical quality, so remote from the Russian winter in which it came, so unreal because in my conscious mind I had no recollection of any such scene. Pleasant dreams I sometimes confided to my mother (the unpleasant ones never) and so I learned that my dream was of Honolulu.

San Francisco, Honolulu, and then Yokohama, where the travelers to revolution were taken to Tokyo and visited the Diet. For my mother and, I suspect, for most of her companions it was the first view of a parliament in session. The parliamentarians did not impress me; I was fascinated by white mice in a cage at the hostel where we stayed. After Japan it was Vladivostok and the Trans-Siberian Railroad for the long journey that proved uneventful except for the occasional fires that lit up the horizon at night. The travelers assumed that the fuel for the flames were residences of the nobility and other big landowners. "The red cock is crowing," some said . . .

Little more than a quarter of a century later this trip to Russia cropped up in an odd interview. I was stationed at Fort Sam Houston, Texas, attending an army training school for surgical technicians. One day in June of 1943 I was summoned from a class and ordered to report to a numbered room at Brooke General Hospital. Reporting as ordered I found a captain from G-2 seated behind a desk in a small, barren room. After some preliminary questions to ascertain that I was indeed the man he was supposed to interrogate, the captain came to the point.

"I understand you have applied for citizenship."

"I have not only applied, I have gotten my citizenship."

Apparently two wheels of the military machine had moved at different and unsynchronized speeds. One wheel had been geared to a World War II law that aliens who were inducted into the military service could obtain their citizenship in ninety days. The other wheel — military intelligence — had moved more slowly, and here was the captain, assigned to investigate whether my politics made me unfit for the grant of citizenship,

*only to learn that he was too late. There was an awkward si-
lence while the captain fumbled with papers on the desk,
finally coming upon one that held his attention.*

"Ah, I see you have been to Russia."

"That's right."

"Were you politically active over there?"

*"I was there between the ages of four and eight. I didn't pull
any political weight, one way or the other."*

*This ended the interview except for some desultory ques-
tions, asked in a southwestern drawl, about the Communist
program in the 1930s for national self-determination for the
Negro people in the black belt. I have sometimes wondered
since what his reaction would have been if, in response to his
final question about Russia, I had said, "As a matter of fact,
Captain, I was a political prisoner while I was there . . ."*

We arrived in European Russia during the "July Days" when
the provisional government employed armed force against
workers' demonstrations in Petrograd and followed this with so
intense a campaign against the Bolsheviks that Lenin went into
hiding. Before the July Days Lenin entertained the possibility
of a peaceful development of the revolution; afterward he concluded that armed insurrection was the sole way forward.
Those days marked a turning point.

My mother (and I) did not go to Petrograd, the vital center
of the revolution, where history was being played out as if on a
stage and the turmoil in the rest of vast Russia supplied offstage
sounds and alarms, occasionally intruding into the spotlight in
the person of delegates reporting from the military fronts or
from the provinces. Instead of going to Petrograd we went to
Kalinkovichi and Mozyr, which you can find on a map if you
look carefully at the southeastern corner of White Russia just
above the Pripet Marshes where White Russia adjoins the
Ukraine to the south and Great Russia to the east. Kalinkovichi
(as I recall her phonetic usage she pronounced it Ka-lein-ko-
vich), my mother's birthplace, a tiny village of several hundred
souls, rated a place on the map because it was situated on a
railroad. Mozyr, seven versts away, perched on the banks of

the Pripet River with its industry and population of 25,000, was the big town of the region.

My mother spent her childhood in Kalinkovichi and early displayed a rare intelligence that her father showed off by having it put to the test by men of the village with arithmetical conundrums and riddles. When she solved some complicated mathematical riddle in her head, without the benefit of pencil or paper, he would exclaim, "Akh! She has the brain of a bookkeeper!" It was meant as a compliment. This male imagination of the ghetto village could conceive of no greater accolade for the mental faculties of a female child. She did not, however, become a bookkeeper; at age thirteen she went to work in a match factory in Mozyr.

The Jewish factory owner honored the Sabbath, but on the other six days of the week his workers worked as God had worked to create the heavens and earth before "he rested on the seventh day from all his work which he had made" and "blessed the seventh day, and sanctified it." For the new thirteen-year-old worker this strict construction of holy precedent meant that after sundown on Saturday she trudged the seven versts from Kalinkovichi to the factory in Mozyr, carrying with her the staple food ration for a week and such other incidentals as she might need before the setting of the sun and the lighting of the ritual candles on the following Friday ushered in another Sabbath. Between the Sabbath visits to her home she worked in the factory for twelve hours a day and slept in the factory barracks. Of the weekly food packet she later remembered with fondness only one item that was occasionally included: halvah, a confection of Turkish origin. In the sparse diet of the ghetto poor the energy-giving nutrition of this mixture of nuts and honey might have had as much to do with its popularity as its flavor or its texture.

Her initiation into wage labor also served as her introduction to ideas and movements that were beginning to stir the younger generation of the Pale at the end of the last century, principally Zionism and its newborn Marxist adversary, the Jewish Workers Alliance, commonly known as the Bund, both of which contested for the allegiance of workers in the factory. By her late teens she chose the Bund, which had held its founding national congress in 1897, the year she entered the factory (and the year before the abortive first congress of the Russian Social–Democratic Labor Party; thus the Bund had seniority, and the RSDLP, Lenin's party, hegemony in the revolution to come).

Yiddish was the language of the Bund and it was the only language she knew. Despite all the joys, nuances, and subtleties that have been discovered in Yiddish, it was not much of a language at the time for young revolutionaries eager to learn revolutionary theory and the social sciences. Hardly any of the written works in this realm were then available in Yiddish (for that matter, hardly any of the world's literature was). They did have the Erfurt Program of the German Social–Democratic Party in Yiddish. Probably they had it, not only because the German party was then regarded as the bellwether of world socialism, but also because the basic text of the Erfurt Program, a condensed statement of Marxist principles, contains only seven hundred words and hence presented a far less formidable problem of translation and publication than Marx's own works. Those seven hundred words the young Bundists studied phrase by phrase, sentence by sentence. If anything was part of the ghetto's culture, exegesis was. Untold generations of Talmudic scholars, teachers, and prophets had pored over scripture to divine and interpret its meaning, and now this highly refined art was applied to words set down under the guidance of two Germans named Wilhelm Liebknecht and August Bebel in Erfurt in 1891.

Study of the written word was accompanied by agitation in the factory, an exercise in which the Bund possessed a practiced skill; a pamphlet based on Bund experiences in Vilna then served as a primer on factory agitation for Russian revolutionaries generally. Not all activity, however, hinged on the word, written or spoken. The Bund was committed to armed self-defense against pogroms, and on Sabbath afternoons its young adherents, male and female, wandered off deep into the woods where they could practice the efficient mastery of an old revolver without surveillance or disturbance.

Theory, agitation, and revolver, these were the instruments

of collective, organized revolutionary endeavor, mastered in common with others. For the girl revolutionary nearing twenty there still remained the range of personal decision where the question is not only what one believes and what one does as social being but how one lives. In private contemplation of a personal ethic she evolved a romanticized asceticism: the pure revolutionary was above marriage, sex, or any solely personal gratification.

At this point in her evolution the 1905 revolution burst forth like the splendid realization of a dream, shaking the Czarist regime enough to loosen its most repressive restrictions, so that revolutionaries at last could address a public, not any more through the whispered word and the surreptitious leaflet but openly and directly in large assemblies. She discovered her gifts as a public orator. She was good and in her best moments she was truly great. I did not hear her speak in public until she was well into her thirties, when the occasions were less exalted, but I have met people who heard her when she was twenty-two and the tribune of the revolution in Mozyr, and something of the excitement of it could still be evoked a half century later. In Mozyr the revolutionaries actually held power for three weeks in 1905.

Three weeks of power, six years of prison, and now she was back in Mozyr in the summer of 1917, a semilegendary figure, the aura of legend heightened among the compatriots she left behind because she had been not only to Siberia but to London and New York, which in the mud and medievalism of the ghetto village shone as centers of culture, enlightenment, and civilization. She was back and a revolutionary leader in the city duma, a transitional organ of municipal government. Early in 1918 the revolution's progress was interrupted in Mozyr because German troops occupied the town. The German military has little tolerance for rival or dual power, and since she continued to function as public spokesman for the duma she was arrested. With her when she was picked up on the street by German intelligence officers I too was marched off to the Mozyr jail.

No one on the outside was permitted to communicate with

her, and she did not attempt to communicate with anyone for fear that the line of communication might lead to further arrests of her coworkers. In this impasse of communication there was no arranging my release and I remained in jail. The Russian jailer, now serving under the Germans as he had served under other regimes, had been my mother's host when she was arrested in Mozyr in 1905. Perhaps for the sake of old acquaintance he treated her with civility, or perhaps it was because the unsettling events since February 1917 had taught him that no one knew when today's prisoners might become tomorrow's rulers. Civility alone, unhappily, could do little about the physical appointments of the Mozyr jail. It was too small to provide separate facilities for political and criminal prisoners; for that matter, she was the only woman political prisoner and we were confined in the one cell for women, which already accommodated nine prisoners before our arrival. All the women bedded down on the stone floor. In such communal circumstances my mother could not, of course, demand any bedding privileges for herself but with fervent indignation she announced that she would not have a five-year-old child sleeping on that stone floor. On this score civility took on the tangible form of a canvas cot for me. The German commandant, on an inspection tour of the prison, fumed at the sight of the cot and fell back on a cliché of jail overseers, "We are not operating a summer resort . . ." But the cot remained.

If you must go to jail and have a choice of the time, you might do well to choose the age of five. It is an adaptable age when the child is inclined to accept the world as it is, not in the way that adults accept it, with passive resignation and the repression of discontent, but with an innocence which assumes that perhaps this is how the real world is supposed to be, for there is always a haven in the superior world of childhood fantasy. Moreover, except in the most cruel or genocidal of regimes, such as reached their abyss in the Nazi death camps, you are likely at five to fan the sparks of kindness and humanity that reside in the drab world of inhuman relationships that embrace the jailers and the jailed.

In my indistinct, tenuous memory of the Mozyr jail, the evil of it is shadowy, a thing of mood, a presentiment rather than a reality; there was an undercurrent of apprehension and a feeling of monotony. Among our cellmates was a peasant woman who was charged with smothering her drunken husband to death with a sack. A sturdy woman, she exhibited no remorse over what she was accused of doing and absolutely no fear of the consequences. On the contrary she was the gayest, most spirited inmate of the cell, occasionally breaking into the refrain of a peasant dancing song and executing a quick dance step to its tempo. She treated me kindly and yet I was afraid of her. I tried to imagine how it was to place the sack over the living, breathing head, to tighten it, to hold it there until the breathing stopped and the life was extinguished, and inevitably in this effort of the imagination I became the victim . . . So I feared her. The German guards — alien, forbidding, strong — were also objects of fear, especially after the commandant's display of temper at the cot. Yet I hazily recall overtures of kindness from a German soldier assigned to guard duty at the jail. To overcome the first barrier of language he taught me German words for things about us. Why does *blumen* stick in my mind?

I do not recall physical hardship and nothing at all about the food, but then there had not been much food on the outside either, and the jail fare would have had to be abominably bad or of skimpiness well below the hunger level to make an impression upon me. As it turned out my term as inadvertent political prisoner was cut short after three weeks. Just how my release was negotiated and arranged I do not know, but a sequel to this episode confirms how stringent the regulations were against any contact between my mother and the outside world.

No one was permitted to visit her, not even I. As a second-best expedient her friends contrived visits from a distance. Overlooking the jail was a hill to which I was brought in the afternoon when the women prisoners were taken out for exercise. From our hilltop vantage point my escort and I waved at my mother who walked, as the other women prisoners walked, in a circle within the jailyard. We could see that she could see us and we understood why she did not wave in return. Each afternoon we were there, I and someone who took me, but we did not stay long, for the German guards pointed their guns at us and on several occasions when we were slow to respond to this sign they fired warning shots over our heads. After the first visit we could see mother looking for us on the hilltop.

Then I came down with influenza. The German authorities lived up to their reputation for rigid, heartless adherence to their own regulations (I was going to throw "mindless" in among those adjectives but one of the horrors in the method of Prussian militarism is the amount of mind that went into devising it); the authorities would not bend the ban on communication with my mother so that she might be informed of my illness. Her friends, knowing her and acquainted with the foreboding capacities of her imagination, could surmise her anxiety at the sudden, unexplained cessation of the hilltop visits. They decided upon a desperate stratagem to let her know what happened to me, choosing a young village daredevil for its execution. One afternoon when the women prisoners were on their circular promenade in the jailyard, he clambered up the wall that enclosed the yard and shouted out my mother's name to attract her attention. Unfortunately he also attracted the attention of a German prison guard.

"Your son —" This was all he blurted out before a rifle butt crashed him off the wall.

A lesser maternal imagination than my mother's could conjure up a variety of morbid endings to that dreadfully truncated sentence. She became totally preoccupied with filling in that void. It was not true that time is a healer, for the obsessive torment of the exercise only grew with the hours, with the days and nights. On the second or third night some male prisoners attempted to break out. German cavalrymen, called in to reinforce the guard, employed their sabers to subdue the attendant rioting in the male section of the jail. The alarms, the sounds of violence, the screams of the slashed men (the women heard that three of the men were hacked to death) filled the small jail through much of the night. This night, coming after the days and nights of her own anguish, made any more tortured suspense unendurable.

She went on a hunger strike, declaring it would not end until she knew what happened to her son. The other nine women in the cell joined in the strike and in passive disobedience to prison regulations. After several days of this revolt by the women the German commandant yielded, and now the concession to the original demand was not enough, for when my mother learned of my illness she also insisted upon the right to visit me. It was arranged. By this time, toward the end of 1918, it was not only a matter of women's power; the power of the German military machine was beginning to disintegrate, its self-assurance shaken, its discipline loosened by defeat and a growing rebellious mood.

She came to visit me in a carriage and the security precautions might have taken on another guise for the townsfolk who witnessed the procession; the two guards on the footboards might have looked like footmen and the cavalry escort like a retinue . . .

Bobruisk. This is my father's birthplace and the home of my paternal grandparents, twice as big as Mozyr and only sixty miles north of it in the Jewish Pale of White Russia. I am in the street, a leaden gray sky above, and beneath it, like water that reflects the colors of the sky, flows a leaden gray human mass. It is the German army withdrawing to the west, not to return until summer's first days in 1941. The infantrymen move with precision and silence, the unpaved street yields little echo to the tramping feet. I, too, am silent, fascinated and frightened, as I was to be when, as a child, I first saw a water snake gliding across a pond in the predawn light that barely signifies the rising of the sun to come. The Germans are going and the scene should evoke elation, but it does not; there is such an inexorable quality in the rhythmic motion of these rows upon even rows of uniformed men that the gray mass seems ominous and indestructible. I feel something of all this but I cannot articulate it. Many years later the scene is brought back upon reading the

description by Richard Harding Davis of the German army as
he saw it marching into Brussels in August 1914 — "like a river
of steel it flowed, gray and ghostlike."

Evening. One lit candle and six of us in the room. A knock
on the door. The three soldiers in the doorway are different
from those I had seen earlier. Their dress is not uniform or
militarily tidy; one does not even have boots or shoes, just rags
wrapped around his feet. A soldier speaks in Russian.

"Good people, do you have food?"

"No, we do not have food; we are sorry, but there is no food
at all."

The soldiers leave. You can sense the relief in the room. My
grandparents and my three aunts, the younger, unmarried sis-
ters of my father, are relieved, especially my grandfather, who
had been the family spokesman. They are relieved because the
soldiers had not searched the house for the food that was in it.
I am more shamed and disturbed than relieved, for my sympathy is with the revolution and those were soldiers of the revolution. I am still a newly come stranger among my father's
people, a visitor from the different world of my mother and her
associates, where I imbibed attitudes and values with the certainty of childhood only to be thrust now among these other
adults who do not share in so much that I was taught to regard
as self-evident assumption. Although I remain in Bobruisk for
one year and the better part of another the sense of estrangement tinged with hostility never leaves me altogether. I am
ever the transient.

My grandmother had a flat, wide, open face, good-natured
but stupid. It is the face of a cow, my mother said once, the
most cowlike face she has ever seen on a human, and since it
was the first time I heard this metaphor its aptness was indel-
ibly impressed upon me. (To add to the mystique of Yiddish,
somehow the word "beheime," which is Hebrew for beast and
gave us "behemoth" in English, conveys more stupidity than
cow does.) My grandfather was a short man, his face completely dominated by small, gleaming eyes and a large, thick
beard. I remember a typical gesture. He forms his right thumb
and forefinger into tweezers, plunging these into his beard, bur-

rowing deeper and deeper, and when he finally catches the louse his eyes gleam with triumph and his lips emit a sound of sensual pleasure, "Tz . . . tz . . . tz . . ."

One of my aunts became a governess during the Polish occupation of Bobruisk. From several glimpses of her little girl charge I could tell by the clothes and the manners that she was of another class. And not only by clothes and manners. One evening my aunt brought home a treat, miniature bagels on a string that was looped as if for a necklace or garland, but the treat was not for me, it was intended for her charge the next morning. I found this treasure and tasted of it, yielding to temptation more than once, although I may say in my own defense that I left more bagels than I ate. When this depredation was discovered I was denounced as a thief. It was a lacerating humiliation, the sting of it sharpened by a feeling of injustice that I dared not assert; confronted by my accusing judges, stern and righteous with the authority of the Torah, I dared not plead: Your honors, I plead innocent on the grounds of hunger.

What is the morality of hunger for a child of six? I knew hunger well as a constant companion and in those years I learned that a hallmark of hunger's companionship is its constancy. True hunger is not fickle; it is with you not only before you eat but after you have finished eating, it not only awakens you in the morning but goes to bed with you at night. Hunger must have been amused by a staple dish my grandmother contrived to shake its fidelity. I was not amused. This dish was a soup with a base of beef fat, onions previously fried in such fat for flavor, and rare, small chunks of potato or turnip for substance. When the beef fat was in a molten state the soup was generally too hot for me to eat, and when it cooled off enough to swallow the fat congealed into a glutinous scum that nauseated me. Only for a swallow or two was there a rare equilibrium between being scalded and being nauseated. I have only circumstantial evidence as to the source of the beef fat. My grandfather was one of those middlemen who proliferated in the bootstrap economy of the Jewish ghetto. Cut off from the land and basic productive enterprise, the ghetto was compelled to subsist in large measure on the economic incest of petty intraghetto trade. He traded in tallow for candles. The soup may have been punishment for the sin of rendering unto the human stomach that which was intended to nourish the flames of sacred ritual.

There is hunger — and there is cold, although for cold it must be said that unlike hunger it is a respecter of seasons. However, this extenuating discrimination is appreciated only during the seasons in which cold does not reign. It does no good on a winter morning. I am awakened by the urge to urinate; the small sphincter muscle is performing a miracle of stubborn courage in resisting the tidal pressures from the bladder, but if in its intrepid spirit the sphincter is emulating Horatius its enemy is more implacable than the Etruscans were at the bridge across the Tiber. It is warm in bed and even without the steamy vapor of my breath I know how cold it is out there. I lie in the warmth of my body, sheathed in the armor of winter underwear behind a bulwark of quilt and miscellaneous cloth. I am curled up and am torn between the growing discomfort of the bladder-sphincter contest and the painful shock of the encounter with cold if I crawl out of bed. Why, I wonder, cannot I slip back into sleep and dream I urinated and so relieve the increasingly unbearable pressure without leaving the comforting warmth? I almost yield to the temptation but I am too old for bed-wetting and inevitably necessity prevails, as it does every winter morning, as I know it will even as I engage in the wishful fantasy that there is some escape from the desperate lunge into the cold.

I have never welcomed spring more ardently or more elementally, simply as the end of winter, as the deliverance from cold, from a state in which one strives for hibernation and, in frustration, envies the animals that achieve it. The poetic compliments that have been paid to spring, the life-birth-love symbols that are attached to it all seemed like embellishments of the main thing about the season that replaces winter.

Toward the end of summer in 1919, Grandfather brought some news home one evening with hand-rubbing cheerfulness and anticipation. The Polish army is swiftly approaching Bobruisk and soon would be in town. He received this intelligence from an important ghetto merchant, who also assured him that arrival of the Poles would signal the revival of free trade and the opportunity to make a profit. What else the Poles might bring with them the important merchant did not say but Grandfather soon found out.

On the second day of the Polish occupation of Bobruisk Grandfather came home in the late afternoon sobbing. His face was bruised; in his luxuriant beard there were naked patches of raw flesh; his black caftan was smeared with mud and dust, but his sobbing told of more than these marks of physical violence: it told of terror and humiliation. He had been walking along the street when three Polish cavalrymen came upon him. They encircled him on their mounts and flicked their whips at him, first at his feet to see the little Jew dance, and then in displays of the virtuosity of their whipmanship they aimed occasional flicks at his face. The most venturesome of the trio devised another exhibition of skill, this time in horsemanship; on the run he leaned far down from his saddle, seized a tuft of the little Jew's beard, and held onto it as he rode on. The others, not to be outdone, took their turns.

After this encounter and others of a kind Grandfather and other adult Jewish males of the town developed toothaches. The common home treatment for a toothache was a compress, really some wadding held in place by a cloth wrapped vertically around the head, encasing the chin (and beard) below and tied in a knot on top of the skull. In this instance the compress was more prophylactic than analgesic, the calculation being that a wrapped beard would be less attractive to Polish soldiers. I do not know how much free trade and profit came my grandfather's way during the Polish occupation. My sensitivity to an atmosphere of fear was keener than my awareness of economics, and I do know of the fear that pervaded the ghetto during our brief interlude in what later was to be called the free world.

Two Polish soldiers were quartered in our house. For occasional amusement they shot at crows on the backyard fence. These soldiers never mistreated any member of the household, but the sound of the rifle shots in the backyard terrified my grandmother.

The summer after the Polish arrival the distant thunder of artillery heralded the advance of the Red army. As the artillery drew closer we slept out of doors; it was warm, and it was said that scattered bodies on the ground provided a lesser target for artillery shells than a house did. There I was, a child of six, looking up with wonder at the infinite luminousness and mystery of a midsummer night's sky, hearing the nearby noises of a summer's night, and listening intently for something else. Then it would come, the sirenlike whine of the shell cutting through the air, becoming louder and more insistent as it drew nearer until it reached its explosive climax. Boom! The fire was not directed at the town, but the targets, whatever they were, were close by on the outskirts and who could tell when a shell might go astray and how wide off the mark it would be? Our household was spared but not the family of my friend, Monek. His two older brothers, lads in their late teens, were sent to fetch water from the well and on their way back one was hit; both his legs were severed and he bled to death. I hardly knew him, for at our respective ages only a few years made for a wide social gap; for me the loss was impersonal except for Monek's grief. I thought about death, as I had tried to think of it when a great aunt of mine died of intestinal typhus in Kalinkovichi, but the enormity of it, its perplexing amalgam of the finite and the infinite, were beyond my comprehension. After my great aunt died, the death having been slow and ugly and I having been part of the vigil or wake that began even before life left, I had nightmares. I had none after the death of Monek's brother.

The Poles departed, leaving a curious rear guard in our house. One morning, when we were still seated at the breakfast table, a platoon of mice marched boldly across the floor, uninhibited by the broad daylight or our presence. We had been unaware of their tenancy in the house but the reason for it was easily surmised. Not only had two Polish soldiers been quartered in the house, sacks of the Polish army's flour had also been stored in it, attracting a large portion of the town's sizable mouse population, for in Bobruisk this was possibly the only food hoard of its kind after years of war and revolution. As long as the flour was there the mice were sated, content, and unseen, but when the Poles withdrew they took their flour with them; hence the demonstrative hunger march of the mice.

Pursuing the retreating Poles the Red army moving through Bobruisk was buoyant and self-confident, the first time I had seen soldiers in such a mood. They were on the offensive and the offensive was rolling. In the long warm summer evenings there were sounds of laughter and music in the town, voices of the soldiers mingling with those of townswomen, and for me there was something tantalizing and mysterious in the flirtation of the male and female tones. A group of soldiers strolled through the street and one, the center of the group, accompanied himself on an accordion as he sang a ballad. One line stuck in my mind. "We are marching on to Warsaw . . ." I moved in the opposite direction. My mother had come to deliver me from Bobruisk and we were on our way to Moscow.

Travel. The memory of it is a series of disjointed scenes, suspended in a void of transit, for I cannot remember the destinations or the points of departure, except for one and then only because the point of departure was implicit in the episode. Only fragments of a journey are recalled and the journey is endowed with fantasy and uncommon intensity; it is a "thing in itself" and having no beginning and no end it evokes the mystery of motion through infinity and eternity.

It is night. The moon is afloat on the sky through shoals of clouds, alternately lighting up the white birches of the Russian landscape or casting them in shadow. Now we are riding through an avenue of trees, which almost touch above the narrow road, and it is very dark and very still, except for occasional gunfire that is so distant it can barely be heard. You cannot see the end of the avenue and you get the feeling it goes on forever, tree trunk after tree trunk on either side and the leafy canopy overhead. Later a stretch of road is paved with white stones

that reflect the moonlight and it is not still, the horses' hooves
and the carriage wheels clatter on the stone . . .

Finally we stop at an inn. It is long past midnight, I am tired
and sleepy but sleep does not exhaust my needs. When we are
settled in a room I break the silence, speaking in Russian.

"I want a little one."

"Yes. Good. You may have one."

My mother has taken a salami from a bag and is slicing it.
She gives me a thin slice. I eat it because I am hungry but this
is not what I meant.

"I want a big one."

She cuts a thicker slice of salami. I take it and eat it because
I am still hungry, although this still is not what I meant. Now
the edge of hunger is dulled and my other need, the one I have
been trying to convey, is much the greater, and my irritation at
the inability to communicate it, at her stupid incomprehension,
is also greater. I am irritated and I am also suffused suddenly
with a sense of bereavement — I am all alone again; there had
been a reassuring warmth and closeness between us, sitting in
silence side by side as we were transported through the night,
and now we are apart, she does not understand and I have hostility for her and pity for myself.

I try again. A little one? Another slice of salami. A big one?
No, she says, you cannot have a big piece, you have to go to
sleep and if you eat too much salami you will not be able to
sleep. I burst into tears. She thinks the tears are occasioned by
vexation at her refusal to give me more salami and she continues to explain. Her patient explanation only grates on my
impatience, heightens my frustration and its tearful expression.
At last the force of my anguish and the manifestations of my
physical discomfort make her understand.

She is penitent, she was not privy to the code, this code my
Bobruisk aunts had taught me with its euphemisms of little and
big for the toilet functions. I am twice relieved, physically and
emotionally, but the episode remains a poignant symbol of
estrangement. She was doing what she had come all the way
from America to do, agitating and organizing for the defense of
the revolution, traveling across White Russia and the Ukraine,

recruiting troops for the Red army in battle against foreign intervention and the Whites, and all the time embroiled in the most exhausting of politics, a ceaseless internal struggle within the Bund. Although at the last moment in New York she resolved to have both the revolution and her child she cannot truly have them both, not at all for long intervals and only imperfectly when they — mother, child, and revolution — are together.

What am I doing in Gomel? I know it is Gomel, although all I can see of it are the walls of a room with nothing to distinguish it from countless rooms in other White Russian towns. I am not supposed to be in Gomel, in the sense that it was not a chosen destination, but illness interrupted the journey to wherever we were going and I am sick in bed. I know it is Gomel because among the bedside stories my mother told me was one about a speech she made here.

Gomel is a railroad town and at some point the railroad workers turned out en masse to acclaim the revolution and its local leaders. Not long afterward White troops attacked Gomel. Only a small band of revolutionaries, barricaded in one building, offered resistance; they were overrun and annihilated by the Whites as the railroad workers stood by, doing nothing to aid those they had acclaimed only shortly before. Addressing the railroad workers after this episode my mother drew a parallel from the Gospel, in the last six days of the life of Jesus, between the Sunday when the multitudes welcomed him to Jerusalem with hosannas and palm leaves and the Friday when he was crucified all alone except for the involuntary company of the two thieves nailed to the crosses on either side of him.

She frequently tells me tales from the New Testament, usually with some contemporary connotation. In the Czarist prisons, where she received her education, her tutors were the cultured daughters of the aristocracy and middle classes, among them the purest of Russian souls in their time. In their culture was the strong strain of Christian mysticism and symbolism that runs through Russian literature, delineating and probing the big questions of Good and Evil, of Spirit and Flesh, of Exaltation and Suffering, of Martyrdom and Resurrection. Upon the fresh, open, thirsting mind of the Jewish girl from the ghetto the Christian symbolism made a profound impression. Its transmuting attraction was intensified by the prison condition, by the deprivation and isolation, by the mortification of the flesh, by the cruelty and heroism she witnessed, by the encounter with the noblest and basest in Russian society.

Years later, confronted with a child's need for storytelling, knowing no fairy tales and very few traditional children's stories, she reverts to tales from the New Testament. So Gomel is inscribed in my memory together with Jerusalem and Calvary.

Somehow I have gotten hold of a small mirror, and lying in my sickbed I have caught in it the sun's rays streaming through a window. Manipulating the mirror I play the sun's reflection upon the wall, moving the light beam methodically at first, back and forth in a horizontal line, then ever more swiftly in ever more irregular patterns so that the spot of light darts all over the wall in dazzling zigzags and flourishes. My mother enters the room. Still absorbed in the game I have been playing I blurt out, "Would it not be wonderful if the Red army had a machine gun that could fire like this mirror?"

The train is moving. We are huddled in a corner but it does not help much. It is not possible for the only woman and child to be inconspicuous in a boxcar filled with soldiers. Even if she were not the only woman in this boxcar my mother would be conspicuous. She has just recovered from typhus and the kerchief on her head does not altogether hide the clean-shaven baldness of her skull. (The depilation is intended to frustrate the louse, which is the principal typhus carrier. At the peak of the typhus epidemic Lenin said, "Either the lice triumph over socialism, or socialism will triumph over the lice.") To augment the grotesquery of the clean-shaven head she also has a black eye. Weak from typhus she had stumbled and fallen badly. You would think that in a face so gaunt from the disease, with the circles under the eyes so deep and pronounced, the traumatic blackness surrounding the one eye would be hardly discernible, and yet it is obtrusive.

We try to diminish our presence in the shadows of the corner, but we attract attention. Soldiers exchange remarks, loudly enough so that we are sure to hear them . . . What do you suppose she did to make her husband so angry? . . . Do you think she is running away? . . . things of this sort. The banter is good-natured and restrained, almost diffident; the vestiges of typhus do not fit in with the suggestiveness of crude male humor about a woman with a black eye. More, this is a troop train during civil war and the odd-looking woman with a child must be of some importance to have secured passage on it.

There is more talk about the train. It does not move with rhythmic harmony, the chug-chug-chug-chug bass of the engine accompanied by the clackety-clack treble of the wheels rolling on the track. The engine groans or coughs consumptively, the wheels register clump-clump, the train is afflicted with shuddering starts and stops as if the effort of locomotion is beyond its strength. Somebody says the trouble is they are burning wood, and poor wood at that, not dry and seasoned as it ought to be. In the old days, says a soldier, this trip took two hours; we'll be lucky if we make it in a day.

The train has sputtered to a halt again. Before this stop I had communicated to my mother a toilet need, a big one in the Bobruisk code. She turned to some nearby soldiers with the problem and one volunteered to help solve it the next time the train stopped.

For modesty's sake my military escort leads me behind a clump of shrubbery some distance from the train, perhaps fifteen or twenty yards. I squat but the circumstances are unsettling and the going is slow. I am still squatting when the engine groans and with a shudder the train begins to move. Above the train's clatter and the human commotion in our boxcar I can hear my mother's shout of alarm. My escort, his rifle slung over one shoulder, seizes me with the other arm around my chest, tight under the armpits, and runs for the train. My pants are down and I am still dripping, I am ashamed, but most of all I am scared. From our boxcar moving ahead of us there are shouts of encouragement and laughter.

Soldiers crowd the doors of other boxcars to watch and cheer the strange race. Running faster my escort has tightened his grip around me, and it increases my discomfort and also my anxiety. For some reason I feel as if I were a rabbit. The near collapse of Russian railroad transport proves our salvation; the locomotive's acceleration is not quick enough to leave us behind. I am passed up to outstretched hands and my escort vaults into the boxcar after me. Hurrahs and more laughter. It is no use at all now to retreat into the corner and huddle there. Good boy (*molodets*), soldiers say to me and pat my shoulder. The moat of uneasiness that separated mother and child from the soldiers is gone. The train continues to move slowly and erratically, but it is not so bad any more.

After the provincial drabness of Mozyr and Bobruisk, Moscow and the Hotel Metropole were resplendent visions out of one of Pushkin's poetic fairy tales. A few steps out of the hotel and there was the majestic expanse of Red Square, seeming even more vast than it does now because this was before the granite eminence of the Lenin Mausoleum on the square; on the right, like sentinels, stood the turrets and towers of the Kremlin and up ahead St. Basil's Cathedral with its disarray of towers that resembled incongruously plump minarets fattened on kasha, potatoes, and borscht, each capped by a dome, two smooth harlequin hats among several burred pine cones and pineapples, and towering about them all a gleaming golden onion.

I did not have to step out of the hotel to see splendor. In my child's eye the Metropole was a montage of dazzling chandeliers in the grand dining room, the grandest room I had ever seen — of marble columns, of an imposing staircase designed for grand entrances. This is the memory I retain of it and perhaps it was like that. Forty-five years later, visiting Moscow again for the first time, I asked our guide to take us to the Metropole and encountered tacit disapproval. Reluctantly he took us by the hotel the next morning but only for a quick, unrevealing look into the foyer. I could have pressed the issue but did not; other members of the party were bent on other sights;

they had no sentimental association with the Metropole. Unwillingness to offend our guide or to impose upon my companions afforded a commendable rationalization for not pressing the issue, but I suspect there were other reasons. In the guide's demeanor I sensed a discretion of national pride beneath the balky resistance to showing the Metropole to foreign visitors. I have seen enough hotels that have aged without grace, deteriorating into an unkempt, pathetic shabbiness, losing any dignity they once might have had. Perhaps this was the fate of the Metropole in the intervening forty-five years, or worse yet, perhaps it never truly was what I remembered. Perhaps it was better to leave with childhood's romantic image intact.

In the autumn of 1920 the Metropole, like so many revolutionaries, had an alternate name, a *nom de revolution:* The Second House of the Soviets. I do not know what The First House of the Soviets was or whether there was a third, but the Metropole was second and this indicated its place in the sociopolitical realm. It was a government hostel for people below the very top ranks in the Soviet social structure, and my mother rated shelter there as a national leader of the Bund. By then the Left Wing's triumph was total in the Bund, which declared that on all essential questions its program coincided with that of the Communist party; indeed, negotiations were under way for the self-dissolution of the Bund and the absorption of its members into the Communist party. Officially recognized as an autonomous political party, and this three years after the revolution, still the Bund did not rate very high in the Soviet scheme of things; its status might have had a bearing on the quality of our accommodations. Moscow's housing problem already was impossible, the Metropole was jammed, and we were quartered in what must have been once a large store room, sharing this windowless chamber with several other persons who were separated from us by curtains.

With residence at the Metropole went the privilege of eating in its dining room twice a day. The cuisine did not match the grandeur of the physical setting. I especially remember a gruel that was served for breakfast as I was convinced at the time that it consisted of the kind of oats that is fed to horses. Cooking did nothing to destroy or soften the tough, stubborn individuality of these grains. I chewed and I chewed them until I was tired of chewing, but the grind of my child molars made no more impression than the cooks had; these grains would not be masticated into a mash and when I finally swallowed them each descended through my gullet as whole and intact as Jonah.

Still, during that autumn and winter in Moscow, especially the winter, it was a privilege to have even such shelter and food as we had. It was a privilege to reside at the Metropole where ebullience and hope at life's brim submerged the gruel and the curtained cubicle. Among the hotel's residents were other returned exiles, and I encountered children from England, Switzerland, France, and other Western European countries. I was the only one from America. My best friend, Tolya, came from England. It was no English-speaking union between us, for by then we had forgotten such English as we had known. Tolya had special status because his father was a Chekist; in our circle the Cheka, the vigilance arm of the revolution that outwitted, ferreted out, and sternly punished counterrevolutionaries, was the glamorous embodiment of courage and honor. Tolya did not tell me exactly what his father did in the Cheka but I was certain it was something clever and dangerous. I respected his reticence, never asked questions, taking pride in my mature self-discipline that did not pry into weighty and confidential matters of the revolutionary state.

That November, when the revolution marked its third birthday and I my seventh, Tolya and I fought with the Red army under the command of Mikhail V. Frunze in the final campaign of the civil war on the European soil of the Soviet Republics. That is, we eagerly read every dispatch and eavesdropped on every snatch of adult conversation about Frunze's offensive against Baron Peter Wrangel's White armies that tried to hole up for the winter on the Crimean Peninsula. We lived by the reports from the front and we marched through the Metropole's hallways singing with fervor: "Bravely we go into battle/ for the power of the Soviets . . ." It was an old romantic song, "White Acacias," transfigured into a militant civil war march.

At the climax of the campaign, when Frunze's troops stormed

the narrow Perekop Isthmus, which attaches the Crimea like a pendant to the mainland, we were transported by one heroic exploit. As we understood it, at one stage of their assault Frunze's men advanced boldly to positions where their backs were to the sea; there was no retreat, they either had to win or to die. They won. And the entire Metropole was in a celebrant mood. Tolya and I generously shared in the celebration with others, although inwardly we felt that our fidelity to Frunze gave us greater title to rejoice.

After the triumph we lapsed into a mood of depression. What, after all, were we doing? Suddenly vicarious heroism was not enough. We talked of running away but our reconnaissance did not extend beyond Alexandrovsky Park only a few blocks away; December had come and with it the cold and snow of a Moscow winter. In this mood Tolya thought of something we could do, right in the Metropole. We could check on the passports of people who came into the hotel. Enlisting some others for our inspection team we stationed ourselves on a staircase to check all persons ascending it. Tolya was our chief and it was he who demanded with stern politeness, "Passport, please." Adults produced them, some with humorous indulgence, others with mock solemnity. It was routine until we stopped one man and a crowd began to gather (as they say in the transcripts of Soviet assemblies, there was animation and laughter). He was short and stocky, wearing glasses and a tuft of beard, and he looked at us with a benign, avuncular smile on an open peasant face. We stood our ground, although from the growing crowd of adults we sensed that this was no ordinary confrontation. He produced his passport and then, amused, he looked at the adult throng, shrugged his shoulders, waved an arm to indicate us, and said, "There is the youth . . ." By then we had learned his identity, Mikhail Kalinin, "President of the Russian Soviet Federated Socialist Republic" (an inexact transliteration of his actual post as chairman of the executive committee of the Supreme Soviet of the R.S.F.S.R. The Union of Soviet Socialist Republics did not come into being until two years later).

In our scale of heroism statecraft did not occupy the first

rank; this was reserved for men of the Red army and the Cheka. But with the catholic imagination of childhood, along with such contemporary heroes of the revolution I also had a private, literary hero, Dubrovsky, in a story of that name by Pushkin. Vladimir Dubrovsky's widowed father is a small landowner who is robbed of his estate and his life by the capricious malice of a wealthy and powerful neighbor after a stupid quarrel. Rather than cede his ancestral home intact to his father's persecutor young Dubrovsky puts the torch to it and flees to the forest to lead the life of a vengeful bandit, gallant and generous, and the scourge of the local establishment. Dubrovsky also falls in love and his beloved, Marya (Masha) Kirilovna Petrovich is, of course, the daughter of the rich and boorish tyrant who wronged his father. In such circumstances their love ends tragically, as it was destined to end. Marya belongs to the ample gallery of pure and tragic heroines in Russian literature, the prototype for which, Tatyana in *Eugene Onegin,* was also Pushkin's creation.

Ordinarily at age seven I would have dismissed Marya as an irrelevant nuisance and would have regarded Dubrovsky's love for her as a perplexing weakness, but Marya (and Dubrovsky) were spared such nonsentimental intolerance. I, too, fell in love.

It happened at a ballet performance in which the artists and spectators were child residents of the Metropole. One ballerina, who gave a solo performance, was about my age, perhaps a year older, and when I saw her, for the first time in my life I had use for the word exquisite, and perhaps for the last time, for never again could it be used with the same perfection; for me it is like those glasses that British officers smashed after a toast to the queen so that they could not be used for another toast or any other purpose. She was exquisite. I had never seen ballet before, or a ballet costume. It might seem odd that the costume so impressed me as to stick in my mind, but in that Moscow winter (and from the photographic evidence I have seen, in other Moscow winters as well) the heavy, bulky garment was in fashion, coarse and ill-fitting and in dark colors; the color frequently defied precise designation but it was unmistakably dark. After the visual monotony of such styles the ballet costume was enchantment, with its pure whiteness, with the frilled, airy lightness of the tutu beneath the tight-fitting bodice, all of it encasing such litheness and grace and revealing so much tantalizing flesh in the bare arms and legs. She danced "The Dying Swan," her arms fluttering in time with the Saint-Saëns music, played on a piano accompanied by the thumps of my heart. My dreams had been martial and in them, as I stormed into the Crimea with Frunze's men, death was no stranger but it was always heroic; it did not occur to me to set it to music, but if I had Tchaikovsky's "1812 Overture" or the finale of one of his symphonies would have been appropriate. Certainly not Saint-Saëns. Now as I watched the swan die, so tragically, with such measured grace and beauty, my martial visions melted away. Oh, to be able to die like this! To share with her this elegant pathos!

After the concert I was feverish. Modesty and the purity of my passion precluded its full revelation to Tolya, but I could not conceal my interest. In an abstracted way. We resided in the same hotel but clearly she inhabited an astral realm far beyond my reach. Tolya was more practical and as the son of a Chekist he ferreted out some intelligence: she came from France and her name was Marya, the same as Pushkin's heroine, and even in the French origin there was coincidence because Pushkin's Marya, as the cultured daughter of a wealthy landowner, conversed in French. The next day Tolya produced more intelligence: her room number.

Bold and inventive Tolya proposed that I communicate with her by telephone. I had seen telephones but never used one and on the several occasions I had observed their use by adults I was impressed by the perseverance of these select adults, by their patience and their intrepid ingenuity in surmounting hurdles and pitfalls that apparently lurked in the tubular instrument; when they finally overcame these obstacles I was struck by the self-importance and loudness of their tone, by its serious, businesslike tenor. In the Moscow of 1920 one did not use a telephone lightly. Had I been on my own I might not have had the daring to do it, but with Tolya instructing me and egging me on I ventured into this mysterious realm of communication. Matters were more awesome because I was to cope with two unknowns, the telephone and Marya; the medium, as it were, compounded the inhibitions that would have attended the message in any event. My voice faltered and my enunciation was unclear, but an understanding operator finally divined that I wanted room number such-and-such. After a few buzzes and clicks I could hear another voice; it was an adult, female voice, and it spoke in French. By this time I had grown bolder and repeated with impatience that I wished to speak to Marya. The only response was a torrent of incomprehensible French. So ended the romantic siege. In time perhaps there would have been recovery and a renewal of the campaign but time ran out. I left the Metropole.

It is not possible, however, to take leave of the Second House of the Soviets without an introduction to Streletz. I cannot remember his physical appearance but this is not important. Streletz was the buoyant spirit of that time in that place. He was a Bundist who was not privileged to reside at the Metropole. Occasionally he visited my mother and always with an anecdote or a topical song, rendered with verve but not loudly. Mostly his performances were a gay mocking of the hardship and hunger in that Moscow winter. The feeling of him that I retain is much larger than the sum of remembered details, which are an odd assortment: a three-line ditty that translates badly from Yiddish into English, a joke you might have heard, an involved story that hinges on a play on words in a foreign tongue, an in-group topical song.

> Hot tea, cold tea,
> There is no sugar,
> One drinks it plain.

Streletz sings the Yiddish rhyme with a gay lilt and I laugh. I laugh because I know all about tea without sugar. This is common. I also know about tea with saccharin, which is not so common, and I am not certain which is worse, tea with saccharin or unsweetened tea. Saccharin is used by those who can get it as a substitute for sugar, and not for any dietetic reason, not to resist obesity or to mollify diabetes. It is used as a substitute when sugar is not to be had. In full-bodied, strong tea saccharin would not be too bad, but there is no such tea. In the lightly tea-flavored boiled water of the time nothing cuts the sickly sweetness. The expertise of experience in these matters makes me relish the insouciance of Streletz's hot tea, cold tea . . .

Maybe you have heard the joke about the rabbi's solution of the housing problem of the Jew who no longer could endure his overcrowded quarters. Ah, but you did not hear it from Streletz. You did not hear it in revolutionary Moscow in the winter of 1920. You did not hear it in a curtained-off portion of a windowless chamber that you shared with six other persons.

You have not heard, I am sure, Streletz's play-on-Russian-words story. It is just as well. I cannot explain why I remember it, not that I really remember *it* so that I can tell it, I only remember about it. The Russian colloquialism for hernia is "blind intestine" and somehow the crux of the story is that someone gets a hernia by eating the meat of a blind horse. There was much talk then in Moscow about horsemeat. If I ate any I was not aware of it, and I suspect that it was more talked about than eaten.

It is very easy to understand why I remember Streletz's political and topical song, which was patterned after a singing catechism traditionally associated with learning the Hebrew alphabet. This was his adaptation:

> What does a little boy learn?
> Aleph (A).
> What does Aleph mean?
> Ai, ai, ai . . .
> Once more.
> . . . a drawn out sickness.
> What does a little boy learn?
> Beth (B).
> What does Beth mean?
> Bund . . .
> Once more.
> . . . buried.

Then you repeat back to the beginning:

> Bund buried
> Ai, ai, ai, a drawn out sickness.

In this catechism, as Streletz sang it, the sixth letter of the Hebrew alphabet — Heh or H — meant Henye Horelick, which is an acceptable rendition of my mother's maiden name although the absence of an H sound in the Russian language and the substitution of G for it (the thirty-first President of the United States, for instance, was known to the Russians as Gerbert Goover) stamped preference on Genya Gorelick.

Sacrificing the actual sequence of letters in the Hebrew alphabet to retain alliteration the reprise from H in the song of Streletz was roughly as follows:

Henye Horelick
Orates orations (darshent droshes)
Mayhem murderers (gvald gazlonim)
Bund buried (Bund bagrobun)
Ai, ai, ai, a drawn out sickness (ai, ai, ai, a farshlepte kreink).

The song is a musical accompaniment for my exit from the Metropole because this departure was an incidental consequence of my mother's final and futile conflict in the Bund. At issue was liquidation of the Bund. The Bund had applied for membership in the Communist International since it accepted the International's fundamental program (i.e., support for Soviet power and the dictatorship of the proletariat). The International responded by establishing a commission to explore amalgamation of the Bund with the Russian Communist party.

The Bund thereupon proposed that in the amalgamation it be granted a large degree of autonomy, including retention of an independent organizational structure and its own name as a Jewish section of the Communist party. The Comintern Commission concurred in the Russian party's objection to such an arrangement, holding that Bund autonomy "would lead to continuation of the organizational and ideological alienation of one portion of the Jewish proletariat from the rest of the proletariat of Russia." The upshot was a Comintern decision that the

Bund membership be absorbed by the Communist party and its leaders be integrated into the leadership of the party's Jewish Section, which conducted agitation and propaganda in the Yiddish language under the direction of the party's central committee.

My mother led a minority group that opposed such a solution. I was not aware of the political intricacies of the conflict but this ignorance did not immunize me from the personal consequences.

The intraparty struggle commanded all my mother's energy and time, and it necessitated many visits to the Bund's major constituencies in White Russia. I could not be left alone in the Metropole and so a temporary place was arranged for me in a Soviet home for orphans. Literary tradition and the dismal realities it reflected make orphanage sound very bad, but it was not bad at all, and there is no need to be suffused with pity or compassion at the mention of it. In a time of famine and epidemic a Soviet orphanage was a good place to be, as good as any place there was, and perhaps the best of all possible places. The tragedy of having been orphaned is something else (there had been more than six years of war, foreign and civil, years of hunger and pestilence, to produce an abundant crop of orphans). For this the orphanage was not accountable (you may charge it to the Czarist regime's plunge into World War, to White Guard armies, and to the invading troops of foreign countries that tried to crush the revolution). The orphanage did not make orphans, it sheltered them, the lucky ones who could get in, and cared for them.

The revolutionary regime did not have much food, medicine, accommodations, and hygienic staples (including soap), but the best of what it had was given to its children. This was not just out of sentimentality. The child of today is the socialist man of tomorrow — everywhere posters conveyed variations on this theme. The future as abstraction assumed corporeal shape in the child, and the future is very important in a revolution. People who have been living almost solely in the past and present (man's fate) are suddenly seized with a vision of the future (man's hope), and then the present is no longer the same. In a special way it was no longer the same for the child.

The orphanage occupied what had been the palatial suburban estate of a Czarist prince ten versts out of Moscow. To get there I advanced beyond the telephone in my utilitarian acquaintance with modern technology as it existed in revolutionary Russia at that time; I rode in an automobile. The other inhabitants of the home were almost all peasant children; an ability to read, for example, was a distinction I shared with only one other child, for literacy at that time was still pretty much an urban achievement. I had never mingled with peasant children before; there was no occasion for it in the ghetto towns of my grandparents or in the cosmopolitan sophistication of the Metropole. Nor, except for the three weeks in jail, which was altogether different because it was an adult world, had I ever been part of institutionalized life. Faced with strangers in a strange setting I was apprehensive.

Very discreetly and unobtrusively I sized up my new companions. They did not bother to be discreet in sizing up the strange, new kid. The time for testing came. An older boy in a group pointed to a chap about my age and size and asked, "Can you lick him?"

I looked him over, thought for a while, and said, "I don't know. Maybe I can lick him. I am not sure."

"Can you lick him?" This time pointing to a bigger and older chap.

"Yes, I can," I replied without hesitation.

"What about him?" This him was the biggest and sturdiest of the lot.

"Of course! Of course I can lick *him.*"

They guffawed and then I also laughed. I was not called upon to lick anybody, maybe because of the preposterous cheekiness of my performance. Except that it was not cheek at all, it was semantics. They had used a Russian word that is like "lick" and with the same colloquial meaning, but I was a stranger to the word in this guise as I was to its users and the locale. I had been exposed to much and yet had inhabited the worlds of the ghetto and the Metropole, insulated from the bigger outer world. Now suddenly this word was thrust at me when I had considerable anxiety and little time. I knew I had to divine its meaning in a hurry and I sensed that it had to do with combat, with a test of physical strength. Pause to think about it and "to lick" is not a prepossessing verb; its ordinary literal meaning is more suggestive of defeat than conquest (e.g., one licks wounds); the tongue (except when employed in speech) is no offensive weapon. Such was the line of my hasty reasoning with its Russian equivalent. If I'd had more time . . . but my quick associations with the word seemed logical enough to transform it into its opposite, and so it was that the bigger the adversary the greater my certainty that I could lick him.*

Physical culture was an important rite at the home. We did our calisthenics outdoors and on some days, in the final ritual, we stripped to the waist and rubbed ourselves down with snow. The only other thing I can remember about the home is that an old oak on the grounds was supposed to bear the scars of artillery fire from the Napoleonic wars. I might have remembered more but my stay there was cut short by scarlet fever. Later I was told that three children came down with the fever. The other two died.

The hospital was near the home and there my mother came to visit. She was still engaged in the Bund's final conflict, but she came. There was no transport and she walked the ten versts from Moscow through the snow and cold. During the crisis stage of the fever she stayed all night in the hospital room. Later, when I was convalescing, she brought a small parcel that was her food ration, in it a variety of fatback that was cured but not cooked. I gnawed at the pig fat with child's teeth.

When I was discharged from the hospital it was not to the home. It was early spring, the struggle in the Bund was over, my mother's group had lost. Not by much. If my memory is right the division in the Bund's central committee was six to

---

* "Lick" is a very free translation. The Russian word was *sladit;* I understood it as "sweeten," but their meaning was to "manage" or "overcome." To sweeten someone did not suggest physical conquest to me.

four, and in the ranks it was 54 to 46 per cent. But she lost. She requested assignment to Poland, where the Bund continued as an independent entity.

We crossed the border at night. The journey across the frontier between two worlds is a series of faint images: a horse and wagon, darkness and stillness, human shadows rising from the ground, whispered conversations. Then it is dawn, we are in a carriage, we stop for breakfast at an inn. On the table are slices of black bread and several white rolls. It has been a very long time since I have seen white rolls. I stare at them. I turn to my mother: "May I — may I have one of those?"

In Poland I am again placed in an orphanage, this one is Jewish and is supported by American Jewish charities. My mother is off on a speaking tour of Poland's Jewish communities for Russian famine relief. Many of my companions at the orphanage are orphans because their parents were killed in pogroms. A boy of thirteen from Vilna is a hero. He is a good athlete, the only one of us who can jump across the length of a canvas cot, but this is not what makes him a hero. It only adds to his stature. The mark of his heroism is a deep gash in his back, the entrance to the wound still unhealed. The story is that he fought back in the pogrom that took his parents' lives and the gash was inflicted by an assailant with a knife. (After I left the orphanage we visited a dentist in the Warsaw ghetto, not for professional services, since my mother talked with him about politics. Sitting in the waiting room I looked out of the window into a refuse-strewn alley; enormous rats poked about in the refuse. Decades later when I visited Warsaw, in 1966, looking at the memorial that stands where the ghetto once was I thought, yes, everybody now remembers who destroyed the ghetto, remembers it so well that another issue of identity is forgotten — who created the ghetto?)

I did not stay in the orphanage for long, and although we remained in Poland for more than a year it was only a way point. My mother reestablished communication with my father in Chicago and he sent us money; the American dollars were exchanged for astronomical but fluctuating sums of Polish zloty in the wild inflation of the time. We ate well and lived in

Otvotsk, a pine-wooded health resort that was said to be good for tuberculars. In time money was accumulated and arrangements were made for our return to the United States, through Berlin and Paris to Le Havre and embarkation for New York. Years later, having to ascertain the exact date of our arrival for some bureaucratic form, I checked it in the *New York Times* and learned that among our fellow-travelers aboard the S.S. *Paris* of the French Line were Isadora Duncan and Sergei Yesenin. We landed in New York on October 1, 1922, on the eve of the Jewish Day of Atonement. It was a portent.

From New York we went on to Chicago, where my father awaited us, and there everything was bad. My father must have worked very hard as a cutter at Hart, Schaffner & Marx to support us in Poland and to save the money for our passage. He was unwell. Although he had been kept from the war theater during his service with the Canadian army he had not escaped injury, one of those stupid injuries of garrison duty. He had fallen off a ladder and incurred some cerebral damage. He suffered severe headaches, which were exacerbated by fatigue, and he was fatigued from overwork. For his ailment he received out-patient treatment at a clinic.

My mother went to work in a garment shop and she was not prepared for it, not for the transition from speaker's tribune to sewing machine, from the role of agitator in revolutionary Russia to that of a finisher in a Chicago sweatshop, not prepared for the strain and tedium of the work, nor for the submissiveness and gratitude expected from a greenhorn who was not proficient at the machine and clearly not Americanized in her ways.

The differences that led to the separation of my parents in 1917 still persisted, and conciliation was not made easier by the separate lives they had led in the intervening years. It was not a good reunion. I did not help. I complained and whined. In this monster city, alien and hostile, I knew no contemporaries. I did not know the language and did not know the customs, and I had no idea of how I would ever overcome this estrangement, how I would ever break out of this utter, terrifying sense of aloneness.

We had been in Chicago two or three weeks when Mother came home from the shop early in the day. A foreman had made an offensive remark. She slapped him and was fired. She told these bare details and then she began to weep. I had never seen her weep before. She wept with huge, heaving sobs. My father talked to her but it did no good. She said nothing and it seemed as if she heard nothing. She continued to weep for a long, long time, it seemed to me, and then my father said that he and I would go for a walk. It was a long walk, we said little, and there was not much companionship between us. When we returned my mother had stopped weeping.

That evening my father went for a regular treatment at the clinic and he did not return. He never returned. I have not seen him or heard from him since. At the time my mother was taken to the morgue to look at unidentified corpses in varying stages of decomposition that had been fished out of Lake Michigan and the rivers and canals of Chicago. None of them was my father's.

Hello, America.

II. The Generations

When Huey P. Newton, principal founder and leader of the Black Panther party, was on trial for his life in 1968, charged with murder in the shooting death of an Oakland cop, his fellow Panthers were saying some very strong things.

Things of this sort: "They will have to kill us before we'll allow them to kill Huey . . . [His execution] would have to be over our dead bodies and their dead bodies . . . If Huey is not set free there is little hope of avoiding open armed war in the streets of California and of preventing it from sweeping across the nation." Sometimes they just said, "The sky's the limit."

Among radicals of my generation, among many and perhaps most, I found the response to the Panther rhetoric ranged from acute discomfort to outrage. Ah yes, the generation gap. Saying this, people mean the biological generations, but there is also another generation gap: it is the subjective contradiction between one's own youth and age that tends to develop within anyone whose years span two generations. In the reactions of my contemporaries I detected frictions with their own past. Men who personified the tradition to which they laid claim had said things that sounded very much like what the Panthers were saying.

A striking parallel is afforded by the most venerated figure of the American socialist movement, Eugene V. Debs, in speaking of the Haywood-Moyer-Pettibone case of 1906. The three men were charged with murder in Idaho and the talk at the time was that "they shall never leave Idaho alive."

"Well, by the gods, if they don't," Debs responded, "the governors of Idaho and Colorado and their masters from Wall

Street, New York, to the Rocky Mountains had better prepare
to follow them."

With a reference to the Haymarket case of 1886 Debs continued:

"Nearly twenty years ago the capitalist tyrants put some innocent men to death for standing up for labor.

"They are now going to try it again. Let them dare!

"There have been twenty years of revolutionary education,
agitation and organization since the Haymarket tragedy, and if
an attempt is made to repeat it, there will be a revolution and I
will do all in my power to precipitate it.

"If they attempt to murder Moyer, Haywood and their brothers, a million revolutionists, at least, will meet them with guns."

(To friends Debs confided, "If they hang Haywood and
Moyer, they'll have to hang me.")

In present-day jargon Debs threatened to "off" two governors
and an untold number of western mine operators and eastern
financiers. Only it did not sound so crude, just as swearing "by
the gods" is not so raw as a reference to mothers and fornica-
tors. "Arouse, Ye Slaves!" was the bold streamer over his manifesto on the front page of the *Appeal to Reason,* March 10,
1906.

Three weeks earlier, on February 17, William D. (Big Bill)
Haywood, secretary-treasurer of the Western Federation of
Miners; Charles Moyer, federation president; and George Petti-
bone, a union sympathizer in Denver, had been arrested in connection with the fatal bombing of former governor Frank
Steunenberg of Idaho. According to the prosecution's theory
the murder was a reprisal for the governor's use of state troops
against the workers in the Coeur d'Alene strike of 1899. The
three men were indicted on March 6.

Manifestly, between the time of the indictment and the deadline for the March 10 edition of the *Appeal,* Debs did not study
lengthy legal documents, setting forth the pro and con evidence, to arrive at an independent judgment as to the legal
guilt or innocence of the accused. His was the swift, passionate
reaction of solidarity with men he regarded as comrades who

had been taken captive and faced death at the hands of the enemy in a war between the classes. Nothing was more vivid in Debs's social imagination and more constant in his political creed than the class struggle. So, recalling the use of federal troops against the Pullman strike that he led, Debs wrote, ". . . in the gleam of every bayonet and the flash of every rifle *the class struggle was revealed.*" On another occasion he exclaimed, "The capitalist class! The working class! The class struggle! These are the supreme economic and political facts of this day and the precise terms that express them."

This conviction molded his response to the threatened execution of Haywood and the others. Certainly his response was not the emotional outburst of youth and inexperience. He was no longer young, having just passed his fiftieth birthday. He was no novice, either in politics or economics, having been a small-time Democratic party politician and a big-time craft union official before he came to industrial unionism and socialism. As Democrat he had been elected Terre Haute city clerk and Indiana state legislator. As craft unionist he had risen to the post of secretary-treasurer of the Brotherhood of Locomotive Firemen and Enginemen and editor of the brotherhood's journal. All this was prelude. He went on to organize the American Railway Union along industrial lines and lead it into battle against the Pullman Company and the nation's railroad corporations, which were promptly reinforced by the United States Attorney General, by federal judges, jailers, and troops. For defying this concentration of power he was imprisoned. In jail he was converted to socialism. By 1906 he was the most celebrated labor orator and strike leader of his time and the standard bearer of American socialism. When Debs spoke of guns and revolution it was not the voice of youth or innocence.

And what of the man in whose behalf he spoke, Big Bill Haywood? To radicals who came of age between the two world wars he was not as important as Debs, but he was important. If some of these radicals are shaken up by revolutionary hyperbole today, Haywood ought to give them at least a twinge of retroactive uneasiness. He came to New York's Cooper Union in the pre-Christmas season of 1911 to speak, he said, about the class struggle. "I don't know of anything that can be applied," he told his audience, "that will bring as much satisfaction to you, and as much anguish to the boss as a little sabotage in the right place at the proper time. Find out what it means. It won't hurt you, and it will cripple the boss." Describing the class struggle as he knew it in the hard-rock mining regions of his native Rocky Mountains, he concluded: ". . . having contended with all the bitter things that we have been called upon to drink to the dregs, do you blame me when I say that I despise the law and I am not a law-abiding citizen? And more than that, no Socialist can be a law-abiding citizen."

Violence was endemic in Haywood's background and experience, as is manifest in his autobiography. He tells, for instance, of a time when he and Moyer visited the Cripple Creek, Colorado, gold-mining district where the National Guard had been called out in a strike and had set up a bullpen to accommodate strikers taken into custody under martial law. Before they left Denver this dialogue took place:

HAYWOOD: I don't propose to spend any time in the bullpen.
MOYER: Well, what are you going to do if they arrest us?
HAYWOOD: Let's shoot it out with them.

As they packed a couple of extra revolvers in a bag Haywood said, "If we don't need these we can leave them with the boys."

That was in the line of duty and, as Haywood reported, "Everything was perfectly quiet in Cripple Creek." Another incident was different on both counts. It happened in Denver on Election Day and involved Dan McDonald, president of the American Labor Union, a short-lived western venture into industrial unionism, and Haywood and Moyer. As the labor trio emerged from the back door of a saloon (all saloons were supposed to be closed on Election Day), they ran into a group of deputy sheriffs, headed by James O'Neill, young nephew of Captain Felix O'Neill of the Denver police. The deputies wore badges.

MOYER: Pretty badges.
O'NEILL: Don't you like 'em?
MOYER: Indeed I do; I'd like to have one for my dog.

That's when the fight started. Moyer was floored with a fist between the eyes ("The man must have had on brass knuckles," Haywood wrote). McDonald went down when O'Neill bashed his forehead with the butt of a big six-shooter. That left Haywood to face the deputies. He was hit on the head with a gun. Then he dropped to his knees and drew a .38-caliber Colt he had slipped into his pocket before setting out for the Election Day rounds. O'Neill came at him and Haywood fired three times in quick succession. "My three bullets hit him in the left arm, permanently crippling it," Haywood later recalled. "Two bullets had lodged in the bone, or I probably would have killed him, as his arm seemed to be across his body when I shot him."

Haywood received this medical report from the surgeon who was stitching his scalp wound after having tended to O'Neill. The surgeon remarked that Haywood was lucky O'Neill's wounds were no worse. "I'm sorry I hurt him so badly," Haywood replied, "but from now on I'll carry a stronger shooting gun."

True, the episode occurred in 1903 when Haywood was thirty-four and a rough-and-tumble union leader who had never been away from his native West with its leftovers of frontier custom. But when he wrote about it in the mid-1920s, with a touch of bravado and without a trace of regret, he was a Communist nearing sixty and living in Moscow, not far from the Kremlin where half his ashes soon were to be interred (the other half, by his request, were taken to Waldheim Cemetery, Chicago, to be placed near the graves of the Haymarket martyrs).

Haywood and Debs — their heyday, it might be objected, was before World War I; but what about the 1920s and '30s, which were my formative years, when the Communist party became the premier force on the American Left? Well, there was the 1929 strike of textile workers at Gastonia, North Carolina, which was led by Communists. In April a gang of masked vigilantes wrecked the union hall and beat up strikers. In June another raid, led by Gastonia police chief F. O. Aderholt, was directed at strike headquarters. This time the strikers and their Communist leaders were armed and ready. They met their assailants with gunfire, killing the police chief and three of his deputies. If any of my youthful associates faulted the Communist strike leaders for having guns and using them in those circumstances I did not hear of it. Indeed our response was expressed in a vignette by William Z. Foster, the Communist leader, in his memoirs *Pages from a Worker's Life*. This was published a decade after the Gastonia episode, so he had time to reflect upon it.

Foster recalled a visit to the Gastonia union hall toward the flickering end of the strike, after the second vigilante foray, after the armed defense of the hall and the consequent imprisonment of the strike leaders. There had been still another raid and an extensive reign of terror in which several union organizers had been flogged and Ella May Wiggin, a strike leader and labor songwriter, had been killed by gunmen on a public highway. There were threats then of one more vigilante assault upon the union hall to finish off the strike.

Foster and a companion drove up to the union headquarters after dusk and were loudly hailed by a union sentinel, all alone and armed. Foster asked the lone sentinel whether he was aware of the threatened raid. He was, he said, and ready for it. He seemed particularly determined to defend a freshly painted union sign on the building front that had replaced one destroyed by vigilantes. "In his Southern drawl," Foster recalled, "he quietly told us that the man who should climb up to take down that sign would surely die, no matter what happened to himself. And I had not the slightest doubt that he would have been as good as his word had the occasion developed."

The incident of the armed sentinel is the core of a brief essay on Jimmie Higgins, "the type of tireless, devoted, disciplined, self-sacrificing and brave worker — the very salt of the working class." Writing of it a decade later Foster said, "In the years that have passed, the figure of that lone union picket has stood out clear and bright to me as Jimmie Higgins at his best." (Jimmie Higgins is a mythical character, originally created by Debs's running mate in the 1904 presidential elections, Ben Hanford. In 1919 Upton Sinclair published a novel called *Jimmie Higgins*. Foster's description of him is consistent with the traditional image.)

As with the white textile workers at Gastonia, so with the black sharecroppers at Camp Hill, Alabama. Led by Communists they defended with guns a meeting of their Sharecroppers Union against a raid by white terrorists in December 1932. The count of known casualties was four dead and more than a score wounded.

What is the point of all this history? Definitely it is not the point imbedded in the folksong line: "I did the same when I was young," which translates: I understand the careless follies of youth because I, too, committed them when I was young. This is the patronizing tolerance that, in the conceit of age, is supposed to establish the link of empathy between generations in a well-ordered world. It does nothing of the sort. Anyway, the historical episodes are not cited as exemplars of youthful folly; there is some folly in them but more wisdom, and neither the wisdom nor the folly is related to any biological cycle. The episodes are cited to illuminate a tradition, and even more important to indicate the continuity of a movement radically opposed to the existing social order and dedicated to its revolutionary overthrow and replacement.

It is of some importance in developing a sense of history that the response of young ghetto militants to the threatened execution of Newton was so similar in essential elements to Debs's response to the threatened execution of Haywood sixty-two years before. It is similarly significant that guns are no radical novelty. Either in rhetoric or in actual use they are part of the American radical tradition in this century. There is historical continuity in this. Call it a continuity of revolutionary temper that is not the exclusive trait of any one generation. But there is also discontinuity, which is well revealed in Debs's appeal on behalf of Haywood and his colleagues.

Debs's first premise was that between the Haymarket tragedy in Chicago and the pending trial in Boise there had been "twenty years of revolutionary education, agitation and organization." It is not simply a matter of his own will, passion, or indignation, but of the cumulative impact of education, agitation, organization. Therefore he speaks not of small, scattered armed bands, which can be fashioned by small numbers of individual wills and passions, but of "a million revolutionists, at least . . . with guns." On a comparable scale he envisions the enemy, not only local cops or even state officials in Idaho and Colorado, but the copper kings of the Rockies and the financial oligarchs of New York. All this is integral to his prophecy of revolution.

Cogent arguments undoubtedly can be made that Debs really could not have delivered on his promise to precipitate a revolution and lead a million revolutionists with guns if Haywood and his fellows were hanged. Such arguments would be a futile exercise. Debs did not write in the spirit of a bookkeeper advising his employer on the sufficiency of his collateral to sign a promissory note. Why then should anyone demand that in this respect young Panthers be more shrewdly calculating and prudent than Debs was with his greater years and experience?

Central in Debs's vision was conscious action by organized millions. Therefore he disagreed with Haywood's sally about the personal gratification of sabotage, with its underlying logic and its many implications. Several years after his acquittal in the Boise trial Haywood set down his thoughts on law and sabotage in a theoretical tract that provoked a sharp polemic by Debs. The difference between the two men was real, but so was the difference between Haywood's practice and his rhetoric.

Typically his insinuating remark about "a little sabotage in the right place at the proper time" was delivered at a Left-Wing meeting in New York. The spirit that moved him at such New York gatherings was revealed in the statement of his theme: "I am going to speak on the class struggle, and I am going to make it so plain that even a lawyer can understand it. I am going to present the class struggle so clearly here tonight that even a preacher will know its meaning . . . Socialism is so plain, so clear, so simple that when a person becomes intellectual he doesn't understand socialism." (In the same vein he delivered his best aphorism, "A Christian Socialist is one who is drunk on religious fanaticism and is trying to sober up on economic truth.") For Haywood the New York socialist movement was the lair of lawyers, preachers, and intellectuals, and in waging serious ideological war with these dilettantes, as he saw them, it was also his proletarian pleasure to taunt them.

He was not tempted by such pleasures in Lawrence, Massachusetts, where he led a strike of 22,000 textile workers. To these workers, who faced 1400 soldiers with bayonets, court injunctions, and modified martial law, Haywood did not talk about sabotage. Instead he talked in the most elementary terms of the power in the unity of the workers, as he did when they finally won. "Everything for your uplift rests in your hands. Single-handed you are helpless, but united you can win everything . . . You have won by massing your brains and your muscle and withholding your labor from the bosses." On this occasion he also said, "No one can point to any striker and say that he committed any violence . . ." Leading the class struggle in Lawrence was different from talking about it in New York, or from writing about it in tracts designed for debate within the Socialist party. Haywood was a phenomenal strike organizer and orator. In the Lawrence woolen mills, workers of seventeen nationalities were employed, most of them foreign-born with only a meager knowledge of the English language. It was said they understood Haywood even when they could understand no one else who addressed them in English.

On the battle line Haywood, like Debs, placed his faith in the organized action of the mass. This was so even when he packed his revolver for the trip to Cripple Creek, for he was then entering a battle zone where thousands of miners and smeltermen were arrayed against troops, private gunmen, and strikebreakers. In that context, if he had resorted to the revolver it would not have been the daring exploit of a lone Western gunslinger; it would have been an episode in a mass confrontation. The guns of the other side already were much in evidence. To the workers Haywood led, an armed encounter, if it came to that, would have been comprehensible and valid resistance to the naked violence of the mining companies and the state government.

The same may be said with even greater certainty about the

white textile workers and black sharecroppers of Gastonia and Camp Hill. They were trying to form unions and win modest economic improvements. The legitimacy of such objectives was self-evident to them and ostensibly was recognized in other regions by society at large. Pursuit of legitimate aims imparted its own logic to armed defense of their right to engage in it against the illegitimate terrorism of their enemies. The means were not superimposed upon the conflict as arbitrary choices of the Communist leaders, they grew out of the conflict and the tactics of the other side; they were, in a sense, incidental to the conflict. Of course the combatants and their leaders had to choose; they could have rejected armed self-defense, but their choice of it derived justification from the circumstances.

What was manifest on a primitive level in Gastonia and Camp Hill was expressed on a sophisticated plane in Debs's broadside on the Haywood-Moyer-Pettibone case. The workers permitted the Haymarket executions, he argued, because they did not recognize them as acts of class vengeance, but then two decades of revolutionary education, agitation, and organization followed. Now the workers could comprehend that the issue in the Boise case was not simply the lives of the three defendants but the fate of their class, that the execution of Haywood and his colleagues would be vengeful violence against the class, and they therefore would respond in kind. A violent confrontation between the classes on a national scale, involving a million revolutionists, at least, with guns — this would be a revolutionary crisis and he would do all in his power to resolve it with the triumph of the revolution.

Such was the essential logic of Debs. As in Gastonia and Camp Hill so here the resort to guns would acquire validity for the mass as a response to the illegitimate violence of the ruling powers. Illegitimate not only in the narrow juridical sense (i.e., legal frame-up in Boise, and extralegal terror in the Southern towns), but also in a profound social sense because the violence was designed to thwart attainment of legitimate objectives: formation and consolidation of effective unions. The Boise prosecution of Haywood, being aimed at the Western Federation of Miners, reflected the national resolve of the big corporations not to tolerate a militant industrial union in basic industry. They were to hew successfully to this line for three more decades.

A common design can be sketched in broad outline from Boise to Gastonia. Large numbers of people are involved in battle to satisfy needs they feel and understand. But their objectives transcend that which the ruling powers are ready to concede in the given time and place. The ruling powers resort to overt violence. The mass of their antagonists responds in kind. This violence has mass sanction because it flows from mass experience.

To Debs, Haywood, and Foster the pattern schematically outlined above would have seemed natural because all three were schooled in industrial battles that involved many thousands of workers. Everything — objectives, tactics, style — had to be related to the mass constituency. Without it there was either no battle or a prior certainty of defeat. They had to reckon with the experience and consciousness of this constituency to make their proposals comprehensible and valid to it. They carried their acquired tactical sense with them from the industrial wars into the much broader and far more complicated arena of revolutionary battle to overturn the existing social order.

Habit was reinforced by logic. To them power was no catchword. They knew it as adversary in its dominant forms, as corporate giant, as government employing its ultimate weapon, military force. Debs had confronted the United States army in the railroad strike of 1894. Haywood had seen the National Guard as an army of occupation in mining towns during the industrial wars that extended over several years in the Rocky Mountain region at the turn of the century. Foster, in the great steel strike of 1919, had to contend with federal troops, state militia, and the Pennsylvania State Constabulary, popularly known as the Coal and Iron Police because it served virtually as the private army of the coal and steel companies. In the union leaders' eyes the intensity of the battle and the enormity of the force marshaled against them attested to the reality and the potential of the power they led. This was the power of thousands, even hundreds of thousands of workers, and indirectly of millions. If such powers clashed in battle for partial stakes, for modest economic reforms in the railroad, metal mining, and steel industries, what would it be like when everything was at stake? It seemed axiomatic to them that the power of the workers en masse — more conscious, more resolute, more inclusive — was prerequisite for a revolutionary assault to gain mastery over the country's productive wealth and political structure. Moreover, in their combat experience they perceived the glimmerings of the greatest consciousness and resolution that would be needed in the final conflict.

The three men are not chosen at random. They were the most prominent personalities of the three major revolutionary organizations on the American scene thus far in the twentieth century: the Socialist Party, the Industrial Workers of the World, the Communist Party. Those organizations were profoundly dissimilar in theory, program, method. The men were strong personalities with distinct personal styles. Haywood's Election Day caper in Denver, for instance, was strictly the mark of personal style; it did not fit into any calculated framework of strategy or tactics. In Debs's personality the quality of human compassion was so pervasive that Horace Traubel, friend and disciple of Walt Whitman, said of him, "When Debs speaks a harsh word it is wet with tears." One of Foster's hallmarks was a purposeful self-discipline that excluded the bravado of Haywood and the conspicuous emotion of Debs. Different organizations, different personalities, and yet the three shared a community of experience and basic attitudes shaped by it. Each possessed a gut sense of class identification and for each the power of the mass was the fulcrum of revolutionary strategy. These attitudes they had in common, along with the qualities of revolutionary temper and integrity.

Those qualities of temper are more easily shared by today's young radicals than the attitudes toward class and mass. And for the most compelling of reasons. Their experience has been so different. Debs could exclaim that in the gleam of U.S. army bayonets and the flash of U.S. army rifles during the Pullman strike he saw the class struggle revealed, but neither the exclamation nor the revelation emerges from the experience of the present generation. It also has seen rifles and bayonets, but typically it has seen them at the 1968 Democratic convention in Chicago, in suppression of ghetto rebellions, in military invasion of campus communities. Such personal witness or encounter may nourish revolutionary temper but it cannot make for the class identification of the predecessors. It cannot make for the same sense of certainty about the human agency for radical change or revolution. In the social miscellany assembled for the Chicago confrontation or in a mass expression of discontent on campus there just is not the latent power that was revealed to Debs and those others. The ghetto represents a more concentrated, more formidable power — more closely resembling, therefore, class power. Yet it is not of the same magnitude, either in numbers or in indispensable function in the social structure. For that matter, young white radicals cannot identify with the ghetto, not in the same intimate, unequivocal sense that those older revolutionaries identified with the working class. They are not of the ghetto, nor can they relate to it in the same way.

The consequence is a gap between commitment to revolution and any coherent conception of the power that can bring it about. Like any gap between desire and fulfillment it creates tension and frustration. The curse of frustration is not dispelled by shouts of "Power to the People!" This slogan has meaning only when joined with the premise that the people have the capacity to take power and to wield it. The indispensable premise dwindles and vanishes as some radicals peel off layer after layer of the population (among them the working class, all white-skinned persons, a great multitude of black Uncle Toms and brown *Tíos Tacos*) and discard these layers as hopeless in a radical contest for power. They may shout "Power to the People" but it lacks meaning. Such rhetorical use of "the people" resembles the conventional usage by the politicians, liberal or reactionary, although the purposes are opposite. The ritualistic reference to "the people" by the status quo politicians is designed to perpetuate the illusion that the people now have power. The challenging thrust of the radical slogan is that the people do not have power and ought to take it. But when the slogan is stripped of the premise that gives it meaning then the future conquest of power by the people becomes as illusory as their present possession of it. You get a conflict of illusions, "power to the people" versus "government of the people," because in both phrases "the people" is invoked as an image, not as a history-making force. The upshot is that power remains where it is, which is fine for those who possess it and for their retainers and beneficiaries.

Debs, Haywood, and Foster might have had reservations about the "power to the people" slogan. In their vision of a class-divided society it would have seemed ambiguous because it avoids the issue: which people? They replied along class lines: the working class, the working people. Actually, in peeling off population layers as useless in the contest for power the contemporary radical also attests to a certain ambiguity in the slogan he employs. Yet those older revolutionaries, with their conception of clear-cut class lines, came closer to embracing "the people" than many present-day radicals do with their classless or class-blurred vision of society. The former, at least, saw a popular majority as their potential constituency; the latter, in their selection of the chosen people, are much more exclusive.

Each conception dictates its own tactical logic. In one conception a majority class, both by virtue of its preponderant numbers and its decisive position in the economic structure of society, is seen as the instrument of social change. Tactics then are related to the realization of this potential. The other conception embraces a miscellaneous assortment of social groupings; neither in numbers nor in social function do they, even in their sum, represent a credible power to overturn the social order. Tactics then are more likely to be molded by subjective factors, to become elements of style of individuals or elite groups. In the matter of violence, for example, the historical record demonstrates that the difference is not about its use in principle or in general, but about the social context and consequence of its practical employment. To the representatives of the former generation it was related and subordinated to what they perceived as the fundamental problem: the enhancement of the strength, cohesion, and self-awareness of the working class. No such compass guides those contemporary radicals for whom violence has become a thing in itself, unrelated to the comprehension or experience of any mass constituency. Indeed, in some instances it has become the deliberate substitute for any serious effort to win a mass constituency, which is dismissed as an illusion in any foreseeable future.

In the succession of generations my own comes between those of Debs, Haywood, and Foster and the younger generation of the present. I have said that some of my contemporaries are discomfited or outraged by the rhetoric and practice that are common among young radicals. What exactly prompts this reaction? Is it the temper that forms a historical bond with the revolutionaries of the day before yesterday? Or is it the divergence from their conceptions of class and mass? The answers cannot be neatly catalogued. For one thing, despite the inclination to package generations, they are not packages of standardized human products. For another, individual motivations are frequently mixed. Still, quite often the negative reaction *is* directed at the quality of revolutionary temper. And even dispute about tactics and the conceptions that underlie them is often marked by a peculiar distemper and hostility, by an irritated conceit that complains about the irrational behavior of crazy kids. There is absolutely no sense of history in that, no confrontation with the changed social reality and experience that shape the social behavior of the present generation.

Also missing is what has been called "compassionate solidarity." Debs exemplified this quality beautifully in the wake of the guilty plea by the McNamara brothers, J.B. and J.J., in the dynamiting of the Los Angeles Times Building that inadvertently took twenty-one lives on the night of October 1, 1910. The dynamite charge was set off as reprisal against the *Times* for its aggressive leadership in a frequently violent open shop campaign against unions in general, and particularly against a

strike of the Structural Iron Workers Union with which the Mc-
Namaras were associated.

During the trial of J. B. McNamara, first to be prosecuted,
the brothers suddenly changed their plea from not guilty to
guilty. They were induced to do so by Lincoln Steffens, the
great muckraker, who enlisted Clarence Darrow, the McNamaras' chief counsel, and others to reinforce his own powers of
persuasion. Steffens believed he had the prior agreement of the
business interests, which dominated Los Angeles, to match the
McNamaras' guilty plea with restraint in the punishment to be
imposed and with abandonment of their intransigent refusal to
deal with unions. Such reasonableness, he hoped, would lead
to the triumph of the golden rule in industrial relations.
Steffens' hope, romantic in its reliance upon pure reason, was
swept away by the anti-union frenzy in the wake of the McNamaras' guilty plea; instead of the golden rule the open shop was
more firmly and vengefully entrenched. More arrests and prosecutions followed despite the supposed understanding that
there would be none. That's a complicated and controversy-
laden story; here we are concerned with certain radical reactions after the guilty plea, after the McNamaras were deserted
in droves by former supporters, who felt they had been deceived or betrayed.

Describing himself as "a working class brother of the McNamara brothers after as well as before their confession and conviction," Debs declared: "I absolutely refuse to join in the capitalist clamor and craft union claque of denunciation of these
condemned unionists . . . As a workingman I absolutely refuse to condemn men as murderers under the moral code of
the capitalist class for fighting according to their lights on the
side of the working class."

Debs referred to the harshness of the industrial wars at the
time, to the ruthlessness of the employers, to the cruel defeats
inflicted upon the craft unions. Then he asked:

"Who shall say that these craft unionists, the McNamara
brothers, defeated at every turn and threatened from every side
by the remorseless power of the trusts and the forces of govern-

ment, are conscienceless criminals when in such a desperate extremity they resort to the brutal methods of self-preservation
which the m⌐ ⌐ers and exploiters of their class have forced
upon them?

"As between this blind and cruel extreme and the opposite
extreme of abject and cowardly surrender, the former is infinitely preferable; for at least the spirit of resistance to oppression, and the poverty and misery which spring from oppression,
keeps the hope alive that the horrors of slavery shall not endure
forever."

Debs injected a historical note: "I utterly abhor murder, but
I have my own idea as to what constitutes murder. John Brown
was an atrocious murderer in the eyes of the slave power, but
today he is one of the greatest heroes of history . . ."

In the above context Debs made clear his own position on the
dynamiting as a class-war tactic. "The acts to which the Mc-
Namaras have confessed . . . I do not approve," he wrote,
"nor does any other Socialist; and such acts would never be
committed if it were in our power to prevent them." His references to the McNamaras as "craft unionists" also serve as a line
of ideological demarcation; in those days "craft unionism" and
"industrial unionism" were employed as alternate labels for
conservatism and radicalism in the labor movement. Indeed,
Debs said, "Their acts are the logical outcome of the impotency
and helplessness of the craft form of unionism," the implication
being that industrial unionism as the more embracing form,
more effectively marshaling the power of the workers, would
persuasively eliminate resort to conspiratorial terrorism. But
all this was subordinated to his passionate affirmation of solidarity with the McNamaras against "the masters and exploiters."

Haywood's response was simpler. "While the capitalist class
is writing the criminal record of the Bridge and Structural Iron
Workers Union," he said, "it is no part of the duty of Socialists
to be assisting them in their work, but it is our duty to compile
the category of crimes perpetrated by the capitalist class. As
for me, I am a defendant in every case where the working class

or its representatives are on trial and the capitalist class is the plaintiff. Therefore my heart is with the McNamara boys as long as they are fighting in the interests of the working class."

As for Foster he developed a long, intimate friendship with J. B. McNamara, visiting him as often as he could at San Quentin and Folsom prisons, where J.B. was confined for more than thirty-one years before he was released to the grave. "His friends," Foster wrote, including himself in that category, "love him with almost limitless devotion and admiration . . . McNamara is a splendid example of the invincible working class spirit . . . His name deserves to stand high indeed on the roster of the heroes of the labor movement." Foster's tributes to McNamara were no testimonials to the 1910 explosion. Asserting that prison was McNamara's university, Foster wrote, "He now realizes that the workers cannot solve their problems by a few heroic trade union battlers, such as he and his co-workers were, carrying on terroristic work, but that the workers must unite as a class, put an end to the capitalist system and erect a new, free socialist society."

Differences in outlook and personal style can be discerned in the responses of Debs, Haywood, and Foster, but once again there is a common bond of elemental class identification and solidarity. Haywood conspicuously refrained from any assessment of the McNamaras' specific act. His declaration that his heart was with them was made during the same speech in which he recommended a little sabotage. Later on he did not bother to dispute the accusation of ideological opponents in the Socialist party that his advocacy of sabotage was espousal of what the McNamaras had done. Debs and Foster, on the other hand, ventured lightly into critical assessments, but with different shadings of emphasis. For them, as well as for Haywood, however, the paramount fact was that the McNamaras were combatants on their side in a relentless war between the classes.

Today individual terror as a radical tactic is not marked with or defined by such elementary class lines. Class motivation and class objective do not seem so clear and simple. In the ghetto, to be sure, the encounter with oppression and injustice is at least as elemental; the impulse to individual violence as protest or retaliation, or even as tactic to attain a specific goal, is comparable to that cited by Debs in the McNamara case. But yielding to the impulse is subject to comparable objections as to its efficacy. Whatever might be said about the ghetto, it does not hold true for white radicals who make a cult of terrorism. Compared with the McNamaras' rationale theirs seems much fuzzier; its very extravagance in justifying acts of terror makes the resort to such acts seem more futile.

The McNamaras, after all, were conservative; they were craft unionists, Democrats, and members of the Militia of Christ, a Catholic organization. They were engaged in war with the National Erectors Association, a combine of construction contractors who employed their craft. It seemed to them that selective use of dynamite, joined with the weapons of organization and strike, would help secure union recognition and the establishment of union standards on the job. These elementary pragmatic aims were not wrapped in radical rhetoric. The McNamaras had no illusion that dynamite would shake or disrupt the system, let alone blow it up. For that matter they were not interested in overthrowing the system. Their aims were infinitely more modest and the very modesty of their aims helped make dynamite more plausible to them. Destruction of property, they reckoned, might induce men of wealth, who valued property above all else, to come to terms, to concede to the workers a little more of the wealth they produced.

Such a rationale for dynamite to compensate for labor's lesser power in the war with capital exerted the attraction of simple logic. The rationale (and dynamite) had been indulged in before. But the consequences of the McNamara episode were the most disastrous. To begin with there was the tragic mischance that took twenty-one lives, magnifying the passion and outrage of the backlash. Then there was the timing; the explosion was touched off just when a powerful movement was gathering for economic and political reform, stimulated and prodded by a spectacular growth in radical strength. In Los Angeles this national trend was expressed dramatically in the candidacy of Job Harriman, attorney and Socialist party leader, for mayor. Before the McNamaras' guilty plea, the political odds, based on the tangible results of the primary vote, were that Harriman would carry the then pending final election. After their plea Harriman's defeat was sealed. The popular movement, which the Socialist campaign embodied and which bore the promise of creating most favorable circumstances for union organization in Los Angeles, was stunned and shattered. Just when it seemed that this open shop citadel might be breached by a popular upsurge it was rendered more impregnable by dynamite and its aftermath.

As it turned out historically the broad-scale realization of the McNamaras' trade union aims nationally a quarter of a century later was not effected with dynamite, it was done with sit-down strikes in the rubber plants of Akron in 1936 and the auto plants of Flint in 1937, in the San Francisco general strike of 1934. Violence marked those battles (in San Francisco the workers improvised barricades to meet police charges up Rincon Hill and police bullets killed two waterfront pickets; in Flint sit-down strikers effectively employed a plant firehose and a barrage of iron bolts, bottles, and coffee mugs to repel massive police efforts to dislodge them from General Motors plants). Those battles spilled out of the bounds of legality, but the decisive factor was the massive power of the workers.

History, as it were, validated the tactical judgments of Debs and Foster. It is also necessary, however, to place in historical perspective their total response to the McNamara case. Allowing for all the difference in circumstance between the time of the McNamaras and the present, the display of compassionate solidarity with them retains the power of suggestion. What is the relation of tactical disagreement to a larger community of aims? How is morality defined in battle against injustice, oppression, exploitation? The questions may be posed as rhetorical abstractions, but they manifest themselves in concrete shapes and they are best answered in these shapes.

Precedent can be useful in arriving at such answers, but to

the degree that the answers are addressed to the questions as they actually arise in social conflict the usefulness of past experience is defined by the sense of history with which it is informed. Somehow this sense of history has been lost or obscured and the burden for this rests upon the older generation whose experience, after all, comprises the history immediately antecedent to the present and is the living link to what had gone on before. Yet some of my contemporaries lament, "The kids don't have a sense of history," and they do so without any tinge of self-criticism, without any apparent awareness that a pertinent question might be, well what have *you* done with history? In reply two diverse witnesses are offered from the American labor movement: Einar Mohn, conservative and shrewd chieftain of the Western Conference of Teamsters, and Harry Bridges, President of the International Longshoremen's and Warehousemen's Union, the foremost personal embodiment of Left-Wing unionism to a whole generation. Addressing his union's convention in 1969 Bridges observed that younger ILWU members "don't understand much about our history, nor do they care — and I'm not so sure they should care." In contrast, Mohn's point was that the older members did not seem to understand or care, not enough to recall their own history in contemplating present-day phenomena.

"Now I don't believe in violence on the campus," Mohn told teamsters and auto workers at the founding conference of the Alliance for Labor Action that year, "but why do we get so thin-skinned about this? I remember when it was a high-risk insurance to cross a picket line or scab. I remember a city on the Great Lakes where buildings were taken over by the workers, held for a number of days, and we weren't so thin-skinned then."

That last remark was aimed especially at auto workers whose union emerged from a wave of sit-down strikes. The teamsters, on the other hand, have been especially proficient in the care and treatment of scabs. Mohn was saying that the modern American labor movement was born in transgressions against legality; there is no law that says you can "dump a scab," and nothing is more sanctified in law than the prerogatives of property, which were violated by the sit-down strikers when they occupied the factories without the sanction of their owners. Confronting men who had done these things, who had employed illegal violence and force, Mohn asked: why are you so thin-skinned now when similar things are done on campus? This question invites another: if you cannot relate your past, the history through which you lived and that you helped make, to the present, then how can you expect those whose total experience is in the present to relate it to a past they do not know? Bridges answers simply that he does not expect them to and is not sure they should and in doing so he avoids the issue posed by Mohn about the capacity or inclination of labor's veterans to invest their history with contemporary meaning, even for themselves, let alone anyone else.

Whichever view you choose — Mohn's or Bridges' — labor history is a luckless, forlorn thing, abandoned by those who knew it in its more spirited days and the object of indifference among those who have no personal acquaintance with it. Radical history encompasses more than labor history but both are intertwined, and a similarity in their fate is illustrated by two episodes of recent times.

The first concerns the labor movement. When the American Federation of Labor was to move from its old headquarters in Washington, D.C., to a new building some years ago, the problem arose of what to do with the old records and correspondence files that had been stored in the basement of the old building. President George Meany decreed he would choose what was to be salvaged and the rest would be destroyed. The bulk of the archives, containing invaluable and irreplaceable material on the history of American labor, was destroyed at Meany's direction. Symptomatic of his values, only the financial records were wholly and scrupulously preserved. The life of the movement was reduced to a fiscal account, to per capita receipts and financial disbursements.

The second episode concerns the Socialist party. Fallen upon lean days it decided some years ago to move its national office to more modest quarters and then it faced the problem of what to do with its records and correspondence files. The people in charge concluded that some of the older files, which could not be fitted into the new quarters, should be junked. Luckily they summoned a junkman who had a better sense of history (or a keener scent for money) than the Socialist functionaries. He consulted a dealer in rare documents and papers with whom he did business on occasion. The consequence was the collection of Socialist party materials at Duke University in North Carolina.

If elder custodians of the historical records of the labor and socialist movements treat their trust as a bookkeeper's dream or a junk dealer's delight, why indeed should the young care about the history of either movement? Something more than a generational gulf is involved here. It is a void in which much is lost, first of all a sense of historic root. Without this sense a movement cannot comprehend itself, cannot understand its development, cannot see itself in historical perspective. Its self-critical faculty is diminished; it is more prone to inertia, more easily buffeted and swayed by any wayward new wave or current.

Narrow-minded lapses of chance custodians of archives as property are at most symbolical or symptomatic. The greater responsibility for the fate of radical history falls upon men who love archives too well, the historians. They have created a historical hiatus. It is the period during which the hegemony of communism on the American Left was visible and recognizable. The dominant historical schools treat this period as an aberrant interlude, as a break in the historical continuum of American radicalism. In terms of the prominent personalities in this essay their formula would be: Debs yes, Haywood maybe, Foster no. And this formula would be offered as judgment of their relevancy to the development of American radicalism. Primary importance attaches to the choice of what is to be judged. Not the inherent strengths or weaknesses of these men and the movements they represented but their legitimacy, as it were, in the historical succession. And the standards for establishing legitimacy concede much to the unique strain in the American tradition that made "un-American" a utilitarian political label. It is not done with the crassness and vulgarity of the professional exploiters of the label. The label itself is not used. It is done with greater sophistication and subtlety, and yet the major radical expression and experience of an American generation is excised from the historical sequence as being alien to it.

Such an approach does violence to a sense of history for it attempts to remove a link in the historical chain by decreeing that it does not properly belong there. But just the same it *is* there, fastened to the links that precede and follow it. Furthermore, in a historical chain the interconnection is not mechanical; each link reflects those that preceded and foreshadows those to come. Each link then, despite probable distortions in reflection and projection, can help toward a deeper understanding of what went on before and what follows.

Failure to come to terms in their historical context with the decades of Communist preeminence on the American Left hobbles the comprehension of history before and after that era. In large part this failure is a legacy of the years of McCarthyism. Not so much in the simplistic acceptance of McCarthyite premises and standards, although there is a good deal of that, as in the more subtle residual influences of McCarthyism, which affect Communists as well as their critics. During the worst of the McCarthyite assault Communists and those within their political orbit were thrown on the defensive and compelled to retreat. For them at least it was a fighting retreat, which is more than can be said for others who ducked, ran, or accommodated McCarthyism. Nonetheless defense and retreat tend to create certain behavior patterns in which a political instinct of self-preservation overshadows all else. As temporary expedients such patterns are understandable and, within certain limits, valid. The trouble arises when these patterns become a way of political life, when a besieged fortress mentality persists even after the siege is breached or lifted in the main. Some Communists and their followers, and ex-Communists, too, have not shed the fortress mentality acquired in the McCarthyite era.

This mentality distorts or obstructs their view of what had

gone on before. They are not likely to tell young radicals, "I did the same when I was young." But this is not out of sensitivity or restraint. They are not likely to say it because they prefer to forget what they did or what they stood for. They are no help in a perception of radical history.

Among non-Communist Leftists and assorted liberals the effects of McCarthyism take other shapes. Some of them acknowledge they behaved badly, either through neutrality during the McCarthyite assault or by abetting it. In their satisfaction at seeing the Communists take a beating they did not calculate all the consequences, and some managed to get in a few licks of their own, contributing to the overall lynch atmosphere. Even among those who regret such behavior one encounters rationalizations and extenuations for it. Yes, we behaved badly, but — If this is what self-critics do, what is to be expected from those radicals and liberals who have expressed no qualms, although their behavior was similar? They have a vested psychological interest in justifying their supporting roles in the McCarthyite spectacle. This need is served by the historical treatment of communism as a foreign substance in the body of American radicalism.

All of the above contributes to the peculiar contours of a generational gap in American radicalism. It does not create the gap. Latent generational contradictions are likely to be exacerbated in a time of profound and swift social change. Just as in a protracted period of social equilibrium and stability, when the environment and experience of successive generations remain pretty much the same, generational friction is imperceptible. Given the character of our time a gap was in the cards. But some of its manifestations in a particular country are influenced by specific circumstances. The concern here is with one such circumstance: the treatment of a significant experience of the generation that is on the receding side of the divide.

What does it matter? What value is there to a personal witness by a participant in that experience? That we be better understood is very important to us, but its importance to anyone else is dubious. If this were the whole matter Bridges might be right in saying he is not sure the younger generation should care. If, however, a better understanding of those times serves to restore and reinforce a sense of history, the value of it is of another magnitude. A sense of history could help the present generation to a better understanding of itself.

III. Semiprofessional
Revolutionary—1

AFTER MY FATHER VANISHED my mother and I spent a long, dismal winter in Chicago. Then we moved to New York where she had more friends and *landsleit*. The country also moved — from normalcy with Harding to prosperity with Coolidge, but these trademarks of a period had little meaning for a widow of forty with a boy child, and with the wage level and insecurity of a semiskilled worker in the garment industry. We roomed with families. Affluent families do not take in roomers to share kitchen, bath, and toilet, to intrude upon the privacy of their lives. Even the moderately well-off, who might rent out a room, tend to draw the line at two-at-a-time mother-and-child package deals.

We roomed with poor families (on three occasions at least in households headed by widows) who were prepared to trade privacy and other familial amenities for the cheap rental we could afford. We had no privacy either, but somehow being the observer was often worse than being the observed. Worst of all was being thrust into the middle of another family's quarrels. Your room was no shelter from the screams, the abuse, the occasional violence, the frequent tears. You sat in the room with the door shut, but it did not shut out the flood of anger and hate. And not a neat hate. It was messy with ambivalence and guilt (especially in a shrill exchange between mother and daughter over something like money or silk stockings, which in the Jewish ghetto culture of the time were extravagant and sinful). You tried to read or find refuge even in homework; it was no good, not with those people out there tormenting each other. You were compelled to listen, to be engulfed by this terrible tension. These people were not your kin or even your friends, you were not truly involved emotionally in their quarrel;

maybe it served as some kind of catharsis for them, but to you it was just ugly and frightening.

Not all the families we roomed with were that explosive. Those disturbances were common, though, bred by the necessity that made families take in roomers. Even without the most abrasive outbursts, which aggravated the nerve-end friction between them and us, the relationship with our landlord hosts by necessity was difficult. We grated on each other in a constant physical proximity that lacked human intimacy. The effort not to grate only made you feel more like the hostage of strangers. Inevitably the time came to move, either voluntarily or by request. We moved so often and some of our tenancies were so brief that I cannot recall all those slum tenement flats in Lower Harlem (the section called Jewish Harlem then) and the Lower Bronx, with its Jewish, Italian, and Irish layers, the young of these ethnic groups forming block gangs that engaged in occasional wars. I do know that in the five years it took to complete the eight elementary-school grades I attended eight schools. The insecurities in this school-hopping were made worse because I was nine, a greenhorn with only one word of English ("potatoes" for some inexplicable reason), when I started school, and it was not until the final year that I was with my own age group.

I was educated. I knew the four seasons of the year, and two more besides: the busy and the slack in the garment trades. (Later, when I came upon the Cuban phrase, dead season, dead seemed so much more apt than slack.) You could tell it was the slack season when there wasn't a dime for the ritual attendance at the movies on Saturday afternoon. Then you never knew how the heroine, bound and helpless, managed to get out of that flaming house in the then current film serial. It was bad luck to wear out a hole in the sole of your shoe in the slack season for you did not know how long you would have to keep on stuffing cardboard into that goddam shoe and you hoped it did not rain or snow because the cardboard sopped up the wet. Then it disintegrated and even before that you felt the damp chill of it, the discomfort, and you felt something else. You called it shame (you would have to grow up to call it the indignity of poverty or something like that). You were aware of poverty even in the busy season, but it became conspicuous in the slack. This was the season of conspicuous underconsumption.

In this world the American Dream was remote, as shadowy as the images you saw on the screen when the garment season was not too slack. Frontier, wilderness, or even nature that was not wild — these cherished legacies of the American Heritage — had little more reality than the interminable chase of cowboys and Indians. You came upon the traditional Tom Sawyer pictures, bare feet dangling, fishing pole in hand, but these were not of the world of Lower Harlem and the Lower Bronx.

When we lived in Harlem, during a solitary exploration of upper Central Park I came upon some kids fishing in a goldfish pond. Fascinated by this discovery I watched them carefully. Next day I was there with a string, a straight pin bent into a hook, and tiny balls of bread for bait. Dropping the baited pin into the pond I could see fish nibble at the bread. But there was no barb on the hook and when the line was snapped up the fish slipped off. I persevered, however, mutilating many a fish mouth but landing no fish. At last one fish, slower than the others, did not slip off the pin until it was over land. There at my feet was a real, live, palpitating goldfish. I was totally unprepared for this contingency. Abandoning the line, hook, and bait, I grabbed the fish, stuffed it in my pocket, and ran for home. The wet feel of it against my thigh served as a spur. I ran faster than I ever had before. Out of the park, across Fifth Avenue, and on to the east, passing under the elevated roadbed of the New York Central, and then turning up toward 107th Street, I think it was. Running, running, twelve or fifteen blocks, I don't remember exactly, but it was a long distance to run at that pace without a pause for breath. Hoping all this time the fish would make it, not daring to stop and look at it.

Gasping desperately now, inhaling so little air when so much was needed, feeling that if I did not pause or slow down there would be no breath at all, I came to our tenement and the four flights of stairs to our flat. A swift ascent seemed impossible, each landing cried pause, but I continued to run, up and up those stairs, finally fumbling with the key, then bursting into the flat and toward the kitchen sink. I threw the fish into a pan and filled the pan with water; slowly, inertly the fish floated to the top. End of the Young Boy and the Goldfish Pond. I did not fish again in Central Park.

Although I was nearly ten at the time this is my only distinct memory of the several months we lived in Lower Harlem. Generally the first three years in the United States, which were the toughest, are a blur. In the fourth year we roomed with a family that took us in, not out of economic necessity but out of friendship. This did not alter the seasonal rhythms of the garment trade. Nor did it create privacy; you became more involved in the family life of your hosts than you cared to be, but the abrasions were smoothed by human communication. The following year my mother married a widower, Robert Shapiro, with two sons, Leo and Yasha approximately my age, who lived in the remnants of an anarchist colony in Stelton, New Jersey.

By the time I arrived in Stelton in autumn 1926, the Ferrer Modern School, initial centerpiece of the colony, had declined to little more than a kindergarten, but the school auditorium continued to serve as a community center, a facility for amateur theatricals, concerts, lectures, dances (to the tune of an old player piano and an unchanging collection of music rolls; again and again, "through the dark of night" the piano wailed for "Chloe"). Whatever ideological energy anarchism supplied in the birth of the colony, it was long since spent. A few colonists retained the old anarchist faith, some had turned to communism, and still others to less distinct shades of radicalism. It was no community of creed. Some of the older residents occasionally entered into ideological argument, but not we adolescents. The young who outgrew adolescence also outgrew the colony; there was nothing for them there. With very few exceptions the population was polarized between the elderly and the very young.

The one resident symbol of the colony's founding faith was Hippolyte Havel, an anarchist of some stature, and also of some glamour; he was a poet and at the turn of the century had been one of Emma Goldman's lovers. He lived the life of a hermit in a shack, comforted by wine, venturing forth only infrequently. To my age group, on those rare occasions when we saw him on the road, he was a sepulchral figure stepped out of a Grecian bas-relief, with a wildly magnificent white mane and beard on an imposing head, clutching his threadbare coat about his short, stocky body as if it were a chiton. Such distant homage as we offered to this apparition was mixed with callow amusement at his weakness for wine.

He was unrelated to our daily lives. We dabbled in amateur theatricals; played games, chess, basketball, pinochle, poker; carried our bag of adolescent spirits and yearnings to the Saturday night socials at the school auditorium. Nothing unusual, yet for me it was important; I experienced a sense of community. There were no politics in this existence and very little social concern. Once, I recall, an adult asked me: since you are going to New Brunswick anyway, will you take a message to Western Union? It was a telegram, signed by several adults, to Governor Fuller of Massachusetts, demanding life and liberty for Sacco and Vanzetti. My involvement in the Sacco-Vanzetti case was peripheral at most, yet enough to make me feel some pride and importance in transmitting this message.

Unfocused and demanding no commitment, still there was a radical aura in Stelton's intellectual climate for my generation, an amorphous mixture of libertarianism, rationalism, humanism. The same mixture as was contained in the endless stream of *Little Blue Books* that issued from the Haldeman-Julius presses in Girard, Kansas. Once Girard had been the home of *The Appeal to Reason,* which in its heyday boasted the biggest circulation of any Socialist periodical on earth. Now Girard poured forth little books, really minipamphlets in size, their blue paper covers enfolding bits and pieces of human reason and soul. The assortment was wide in range and time, from sex and science to philosophy and fiction, from Plato to Frank Harris (Harris' pen portraits of his contemporaries were Haldeman-Julius staples). I was an avid reader, not a discerning critic, swallowing these blue books as they came. They were a hodgepodge, but the selective process that created this hodgepodge was influenced by the socialist background of Emanuel Halde-man-Julius. In a thirteen-year-old mind these little books, for all their mixture of taste and theme, cultivated the attitude that rationalism and rebellion were not only virtues but companion virtues. Other intellectual influences made the same imprint: Jack London, Upton Sinclair, the great Russian writers, and that blend of romanticism and radicalism called *The Gadfly*, a novel by Ethel Voynich. Such a literary catalogue was part of the environment in our new home and in the vestiges of the Ferrer colony.

Beyond the colony was rustic America, as rustic as it was then in the strip of New Jersey that straddles the main line between New York and Philadelphia. The spaces were not very open or wide but there was a cherished symbol of rusticity: the one-room Randolphville school where one teacher presided over seven elementary grades. She was a Christian woman from the South. After our morning recital of the Lord's Prayer she daily read to us with a soft Southern accent from Hugo's *Les Misérables*. For the eighth grade and graduation I was transferred to the larger school in New Market. Those of my friends who attended high school traveled to New Brunswick, home of Rutgers University and Johnson & Johnson, the medical supply manufacturers. At the time New Brunswick and its environs on the banks of the Raritan River were also celebrated as the locale of the Hall-Mills murder case, a tabloid sensation of the 1920s. The murder victims were the Reverend Edward Wheeler Hall and his sweetheart, Mrs. Eleanor Mills. At night huge, blood-red, neon crosses dotted the sky over the town, but these were not memorials to the Christian pastor, who got mixed up in adultery and murder. They were trademarks over the Johnson & Johnson plants.

I did not go on to high school in New Brunswick. After only a year in Stelton we moved to Jersey City, from the shades of Peter Kropotkin to the realities of Mayor Frank Hague. A political boss of the old school, still Hague was ahead of his time; most cities required several more decades to reach the depths of urban decay that already prevailed in his domain. The high school I entered, Dickinson, was on double sessions in 1927. I attended the afternoon shift; in the mornings I worked as an errand boy for the small dental laboratory my stepfather operated.

A year in Jersey City, then back to the Bronx. This time to the Upper Bronx, to the cooperative apartments at Bronx Park East and Allerton Avenue. The "coops" (rhyming with hoops) were a housing venture organized by Communists. Later on, after the stock-market crash of 1929, they were referred to by some of their patrons as monuments to illusions bred by "Coolidge prosperity." In the coops Communist influence was visible and assertive, and I was responsive. I knew little about political theory but I knew what I believed: there is a war between the classes and it is irreconcilable, the capitalist system has to be overthrown, the Russian Revolution is the trailblazing example of what is to be done. The step from ideological affinity to organizational affiliation was hastened by the discovery that my two closest friends during my earlier residence in the Lower Bronx were now Young Communists.

Looking back at it more than four decades later I know how momentous that decision was for me, how it shaped my life. For the man nearing sixty years there is a great temptation to assign to the boy of fifteen reasons and motivations of comparable moment and solemnity. I have peered again into the boy's mind and soul to seek the reasons for his choice and they are as I have stated them: family background (which also includes the social environment, the family friends, some of whom he admired, their conversations and interests), random reading and other intellectual influences, and experience. But how much experience did the boy have that was relevant to his decision? Childhood impressions of a great revolution, and a prolonged encounter with the seamier side of American life, which taught him that poverty can deform human beings, that the existence of a worker is hard and insecure.

I regard that boy with some compassion and much respect, for I know the sincerity with which he acted and his exalted feeling of fulfillment and liberation in dedicating himself to a transcendent cause. It did not even occur to him that it might

Factions
w/in Comm.
Party

not be for a lifetime. I know this, but I also know that in politics (a soiled word, but it will serve), as in love, the eternal
vows, until death do us part, sincerely taken, are often
breached. Except for those who have luck or a particular genius, the irrevocable lifetime decision is frequently a myth; if
there is constancy, in the good sense, it is a consequence of renewal and reaffirmation in which the choice, once made forever, has to be made anew, and most often with more pain and
thought than the first time. The boy did not know this.

The late autumn of 1928 was an inauspicious time to join the
Young Communist League. Eternal prosperity was being
toasted with bootleg liquor. Celebration of the American economic miracle was little disturbed by mordant literary critics of
reigning values and ethics, or by the postwar disillusion of the
"lost generation" expatriates. Radicals were scoffed at; Henry
Ford, not Karl Marx, was the true prophet. The country was on
the crest of an economic boom — and the Communist party
was at the climax or fag end of a factional struggle that had
dragged on for six years. This last fact dominated the life of the
YCL. I was bewildered and fascinated by the factional debate.
Bewildered by its substance, fascinated by its style. There is
no need to apologize for being bewildered at age fifteen upon
falling into an involved political argument that had begun
when you were nine. The veteran protagonists of the majority
faction (led by Jay Lovestone) and the minority (led by William Z. Foster and Alexander Bittelman) larded the debate
with references and allusions to episodes and positions that
were obscure or unknown to me. Aside from my unfamiliarity
with what had gone on before, which was a handicap in following this marathon argument, there was my unpreparedness for
coping with theoretical concepts in dispute. Like the apex, for
example. The apex, that is, of American imperialism. The
question was: where is American imperialism in relation to its
apex? Past it, at it, nearing it, or still a fair distance from it? I
was not sure just what American imperialism is, even more uncertain as to what might constitute its apex, and totally mysti-
fied about ascertaining the precise relationship between two
nebulous quantities.

I succumbed to a common failing: attributing profundity to something simply because you cannot understand it. This heightened my fascination with the style of the debate, with the freedom of it, with its vigor, the frequent irony, the verbal thrust and parry. It was my first exposure to serious political dispute and all the devices of the debater's art seemed the more imposing because of the sense that they were being employed in a profound clash of momentous ideas. It was mind-sharpening and stimulating. The adversaries, especially in long, written polemics, invoked the authority of citations from Lenin. When a citation was unusually striking to me I hunted for it in its original context. This was not the best introduction to Lenin's work. Still it was an encounter with the supreme revolutionary mind of the century, with all its range, audacity, and power of concentration, so devoid of illusions or frills, tough, tenacious, supple, absolutely uncompromising in its revolutionary will and its insistence upon confrontation with reality.

It would have taken far more sophistication than I possessed to have found in this initial encounter with Lenin the key to an understanding of the factional fight. Indeed, the fight was over before I understood it. During it I yielded to another common failing: when you don't really know what an argument is about, side with the majority. It is the easier way out and you have the handy rationale of the democratic premise that the greater wisdom is more likely to reside in the greater number. In this instance the premise proved false, or perhaps irrelevant. The factional conflict was resolved in the late spring of 1929 by a special commission of the Communist International sitting in Moscow. Joseph Stalin participated in the commission's deliberations. When Lovestone challenged the solution proposed by the International his majority evaporated and the residuum — he and some two hundred associates — was expelled from the party.

Perhaps the aftermath of the long factional war and its sudden resolution would have been more painful and more protracted if the American party had not received an inadvertent assist from Wall Street. The stock-market crash in October

1929 and the economic crisis it heralded exerted two immediate influences. Ideologically they were offered as prima facie evidence to sustain the indictment of the Lovestone group as having been egregiously mistaken in its sanguine perspectives for American capitalist development. Practically, the party found unity in its activist response to the crisis and its consequences.

In the broader perspective the crisis was shattering confirmation of the Communist critique of the capitalist system. During one of his speeches on the American party Stalin said, "The three million now unemployed in America are the first swallows indicating the ripening of the economic crisis in America." That was said in May. Only five months later, in October, it was brilliant prophecy fulfilled. We were proven right, demonstrably and visibly right. Had we not said the system was rent by internal contradictions that would produce a major economic crisis? And now the system was performing as we had said it would. Each day adduced fresh, damning, conclusive evidence, not only that the system was cruel and irrational, but that this irrationality and cruelty assumed the contours sketched in the Marxist analysis.

We had élan. We had the exhilarating sense of being on the offensive, ideologically and morally. As we carried the offensive into the public arena our élan was heightened by the responses — by the confusions and repressive reflexes among the financial, political, and ideological pillars of society. By the manifestations of sympathy from the deprived and humiliated. Our great public debut came on March 6, 1930, exactly 130 days after Wall Street began its $50 billion pratfall on October 29, 1929. If, economically, it may be said that the decade of the thirties was ushered in on that earlier date, politically its beginning may be marked at March 6. The character and fate of the decade may be read in the portents of that March day when the unemployed massed in the streets and squares, battling with police in many cities and towns.

The call for a worldwide demonstration of the unemployed had been issued in January from Communist International headquarters in Moscow. A long way from the Bronx, but for six weeks, from the end of January to the sixth of March, that

International initiative filled the life of a sixteen-year-old Communist in the Bronx with growing suspense and tension, and with a vague expectation. In the six weeks there was an accelerated interplay between the small things you did and the big pressures and influences that converged upon you . . .

Skirmishes. An effective build-up for a major demonstration is a series of smaller ones. Call it reconnaissance in force. Or rehearsal. Similar purposes are served. Testing, heightened preparedness. But political mass action is not formalized as the military and theatrical; the human material is not previously assembled in mechanically ordered ranks or in a cast. Preliminary skirmishes also serve the purpose of propaganda and mobilization.

In the first skirmish 3000 demonstrators and 200 cops battled in New York's City Hall Park on January 25. The occasion was a protest against the police killing of a striking bakery worker named Steve Katovis. Not directly related to issues of unemployment, still the incident occurred during the period of preparation for March 6.

A month later (February 27) police attacked thousands of unemployed massed at City Hall to demand immediate relief. In the final skirmish, Saturday, March 1, several hundred women and children demonstrated at City Hall. Or as near City Hall as they could get. They were met by 100 uniformed policemen and detectives with orders to prevent the demonstration. There was naive candor then in establishment press coverage of such events. The *New York Times* story said: ". . . women and children of from eight to fifteen years were roughly handled and beaten by the police, who used their fists." (They used their fists because, in a display of chivalry, police commanders decreed that clubs not be used against women and children.) "In their mad rush to escape being hurt, the would-be demonstrators . . . fell over each other. Many were helped to their feet by police and sent on their way after being kicked . . . Members of the radical squad from Police Headquarters, with newspaper reporters' cards in their hatbands, were on the City Hall steps . . ."

A statement from the New York District of the Communist party commented: "The police of New York, like Czarist Cossacks, brutally attacked the women and children . . . who went to City Hall in support of their unemployed husbands and fathers. This is the method the Czar in Russia used against the hungry workers when they demanded bread."

Three skirmishes, three bloody clashes with the cops at City Hall in one month.

I could read in the *Daily Worker* about similar encounters all over the country. Typically:

> LOS ANGELES — Scenes somewhat reminiscent of hand to hand fighting on the front occurred here on Feb. 26 when the Los Angeles police, infamous for their brutality, attacked some 8,000 workers in an unemployed demonstration . . . All reserves were called out and they used tear gas bombs . . . For over an hour the battle raged, the police spilling some of their own blood before the battle was done . . .

> SEATTLE — Police attacked a demonstration of the Unemployed Council marching to City Hall. At least 5,000 [unemployed workers] participated and severe collisions took place with the police who rode savagely into the crowd, clubbing and mauling from horses' backs . . . Over 150 police took part in the attack . . .

My YCL club of some twenty-five members in the Upper Bronx is broken up into teams of five, each with a captain. I am a captain. We are told the teams will be more efficient functionally in the preparations for March 6. We are also told that the division into small groups is a security measure in the event of police raids and mass arrests. The security precaution is made credible by the encounters with the police. If this is how they behave in skirmishes, what will they do in the major battle? What will be the aftermath? Prickly questions. And the atmosphere crackles with possible provocations . . .

ITEM:"All explosive stores in the Bronx were put under heavy guard yesterday following the theft of eighty-six sticks of dynamite from a construction company, which the police feared were taken by Reds for use in further demonstrations" (*New York Times*).

ITEM: Police Commissioner Grover Whalen released to the press the text of an anonymous letter received by the Justice Department. The letter warned of bombings to take place on March 6 and after. "The Reds," it said, had instructions "direct from Moscow" to destroy the City Hall, the Woolworth Building (then the tallest building in the world), Police Headquarters, the New York Stock Exchange, the House of Morgan, and other unnamed buildings. Also to kill President Hoover, Alfred E. Smith (Hoover's Democratic opponent in 1928), John D. Rockefeller, John D. Rockefeller, Jr., Mayor James J. Walker, and others. Among the others was Maurice Campbell. He was the federal prohibition administrator.

My YCL team of five is in the Bronx, where all dynamite stores are under police guard. It is midnight and our behavior is furtive. But we do not have dynamite. We are armed with posters, a jar filled with paste, and a brush. We are not in the vicinity of symbolic buildings or the residences of important people. We are near the factory of the Dubilier Condenser Corporation, incongruously planted in the upper residential reaches of the Bronx. There is not another industrial plant within a radius of several miles. Indeed, aside from an umbrella factory someone discovered on the shores of Pelham Bay, Dubilier is the only industrial plant we know of in the Upper Bronx domain of my YCL branch. (After the discovery of the umbrella factory, a girl comrade and I were dispatched to explore it, to "make contact" with its workers. Stationed at the exit from the factory at quitting time we passed out leaflets and tried to strike up verbal exchanges. Some workers took our leaflets but none responded to our conversational overtures. I had passed out enough leaflets to be no stranger to nonresponsiveness and occasional hostility. But there was something odd about the nonresponsiveness of these workers. Very soon my comrade and I became aware that the workers who passed us by were engaged in animated conversations among themselves.

In sign language. At a lunchroom we learned that the entire work force of the umbrella factory was recruited from a nearby school for the deaf and dumb. So it was back to Dubilier for my YCL branch. Guided by the Marxist conception of the historical role and mission of industrial workers we focused our attention on this wayward industrial outpost.)

On this night in early March we are bent on putting up our posters where they will be seen by Dubilier workers and others who come to seek work at the plant. I am carrying the posters, rolled up in a newspaper. I carry posters — and I think about dynamite. Or, more exactly, about the newspaper stories of stolen dynamite and the police insinuations. The treatment in the tabloids was more lurid than in the Times. Somehow these stories make our mission seem more daring on this cold, blustery March night. In this weather at this time of night these streets are absolutely quiet and empty. It is good, I think, there are no passers-by. But it also makes our presence so conspicuous. We are on foot. Automobiles are a rare luxury. I do not know of even one YCL member in the Bronx who owns a car. Five of us in this empty street; I with the posters under my arm, someone else with a jar of paste in a brown paper bag, and a third comrade with the brush wrapped in rags.

The silhouette of the Dubilier plant towers in the dark among the lesser residential dwellings. Should we plaster some posters on the plant walls? It is tempting. After a brief huddle we decide against it. There might be a watchman or some other personnel in the plant to call the cops. We decide to plaster the approaches to the plant. The posters are beautiful. Bold red and black on white. DON'T STARVE, FIGHT! WORK OR WAGES! These are the slogans along with the summons to Union Square, 12 noon, March 6. Hugo Gellert's worker, sketched on the poster, is strong, courageous. He'll fight. The three of us with the paraphernalia are to put up the posters. The other two are to serve as lookouts. One lookout is Brooklyn-born and bred, the purity of his Brooklynese accent unblemished by the efforts of New York's schools. At the first poster-pasting locale he is to take the more distant observation post at a street corner. "If someone is coming," I ask, "what will be

*your signal?" He replies, "I'll whistle da sextet from Lucia di
Lammermoor." That cuts the tension. But there is enough of it
left so that between our nervousness and a strong breeze we
have trouble with the flutter of the first poster. The rest, about
a dozen, go up smoothly and quickly on walls and fences.
Donizetti's sextet is not whistled that night . . .*

Tensions. The closer to March 6 the greater the political
pressures and tensions.

Matthew Woll, Vice President of the American Federation of
Labor, dispatched a letter to "commercial organizations" in 500
United States cities and to all members of Congress. Woll said
that Soviet Russia is responsible "for the continued riots of so-
called 'unemployed' staged by Communists in New York and
other cities." The purpose, he said, is "to fan the fires of class
hatred and to destroy all civilized governments of the earth."

Woll repeated a charge, earlier made by the Justice Department, that William Z. Foster brought $1.25 million from Mos-
cow to foment disorder. Communists had done considerable
translation from Russian into English; Woll now reciprocated
by translating from English into Russian. A manifesto of the
Trade Union Unity League, the Communist labor center
headed by Foster, had appealed, "Organize councils of the unemployed . . ." In Woll's rendition of it, the phrase read, "Organize soviets (councils) of the unemployed . . ."

Woll's letter got the main play on the front page of the *New
York Times*. The *Times* later served up a sensation of its own:

"It was reported but not confirmed that the Communist International several weeks ago sent a special emissary to New
York . . . and that it is this agent who, remaining behind the
scenes, has been directing the preparations for this demonstration . . . His name was mentioned in well-informed circles as
the name of a prominent Russian Bolshevik who under various
aliases has held important posts in the Soviet Government and
in the Red Army."

The story gave no name, no alias (and no explanation as to
why a Russian Bolshevik would employ various aliases to work
for the Soviet government and the Red army).

The people are in a hurry, most of the men keep their hands in their pockets against the morning cold. It is not easy to pass a leaflet to a handless human bundle moving swiftly to the stairs that lead to the elevated platforms for the trains to Manhattan. To make it tougher, on this cold March morning the mood of the procession is a mix of sullenness, irritation, resentment, all of this wrapped in a half-awake daze. It is something of a contest; to penetrate those shells, to establish that minimum human contact involved in the offer and acceptance of a leaflet, to do it in the split second you have. The trick, I have learned, is to thrust the leaflet at the passer-by with authority, with the air of confident expectation that it will be taken.

I got to the el station before 7 A.M. To catch shop and industrial workers. Later on white-collar employes and sales personnel predominate in the workbound human flow from the Bronx. I was up two hours before my usual get-up time for school. A small irritant. Still I chalk it up as one more reason why industrial workers ought to be more discontented with the system. I begin an observation game. Which of the people going by are bound for work, which are job hunting? Ah, there is a newspaper opened at the classified ads. A giveaway. The spruced-up look is a more subtle and elusive clue. Wage slave is part of my vocabulary. Which wage slave is trying to sell himself, which is already sold? I look for hints in dress and toilet for the extra care taken to impress a prospective buyer of labor. Most elusive of all are the psychological clues. As amateur psychologist and sociologist I assume there must be differences in the bearing and behavior of job-holders and job-hunters. But what are they? Are the hunters more alert, more tense? Or more hangdog? Am I looking for winners and losers in the economic lottery? The answers are not conclusive, but the questions help pass the time. So I appraise the pedestrians as I thrust leaflets at them with confident authority and with what I think is a blend of good humor and militancy.

All the time something else is on my mind. Except for rare instances of overt sympathy or hostility, there is no feedback in the fleeting encounters with the human bundles going by. What are they thinking? What will be the impact of the leaflets upon them? I feel I am contending with a ubiquitous power. Those press stories. The psychological blows in them, the play on fear (dynamite) and prejudice (Moscow gold). These workers shuffling past me, these are the masses we talk about, and I do not know what the stories did to them. I thrust another leaflet forward. Don't starve, fight! Work or Wages!

Three of my team members have left for work. The remaining member and I pass out the last of the leaflets. It is after eight o'clock and I head for James Monroe High School, for logarithms and French verbs. It seems absurd. At that moment the absurdity extends even to the English class where the teacher has us doing a choral recitation of "When Lilacs Last in the Dooryard Bloomed" . . .

Politics. In the initial call for the March 6 demonstration the Communist Party's Central Committee emphasized these slogans: "Work or Wages! . . . Unemployment insurance financed by taxes on profits and inheritances and administered by the workers . . . Immediate relief for the unemployed by grants from government funds! . . . The seven-hour day; five-day week! No overtime!"

The Trade Union Unity League appealed:

"Organize councils of the unemployed, prepare for huge, militant demonstrations in every city of the United States, not a mere protest demonstration, but an organized fighting demonstration of all workers to fight for 'WORK OR WAGES' — 'IMMEDIATE RELIEF.'"

At the time, according to Communist estimates, there were six million unemployed (in a labor force of forty million). Since the government compiled no statistics on unemployment, independent estimates had to do without the benefit of an official yardstick. The government's failure to keep an unemployed count was more than a bookkeeping lapse. It reflected a fundamental policy: the government did not have to count them because it assumed no responsibility to them. This was the American way. We had financial panics and economic depressions in 1907, 1893, 1873, and before that. The unemployed got by somehow — with private charity, individual ingenuity, and the sheer capacity to suffer and endure. True, there had been social unrest and disturbances in such times, but the country survived, the economy recovered and expanded. What was then extolled as the supreme American virtue — rugged individualism — would carry us through again. So deeply imbedded was all this in the reigning ideology of the time that the American Federation of Labor officially opposed proposals for unemployment insurance on the ground the American worker was too proud and independent to accept a dole.

In the Communist agitation the principal focus was on the demands and the organization of the unemployed. However, this focus was placed in the context of the party's overall program, or political line, of that time. On March 6 the front page of the *Daily Worker* was dominated by a manifesto of the party's Central Committee. Each paragraph contained a brief analysis and argument, followed by a sloganized conclusion. These summary slogans, therefore, conveyed the sense and flavor of the document. They were:

> Only the mass action of the workers can wrest a realization of their demands. Forward to revolutionary mass action!
> Down with the social-fascists of the A. F. of L. and the Socialist Party! Organize in the revolutionary trade unions! Join the Communist Party!
> Down with the government — watchdog of capitalists!
> Down with the beggarly charity of bourgeois fakers! Demand work or wages, unemployment insurance equal for white and Negro, administered by the workers themselves.
> Strengthen your fight against capitalism! Prepare the powerful arm of the political mass strike!
> Fight against the imperialist war now being prepared! Defend the Soviet Union, stronghold of the world revolution!
> Long live the Communist International, the leader of the toiling masses of the world!

This was the message to the many thousands who were expected to take to the streets that day.

On the eve. Between five-thirty and six P.M. on Wednesday, March 5, I report to a Bronx apartment to receive final, pre-

demonstration instructions for team captains. Leafletting the next morning as previously arranged. At the demonstration in Union Square the team should try to stick together. If you or other team members own pocket knives, the man says, they might be handy against fire hoses if these are used against the demonstration. I own a pocket knife and I have seen fire hoses; I have grave doubts about the utility of the former against the latter. Another suggestion is more practical and more obvious. The wooden staves to which placards are nailed can be used for defense against police attack . . .

Later that evening I head for a Ruthenberg Memorial Meeting [C. E. Ruthenberg, General Secretary of the Communist Party, had died three years earlier on March 2, 1927]. The next morning's tabloids are on the newsstands. Their headlines blare: 25,000 POLICE AND FIREMEN SET FOR RED RIOT. *(The* New York Times *reported: "The most extensive preparations ever made by the police here to meet a possible emergency were worked out . . . for the unemployment demonstration to be staged by Communists . . ." Other* Times *reports: No permits for any demonstrations at all had been granted in Chicago, Berlin, Paris, Riga, Prague . . . "Throughout Prussia and Estonia the police will be on the alert for disturbances . . . Trouble is expected in Athens, where agents of the Communist International have been particularly active . . ." Police guards have been posted at the homes of Mayor Walker, Police Commissioner Whalen, and "other prominent citizens"; also at various public and commercial buildings.)*

There has been little publicity for the Ruthenberg Memorial. Essentially it is a gathering of New York's Communists. Several thousands of them jam the public hall in midtown Manhattan, somewhere in the vicinity of Hunter College. Many, I suppose, have just been to a briefing like the one I attended. Certainly all have seen the tabloid headlines. All, or almost all, have been in a state of emergency during the preceding weeks. Now we are on the eve. Of what? Something enormous, unpredictable. This assembly is charged with suspense and expectation.

Foster is the principal speaker. He is a tall, slender, hand-

*some Irishman, then a few days past his forty-ninth birthday.
He has physical vitality and great platform poise. In the very
expressive use of his hands when he speaks there is a characteristic gesture: a chopping motion with his right hand. The moving hand keeps cadence, registers emphasis; it seems to clip his
sentences, and they are clipped. Leader of the Great Steel
Strike of 1919, director of the successful campaign to organize
the meat-packing industry during the First World War, railroad
worker, seaman, migrant laborer in lumber, agriculture, metal
mining, and I do not recall what else, Foster is a hero of mine.
He is the embodiment of the American working class, the living
confirmation of the historic mission of the proletariat.*

*On this evening he displays the wisdom and psychological
insight acquired on thousands of soapboxes and public platforms. Or so it seems to me. He does not agitate his audience
or try to arouse it. It is already about as taut emotionally as it
possibly could be. He resorts to anecdote and irony.*

*On his recent visit to Europe he stopped in Paris and was
taken to a* café *chantant. During the evening his host and guide
kept pointing to people. See that cigarette girl? She is princess
so-and-so of Russia. See that busboy? He is count so-and-so.
Remember the hatcheck girl when we came in? She is countess
so-and-so . . . "I want to tell Grover Whalen, the floorwalker
from Wanamaker's, that many people who were mightier than
he are now peddling shoelaces in the streets of Europe!" Foster
now turns to Matthew Woll and the $1.25 million from Moscow.
Against the tale of foreign money he invokes native idiom. "To
use a good old American expression — Matthew Woll, you are
a liar by the clock!"*

*The crowd roars. (I must have loved it; forty years have
gone by and hundreds, perhaps thousands, of speeches heard
and forgotten, but I still remember those passages.)*

I can recall very little of March 6 itself, and even this little
only dimly. It overwhelmed, I suppose, the already overloaded
circuits of my central nervous system. I moved through the day
as if in a trance.

Hazily I was aware of massive police concentrations, becoming thicker as I approached Union Square . . . aware of police on the rooftops of the buildings flanking the north end of the square where the demonstration assembled . . . of hearing and believing that they had machine guns up there . . . of the crowd, enormous, tightly packed, spilling beyond the vast allotted space into adjoining streets (demonstration leaders estimated 100,000 were there) . . .

Five platforms (as I learned later) were scattered through the square to enable speakers to reach every part of the huge assembly. I was in the orbit of one in the eastern half of the square, but the oratory washed past me, leaving one distinct impression in its wake: indignation at official refusal to permit a march to City Hall. The royal and militarist scum of Europe and Asia is permitted to strut on the streets of New York, orators shouted, but the city's unemployed workers cannot march on them. The anger peaked with mentions of Queen Marie. (Marie, queen dowager of Rumania, had been accorded a lavish reception by city officials several years before. In gratitude the Rumanian government bestowed decorations upon Mayor Walker and Police Commissioner Whalen. But a man named Dave Gordon was rewarded with a six-month jail sentence. In a poem published in the *Daily Worker* Gordon called the queen a bitch.)

I barely heard the words. They were not important and I did not think about them. I was totally possessed by two conflicting emotions that were numbing in their power: exultation and apprehensive suspense. The magnitude of this crowd, being part of this mass — the wonder of it never left me. Nor did the sense of foreboding. All the tensions that had been gathering in the prior weeks were present in the square and now the confrontation was direct, physical. This human mass and encircling it an army of police, machine guns on the roofs. Was a clash inevitable, and how blood-spilling would it be? I sensed the answer might come at any moment and there was no way of telling what it would be until it came.

Then Foster stood on the central platform, tall and erect, his figure etched against the sun. He was a long way off and I could not make out what he said, but when he finished speaking a roar of "No!" from those nearer him was audible. With a long arm outstretched, he pointed to the southwest corner of the square, to Broadway that leads to City Hall. The crowd surged in the pointed direction. What followed is a hazy jumble in my mind . . . the roar of police motorcycles, the whine of sirens . . . shouts and screams, and the thud of police clubs against human bodies . . . mounted cops swinging away with their clubs as their trained horses maneuvered through the crowd . . .

("Hundreds of policemen and detectives," the *New York Times* story reported, "swinging nightsticks, blackjacks and bare fists, rushed into the crowd, hitting out at all with whom they came in contact . . . From all parts of the scene of battle came the screams of women and cries of men with bloody heads and faces.")

I was pushed back by people recoiling from the police assault, several layers of them between charging cops and me. The retreat gained momentum and we were driven eastward from the square. It was over, the suspense was ended, the excruciating tension at the moment of the police attack ebbed slowly, but the conflict of emotions was no more. The exultation remained.

Later, from press accounts, I learned that Foster and a committee had gone to a construction shack on the square where Whalen had set up his police command post. (The center of the square was then torn up for reconstruction and landscaping, which accounted for the construction shack.) The committee made a final demand for a permit to march to City Hall to present a petition to city authorities. Upon returning from the session with Whalen, Foster mounted the central platform.

"Whalen and the city officials have handed Broadway and other streets over to every monarchist and militarist exploiter of Europe and Asia to parade on," Foster said, "but now when the workers and the unemployed workers of New York demand the use of these streets Whalen's answer is that they cannot have them. Will you take that for an answer?"

"No!" roared the crowd.

"Then I advise you to fall in line and proceed," he said and pointed toward Broadway.

According to the *Times*, 1000 policemen, mounted and on foot, reinforced by scores of detectives, motorcycle men, and emergency service crews, "barred the advance of the mob and fifteen minutes of spectacular fighting scattered it in all directions."

A delegation that attempted to present the demonstration demands at City Hall was arrested. Foster and two colleagues in the Communist leadership, Robert Minor and Israel Amter, served six months in jail; Harry Raymond, then an unemployed seaman and later a reporter for the *Daily Worker*, served ten.

Throughout the country, Communist leaders estimated, 1.25 million demonstrated on March 6. The demonstration jarred the country. The day after its reports of March 6 the *New York Times* featured two headlines on its front page:

> More Work, Says Hoover,
> And Depression Is Passing;
> 36 States Are Now Normal
>
> Labor Sets March 19
> For Jobless Parley

The second story was about a call for a conference by an Emergency Committee on Unemployment, consisting of American Federation of Labor officials, with Socialists conspicuous among them. Different in tone, still both headlines recorded a reaction to March 6, attesting to the political impact of the demonstrations. Despite Hoover's reiteration that things were not really bad and were getting better, unemployment now was inescapably the major issue before the country. The effect of the Communist initiative was a harbinger of Communist hegemony on the Left in the decade to come. March 6 was prelude to massive organization of the unemployed, to a thousand battles, large and small, in streets, in statehouses, and city halls. It was a precursor of the New Deal reform era.

To me at sixteen, however, its meaning transcended calculated political analysis. It was a portent of revolution, or at least it rendered my own vision of revolution more credible. This vision was inspired by my image of the Russian Revolution, as derived from John Reed's account, from early Soviet films and literary miscellany. In this image the principal protagonists were ordinary people: workers, soldiers (peasants in uniform), and sailors. The genius of the Bolsheviks lay in their ability to articulate the moods and needs of these ordinary people, to express them in clear political terms, to generate from this inchoate power a collective will and purpose, to chart a firm course of political action. But revolution is an act of the mass. Leaders do not make revolution; if they have the wisdom and the daring and a historical identity with the mass, they can insure the revolution's fulfillment.

In this conception the vast mystery of revolution resides in currents that flow at the bottom depths of the mass, where they are least fathomable and perceptible. At what point do these currents surface in a dramatic transformation from passivity, resignation, acquiescence, fear into defiant discontent, and a bold assault upon the status quo? This is the riddle of revolution. On March 6, it seemed to me, I witnessed such a transformation. Not on the ultimate plane of revolutionary apocalypse, but still it was a revelation of profound change in mass mind and mood. In the terminology of our dialectic this was a qualitative leap in mass consciousness. A radical leap from officially prescribed canons of etiquette and outlook for the unemployed worker. And if masses negotiated this leap, was it not proof and token of the great historical metamorphosis to come?

To understand my frame of mind at the time another tenet is essential. The transfiguration of the mass seems spontaneous, but it is not. It is the product of a molecular process and what you do from week to week influences this process. The imagery of revolutionary rhetoric abounds in sparks and seeds. In all the dull detail of your political existence you fanned and you sowed, not knowing when or how the flame would burst or the seed would sprout, and then along came a nodal event like March 6 to reinforce your faith, not only in the volatility of the spark and the viability of the seed, but in the related efficacy of what you were doing. It supplied rationale and sustenance for your routine chores as a YCL member, which for the most part were tedious. Meetings and more meetings, organizational housekeeping, assignments (and checkup): leafletting, sales of the *Young Worker*, petitions, collections of money for varied causes. Occasional socials and hikes in the Alpine Woods on the west bank of the Hudson were diversions.

Another break in routine for me was initiation into soapboxing. You will break in as chairman, I was coaxed, there is nothing to it. All you have to say is that this meeting is being held under the auspices of the Young Communist League, a few words about the league, and then you introduce the speaker. This evaded the issue. What bothered me was not what to say but the circumstances in which I would have to say it. Despite my subjective trepidation I could think of no good objective reason for declining. So it was arranged. Next Friday our YCL branch would hold a street meeting on Allerton Avenue and I would be chairman. I composed and polished my few words, memorized them, rehearsed them again and again to myself. I tried to imagine what it would be like to get up on the box and to shout into the night at indifferent, perhaps hostile strangers passing by. The impending debut was never totally out of my mind in all the days until Friday. I was nervous. Then Friday came and with it a heavy rain that did not let up by evening. Reprieved. No drought-stricken agrarian people ever welcomed rain with a greater sense of deliverance.

The relief was short-lived. At the next branch meeting we again went through the arrangements for the street-corner rally, doling out the responsibilities for bringing the platform, the flag, the literature, and getting "the speaker from downtown." Again I polished, rehearsed, imagined, with no letup in the obsession and the nervousness. Skies were clear on Friday as we assembled on the street corner, all of us who were supposed to be there. All, that is, except "the speaker from downtown." A fidgety half-hour went by and he still did not show. None of us was prepared to substitute; his speech was to have been the substance of the meeting. Nothing to do but disband. This time I had mixed feelings about my reprieve. Wiser than

I had been that rainy Friday, I foresaw still another appointed hour and before me stretched still more days and weeks of preparation and anxiety, on and on . . .

Several evenings later, being lower down in the Bronx, I came upon a group of my comrades from another YCL branch. They were gathered for a street meeting, lacking only one essential for it, a chairman. Would I do it? Up on the platform so suddenly, there just wasn't time for all my latent anxieties to assert themselves. I found my vocal pitch after a rather high-octave "Comrades and fellow workers . . ." which was our standard salutation. (According to Bill Haywood, he coined it in opening the founding convention of the Industrial Workers of the World in 1905.) My well-rehearsed few words issued forth without stammer or stumble. I was a soapboxer.

Soapboxing is a lost art, done in partly by electronics. Through the sheer effort of projecting your voice into outdoor space, over the noises of the street and without the aid of mechanical amplification, you imparted a physical force to the qualities of passion and conviction. Those qualities you had in abundance and they were not filtered through any electronic gadget; you had to speak from your guts (or at least from your diaphragm) to launch the words on a trajectory that reached to the periphery of the crowd and beyond.

More than technology, or the lack of it, was involved, however. Street-corner soapboxing is different from speaking in a hall where the seated audience is, in a sense, captive in its chairs. It is different from speaking out of doors to an audience you had assembled by prior efforts, and which by coming is already committed implicitly to listen to what you say. On a street corner you have to create your audience; to attract the casual passer-by, make him pause, and then hold him as long as you can.

If you are to hold the soapbox down for a half-hour you do not make a half-hour speech. If you are good you make a half-dozen five-minute speeches. If you are very good it might be ten three-minute speeches. Statement of theme, argument, conclusion. Bang! Next speech. The technique is more likely to attract and hold the chance pedestrian. And even if you hold him for only ten minutes you have communicated three complete messages to him, rather than an unfinished and possibly pointless fragment from an integrated half-hour oration.

It was great training in communication, and not just communication in the abstract, but the particular communication with which you were concerned: communication with the mass. In a hall it requires some sensitivity to know when you are not getting through to the audience. On a street corner you do not need sensitivity. All you need is eyesight. The audience melts away before your eyes. In your battle for the audience, depending upon your bent, you cultivate certain devices. I leaned heavily upon irony and villainy. Better soapboxers than I employed wit and humor. But at seventeen you are much too earnest for humor, you do not have the poise or grace for it. So I fell back on irony. What I call villainy entailed the selection of a villain, usually a politician (Herbert Hoover was a providential gift) or a capitalist. You referred to something especially outrageous or stupid your chosen villain had said or done (it did not take much research to find such references), and then you poured it on. In your conception this personalized the class confrontation, and for audience interest it also had the dramatic value of direct encounter.

I soapboxed around the Bronx through much of 1930 and the first half of 1931. Unemployment and the economic crisis were major themes, but there were others: preparations for imperialist war, especially the danger of attack upon the Soviet Union, and the obligation of the working class to defend the first Socialist land. Toward the end of spring and the beginning of summer 1931, the Scottsboro Case became a principal theme. This was the case of nine young blacks (the youngest was only thirteen), hauled off a freight train in Scottsboro, Alabama, and charged with raping two white women who had been riding on the same train. Many elements converged to make the case a symbol, a battle cry. The ugly, traditional accusation, so deeply rooted in the prejudices, guilts, and fears of the pathological sexuality in the owner-slave relation. The young lives at stake, for the penalty was death, and eight of the defendants were sentenced to die in a trial that transformed the rural Alabama village into part carnival and part lynch mob. Even the circumstance that the defendants and their alleged victims were pulled off a freight train was symptomatic of the times. Jobless, destitute, uprooted, millions had taken to the road to seek work somewhere, or at least to get away from the corrosive hopelessness of where they were.

One of our principal slogans then was: "black and white, unite and fight." It was simple to argue the logic of such cooperation to ameliorate an economic misery that cut across the color line. But economics is one thing and rape is another. It was not simple to persuade white workers that interracial effort also entailed their defense of nine young blacks facing death on the charge of raping two white women. It became easier after one of the white women, allegedly violated, confessed that neither she nor her companion was raped. Even then, when you talked about it, you could sense deep-seated prejudice, skepticism, the almost defensive resistance to a recognition of the monstrous oppression that this case illuminated. I know, for when I shouted, "The Scottsboro boys shall not die!" on a Bronx street corner, the words fell on white ears. There was no black ghetto then in the Bronx.

IV. Semiprofessional Revolutionary—2

GRADUATED FROM James Monroe High School in January 1931, I did not even consider the possibility of going on to college. Some of my Young Communist contemporaries did go to college (this fact was impressed upon me when several of them were expelled from the City College of New York). So my total rejection of formal higher education was not universal in the ranks, but it was prevalent. Going into industry or "into the field" as an organizer was the thing to do. Out of school I marked time with a couple of odd jobs that winter and spring until after the YCL national convention in June when I volunteered to go "into the field."

In July I was in Philadelphia, bedding down on a rolltop desk in the YCL office. My immediate chief, the YCL district organizer, was a fellow named Leonard Patterson. His domain embraced Eastern Pennsylvania, all of Maryland, Delaware, the District of Columbia, and everything in New Jersey that was closer to Philadelphia than New York, which included Camden, Trenton, and Atlantic City. This territorial expanse was far more imposing than the organization. The YCL in the district was a meager mess; my wooden bed attested as much to this as it did to my inexperience. Don't mourn, said the Wobbly poet, organize. When I came upon him Patterson wholeheartedly obeyed half of that injunction. He did not mourn. He was leaving Philadelphia, which already impressed me as cause for rejoicing although I had been in the city only a few days. And he was going to Moscow, to a school.

In his celebrant mood Patterson invited me to a farewell party, which turned out to be a small party and my first introduction to hard liquor. He, another black companion, and I crawled through several "parlor speakeasies" in the black ghetto of North Philadelphia.

You entered a private home, sat down at a table, and the host or hostess poured you a shot of corn liquor. In none of these home speakeasies did I see anyone except the proprietors and the three of us. You sat in a bleak, dimly lit room, drank the liquid slowly, waiting for its effects. It being my first time I was not sure what the effects would be, but vaguely I anticipated animation, perhaps vivacity, and conversation that would be engrossing or at least entertaining; there was no other entertainment, no music or any other diversion. It did not work that way. Patterson's euphoria grated on me, deepening the depression of Philadelphia's initial impact. In the beginning there was excitement in illegal and illicit drinking, in the burning taste of the liquid, in being in a speakeasy, and a ghetto speakeasy at that with two black companions. For the seventeen-year-old kid from the Bronx this was high adventure; in different circumstances this was all it might have been. But such romanticism did not wear well beyond the reality of the first two parlors. Patterson became more boisterous, and I became more melancholy.

That night I did not ponder this dialectical contradiction in drinking. By the end of the night I was not in condition to ponder anything. It was not vomiting sickness, but the rolltop desk rolled. It was the end of my first week as a semiprofessional revolutionary in Philadelphia and all I had to show for it the next morning, a Sunday, was a dreadful hangover, which was not helped by the stench from the Schuylkill River and the heavy heat of a Philadelphian summer. It was not helped either by the lack of sleep for I had to be up for an early-morning appointment with Miss Anna W. Pennypacker. She, I had been told, was the middle-aged daughter of a very old, very distinguished Philadelphia family. Her father, Samuel W. Pennypacker, had been a governor of Pennsylvania. I was to accompany her on a trip to a summer camp for workers' children. Even in better shape I would have been ill at ease with a daughter of Pennsylvania's aristocracy, but this morning the encounter seemed like onerous punishment. Mercifully, Miss Pennypacker and a woman companion drove up in a roadster, consigning me to the rumble seat where I could nurse my hangover without having to essay the role of a model young Communist in conversation with a sympathetic stranger from another class and another culture . . .

Hardly anyone dropped in at the YCL office. The sole exception, who visited at least once a week, was a YCL member with sharp features and a conspiratorial air. On the older end of the YCL age spectrum he was, he said, a peddler of "candy, chewing gum, cigarettes" (reciting this in a professional singsong) on Pennsylvania Railroad trains. Being away from the city so much of the time he wanted to know what was doing. For his briefings he always invited me to lunch at Linton's cafeteria. (Linton's had the pioneering spirit of American economic legend; in the depths of the depression it must have had some private vision of affluence to come. It served mentholated toothpicks.) After a couple of months of this arrangement an older Communist recognized my inquisitive luncheon host as a former company spotter in Philadelphia's transit system. We assumed he was performing the same office for the Pennsylvania Railroad and that his interest in the YCL was a moonlighting sideline for a party or parties unknown. Somebody else, experienced in such matters, was delegated to tell off the candy man and I never saw him again.

(I also did not see Patterson again until he walked into a federal courtroom in Los Angeles in 1952 with the cocksure air of a practiced government witness. On cross-examination my attorney, A. L. Wirin, asked: "You have not seen Richmond for twenty years but you walked up on that witness stand and without a moment's hesitation picked him out among all these people in court; how do you explain that?" "Easy," Patterson answered. "If Richmond doesn't change any more in the next twenty years than he did in the last twenty, I'll be able to do it again twenty years from now." I always remember this colloquy when someone, who has not seen me for a long time, says: you haven't changed a bit.)

I've wondered about the *quid pro quo* in those Linton

lunches. The cafeteria food wasn't much, but then what I had to tell him wasn't much either. As a direct barter of exceedingly small values it was no bargain either way. One intangible is how much social value is to be attached to feeding me at the time. I have tried but have not been able to recall or reconstruct just how I managed to eat during those early weeks in Philadelphia. That I managed poorly is suggested to me by the memory of an almost salivary reflex to the appearance of the candy man with his standard greeting: what's doing? The same suggestion is conveyed by another recollection.

I was walking from West Philadelphia to Strawberry Mansion where I finally found a place to flop. It was a long walk and I was taking it because I did not have the streetcar fare. As I cut into Fairmount Park, passing an area where there were benches and concessions, a man hailed me.

"Hey, Slim, you gotta light?"

"Yeh, I gotta light."

"You hungry, Slim?"

"Yeh, I'm hungry."

He bought me a hot dog and watched me eat it.

"You sure are hungry."

My feeling that there was something odd about all this grew when he began to talk about the balmy evening, about the moon that had just appeared, about the sex longings young fellows have on evenings like this. Then he popped the question. "Have you ever been blowed?" Sensing that I did not know the meaning of the question, he explained. He told me he was employed by a man who was so eccentric and so rich that he paid young fellows very well for accepting his pleasure-giving service. I disengaged myself and continued on to Strawberry Mansion.

At the time this, too, was part of a collage: this solicitation by a runner for a rich homosexual, along with the dismal drinking party and the Linton lunches on a stool pigeon's expense account. Philadelphia dispirited me and I hated it. A little later I was struck by a remark attributed to a Philadelphia mayor of that era. When some citizens complained about the city's slums the mayor is said to have replied: "There are no slums in

Philadelphia. There are only historic landmarks." My vision
was the exact opposite. I did not see historic landmarks. If I
visited Independence Hall, it must have been casual; I do not
remember it. Certainly there was no spirit of pilgrimage to the
shrines of American history, not even to those associated with
the American Revolution. This was only five years after the
Sesquicentennial Exposition and I had been aware of the fanfare that celebrated the one-hundred-fiftieth anniversary of
the Declaration of Independence. Residual landmarks of the
Exposition were still fresh, but in my scale of cultural values as
a young Communist at that moment these, along with older
traces of the nation's history, were of no importance.

I remained ignorant of the city's historical lore but I did pick
up tidbits of the youth folklore in the slums. Especially the
vast expanse of slum that covered Philadelphia's southern end.
First, below the city's center of fashion and business, came the
old black ghetto, and below that, stretching on and on to
the Navy Yard, where the Schuylkill flows into the Delaware,
was the slum inhabited by the Irish, Italians, and others. Beginning with the heyday of Philadelphia Jack O'Brien (light-
heavyweight champion of the world before World War I),
South Philadelphia slums produced an impressive number of
professional boxers who crowded the top of their divisions.
Whether South Philadelphia actually was more prolific in this
than the slums of other cities I do not know, but it seemed so,
and certainly South Philadelphia was convinced of it. According to folklore at least every other boy in South Philadelphia
dreamed of becoming a prize fighter; a good many went beyond
dreaming, and of these a tragically high percentage were slow
in realizing they couldn't make it. Telltale marks of such poor
judgment were abundant. If cauliflower ears and mashed noses
were edible, South Philadelphia would have been an eternal
feast.

As a folk symbol the ring was matched by the jail. It was a
tossup as to which represented the more typical experience. In
the folklore the law was personified by Judge McDevitt. A
popular ballad (a parody of "That Old Gang of Mine") related

how each member of the gang was sent away and its refrain was ". . . for Judge McDevitt's broken up that old gang of mine." When the film *20,000 Years in Sing Sing* played in Philadelphia the folk witticism was "That sounds like one of Judge McDevitt's sentences . . ."

Such bits of lore stick in my mind because they are associated with the discovery of South Philadelphia. It began with a telephone call to the YCL office about some young fellows who congregated on a certain street corner, talked radical, and called themselves Communists. By this time Patterson was in Moscow and his successor, Dave Davis, was in Philadelphia. An experienced and able organizer, earnest and sincere, Davis set forth to explore. The telephonic intelligence was true. The leader of the gang, Ben, was a South Philadelphia prototype; a big Irishman, he had fought in the ring and was facing jail then for slugging a couple of cops who tried to curb his exuberance at a church street fair. He had picked up his radicalism on several trips to sea aboard Atlantic Refining oil tankers. With Ben's help, Davis recruited several members of the gang into the YCL. Irish and Italian, authentic products of South Philadelphia's slums, to me they truly represented the human material that could and would overturn the world.

As low as my morale was even this small conquest provided an important lift, although I had little to do with it because my assigned duties lay elsewhere. My official title was District Pioneer Director. I was chief of the Young Pioneers, the Communist-sponsored children's organization, in the district that stretched from the Appalachias to the sea, from Washington to Trenton. An inventory of the physical assets that came with the office yielded only the rolltop desk — and two pairs of boxing gloves. My organized constituency comprised a small scattering of children from Communist families.

The Young Pioneers, where they actually existed, were a bizarre mix of childish élan and more childish sectarianism; of hikes, games, handicrafts, songs, cheers, and Marxist education that, in accord with the learning-by-doing principle, was enriched with plunges into political activism (demonstrations, leaflets, and in the case of some select older boys "infiltration" into the Boy Scouts for "antimilitarist" activity). A few years later the organization was permitted to wither away, but in 1931 it was not considered quixotic for a seventeen-year-old to go to Philadelphia to attempt, mostly on his own, to put it together. How to do it? My facility in answering this question was on par with my preparation for coping with the elementary problems of creature survival. I was too inexperienced and too diffident to be aggressive about seeking counsel and assistance. In the YCL organizational chaos into which I fell, if you were not aggressive in demanding help you got none. (This, of course, is an indispensable learning experience in any organizational system subject to many pulls and pressures.) After Davis arrived, he was a point of support (moral) and reference (political); as for material help he had his own troubles getting by. All he could offer was advice: get a job. In midautumn I got a job as shipping clerk in a shop that manufactured suspenders and garters. It paid eight dollars for a forty-four-hour week, which averages out to less than twenty cents an hour. This took care of subsistence and by then I was also on the way toward solving the problem of what to do about the Young Pioneers.

It was done with the boxing gloves I inherited. In retrospect it might seem incredibly brash or naive for a white boy with four boxing gloves, one contact, and only a trace of self-consciousness about the black-white relation to barge into a black ghetto. But this was another time. With the gloves I set out for a ghetto enclave in Southwest Philadelphia where the home of an elderly black Communist, Mr. W., could serve as a base of operations. Later I was told this was the neighborhood Marian Anderson came from. At the time I was told something else. "Look at old man W. You can tell he worked for Du Pont. Look at his face. Looks like the yellow jaundice, don't it? But it ain't. It's the dye and the chemicals that's eaten into his skin." When it appeared the dye and chemicals might be eating deeper than the skin, the company, in a burst of paternalism, took Mr. W. out of the plant and put him to driving a team of mules in the yard. When motor transport was introduced into the operation he was performing, Mr. W. was let go, along with the mules. What happened to the mules he did not know. He moved up the Delaware to Philadelphia from the Du Pont domain that sits astride the river to the south, one foot planted on the left bank in New Jersey and all the rest, including the massive corporate rump, spread all over the state of Delaware.

Short but powerfully built, Mr. W. had the dignity and self-assurance encountered in some men who acquire a sense of their own worth in a lifetime of work that tests strength and skill. His home was an informal community center. With his help it was not much of a trick to induce a couple of kids on the block to put on the gloves. This done it was no trick at all to assemble a crowd; it just grew and soon kids were competing for, and with, the gloves. Thus left jabs and some very wild haymakers attended the fighting rebirth of the Young Pioneers in Philadelphia. I cannot recall what I said to the kids on that occasion, or subsequently, but the association had a vitality that was revealed in one memorable venture.

One thing you did not have to tell most of these kids was that they were hungry. You did not have to agitate them about how good it would be if free lunches were served in the schools. Out of their need and their knowledge grew the idea for a children's hunger march. They helped to prepare and produce the leaflets, and they distributed them in the schools and in the streets.

It was an early Saturday afternoon in December. This time was chosen because it coincided with a scheduled meeting of the Board of Education. If anyone had asked me how many children would have turned up, I would have answered, "I haven't the slightest idea." With no precedent to go by, with very loose and very limited organization, I did not know what to expect. When 500 children assembled, with a fair sprinkling of mothers attending the younger ones, I was astonished. Most were black, but the white minority, produced by mobilization in Communist ranks, was sizable. As lines began to form for the march there were spots of extraordinary confusion. It turned out that some black mothers, accompanying children of six or seven, misread the handbills. The phrase FREE HOT LUNCHES was prominently displayed, and so were the time and place for assembly. The desperate wish and an unfamiliarity with the written word made it easy to overlook MARCH FOR and to skip the smaller type. Mothers brought their children, expecting free hot lunches to be served then and there. When the misunderstanding was explained they joined in the march.

The kids were spirited. They improvised a rhythmic chant.

> Stands 'em on their head, stands 'em on their feet,
> Mayor Mackey, when do we eat?

I brooded about the misunderstanding. I looked at the handbill to reassure myself that it was not designed, even inadvertently, to deceive. Still those mothers were misled, they must have been disappointed. This rankled. In all the weeks with the kids at Mr. W.'s place I thought I knew the hunger and distress in the ghetto. When the demonstration turnout surprised me (even though I did not know what to expect), the thought flashed: you underestimated the desperation. But somehow the misunderstanding made me feel with the intensity of revelation what I thought I knew all along.

Familiar now with the chant, having achieved unison, the hundreds of childish voices were at peak pitch . . . *Mayor Mackey, when do we eat?* At the Board of Education building some mothers and children were selected informally as a delegation to present the demand for free hot lunches in the schools. As spokesman I did not tell the board about the mothers' misunderstanding, but the rankling incident was the force behind the lash of bitterness and anger. Board members replied. They appreciated the eloquence and sincerity of the young man, but regrettably they could not do much . . . They shared the concern, but they did not have money . . . They would look into the situation, of course, and see what could be done, but they did not want to arouse false hopes, their authority was limited . . .

This was my first such confrontation with officialdom, the

first encounter with the ubiquitous "but" of liberalism. It was also my farewell to Philadelphia. Soon afterward, the proposal was made that I go to Baltimore as YCL section organizer. I eagerly accepted.

You must see Sparrows Point. Soon after arriving in Baltimore you obeyed this injunction.

To see Sparrows Point you traveled five miles southeast from Baltimore and on to one of several fingers protruding from a peninsula at the confluence of the Patapsco River and Chesapeake Bay. You were there after you crossed a bridge over Bear Creek. Some miles to the northeast there was a backdoor entrance to Sparrows Point via a neck of land that joins it to the mainland, but at the entrance you used Bear Creek seemed like a moat and the bridge like a single link with the rest of the world. Instead of turrets and spires, however, blast furnaces and smoking chimneys stood tall on the other side of the moat.

Sparrows Point is one name, but it is three things. It is the tip of the peninsular finger, it is a town, and most important, for this is what you came to see, it is the largest production complex of the Bethlehem Steel Corporation.

You approached the massive array of furnaces and mills and you thought: what a fantastic locale for a feudal castle, water on three sides and a narrow strip of land on the fourth. Heightening the impression of a feudal stronghold was a protective semicircle of military forts. You passed Fort Holabird and en route you also spotted Fort Carroll, perched on an island in the Patapsco River, due west of Sparrows Point, commanding the water passage to it from the Port of Baltimore. Dimly you were aware that on the other side of Sparrows Point, on another finger of the peninsula, Fort Howard stood as sentinel at the juncture of the river and Chesapeake Bay.

Perhaps I was so struck by this geography, physical and military, because I envisioned Sparrows Point as a fortress even before I saw it. At Sparrows Point there were 17,000 workers in 1932. Of these 17,000, eight were YCL members and about twice that number were members of the Communist party. When the numerical ratio is 17,000 to 25, and you are engaged in combat with the second-largest steel corporation in the country, you are prone to think in fortress images.

The 17,000 were on the Bethlehem payroll, but they were not employed, they were underemployed. By mid-1932 steel production plummeted to 20 per cent of capacity. Some of the men said they were working "two days a pay." Bethlehem paid twice a month and the semimonthly pay period, or "pay" for short, was a unit of time as real as the lunar month or the Biblical week. The basic steel wage had been slashed to thirty-four cents an hour; a man who worked two days at that price had $5.44 to show for it at the end of a pay. He was not unemployed; neither was he truly employed. He existed in economic purgatory.

One YCL member, a Finn from Ohio, fled from purgatory, but not to heaven. He became a runner for a bootlegger, servicing the troops at military installations in the vicinity. Another took to making home brew. But not for sale. This was his pride. "It is only for me and my friends," he said. "I do not sell it." The quality was also his pride. "You cannot buy stuff like this, eh?" He had time, so much time, and the patience of a true craftsman.

Carlos the brewmaker was a dark, sinewy Spaniard, a rougher in the hot mill, a job that required the physical strength and dexterity to handle white-hot steel slabs with tongs and feed them between mammoth rollers that pressed them into plate of specified thickness. He lived in Dundalk, one of about half-a-dozen villages inhabited by Bethlehem's vassals. In Dundalk there was a single men's settlement, a sprawl of wooden shacks along the water's edge. Most single men hired bed and board; only those who placed a high premium on privacy took on the household chores and loneliness that went with keeping their own house. Carlos kept a tidy shack, too tidy perhaps in what it told of the time on his hands. Yet, in the tidiness, as in the brew, there was pride. Only two days' work, pay after pay, with all the dead time, with the humiliating wage that kept you from starving and kept you from living; it pressed upon a man's dignity, threatened to crumble it. A man had to find his own ways to keep it whole.

Carlos had one constant companion, a huge German shepherd, and the dog accentuated the loneliness of the man in his twenties. A brooding loneliness, I thought. But then I knew Carlos only in 1932 and it may have been a symptom of the times. There was time for brooding. What he was like in other times I do not know. He offered you the beer with ceremonial hospitality and you drank it slowly, as if the drinking of it was a ritual, not like the drinking of the "rotgut" that sold in the steel settlement for twenty-five cents a half pint. That you bolted, partly because it had a machine-oil smell, and you joked that the stuff was so raw, maybe they had to put a little oil in it so you could get it down.

Carlos did not talk much, except about one thing. The Immigration and Naturalization Service had set up shop at one end of the hot mill, which was a very long shedlike structure housing many rolling mills arrayed in a straight line that, some said, extended for a half mile. Every now and then two Immigration dicks left the desk at their command post and marched through the hot mill, past rolling mills and crews at those that were in operation, until they reached a mill where they beckoned to a man. Then, with the man between them, they marched back, once more past crews of men, many of whom, like Carlos, were foreign-born. Sometimes it was a very long march. Sometimes a man who was picked up came back. Sometimes he did not.

Like the thick smoke, fear was in the Sparrows Point atmosphere. Because of it my visits to YCL steelworkers were rare and discreet (those who boarded I did not visit at all, not at their residence). Work may have been reduced to two days a pay but we assumed there was no comparable slack in company espionage. This was no imaginary fear. A short while before, a steelworker named Carl Bradley was spotted by company spies and fired. Now Bradley doubled as Baltimore secretary of the Trade Union Unity League and its affiliate, the Metal Workers Industrial Union. He also edited the mimeographed Communist paper published monthly for Sparrows Point workers.

The union and the paper were at the hub of Communist activity at Sparrows Point, and that's what we talked about mostly on the rare visits with my comrades in steel. Those were the conversational staples, the matters of course, so much so that I cannot remember what was said about them. Memory tends to retain the extraordinary (which is not necessarily atypical). What I remember is not the political detail, our principal preoccupation, but what struck me as extraordinary in its matrix.

Along with bitterness and fear there was anger and frustration in this matrix, and on the outer edges demoralization. Men cursed the corporation and it was not always a faceless omnipotence; occasionally it took on human guise in the person of Charles Schwab, Chairman of the Board. Having transferred the reins of active management to Eugene Grace, Bethlehem President, Schwab essayed the role of elder industrial statesman, issuing pronouncements on the state of the nation and the world.

Among Schwab's intellectual ingots of 1932 were these:

"We mustn't complain if we have five or six years of very great depression. We mustn't complain if we go broke and all sorts of things happen."

"There are no rich men in America today . . . The happy man and the happy woman are the ones who have no obligations to meet because they can always conduct their affairs to suit their income and conditions of life, however poor they may be."

"There is one great thing for the real man today and that is to sweat . . . That is the only remedy for the depression."

Good old Charlie Schwab. He supplied the text for many a soapbox oration. You did not soapbox in Bethlehem's domain, neither in Sparrows Point, nor in its tributary villages. It was forbidden there and you knew you did not have enough steelworker muscle to shatter the prohibition. You soapboxed in Baltimore, beyond the boundaries of Bethlehem's absolute rule, where only a stray steelworker might hear you, but just the same you had a powerful sense of obligation to articulate the pent-up, hidden anger at Sparrows Point. Maybe it was a vicarious release of the frustration you encountered in the dreary shacks along Dundalk's waterside.

Soapboxing. Have you heard Dr. Charlie Schwab's depres-

*sion remedy? Sweat! That's what it says in the paper (holding
aloft the newspaper clipping, and reading the headline: "Sweat"
Depression Cure, Says Schwab). Sweat! Put it in bottles. It's
good for what ails you. My God, Charlie Schwab has cut his
workers out at Sparrows Point down to one day's work a week.
And he's telling 'em to sweat. With brains like his running the
steel industry, don't you think the workers can do a better job
of it?*

Good old Charlie Schwab. Star of Bethlehem. You lighted
the way and lightened the burden for a young Communist organizer in Maryland and the District of Columbia.

Only once did I cease tiptoeing around Sparrows Point, or in
and out it, going into the steel country this once as if it were not
behind enemy lines. The occasion was a wage cut decreed by
the steel corporations in May 1932. There had been rumors of
a wage cut, the workers expected it, and yet when it came there
was an unexpected twist. Advance rumors pegged it at 10 per
cent; the announcement said 15 per cent. This was the second
wage cut in eight months. The previous October wages were
slashed by 10 per cent, from a base hourly rate of forty-four
cents down to forty cents, and now it was to be thirty-four
cents. Older workers could remember the peak base rate of
fifty-one cents during World War I; the new rate was one-third
less.

The cut came little more than a fortnight after Charlie
Schwab said, "We mustn't complain if we go broke and all sorts
of things happen . . ." You were outraged at the arrogance of
it, at the cruelty, but what could you do? What Carl Bradley
did was to throw off our customary caution and prudence. Taking me along he tore through the steel settlements on an indignation trip; picking houses at random he knocked on doors,
many doors in broad daylight, not caring who saw him, having
no prior briefing on the people behind those doors, heedless
of all the rules of security we had so painstakingly observed.

Bradley was a bull of a man; massive head, thick neck,
muscle-bulging shoulders. His round, open, olive-complex-
ioned face resembled Indian faces you see in the Southwest or
below the border. When Bradley was feeling good and outgo-

ing he exuded a human kindness that enveloped you and a kind of joy that was almost childlike in its purity. Bradley didn't always feel good, and when he didn't there were times when he was a bundle of moods and idiosyncrasies. That year, for example, he was the Communist candidate for United States senator from Maryland, and he would come into the party's office to announce: "I've got to speak tonight. What am I going to say?" He was serious, almost plaintive. The answer he got from the party organizer, Oscar (The Kid) Everett, was a burst of profanity and a threat to throw him down the stairs. Exhibiting his hurt at such rejection Bradley left, but he always managed to think of something to say, enough to soapbox for an hour or two.

One evening, when Bradley invited questions, a Communist seaman on the fringes of the crowd, hidden in shadows beyond the glow of the street-corner lamp, shouted out, "Mr. Candidate, what is your position on water?" It was a thoroughly mischievous question. But Bradley was stumped for only a moment. Then he boomed, "I'm for more water to the people!" He bellowed it, and Bradley was not one of your strong men who startle you with the thin falsetto of a voice. His voice box and vocal cords were of a piece with his powerful torso. The resonance of water to the people flooded four Baltimore city blocks.

He may not have known the politics of water but Bradley was a man of the people. As we went from house to house in the steel settlements he was uncanny, amazing the woman of one house with his clairvoyance; he guessed every ingredient that was in the lidded pots on the stove for supper. I asked him later how he knew. Luck, he smiled, and a little savvy — after all, he added, on two days a pay, how much choice is there? He was home. Observing the decorum appropriate to an uninvited guest, but not as a stranger. I knew the anger that was in him because we talked about it on the way out to the steel settlements. Once there it was controlled. No bellowing now. At first the talk would be easy and soft, Bradley with his singular human warmth thawing out the protective reserve and fear.

Then the other man opened up. The conversation, still quiet, was intense now. The steelworker translated the catchwords — organize, fight — into the practicalities: join the union, strike. Yes, it should be done, but you can't do it, not now. Strike? He was idle involuntarily four days out of five, and he was not sure how much he would hurt the company by voluntary idleness on the fifth day. Assuming the men would stick together, which they won't.

One man, having repeated this litany of frustration, tried to soften it, to establish a special bond of intimacy by telling us his big secret, almost in a whisper. "I've got every son of a bitch spotted in my mill who scabbed in nineteen nineteen." His confidence answered a question that had occurred to me on occasion. Reading of great labor battles I had wondered: where are they now, the veterans of those battles? Now I knew where one was, thirteen years after the Great Steel Strike, still keeping his accounts and biding his time.

Maybe our foray into the steel country was an exercise in desperation and frustration. Maybe, more charitably, it was reconnaissance. It yielded nothing at the time. Still I came away from it knowing something, no longer as projection of theory or as tenet of faith, but with a tactile certainty. I knew Sparrows Point was going to blow. I could not tell when or how, but I knew it would blow. Five years later it did blow when the CIO stormed the steel country. I was not there when the workers finally did what they knew they ought to do, but thought they couldn't. Yet the fleeting glimpse of the metamorphosis barely in the making became, in my mind, a companion to what I had sensed March 6, an augury of the final conflict.

The walls of this enormous room were lined with book-filled shelves from the floor to tall ceiling. It was the biggest private library I had ever seen. A phonograph emitted the tremulous sentimentality of Helen Morgan singing "My Bill." I was living in this house, a typical example of old Baltimore residential architecture, a three-floor box encased in brick monotony, its exterior different from those of several neighbors on East Pratt

Street in one particular: the outdoor steps were dark gray, not white. And a good thing it was because there was no one in the house to keep the steps white.

There was an odd thing about my residence. My host did not know I was his house guest. His name was V. F. Calverton, a name of some importance in the intellectual and radical circles of this time. The deception, if that's the word for living in a man's house without his knowledge, was not as ingenious as it seems. Although Calverton regarded the house on Pratt Street as his home, he spent most of his time in New York, visiting Baltimore for brief intervals, generally on weekends.

I moved in at the suggestion of Arthur, an Englishman and one of a group of young intellectuals who had clustered around Calverton. All the others were scattered by then, most to New York, but at least one must have made it as far west as Montana because he wrote a poem about it. Only Arthur remained and he was given shelter by Calverton. The other occupant of the big house was Calverton's brother, Charles, a civil engineer, but he did not live in it; he only came in to sleep in his top-floor quarters. A lot of living space was going to waste and Arthur said I ought to use some of it, which seemed reasonable to me. Nights on a rolltop desk in Philadelphia had been a learning experience.

My tenancy was clandestine but there was no one to keep the secret from except a woman who favored Calverton by looking after the house although she did not live in it. Afraid that our arrangement would not long escape her notice, Arthur decided to tell her and bind her to secrecy. She won't tell, he assured me afterward. She was a Russian émigrée and most of her White Guard family, according to Arthur, had perished in the revolution and civil war. This was a very traumatic experience for her, he said, and so he promised her that if she were discreet about my presence in the house it would weigh heavily in her favor when the American revolution came.

On Calverton's weekends in Baltimore I slept elsewhere, dropping in occasionally as Arthur's friend to observe this intellectual lion. Arthur insisted there were only three authentic intellectual lions in Baltimore: Calverton, H. L. Mencken, and a man named A. D. Emart, who then was the Baltimore *Sun's* literary critic. They were fiercely competitive, Arthur said, but I noted they had at least one foible in common: a preference for initials over first names.

Then in his early thirties Calverton had prodigious energy. Literary critic, novelist, sociologist, sexologist, free-lance radical (he was on bad terms with the Communist party), he had by then authored at least eight published books, coedited some others, and was editor of *The Modern Quarterly*, a radical literary journal he had founded at age twenty-three. I was additionally impressed because he had worked out at Sparrows Point as timekeeper for Bethlehem, a job that carried him through Johns Hopkins where he reputedly had compiled the most brilliant academic record of any undergraduate in the university's history. Seeing him then in 1932 you would not have divined he had so few years left; he died in 1940 at the age of forty.

He roared into Baltimore, throttles wide open, with entourage and baggage that typically included: one intellectual attraction, one woman, one box of cigars, two bottles of whiskey, and the manuscript of the book on which he was then working. By the end of the weekend, it was said, he had smoked all the cigars, drunk the whiskey, slept with the woman, kept open house for much of the time to display his intellectual attraction (and, not incidentally, himself), and added fifty or sixty pages to his manuscript. I readily believed all the rest, but how could he write all those pages at the same time? Several years later my skepticism on this score was abated somewhat when two of his former young disciples, part of the group that had included Arthur, did a devastating documentation of his plagiarism. He had a picaresque quality and apparently it extended to other men's writings as it did, for example, to envelopes. He delighted in telling how he relieved a publisher of 5000 envelopes with the connivance of a secretary he had charmed.

Another curious boast of his I remember is that he was the second most popular American author in Japan. I did not ask him who was the first. Indeed, I never asked him anything. I was fascinated and awed by the man's intelligence and vitality, which strained my young Communist disdain for him as a radical dilettante. Anyway, in the bizarre mix of Baltimore intelligentsia and radical miscellany at his salons, it would have taken greater temerity than I had as a clandestine squatter at eighteen to break into the conversational babble. I did not even rise to the bait of the oft-told story by a Socialist doctor of how it was in 1919 when the American Legion threatened to raid the local Socialist headquarters. He and some other Socialists barricaded themselves in the headquarters all night, guns in hand, waiting for the raiders, who never came. He always looked directly at me when he told this story, as if to say, "You young Communist punk, with your talk of revolution and your snide remarks about yellow Socialists, how about that?"

After a Calverton weekend the house on Pratt Street seemed more quiet and restful than ever. For a young organizer, beset with tensions and problems, the magnificent library was a haven. Books and music, too; under Arthur's tutelage I developed a taste for Helen Morgan records, although I could never quite share his enthusiasm for "My Bill." He thought the lyrics contained a profound psychological insight into romanticism and realism in love. Arthur was restful, too. He talked slowly, distinctly, and dispassionately. He had a habit of recitation, as if he were perfecting his diction, and it could be almost anything: a slogan on a poster or a line from a verse. "The Pope is dying, dying is the Pope . . ." was a favorite of his. He was some years older than I and knew much that I didn't about things as varied as Baltimore and English literature. We talked young talk about life, love, books, people, and the politics we shared. Neither of us was a cook, but you could get two fresh eggs for a nickel down at the corner store; we consumed an incredible number of hard-boiled eggs.

This idyll did not last, political discord intruded. Arthur had taken a couple of trips to sea aboard an oil tanker and considered himself an authority on seamen. When some other YCL members and I proposed that we throw some energy into the organization of unemployed seamen Arthur invoked his expertise. "Oh no," he said, "try other workers, but not seamen; you cannot organize seamen to fight for relief or government assist-

ance, they are much too expert at panhandling." At first I
thought he was joking, but when the project was presented formally at a meeting he repeated his argument. I tried to reason
with him in private conversation. I called him a goddamn intellectual and he retorted that I was more of an intellectual than he
because I was more taken up with ideas as ideas. It was no use.
My duty was to press the formal charges against him that re-
sulted in his severance from the YCL.

This was my first friendship ruptured by politics, but not the
last. In retrospect it seems that Marx's observation on the repetition of history — the first time as tragedy, the second time as
farce — is susceptible of dialectical inversion. That first rupture had the elements of farce.

My own aptitude for panhandling was poor in the one test of
it at that time. It happened in Cumberland, an industrial town
in the thin western neck of Maryland, wedged between Pennsylvania and West Virginia. I went to Cumberland with Bradley. The moribund Amalgamated Association of Iron, Steel and
Tin Workers of North America had a strike going at a small
specialty mill in Cumberland and Bradley wanted to look into
it. I eagerly accepted his invitation to go along because for me
Cumberland and Western Maryland had about them the aura
of legend, fashioned mostly from tales told by Arthur. Like the
tale of two brothers, railroad workers and militant Socialists
during World War I, who also were reputed to be the best rifle
shots in a country where guns were staple and men took pride
in their marksmanship. The brothers announced they would
not be drafted for the war and would shoot anyone who came
to get them. No one came. This tale, I suppose, is apocryphal,
as is another I heard a couple of years later. When provisions
were made for state relief to the destitute, some pioneer families
in rural Maryland deigned to accept it. They were broke but
they also had valuable heirlooms, antiques, and old documents,
including letters from historic personages, perhaps a Supreme
Court justice or even a President. Sufficient was the indignity
of accepting relief without having it compounded by some state
investigator pawing through the family possessions. They let it
be known that any state snooper who set foot in the county

would be shot on sight as soon as his or her identity was established. This later tale fitted into my earlier vision of Western Maryland as a hidden frontier where the native pioneer spirit came through the barrel of a gun to keep at bay the bureaucratic impositions of twentieth-century American civilization.

Bradley and I set out long before dawn. I got my first glimpse of the Blue Ridge Mountains in the reflection of the rising sun, the sunlit patches set off by long morning shadows, the green loveliness of these hills so fresh, so glad in the dawn that any legend was believable. Cumberland, though, was hard to believe, a disordered cluster of mills and factories, of shops and a railroad yard, a discordant industrial mirage in this magnificent natural setting. We arrived there in the morning and the man who met us asked the practical question: what about breakfast? We had eaten none. An inventory confirmed we had just enough money for gas to get us back to Baltimore. Our host apologized that he could not be as hospitable as he would like. He could take care of Bradley but, pointing to me, "This young fellow. He needs his vittles, more than I can fetch. But we'll fix him up."

Fixing me up consisted of directions. An aunt of his lived down the street, the second house on the right past the next corner, the one with the big back porch. She did not agree with his politics but she was a kind, Christian soul who never turned a fellow down for a handout. With this our host and Bradley walked off and I set out for the backdoor of the kind, Christian aunt.

I was embarrassed and very annoyed at my embarrassment. What the hell, I scolded myself, this is petty bourgeois weakness, rotten liberalism. That last phrase came to me because I had once heard a party organizer rebuke someone for being timorous about soliciting funds for the cause; the organizer said such timidity reflected a rotten liberal approach toward money. I marshaled the arguments all right, and I persuaded myself intellectually, but this did not dispel the sense of shame of which I was so ashamed. With a gnawing stomach and a raging ideological dispute inside of me, I knocked on the backdoor, then stammered out my story . . . going to Pittsburgh

. . . from Baltimore . . . looking for work . . . hungry . . . can you spare something to eat?

The aunt was a big woman, kind as her nephew said she was, but she was no talker. Having said just enough to set me down at the table on the back porch she busied herself with a huge platter of scrambled eggs and fried potatoes. I tried to break the awkward silence with several fitful starts of talk about how bad things were in Baltimore. She still said nothing and I stopped trying. In the stillness I could hear the clank of coupling boxcars and the snort of an engine in a railroad yard. I also heard the rumbles in my stomach and wondered if she could hear them, or if she noticed how my hand shook when it brought the cup of coffee to my lips. I said nothing until I said, "Thank you, ma'am." She said, "Good luck."

When I rejoined Bradley and the local man they had ascertained there was nothing they could do about the strike and Bradley wanted to get back to Baltimore. I picked up no more Western Maryland lore.

The break with Arthur also meant farewell to the Calverton library and Helen Morgan. I moved into a flat with some seamen, who were part of the organizing cadre of the Marine Workers' Industrial Union. Arthur had been egregiously wrong about the organizing potential among unemployed seamen.

This was another world, different from Pratt Street only a few blocks to the north, yet separated by the invisible boundary between the waterfront and uptown. This world became mine. In uptown Baltimore the main arteries were Charles and Baltimore Streets, quartering the city into east and west, north and south. My life flowed from the foot of Broadway out along Thames Street where the MWIU hall faced a cluster of docks. Here began an active involvement that extended for three years and many threads of personal association that endured for many years more, enough to comprise a distinct chapter later on. For the moment it is pertinent to relate that for the young organizer it was heady stuff to go down to the waterfront and in one day recruit seventeen seamen into the YCL. Here was a sense of tangible accomplishment, and also a sense of camaraderie. Here was the excitement of discovery, for these men came from many regions of the United States, from places that were bizarre to me then, like Texas, or exotic, like Hawaii; they came from foreign lands and they had sailed to every part of the world, prone to argue about the quality and location of a whorehouse in Capetown or a cafe in Marseille, or about what really happened during the big seamen's strike in Buenos Aires.

Only one event that late spring and summer seriously distracted my mind from the waterfront.

It was toward the middle of May that we first began to notice them, these men wandering the streets in the evening, sometimes in pairs, more often in larger groups, but seldom more than a dozen together. They drifted aimlessly up and down Baltimore Street, manifestly strangers in the city. These were veterans of the World War (we did not call it the first then or append the Roman numeral I), on their way to Washington to demand immediate payment of the bonus that was promised them.

There seemed to be more of them each successive evening and The Kid (this is how everyone referred to Oscar Everett, the Communist party organizer for Maryland and the District of Columbia) began telephoning the national party center in New York: Get someone down to Washington, this bonus thing is getting big and it has no leadership, these guys are just coming. I did not eavesdrop on The Kid's telephone conversations, so I don't know exactly how he put it, but I suspect that whoever answered the third or fourth call didn't like it. The Kid was irreverent, profane, tough, and very bright.

I suppose he got his nickname because of his round cheeks, the kind that are commonly called baby-faced, and the upward tilt of his nose. These cherubic features were offset by an impish glint in his dark eyes, and by his very thick, very black hair. There was much more imp than cherub in this short, stocky upholsterer from Philadelphia. He could shock me by saying in mixed company about a woman he disliked, "If I had a wooden prick I'd split it in two and fuck her in the nose." And he could surprise me with displays of theoretical knowledge and political acumen.

His successor in Baltimore, fresh from school in Moscow and eager to exhibit his learning, decided to put The Kid through a catechism in Marxist economics. Watching it I waited for the explosion of profanity at this patronizing impertinence. But The Kid chose to be amused. He answered the questions, not playing at one-upmanship, and yet establishing that he knew more than his interrogator. Later that year, during those days before Hitler's seizure of power, I invoked our then pat phrase about "the united front from below." The Kid snapped back, "From below, from above, from the middle — it's not the time to quibble about that crap. They should make a united front."

The Kid referred to himself as a roughneck organizer: "That's all I am, a roughneck organizer." In any organization, especially in one as centralized as the Communist party, the head man on the scene tends to set the tone. The Kid set the tone in Baltimore and it harmonized with the spirit of the waterfront, then the most viable and visible sector of the movement. In fact, after he left Baltimore The Kid went to sea as a rank-and-file Communist and did not again assume a leadership post at any level.

Back in mid-May 1932 The Kid did a little more about the gathering bonus army than just make phone calls to New York. On his initiative we began to round up the veterans on the streets at night into large groups, twenty or more, and direct them to the Salvation Army or police headquarters to demand lodging and food. He and Bradley, Joe Bianca, gruff port secretary of the Marine Workers' Industrial Union, some others, and I joined in these nocturnal roundups. The men were fed and sheltered. Very soon, when the trickle of veterans became a tide and the bonus march splashed into national headlines, the city set up a special shelter for them.

Washington was in my organizational domain and there was a small group of young Communists there, mostly daughters of Jewish middle-class families. This is not said in disparagement; it required a particular courage to be a Communist in the political and intellectual antisepsis that was Washington at that time. Ordinarily I would not have bothered much with Washington, not when there was the waterfront and Sparrows Point in Baltimore, but with the Bonus Expeditionary Force camped in the capital I discovered organizational reasons for visiting it.

I had been to Washington the year before, including it in the itinerary of a hitchhiking tour of my district shortly after arrival in Philadelphia. On that occasion I spent the previous night in Baltimore. Sleeping on newspapers spread on the floor did not bother me much. Nor did the heat of an August night in a poorly ventilated, overpopulated Baltimore flat. Tired as I was, and conditioned by Philadelphia, I would have slept with these discomforts. What disturbed me were the bedbugs. I had known bedbugs before, and could even claim familiarity with them, having driven them out of bedsprings with a lighted match and having ferreted them out of mattress seams and cracks in the walls. But I never became adjusted to them, to their crawl on the skin, to the petty sting, to the welt and itch that followed, or to the repellent staleness of the odor when you squashed them. It was a bad night in Baltimore.

Out on the highway early next morning a sporting type stopped at the wave of my thumb. Being picked up by sporting types, as I learned later, was not unusual because Baltimore is a horse racing center; Pimlico within the city limits, Bowie and Laurel on the way to Washington, and Havre de Grace to the north, where you cross the mouth of the Susquehanna on the road to Philadelphia. If you were lucky you were picked up by a man who had a good day at the track and then sometimes there was a good meal in it, even drinks. So pervasive is horse racing in the Baltimore environment that it infiltrated into the YCL membership in the form of an ex-jockey who no longer could make the weight and a printer in a shop that put out scratch sheets.

The sporting type on the morning after the bad night in Baltimore was different. His sport was not with horses; it was with automobiles. He was driving a roadster, top down — and no windshield. He wore racing goggles, and that's how he drove, pushing the speedometer past sixty, then past seventy (and this at a time when "a mile a minute" meant speed). His goggles protected his eyes but there was nothing to shield mine from the headwind of sixty and seventy miles an hour. I turned my head, I bowed it, but the gale was relentless in finding and whipping those tired, dirty, bloodshot eyes of mine. I could have crouched beneath the dashboard or just held my hands over my eyes, but sitting next to the dashing fellow at the wheel that did not seem proper. I paid for my pride. By the time we got to Washington the right eye was inflamed, oozing matter that looked like mucus or pus.

I had only one address in Washington and it turned out to be in a quiet, middle-class, residential neighborhood in the northwest quarter. It also turned out, when I got there at about ten A.M., that no one was home. Having no money and no other place to go there was nothing to do but wait. By this time the bad eye no longer oozed, it flowed. My handkerchief, dirty to start with, was saturated with the matter; my shirt-sleeve was drenched and coated with it, and the nonabsorbent skin of my forearm only smeared it. So I waited. I had never met my "contact"; waiting for the unknown makes it more difficult. At every approaching pedestrian I perked up, especially at every young female because of the only two facts I knew about the person I was waiting for: name Sophie, and she was a YCL member. Maybe, I hoped each time, this was somebody for me at last, but it wasn't. By noon of this Washington summer's day sweat began to mix with the matter, the brine in it adding sting to the inflammation. If only time flowed as swiftly, but it didn't; it moved slowly, as if it had become aware that its ultimate measure was eternity, and what was the use of hurrying? Slowly the hours passed, one by one, five of them at last, and then eternity punched the time clock shortly past three P.M.; my "contact" came home. In my condition I noticed her attributes in the following order: clean, cool, gracious, kind. My unclean wretchedness did no good for the male ego at seventeen. But Sophie had the tactful kindness to put me at ease. I was grateful.

Such was my introduction to the nation's capital; I saw it first with an inflamed eye through a murky film. Maybe it was a good way to see it the first time, this artificially conceived city, where bureaucracy is the principal industry. I saw it differently in 1932.

June 7. This evening the Bonus Expeditionary Force staged its grand parade up Pennsylvania Avenue. It is a traditional parade route but tradition was modified: the parade began from The Ellipse and flowed into Pennsylvania Avenue without passing the White House and it disbanded at the Peace Monument, just before it reached the Capitol. The veterans were in Washington to impress upon the Congress and the President their demand for immediate payment of the bonus, but they were not permitted to approach the seat of either.

The veterans, 7000 of them, were men in their thirties or early forties, out of the military service for some thirteen years. For this parade they tried to remember what they had forgotten about military bearing and close-order drill. Shoulders back, chest out, face impassive; ranks dressed to the right, files straight; they tried to keep in step to the cadence blasting forth from two bands. The men tried but memory and reflexes were rusty; there was something compelling and pathetic about their effort. A few had dug up their military uniforms for the occasion, but far more common were the vocational uniforms of America: farmers in blue overalls, railroad men in striped ones, carpenters in their distinctive coveralls with pocket pouches for tools, gas station attendants in their livery, and many more.

They were formed in six regiments. They carried no placards. I remember a little boy leading a little dog wrapped in a white cloth with one word inscribed on it: "Bonus." I cannot recall for certain whether there was any sign of their motto: "Heroes of '17, Bums of '32." They did not shout slogans. Silent, impassive, almost grim, they marched up Pennsylvania Avenue toward the Capitol dome, past 100,000 spectators jamming the sidewalks.

Behind me, on the steps of a government building, was a group of women. Thickly rouged and lipsticked, to my eighteen-year-old eyes they looked middle-aged, in the same age range as the men parading by, too old for the flapperish summer clothes they were wearing. I imagined they were pros- titutes who entertained these marching men when they all were younger and the occupation of each was patriotic. (What Price, Gloria?) These women were more shrill in their enthusi- asm than other spectators. In the monotony of the marching ranks there was not much to inspire cheers, but some of the companies in the regiments did carry a sign with the name of the city they came from. So the shrill voices cried out, "Hoo- ray for Portland! . . . Hoo-ray for Columbus! . . ." Just these cries and the soft thud of marching feet and in the distance the brass and the drums of the bands.

I felt an eerie strength in this parade, so strange to me, so different from any I had imagined; without placards or shouted slogans, those recognizable symptoms of conscious organiza- tion. This was spontaneous. True, at a congressional hearing back in April a representative of the Communist-led Workers Ex-Servicemen's League (in common usage the initials, WESL, became the Weasels) called for a national march on Washing- ton. But I knew from evening roundups on Baltimore Street and from watching the march up Pennsylvania Avenue that at least four out of five of these men had never heard of the Wea- sels or their April call. What prompted these men in widely scattered regions of a vast country, men of the most varied oc- cupations, suddenly to descend on Washington in boxcars, trucks, autos, buses, or on foot? It was a mystery. Sure, I knew of the economic distress and of the tantalizing lump sum attrac- tion of the bonus. Motivation was no mystery. The concert of the action was; the spread of the word whose origin was so soon lost; the sudden, simultaneous initiative of men in Oregon and men in Alabama to embark upon the long, uncertain trek to Washington, without any ties of organization, or any bond of identifiable leadership.

In the press small items appeared at the beginning of May about veterans leaving for Washington from Portland, Oregon. Not until May 20, when 400 Oregon veterans commandeered five freight cars of the Wabash Railway from Council Bluffs, Iowa, to St. Louis, Missouri, did the bonus march make headlines. By then, as I had seen on the streets of Baltimore, the convergence on Washington was under way; the sensational headlines only augmented and accelerated it.

All this I knew as the parade went by. And these were veterans, which meant more then than it was to mean later. This was before thirty years and more of a conscript army institutionalized it in national life; before the war of the decade became a hallmark of three successive decades. People referred to *the* war and they did not have to explain which war they meant. Among the living (except for the few survivors of the Civil War) memory encompassed a fleeting interval of conscription, less than two years of it. The country was not yet glutted with veterans, the term retained some social value. Thanks to the professional veterans' organizations the term also conveyed an image of patriotism and conservatism.

Here they were, ex-soldiers and ex-sailors, trained in the use of arms, popular paragons of patriotism, spontaneously self-marshaled and marching from the shadow of the White House to the shadow of the Capitol, insistently demanding something that neither the President nor the Congress was disposed to give them. To the teen-age revolutionary this was "rank and file America"; behind the restraint of these men, behind their awkward efforts to sheathe their pride in military trappings, behind their patent unfamiliarity with the conventions of the demonstrative act, there was a latent, menacing power.

This was my first impression and it grew stronger in the weeks to come. The day after the June 7 parade the official Washington line for the veterans was: you came, you put on your show, now go home. To bolster this line there were scare stories in the press that the food supply was near exhaustion and only $100 remained to buy food for the thousands of veterans, some with wives and children, sheltered in tents and a motley sprawl of improvised shacks on the marshes of Anacostia Flats across the Anacostia River. Free passage and one day's rations were offered as enticements to go home. But the veterans did not leave. Instead, by the end of the week the 7000 there on June 7 (a Tuesday) were reinforced by 4000 more.

On subsequent visits to Washington I felt as if I were in a besieged city. The sense of siege became increasingly more acute. On June 17, with thousands of veterans milling around the Capitol, the Senate voted to kill the bonus. In legislative jargon the bill was dead for this session. But the veterans stayed and more came; by the end of June the besieging army numbered between 20,000 and 25,000 men. On July 16 Congress adjourned and the congressmen went home for the politicking of a presidential election year. But still the veterans stayed.

They were everywhere in downtown Washington, hawking the *BEF News* and other souvenirs, panhandling, or just wandering around. You could overhear the nervous conversations of petty government clerks, Southern accents common among them. How is it going to end? What is going to happen? These clerks had turned out to watch and cheer the parade on June 7, but now they were disturbed, worried, filled with foreboding. I heard the rumors. President Hoover was scared witless. The Quantico marines were on a constant alert. No, marine platoons were concealed in the White House. After congressional adjournment the rumor became more persistent and widespread: the army will be called out.

The bulk of the BEF was camped out at Anacostia Flats, out of sight and far away, separated from Washington proper by the river, and it was always possible to raise the bridges over the river. Indeed, the Anacostia Bridge was raised on the night of the Senate vote to kill the bonus and thousands of veterans were kept from the Capitol.

In mid-June, however, some veteran contingents, led by Communists and others of the Left, occupied sites within the city. One camp was on a cleared lot at Pennsylvania Avenue and Third Street. From this redoubt men moving on the double could storm the Capitol in less than a minute. The larger contingent occupied buildings, emptied for demolition and replacement, on B Street, between 13th and 14th, only a few blocks south of the White House. In a newspaper article later that year General Pelham D. Glassford, Washington's police chief, observed, ". . . some members of the wealthy classes throughout the country looked upon the occupation of the nation's capital as a revolutionary action." If this is what they thought far away, on the scene it was tempting to fantasize: suppose those men off 14th Street took that short march to the White House?

That was fantasy, the kind of joke you keep to yourself. Close up, even with my powers of observation, this was no revolutionary action. And yet these men had seized freight trains, defied the law; some, like the Communist-led Michigan contingent, had fought their way to Washington over two weeks and 600 miles despite every effort to stop them. There was something elemental in this spontaneous eruption, something that struck a deep chord in a distressed and troubled country. It was enough to make me think again about something of Lenin's I had read . . . "We do not and cannot know which spark . . . will kindle the conflagration." There was no fire this time but I thought I discerned in Washington how it might be kindled.

The coveys of civil servants did not think about Lenin; from what I overheard most of them, unlike General Glassford's scattered men of wealth, did not think of revolution. They were just nervous. The press did not soothe their nerves. Every time I arrived there during those weeks some sensation was headlined: 1,000 ARMED REDS EN ROUTE . . . DYNAMITE SEIZED IN ANACOSTIA CAMP . . . FEAR WATER SUPPLY POLLUTED (some conduits of the capital's water system ran under Anacostia Flats, the story said, and might be vulnerable to the primitive sanitation of the veterans' camp) . . . 200 VETS DISARMED IN ALEXANDRIA (this about a contingent of Alabama veterans who rode in on a freight train) . . . The details might be distorted by memory, but not the tenor. Fears of Reds and fears of an epidemic in the Anacostia camp were good for recurrent headlines.

As the end of July neared Washington was oppressed with a fatalistic sense of impending catastrophe. Only one certainty was heard everywhere: things cannot go on as they are. And the only noncatastrophic means of lifting the siege seemed categorically foreclosed. The President would not yield, the veterans would not leave (some talked of staying until 1945, which was the date they were then promised the bonus).

I was not there on July 28 when the catastrophe finally came, when cavalrymen with sabers, infantrymen with bayonets and gas grenades, supported by a platoon of tanks, all commanded by General Douglas MacArthur, drove the "Heroes of '17" out of Washington. The next day, at a protest street meeting on Baltimore's waterfront, a couple of carloads of veterans drove up. One veteran consented to speak. Shaken, still in a state of shock, he sounded no ringing call for retribution. He muttered something, barely audible, about there being a dead baby in one of the cars. (I did not go to look. But the only two fatalities of the army gas attack were two babies. The two men who died were killed by bullets of the Metropolitan Police.)

You were shaped primarily by what you did, what you observed, what you experienced, but there were also more purely intellectual influences.

You tried to learn the rudiments of Communist theory. In New York you went to the Workers' School, which occupied a large loft in a building on Union Square. The loft could serve as an auditorium or it could be partitioned into classroom cubicles.

I remember best an evening class in "Marxism-Leninism I" with a teacher named Campbell, who later turned out to be Earl Browder. Our text was *Leninism* by Joseph Stalin. Browder spoke very slowly, very deliberately, weighing each phrase and sentence before he expelled it with the force of an oracular pronouncement. Sometimes I inhaled a deep breath at the end of one of his sentences just to see if I could hold it until he launched into the next. In later years, with much application and practice, he perfected his oratorical technique but when I had him as teacher his deliberateness was tortured.

The partitions were very thin and through the one on our left we could hear Dr. Markoff, a Marxist dentist who taught an elementary introduction to Marxism. If Browder's delivery was like that of a heavy gun that has to be primed and reloaded after each shot, Markoff's was like that of a rapid-fire machine gun. Between each of Browder's sentences Markoff rattled off a paragraph. Behind the partition on our right, speaking at a normal pace, an old Communist named George Siskind taught "Marxism-Leninism II." Students joked about this novel experiment in education; you were taking one course and simultaneously, if you only had three ears, you could review what preceded it and preview what was to come. Not that there was much joking; Browder was solemn and we students were earnest.

One rudiment you learned was that revolutionary theory and practice must be joined if either is to be effective. For you this became a truism. This is why you read, studied, went to classes. And yet there was also tacit acceptance of a division of labor. You wanted to know enough of the rudiments to be able to comprehend a theoretical exposition or argument and to relate it to what you were doing, but you also were content to leave the formulation or development of theory to wiser men. The intellectual discipline and range of knowledge required for serious theoretical work were enough to make it tempting to leave theory to others and this normally beckoning temptation was enhanced by two particular circumstances.

One was the limitless opportunity for activism that was rewarded with quick, tangible results. It was a time of burgeoning movements and conflicts. Organizational, tactical, agitational skills were at a premium; there was no lack of work even for apprentices in these crafts. There were unemployed councils and unions to be organized and led in battle, your own organization had to be staffed. The demand for the "roughneck organizer," as The Kid styled himself in Baltimore, far exceeded the supply. In following your inclination to plunge into this activist whirlpool you could invoke authority. Like Lenin's approving reference to Goethe's lines, ". . . theory is all gray,/ And the golden tree of life is green." Or Lenin's semiplayful explanation that he did not complete his original design of *State and Revolution* because the Soviet revolution "interfered." "It is more pleasant and useful," he wrote, "to go through the 'experience of the revolution' than to write about it." Amen, you said. In your late teens and early twenties the green of life was far more alluring than the gray of theory.

More brilliant than green, gray, or any other color in your intellectual spectrum was the red of Lenin's revolution, which more than all else tinted what you thought and did. Among other things you saw in this revolution the supreme confirmation of the indivisibility of theory and practice. At first blush then it was a curious contradiction that this same revolution encouraged a dichotomy between practitioners and theoreticians. This was not as strange as it seems at first. In accepting the revolution as the model you tacitly accepted a corollary: this revolution solved in practice all the fundamental problems of revolutionary theory. You needed only to drink at this fountain of eternal theory. True, political reports and resolutions you read generally contained sections on *The World Situation* and *The Economic Situation;* these were variables, but at most they called for skills of analysis, derived from the theory, or of adjustment in the application of fixed theoretical premises. And the men who proved their mastery of the theory in practical leadership of the Russian Revolution were clearly best equipped to employ it in the functions of analysis and application.

All that, however, is much too gray. The revolution was more than a theoretical model, more than the most momentous episode in history; it was a living, vibrant, emotional presence. It came alive in economic charts and graphs; the black lines — precise, stark, implacable — defining the fate of two worlds, the decline of one and the ascent of the other. You pored over economic data — and you sang Soviet songs. You read Soviet literature, but most vivid of all were the Soviet films, epic in style, possessed with the energy and grandeur of the revolution. I had been there and still retained enough of the language to catch some of the dialogue and most of the lyrics in Soviet films. It was easy for me to be a Russophile, but others were too and in strange ways sometimes. I say strange because, as one example, I remember a girl in New York, sensitive and bright, who had just discovered Dostoevski and was immersed in his anguish. For her, somehow, his tormented genius was mixed up with the revolution as testimonial to the greatness of the people who had been chosen by history to blaze the path to man's future. Dostoevskian tragedy served, and so did touches of American burlesque, as in lyrics that originated with some girls at Hunter:

> What can be more sheiky
> Than a well-dressed Bolsheviki?
> What can be more Rooshian
> Than a little revolution?

Peripheral absurdities were not lacking, but these were peripheral, and at the heart of it all was a devotion with the purity and passion of a first love. A depth of feeling that Sean O'Casey tried to capture in a hymn.

Morning star, hope of the people, shine on us!
. . . Red Star extending till thy five rays, covering the world, give a great light to those who still sit in the darkness of poverty's persecution.
Herald of a new life, of true endeavour, of commonsense, of a world's peace, of man's ascent, of things to do bettering all things done;
The sign of Labour's shield, the symbol on the people's banner;
Red Star, shine on us all!

As the Red Star shone for the Irish poet over the slums of Dublin so it shone for me in Sparrows Point or the ghettos of Philadelphia; so, I knew, it shone over London's East End, where I was born, and over all the cities I had traversed, Yokohama, Warsaw, Berlin, Paris, and many more I had never seen. "The Red Star shines over the Kremlin," O'Casey wrote. Yet the power and the splendor of its rays derived not just from their point of origin, but also from the universality of their reach. The star was the symbol of the nascent world brotherhood of man. It made you one with the peoples you read about on the onionskin pages of *International Press Correspondence* (*Inprecor*), a news service publication of the Communist International, and the more remote they were from you in space and sociological time the greater the thrill in the sense of kinship with them. A mutiny aboard a Dutch cruiser in waters off the Dutch East Indies, a strike of diamond miners in South Africa, peasant uprisings in French Indochina — you came upon such events in *Inprecor*, not as a distant observer, but as allied combatant. In the revolutionary zodiac we were all born under the Red Star.

You got varied refractions of its light. Through books sometimes — and one book that exerted a singular influence was Vincent Sheean's *Personal History*. You were captivated by the portrait of Michael Borodin, chief Soviet representative in China, couch-ridden with malaria in Hankow, isolated outpost of a waning revolution, which even then, in 1927, was being butchered farther down the Yangtze. His hopes, his labors sinking in blood, his own life in danger, still Borodin lay there talking with calm detachment and self-assurance about the revolutionary wisdom of taking "the long view." You were intrigued by the romanticism of Sheean's relationship with Rayna Prohme and enchanted by the portrait of her as the incandescent revolutionary flame that consumed itself. Stronger than the empathy evoked by these portraits was the supreme sense of historical rectitude evoked by Sheean's confession that he perceived the inevitability and justice of revolution but could not join in it because he was not "prepared to give up all the pleasures of modern Western culture, everything from good food and sexual liberty to Bach and Stravinsky." By the time you read this you were nearing twenty-two and had served a revolutionary apprenticeship of four years, long enough to make you feel you were a journeyman with an earned right to moral superiority over this liberal intellectual, who was intelligent enough to recognize revolution as the historical imperative of our time and honest enough to acknowledge that he did not have the mettle for it, being too attached to the bourgeois comforts and refinements of a dying society.

Borodin epitomized the serene wisdom of revolution; in his "long view" was the certitude that no matter the vicissitudes, the defeats, the setbacks, the future was yours because you were the conscious instrument of an inexorable historical process. This same sense was more crudely conveyed in the lyrics of a YCL song, "The world is like a sailing boat,/ And we are at its rudder . . ." Rayna Prohme, in her purity, embodied the transcendent morality of revolution. Wisdom, serenity, morality, history — all these were with you, and you were at the rudder.

In this bright canvas there were also dark shadows. Sheean wrote of the pleasures he was not prepared to give up, but not of the hazards to be assumed. These, with their horror and heroism, were etched in another book that appeared at about the same time, Andre Malraux's *Man's Fate*. You were transfixed by the climactic scene in the novel, in which the veteran Russian revolutionary, Katov, and several associates in the last-ditch Shanghai insurrection of 1927 wait to be taken from an improvised prison compound to be stuffed into the furnaces of railroad locomotives. The experienced Bolshevik carries with him a suicide dose of cyanide for such contingencies, but in an ultimate gesture of revolutionary courage and self-sacrificing comradeship he gives the cyanide to two younger Chinese revolutionaries.

You came upon the practice of human incineration in one of Mayakovski's poems: "The Japanese/ 'pacifying'/ for the yen/ fuelled/ their locomotives/ with our men." Maybe the locomotive furnace as an execution chamber was an Asian refinement (this was an innocent time before the Nazi crematoria), but there was nothing exotic or far removed about torture and death. You had heard too many stories about the sadistic pleasures of police Red squads, notably those in Chicago and Los Angeles. You had met Joe York, a rangy towhead, modest, simple, and you liked him; you also knew that he was one of five killed by police during a march of the unemployed on the Ford plant in Dearborn. You had not met Harry Simms, another young Communist, but you knew he was your age when he was shot down by company gunmen in Harlan, Kentucky. It was not a matter of melodramatic heroics, certainly not one of craving martyrdom; it seemed like an elementary recognition of reality that you were engaged in an implacable, cruel conflict with ruthless antagonists who would give you no more dispensation than they gave York or Simms in similar circumstances, and such circumstances were within your range of expectations.

To try to recreate now the impressions made by Sheean and Malraux is not to say they were seminal influences. Indeed, I responded to them as strongly as I did because they confirmed or reinforced the conception I already had of the time and my relationship to it. In the people they wrote about, real and fictional, were idealized reflections of my own aspirations. I had known physical fear and so did not assume I could be as brave as Katov. I knew myself too well to claim the serene wisdom of Borodin or the revolutionary purity of Rayna Prohme. Yet, in their sum, they defined the compass of what I reached for, and there was enormous pride in the consciousness that I was joined with them in a world fraternity, that I had earned the privilege to call them comrade.

Both Malraux and Sheean wrote of revolutionary defeat. Malraux's heroes die, so does Sheean's heroine. The tragedy of defeat, of death, pervades their narratives. All that happened in 1927, before my political awareness. Shortly after I became aware and involved there were symptoms of revival in the Chinese revolution. The long civil war had begun; the Communist armies had established Soviet regions and were resisting the annihilation campaigns by Chiang Kai-shek's troops. Maybe this softened the impact of the defeat. Or maybe it was a Western bias about the antiquity of China that made it easier to place defeat there in the philosophical perspective of the long view. Whatever the reason, defeat in China was nowhere near as shattering as the defeat inflicted in Germany by Hitler's conquest of power.

People speak of the thirties as if the arbitrary decimal structure of our arithmetic, which makes a decade a unit of time, also makes it a homogeneous historical entity. This isn't true. The thirties were one decade — and two historical periods. Hitler's conquest and the responses to it split the decade in two. To comprehend the traumatic shock of the Nazi triumph one must know something of Germany's place in the Communist firmament at that time. If a poll had been taken among

Communists as to where the next revolution was most likely to succeed, the consensus would have been overwhelming: Germany. It was the locale of the one mass Communist party outside of the Soviet Union. Its working class was the most organized, the most disciplined, the most developed politically, heir to a great revolutionary tradition that extended from Marx to Karl Liebknecht and Rosa Luxemburg. In the celebrated clenched-fist "Red Front" salute of the German movement, in the marching beat of its songs, you sensed a combative militancy. In its cultural sector (Brecht, Piscator, and others) you felt a powerful ideological force. In all the strategic and tactical considerations that informed your political thought the German Communist party was in the van of all others in the capitalist world. And Germany was the country in deepest crisis, with the sharpest class battles. You had read Lenin's observation that when the revolution triumphed in a more advanced country it would become the Socialist model. And you had heard friendly gossip that some German Communists occasonally speculated about when Berlin would be the revolutionary capital.

Instead, Berlin became the captured capital of world counterrevolution. Germany had fallen to counterrevolution in its most grotesque and savage forms, spearheaded by a movement with a pimp as its martyr saint and a raving mountebank as its leader. A movement that in its style, rhetoric, and ideological excrement dragged a civilized, cultured nation into a barbarism without precedent or parallel.

Confronted with this historic twist, only an abysmal lack of intelligence and sensitivity could have kept you from being tormented by the questions: Why? Could this catastrophe have been averted? How? How can its repetition be prevented?

It was the end of an era. Slowly, haltingly, two years in gestation, a new era was born. It was to be christened "Popular Front," this being the composite political answer that emerged to the searing questions occasioned by the German debacle. The end of the old era coincided with the end of that phase of my life that comes under the heading of the semiprofessional revolutionary as a Young Communist.

V. An Old Problem
of American Radicalism

WITH ITS DRAMATIC PRINCIPALS, a Russian nobleman and a beautiful Central European countess, with its echoes of a celebrated romantic duel in the nineteenth century, the Serge Schewitsch affair seems incongruous in an American radical setting. Yet this is the stage for important scenes in this intercontinental tragedy.

Serge Schewitsch was a son of Russian nobility (newspaper stories used the title Baron) who became a revolutionary and migrated to the United States in 1877. A gifted journalist and orator in English and German, as well as Russian, he was a prominent figure in the American socialist movement for more than a decade, serving as an editor of the *New Yorker Volkzeitung*, a German-language Socialist paper. In 1890 he returned to Europe and finally settled in Germany. According to the story current among his New York comrades Schewitsch intended to secure German citizenship and to stand for election as Social Democrat to the Reichstag, which was the world pinnacle of Socialist parliamentary ambition.

By then he had attained a romantic pinnacle. When he came to the United States he was accompanied by Countess Helene von Racowitza, and here they were married. She was the golden redhead for whom Ferdinand Lassalle, brilliant and gallant pioneer of German socialism, fought the duel in which he was fatally wounded. Her love affair with Lassalle, her marriage within six months to the Rumanian count who fired the fatal shot at her lover, a union that in its haste scandalized European society, and her own gifts made her a famous, glamorous personage. She was used (poorly, critics said) by George Meredith as the model for his heroine in the novel *The Tragic Comedians*. An American magazine, *Current Literature*, published this contemporary appraisal of her: "There can be no doubt that in Helene von Racowitza we have one of the great enchantresses of history, the peer of Helen of Troy, Cleopatra, and poor Mary Stuart."

Schewitsch's world of romantic enchantment and political ambition was shattered with one stroke. The Berlin *Vorwärts*, central organ of the German Social Democratic party, published a sensational story exposing Schewitsch as a spy and agent provocateur in the pay of the Russian Czarist government. At this juncture it is pertinent to introduce the testimony of Morris Hillquit, possibly the most astute of American Socialist party leaders.

"The charge was absurd," Hillquit has testified. "It was inspired by a rancorous party opponent in the United States and was accepted by the credulous and impulsive veteran leader of the German movement and editor-in-chief of the *Vorwärts*, Wilhelm Liebknecht, without investigation or verification.

"The publication caused a storm among the Socialists of New York, who knew and trusted Schewitsch, but it was characteristic of their awe and respect for the German party and its venerated leader that they were reluctant to engage in an open controversy with them. It was left to me, a mere youngster, to introduce and advocate at the next general party meeting a resolution of protest against the outrageous libel and an expression of confidence in the loyalty and integrity of our maligned comrade."

Largely as a result of the American protest, Hillquit said, "The *Vorwärts* charges were practically withdrawn by the editor." Practically withdrawn? The qualification and ambiguity leave a nagging doubt about the quality of the withdrawal, especially because Hillquit was an able lawyer with a gift for precise expression when he put his mind to it. In any event, as Hillquit noted, "The damage was done," and the equivocal *Vorwärts* retraction did not mend it, as the dénouement attests.

"The political career of Serge Schewitsch was blasted," Hillquit related. "He and his wife remained living in Munich; having spent their fortune, they found themselves destitute and friendless and ended the misery of their lives by their own hands. They died in mutual pact of suicide in 1912 . . ."*

In the light of all that has since transpired, how frightfully evocative is the reference in this poignant story to the "awe and respect for the German party and its venerated leader" among the prestigious, veteran leaders of socialism in New York. The episode, it seems to me, is related to a fundamental, historical problem of American radicalism, which is the creation of an indigenous revolutionary movement with the theoretical capacity and practical skills to make it effective and viable in the American environment. Unfortunately the Communist experience has been used to obfuscate the true proportions of the problem. To dispel this obfuscation it is necessary to place both the problem and the Communist experience in historical perspective. It is necessary to examine the antecedents of communism.

The objection might be made that the nasty turn in the Schewitsch affair, coming at the turn of the century, revealed attitudes that were a throwback to the nineteenth century and not typical of the pre-Communist Socialist movement in the twentieth. Everyone who has dipped into the subject recognizes that the major radical ventures and experiments on American soil in the nineteenth century were foreign importations that acclimated themselves poorly.

The first half of the century was marked by utopian communes and colonies, original "counter-communities," inspired by European religious sects or such secular thinkers as the Frenchmen, Charles Fourier and Étienne Cabet, and the Scotsman, Robert Owen. They proliferated for a time and ultimately vanished. Just past midcentury the first Communist

* Memory may have played tricks with Hillquit. The couple died in 1911, not 1912. Contemporary newspaper accounts do not indicate double suicide. *The London Times* (October 4, 1911), citing a Reuter dispatch from Berlin, reported: "Her third husband [Schewitsch] died quite recently at Munich, and a few days later, overcome, it is said, by grief and financial difficulties, she committed suicide by taking chloral hydrate." It may be reasonably assumed, however, that Hillquit's recollection of the atmosphere in the New York Socialist party, which he knew firsthand, was more exact than his memory of some remote deaths in Munich.

clubs, influenced by Marxism, were formed by German immigrants who fled their native land after the aborted revolution of 1848. From such origins the Socialist Labor party emerged in the final quarter of the century. It was dominated by German immigrants who were constantly reproached by Friedrich Engels for their doctrinaire, sectarian, self-imposed isolation from the mainstreams of American life.

With the advent of the twentieth century the Socialist party was born in 1901 at a convention in Indianapolis, smack in the middle of Indiana, and you would be hard put to find a more American birthplace. Radical historians are agreed on the foreign flavor and sectarian character of the nineteenth-century Socialist movement. They also agree that the new party in the new century represented a sharp break with the past. Indeed, it did, and yet a close examination of the Socialist party reveals significant traces of a reverential deference, ideological and political, to the German Social Democratic party, then the model party of the world movement. This reverence was manifested not only in the party's infancy, which was the time of the Schewitsch affair, but also in its maturity, in 1912, the year that marked its peak, according to most historians. (Even the dissenters concede 1912 was a high point although they dispute it was a peak in the sense that the party's subsequent course was downhill all the way.)

In 1912 the party was agitated by an internal struggle over the Socialist attitude toward capitalist law and capitalist property, and the uses of violence, all of which was frequently capsulated in one provocatively suggestive word — sabotage. The struggle was climaxed by the adoption of an "antisabotage" clause in the party's constitution at its national convention, the subsequent recall of William D. Haywood from the party's national executive committee on charges of violating the new clause, and the exodus of Haywood and thousands of his followers from the party.

It was a critical juncture in the party's development and the intrusion of German authority in the American controversy was overt. An aura of intrigue attends the intervention from Berlin. Consider the Kautsky letter.

Toward the end of 1911 a man named Louis Tarzai, editor of *Testveriseg*, a Hungarian-language Socialist paper in the United States, solicited an expression of opinion by Karl Kautsky on the American controversy about "sabotage." Kautsky, the German party's premier theoretician who was regarded as the world's greatest living authority on Marxism, obliged. His letter, dated from Berlin, December 13, 1911, was also published in the *New Yorker Volkszeitung;* then an English translation appeared in the *Chicago Socialist* (January 4, 1912) and other Socialist periodicals. The principal protagonists in the American debate had been Haywood and Hillquit. Kautsky's enormous authority was thrown unequivocally behind Hillquit's position.

This solicited intervention provoked a protest from a prominent Left-Winger of the time, Robert Rives La Monte, who wrote:

> Was there ever anything more characteristic of the immaturity of the American movement than the attempt to drag Comrade Kautsky into this tempest in a teapot? We will not trust our own brains. A question arises on which we are divided. Instead of using our own brains to reason about it and see what is right, we are so used to getting our opinions ready made, like our clothes, that we at once appeal to some intellectual, to some infallible Pope to tell us what to think about it . . . While I admire Kautsky as the greatest living Marxian scholar, I do not recognize him as my Pope, and I take issue with him on many points in his Papal Bull.

Kautsky was not the only Big Bertha of German socialism to be rolled into the American battle. Another was Karl Legien, President of the German Federation of Trade Unions. He appeared in person before the Socialist national convention of 1912. His presence in the country at the time of the convention might have been fortuitous (he was in the United States for a lecture tour arranged by President Samuel Gompers of the American Federation of Labor), but there was nothing fortuitous about his speech. *The International Socialist Review,* a Left organ, described the speech as "quite evidently 'inspired.' " Referring to Legien's statement that he had been briefed on the principal convention issues by "prominent members of the party," *The Review* added with factional malice: "And nearly everybody knows who the 'prominent members of the party' are who speak German fluently."

In his address to the convention Legien first invoked authority. Acknowledging he was not officially delegated to represent his party, he went on:

"I dare say, however, that I should all the same be entitled to speak on behalf of our party and also on behalf of its Executive Council, not only because I am one of the representatives of the German Social Democratic Party in our Reichstag, but also on account of the fact that I am the President of the German Federation of Trade Unions, and for this reason in constant touch with the Executive Council of the Socialist Party of Germany."

Then Legien essayed flattery.

". . . the Socialist movement of our country is closely and with much interest watching the movement in the United States; partly because it is largely believed that the United States may possibly be or become the first nation of practical socialism as a result of the rapid concentration and growth of capitalism and the privileges and possibilities that are open to the workers of this country."

Finally Legien leveled his shots at Haywood, his followers, and the Industrial Workers of the World.

". . . In our German movement we have no room for sabotage and similar syndicalist and destructive tendencies . . . Our party never tried and never permitted the creation of new or rival trade unions . . ."

The *New York Call,* a Socialist daily, reported the Legien speech evoked "the greatest enthusiasm that has yet broken forth in the national convention." Two days after Legien's speech the "antisabotage" clause was adopted by a margin of slightly better than two to one. Given the alignment of delegates it may be assumed the clause would have been approved without Legien's appearance, but there is no doubt he added moral and theoretical weight to the action.

Kautsky and Legien were concerned with the big issues be-

fore the convention, but there was also a petty issue that provoked an illuminating exchange.

Tom Hickey, an iconoclastic Irish rebel from Texas, proposed
a rule that anyone elected to public office should not at the same
time hold an executive post in the party. Arguing for his proposition, Hickey said such was the law in Texas, and the following
exchange ensued.

HICKEY: "I am not concerned with what they do in Germany.
I am concerned with an elementary principle of democracy that is
recognized in every portion of the United States."

HILLQUIT: "When Comrade Hickey says that he is not concerned
with Germany, but he is concerned with Texas, I simply wish to
call Comrade Hickey's attention to the fact that the Socialist comrades in Germany have made somewhat better progress than the
comrades in Texas. We can well afford to imitate the comrades
in Germany rather than those in Texas."

So Hillquit, who essayed a centrist role and aligned himself
with the Right Wing in inner party showdowns, defended the
model party against the irreverence of the Left-Winger,
Hickey. Hillquit's retort may also serve as an explanatory foot-
note to his opening remarks as the convention's first chairman.
He recited the measures of the party's growth — in members,
votes, publications.

"But, comrades," he continued, "it is not merely our physical
growth, it is not merely our large strength, upon which we con-
gratulate ourselves . . . It is the fact that the Socialist Party
has at all times remained true to its trust and carried the banner
of International Socialism aloft in this country, unsullied and
unstained."

From his rebuke to Hickey it is a fair inference that in Hillquit's mind the integrity of international Socialist principle was
better defined in Germany than in Texas or in any other American locale, for all such locales were similarly vulnerable to invidious comparison with German achievement. Hillquit took
pride in what he represented as Marxist orthodoxy. But the
most prominent and most candid deviationist from orthodoxy
also invoked a German model. Victor Berger declared he was

"rather proud of being called the 'American Bernstein.'"
Berger said: "The tactic of the American Socialist Party, if that
party is to live and succeed — can only be the much abused
and much misunderstood Bernstein doctrine." Berger was
pragmatic and parochial, immersed in the practical politics of
Milwaukee and Wisconsin, but when it came to a theoretical
framework for his tactical line he also referred to German authority in the person of Eduard Bernstein, premier theoretician
of "revisionism" in the German party.

The evidence, and there is much more of it, shows the considerable extent to which the German party represented a
model for American Socialists and some of their most influential
leaders. They saw no contradiction between their model-
acceptance and their energetic, dedicated effort in the United
States. Certainly Hillquit, who so strongly recommended imitation of the German comrades, saw no such contradiction, and
he was astutely aware that the big challenge was creation of an
indigenous movement that responded effectively to its native
environment. His awareness was articulated in an assessment
of where American socialism stood at the end of 1912.

For years, he wrote, social philosophers and statesmen
viewed socialism as "a specific European product [that] will
never take root in American soil . . . And for a long time the
belief seemed to be justified." Now all that was changing.

"The Socialist movement has become fully acclimatized on
American soil. According to a recent census, over 71 per cent
of the members of the Socialist Party are native citizens of the
United States. The Socialist movement is today at least as
much 'American' as any other social or political movement in
this country . . .

"And still American Socialism is only in the making . . .
American Socialism has not yet evolved definite and settled
policies and methods, but the more recent phases of its development tend to indicate that it is beginning to solve its problems and to overcome its obstacles."

That last sentence is a marvelous example of the lawyer's
caution — it does not claim a solution to the party's problems,
not even the beginning of a solution, nor an indication of a be-

ginning, but merely a tendency to indicate the beginning of a solution. And the problems, for which the solution still was so qualified and tentative, were those of evolving "policies and methods" for American socialism. Hillquit's Left critics used to sneer at him as a mere "tactician." This pejorative label is evoked by his definition of the problem. It was not simply a matter of policies and methods; if these are to have substance and validity they require a foundation of theory. Hillquit pointed only to symptomatic manifestations of a more profound lack, which was theoretical and programmatic, entailing analytical comprehension of American society, its economy, political structure, history, culture, tradition. Anyone surveying the theoretical labors of pre-World War I American socialism is struck not only by their paucity, but by their bizarre vagaries.

In this connection the point might be sharpened by a reference to Louis Althusser, the French Marxist scholar and Communist. He deplored "the stubborn, profound absence of any real *theoretical* culture in the history of the French workers' movement." Later on Althusser contended the theoretical vacuum was filled partially by the French "political tradition for which Marx had the most profound respect." Central to this political tradition is the French revolutionary experience, ranging from the classical bourgeois revolution of 1789 to the precursor of Socialist revolutions, the Paris Commune of 1871. In the United States, however, the theoretical vacuum is bigger and a revolution-rooted political tradition is smaller.

Althusser referred to giant figures of theoretical culture in working-class movements of other European lands — to Marx and Engels and "the earlier Kautsky" in Germany; to Rosa Luxemburg in Poland; to Plekhanov and Lenin in Russia; to Labriola and Gramsci in Italy. And then he asked, "Who were our theoreticians?"

The same question can be asked, with even greater force, in the United States. Althusser was specially concerned with philosophy and the absence of any French masters in Marxist philosophy. Therefore, in answering the question — who were our American theoreticians? — one may refer to William English Walling. He was an important, prolific, Socialist intellectual and in the pre-World War I era he was loosely associated with the loose Left Wing.

Walling, according to Irving Howe, was "one of the few serious theoretical minds American socialism has produced." He was one of the rare Socialist intellectuals who ventured into the realm of philosophy, and more presumptuously than any other in a book called *The Larger Aspects of Socialism*.

It was Walling's thesis that Marx and Engels were groping toward a philosophy but never quite made it for two reasons: (a) they were encumbered with the Hegelian dialectic and (b) they did not live long enough. That is, they did not live to see the appearance of the philosophy toward which they were groping. This, Walling said, was pragmatic.

Having anointed John Dewey and William James as the true philosophers of socialism, Walling went on to crown Friedrich Nietzsche as the father of the true Socialist ethic. "Nietzsche goes as far as James," Walling wrote, "when he says the falseness of an opinion does not necessarily take anything away from its value . . . His view is at least social, or, as Nietzsche himself would say, moral." To prove his point Walling cited Nietzsche's dictum: "The falseness of an opinion is not for us any objection to it . . . The question is, how far an opinion is life-furthering, life-preserving, species-serving, perhaps species-rearing . . ."

Walling celebrated this Nietzschean citation as a triumphant ethical quintessence of pragmatism. The trouble is, of course, that pragmatism has been the distinctive, utilitarian philosophy of American corporate liberalism, and as such the most formidable native antagonist of revolutionary ideology. Yet Walling is typical of what passed for a theoretical culture even in the revolutionary wing of the Socialist party in its heyday.

To avoid misunderstanding, I suppose it should be noted that the Socialist party had impressive achievements. It had a genius for popular agitation and it was reaching a mass audience. It was a moral force, which was best personified in Eugene V. Debs. Its members and supporters represented a formidable native constituency. Its electoral victories and growing vote made it an increasingly significant factor in American politics. It exerted considerable influence in the trade unions. Hillquit recited his party's achievements at length, but at the same time he attested it was some steps removed from evolving the theory and program of an American Socialist movement. In this sense La Monte was perceptive when he saw in the appeal to Kautsky as an infallible pope a symptom of the immaturity of the American movement. After all, an inclination to dependency bears some relation to a capacity for self-reliance.

American Socialist attitudes toward the German Social Democratic party have been treated in some detail because this aspect of Socialist history is little known and appreciated even less. And yet it is indispensable in placing the Communist experience in a historical perspective. The Communist experience may be approached with provocative questions.

If in 1912 Hillquit could urge imitation of the German Socialists because of their progress, how much worthier of imitation must the Russian Bolsheviks have seemed to the neophyte American Communists of 1919? Surely the German achievements in 1912 — members, votes, Reichstag deputies — were microscopic when compared with the conquest of political power in the epochal revolution of 1917, a great turning point in human history. (This is so even if German achievements are taken at face value without reference to the rotten core revealed with the outbreak of World War I and German Social Democratic betrayal of professed Socialist principles in supporting German prosecution of that war.)

If at the turn of the century the most venerated and authoritative Socialist leaders in New York regarded the Germans with such awe and respect that they hesitated to defend a comrade falsely accused of the most heinous crime in the Socialist code of ethics, how much awe and respect was properly due the Russian Bolsheviks in 1919? At that time, remember, these Bolsheviks, ragged and hungry, beset by epidemic and economic chaos, were defending, gun in hand, the infant Socialist republic against armed onslaught by a host of enemies, foreign and domestic.

In posing these questions it is not suggested the Communist

experience was simply a continuation of what had gone on before, just more of the same. It was radically different, and not least of all in the sphere of international relations.

In the world Communist movement the conception of the model party was no longer informal, it was formalized as credo and institutionalized in a system of organization that was distinguished by a high degree of centralism and discipline. The old Socialist International was a loose confederation of national parties; it did not regard itself as an operative leadership center for its national affiliates with the corollary authority to make policy and exert discipline. The new Communist International was a tightly knit association, in which the national parties were seen as detachments of one worldwide revolutionary army with one general staff, vested with the authority to chart strategy and to exercise all the prerogatives of command, including discipline, to effect its strategy. The new international was also conceived as a crucible in which the flames of bolshevism would purify the world movement of the accumulations of opportunist dross.

The treachery and decomposition of the old international made the new more resplendent. The contrast was stark: ignominious betrayal on one side, triumphant revolution on the other, and over all towered the architects of the revolutionary triumph, the redeemers of Socialist honor and faith, the human guarantors of the new international, the only figures on the world revolutionary stage whose authority and leadership were validated by such incomparable deeds. After the World War I performance of the Western European Socialist parties, marching off to war behind their respective ruling classes, one international with one strategy, subordinating its national components to a global leadership center, seemed like a welcome surety for fidelity to internationalism and against the descent into chauvinism that disintegrated the old international.

Finally, the Russian Revolution necessitated a revision of Marx's celebrated slogan; the workers of the world no longer had nothing to lose but their chains, they possessed one sixth of the world. Defense of the first Socialist conquest, governed by the infant Soviet state that was surrounded by far more powerful enemies, was a primary imperative for cohesion of the new international. The determination not to yield this revolutionary ground, purchased with incredible sacrifice and heroism, not to permit destruction or strangulation of this trail-blazing venture into a new society, was vested with historical logic. It was also animated by the emotional responses to the epic of revolution, by the moral fervor that is an essential quality of any truly revolutionary movement. At the same time this overriding commitment inevitably accentuated the centralism and the decisive authority of the Bolsheviks as the model party at the pinnacle of the pyramidal structure. And this was so not only for American Communists, but for Communists everywhere.

One coordinated revolutionary army, embracing the entire globe, from remote villages of the Chinese interior to the industrial capitals of Europe, and yet centrally directed — the sheer daring and magnitude of the design are overwhelming. And there was the revolutionary genius of its great conceiver, Lenin, to make it real and authentic. In the exhilarating sweep of the conception it was easy to disregard the possible pitfalls and hazards that inhere in a tightly centralized structure that attempts to embrace so much, so much diversity, such dispersed and heterogeneous components. In the beginning, indeed, when the new international served as marshaling and training ground for a new assembly of revolutionary forces, the possible pitfalls seemed of small consequence.

It was into this powerful vortex, into this totally new international system of political and organizational relationships that American Communists voluntarily plunged in 1919. What did they bring with them? Most of them came out of the Socialist party and they bore the marks of where they came from, including those reflected in the provocative questions posed above. To be sure, the manifestations of awe, respect, and imitation were nonsystematic in the old Socialist party; they represented one current among many and it could not have been otherwise in the party's heterogeneous mix of populism, syndicalism, reformism, Marxism, and lesser isms. However, aside from their intrinsic significance those manifestations were symptomatic of something more profound and universal in the party. This was the poverty of theoretical culture and political tradition, which was also the legacy of the neophyte Communists as they entered the new international that was led by a group of revolutionaries who possessed in unparalleled abundance exactly that which the Americans lacked.

Subsequently the pioneer Communists and those who joined with them were also shaped by the internal development of their party. That's an involved history extending over more than half a century and in selecting two critical episodes from it there is no pretense of encompassing all of it. Nonetheless the two episodes marked important turning points. In 1929 a special commission of the Communist International, in which Stalin personally played a dominant role, was the decisive instrument in the political surgery that excised Jay Lovestone, the party's general secretary, and some two hundred of his followers from the party's ranks. In 1945 Earl Browder was deposed as general secretary and subsequently expelled from the party, and once again international intervention was decisive. This second time the Communist International no longer existed and the intervention from abroad took the form of an article by the French Communist leader, Jacques Duclos, who condemned Browder's policies and their theoretical rationale as "a notorious revision of Marxism."

The years 1929 and 1945 are important because they embrace the period of the greatest Communist influence in American life, and this period was thus ushered out, as it was ushered in, with a decisive push from abroad. Moreover, the two episodes represent the only instances of such drastic and dramatic change in the party's leadership. In both 1929 and 1945 American Communists faced critical, difficult problems of leadership and orientation. The incumbent leadership pointed in one direction but, as was soon revealed, the actual course of national and world events, as well as the policies of the international movement, took another direction. The problems were real, but the pertinent point in this context is that they were not resolved independently with the inner resources of American communism.

To be sure, before both 1929 and 1945 there was articulate opposition within the party to the dominant leadership and policy, far more formidable in the first instance than in the other. It can be argued then that with the unfolding of events (the economic crisis in 1929, the Cold War post-1945), in the normal course of inner party conflict, a resolution of the issues would have been reached with an appropriate rectification of the party's course. Such argument, as persuasive as it may be, must remain hypothetical, for the inner conflict was not permitted to run its normal course to a definitive conclusion. A resolution was abruptly induced by external influences. A line possibly thrown away earlier may register with greater impact here: after all, an inclination to dependency bears some relation to a capacity for self-reliance. This capacity was not given a fair test.

That line was first employed in relation to La Monte's comment that resort to higher authority abroad, in the person of Kautsky, was characteristic of the American movement's immaturity in 1912. Was not immaturity also indicated in the episodes of 1929 and 1945? The immaturity was manifest in 1929; the first decade after the Communist party's birth in 1919 was a formative period, marked by virtually incessant factional strife. Matters were different in 1945; the party had sixteen years of cohesion behind it and the enormously rich experience of the 1930s.

Like the Socialists of 1912 the Communists of 1945 had impressive credits. They had shown great political initiative and energy, great organizational and tactical skills. With these attributes they were a dynamic force in the unionization of the workers in the basic, mass production industries; in placing the issue of black liberation on a new plateau; in triggering and stimulating varied mass movements that fought through for the significant social reforms of the New Deal era. They offered the most credible radical program for coping with the two primary immediate problems before the country — the consequences of the economic crisis and the threat of fascism, both here and abroad.

Deeply, intimately involved in varied mass movements, they

were compelled to confront the historical traditions and contemporary realities of the American environment. They began to probe these, and despite some self-serving banalities and theoretical vulgarizations, their endeavor charted new directions in exploring the country's traditions and institutions. They exerted an important influence on the national culture. They were a political and ideological force. And yet, as was revealed in the Browder crisis, which involved alternatives of long-range perspective and orientation, they had not solved fundamental theoretical and programmatic problems of American socialism.

In 1945, even to a greater degree than in 1929, the essential discussion in the ranks took place after the fact of decision. It was an exercise in post mortem, rather than in diagnosis. One can only speculate about the possible effects upon American communism, upon its theoretical and programmatic capacities, upon its ability to face subsequent crises, if it had been compelled to rely upon its own resources to resolve the critical problems it faced in 1945.

Of course, the 1945 episode and the way it occurred are explicable only against the background of the methodology and relationships established in the organizational and political system of the Communist International, which had been dissolved only two years earlier. Yet, to see only this, without simultaneously taking into account the antecedents of American communism and its internal developments, is to see a distortion. The supreme importance of this point is underscored by recent history. Since Stalin's death in 1953, and more particularly since the 20th Congress of the Soviet party in 1956, it has become apparent that various Communist parties have distinct profiles of their own. What previously was latent but obscured by the monolithic structure of the International (and the patterns established by the International outlasted its organizational existence) has now become unmistakably visible; among the various parties there are distinctions in style, method, theoretical analysis, and programmatic action. The amazing thing is not that it is so, but that many people believed it would not be so — as if the development of Communist parties, unlike that of other organisms, would not be influenced by heredity and environment. True, as proponents of communism they represent a theoretical and political community, and almost all of them, moreover, were taught in the exacting school of the Communist International; they were shaped by such common influences, but simultaneously each was molded by its antecedents, by its experience and inner development, and most of all by all the factors — economic, political, historical, cultural — that make up its particular national environment. The consequences are manifest today in the diversity encompassed by world communism.

The academically dominant historians of American communism are so preoccupied, however, with the hegemonic influences of Moscow that they make no real effort to explore why an American party responded as it did to external stimuli. The fatal defect of this historical method becomes glaring when one attempts to use it to comprehend the differentiated development of such Communist movements as the Chinese, Cuban, Polish, Yugoslav, Vietnamese, Italian, Korean, French, to cite a select few. The method that focuses almost solely on external stimuli and influences is absolutely useless in explaining the real, manifest diversity of these movements. The variegation is explicable only in terms of their particular backgrounds, experiences, and national environments. These are the factors that ultimately determined the specific responses of the respective parties to external influences. The key to understanding the several parties listed lies in the interaction between stimulus and response, and in the recognition that the external stimuli, even in the tightly knit and highly centralized structure of the Communist International, were only one element in the total environment that molded these parties.

The same methodological principle is applicable to any serious study of American communism, especially if the study is concerned with a solution to the problems of creating an indigenous revolutionary movement that is viable and effective. Such a serious study involves a searching examination of the factors in the national environment that influenced the evolution of American communism. These factors are pertinent because the most salient of them are operative today: the absence of a theoretical culture, the absence of class and Socialist consciousness in the American working class, the roots of these phenomena in the economic, political, ideological development of American capitalism.

In approaching such a study some more of Althusser's observations may be useful. After sketching French Communist experience in the theoretical domain he added, ". . . the end of Stalinist dogmatism has not restored Marxist philosophy to us in its integrity. After all, it is never possible to liberate, even from dogmatism, more than already *exists*. . . . What the end of dogmatism has restored to us is the right to assess exactly what we have, to give both our wealth and our poverty their true names, to think and pose our problems in the open, and to undertake in rigor a true investigation. It makes it possible for us to emerge partly from our theoretical provincialism, to recognize and acquaint ourselves with those who did exist and do exist outside us, and as we see this outside, we can begin to see ourselves from the outside and discover the place we occupy in the knowledge and ignorance of Marxism, and thereby begin to know ourselves."

Sorting out thoughts in the above passage and relating them to the United States the following may be said: First, the inhibition and stultification of theoretical development, which is implicit in "Stalinist dogmatism," were particularly deadening in the United States for historical reasons previously discussed. Second, that which was liberated from dogmatism, that which exists as theoretical accumulation, is not much. Third, it may be suggested also to "those who do exist outside" the Communist sphere that they, too, give their wealth and their poverty their true names.

The radical ferment of the 1960s has stimulated theoretical exploration. I appreciate the importance and potential of such labors by the non-Communist Left (and here Communist is used in the restricted sense of association with the Communist party). But I still believe that in their sum such labors fall far short of comprising the evidence to disprove the thesis that the poverty of American radical theory transcends the Communist

orbit and "Stalinist dogmatism." Indeed, traditional weaknesses crop up in new guises.

I have, for example, Volume 1, Number 1, of still another
revolutionary publication of recent vintage. Staring at me from
its cover are the portraits of five men: Marx, Engels, Lenin,
Stalin, and Mao.

This publication, complete with a statement of principles
and a polemic against the principles and/or practices of other
groups and parties, was issued by one of those revolutionary
youth collectives that have sprouted throughout the country in
the past several years. Some other collectives might have
amended the choice of cover photos, adding or substituting
Che or Fidel, Ho or possibly Kim Il Sung. But the odds are
overwhelming against so radical an amendment as the inclusion
of an American in that gallery. The cover display is thus a pic-
torial illustration of the fundamental, historical problem I have
been discussing.

Certainly the editors of the publication can justify their gallery by saying no American has been the peer of their choices in
revolutionary theory or the conquests of revolutionary practice.
This is an objective fact. There is also a secondary subjective
element, however, in the indisposition to attach sufficient value
to the projection of native root and tradition so as to use an
American as a cover symbol even at the sacrifice of something
in stature. Indeed, reading the matter in the publication, it is
doubtful that the latter issue even arose. The combination of
historical reality and subjective reaction to it tends to induce,
at the very least, a dependency upon theory and inspirational
example from abroad.

As symbolism, the picture gallery is rendered the more significant by the autonomy of the collective that assembled it.
The collective is not part of any national organization, let
alone any on the international plane. Its choice of portraits to
project its self-image was not influenced by any compact or loyalties implicit in organizational affiliation. Its exercise of "free
will" reflects, therefore, in pure form historical problems of the
American movement, not the least of which is the absence of
a theoretical culture that could have produced one credible

nominee for a cover photo. The same lack and the related problems are manifested in less symbolical ways; for example, in the almost promiscuous embrace of precepts from abroad. Whether these be quotations from Mao or maxims of Che, there seems to be little effort at a critical comprehension of them in their specific historical context, and even less effort at any critical analysis of what may or may not be relevant in the United States, and with what modifications or adaptations.

The argument is not whether anything can be learned from revolutionaries in other lands, including Mao and Che. Much can be learned. For that matter, as Marxist scholar and thinker, the early Kautsky stood head, shoulders, and torso above his American contemporaries, and by then prevailing standards the German party was much more accomplished than the American. The American Socialists had much to learn from Kautsky and the German party. Later on there was an even greater contrast between the towering historical stature of Lenin and the Bolsheviks and the modest height of American Communists. At issue are not the teaching credentials of thinkers, leaders, and parties in other lands; at issue is the capacity of American revolutionaries to learn, or more exactly perhaps their recognition of the essential prerequisites for such a capacity. And a primary prerequisite is a theoretical culture.

As Althusser observed, "A real theoretical culture can [not] be created overnight or by simple fiat." The same point was illustrated historically by Lenin. Sketching the reasons for Bolshevik success he recalled that between the 1840s and 1890s "advanced thinkers in Russia . . . eagerly sought for the correct revolutionary theory and followed each and every 'last word' in Europe and America in this sphere with astonishing diligence and thoroughness . . . Thanks to the enforced emigration caused by tsardom, revolutionary Russia in the second half of the nineteenth century possessed a wealth of international connections and excellent information about world forms and theories of the revolutionary movement such as no other country in the world possessed." But the incomparable fund of information and the diligent pursuit of every "last word" were not enough. "Russia," he wrote, "achieved Marxism, the only correct revolutionary theory, virtually through agony, by a half century of unprecedented torment and sacrifice, of unprecedented revolutionary heroism, incredible energy, devoted searching, study, testing in practice, disappointment, verification and comparison with European experience."

Out of the torment and heroism, out of the study, testing, verification, and comparison — out of all this and yet, in a sense, transcending all this, first Plekhanov and then Lenin led in the creation of a theoretical culture that made possible the critical assimilation of world revolutionary experience in solving the problems of the Russian revolution. What is one to make of all this if one compares czarist Russia and American monopoly capitalism with its vastly superior economy, its infinitely more subtle and sophisticated ideological defenses, its incomparably greater resources, intellectual and technical, for the imposition and exercise of ideological domination? Surely all the talk of revolution here is rhetoric or posturing if it is not related to creation of a movement with the theoretical maturity to derive strength from the assimilation of world experience, instead of perpetuating weakness by the dependency upon diverse "last words" from abroad.

Modern means of communication and travel make access to such "last words" easier and swifter, and the supply of them is more abundant because for the first time in history a revolutionary process is truly global, extending to the most remote regions of the earth, remote in a cultural as well as geographic sense from the dominant Western culture of the United States as Asia and Africa and Latin America are. There is virtually a supermarket profusion of "last words" and no commensurate development of the theoretical discrimination to consume them rationally. Often they are swallowed whole, neither chewed nor digested, let alone assimilated.

I hesitate to propound any axioms but will venture one: To the degree that a theoretical culture is lacking here, to the same degree dogmatism is likely in latching onto "last words" from abroad; for the lack is a measure of incapacity to assimilate foreign experience and therefore what is imported tends to be a mechanical model.

Alongside dogmatic importation there has been a contrary tendency to embargo. At its most sophisticated this tendency offers the following rationale: since the most advanced revolutionary experience of this century occurred in countries that provide a striking contrast with the United States in economic development, in political tradition and structure, therefore the theoretical synthesis of their experience is irrelevant here. The truth of the premise casts an aura of plausibility around the conclusion. Unfortunately this plausibility is reinforced by negative experience with mechanical imitation of foreign models. Just the same the conclusion is false and its peremptory character smacks of dogmatism. What should flow from the premise is not the a priori assumption of irrelevancy, but a caution against mechanical imitation, and a command to the exercise of a critical theoretical intelligence in the differentiation, assimilation, and adaptation of world revolutionary experience and its embodiment in theory.

One may recall that when the Russians were diligently following every "last word" of revolutionary theory in Europe and America, they were acutely aware of the contrasting circumstances that obtained in their country. This is why they subjected the acquisitions from abroad to study, testing in practice, verification, and comparison. A similar process was manifested in the Chinese revolution and, in a different way, in the Cuban. Because those revolutions were so strikingly dissimilar in setting and unfolding, it is the more impressive that all three claim a common patrimony in the work of Marx and Lenin and their lesser followers, in Marxism-Leninism that is, as the most profound, most comprehensive, most advanced theoretical embodiment of world revolutionary experience. Still one encounters suggestions that the Cubans, for example, espouse Marxism-Leninism out of ignorance or affectation. One American Left intellectual decreed Marxism-Leninism irrelevant to the Cuban revolution, thus inviting two inferences about the Cubans: either they were unaware of it, or they were aware and pretended not to be. Either inference, it seems to me, is gratuitous presumption, given the intellectual capacities of the Cuban revolutionaries, their courage, and their candor.

Similar suggestions of irrelevancy are conveyed more widely by the gaggle of sociologists, whose praise of Marxism as a brilliant theoretical dissection of nineteenth-century European capitalism is capped by the judgment that the time and place of its origins render it obsolescent in the twentieth century. This poses an intriguing question. Whom to believe? These sociologists or the contemporary revolutionaries who assert, despite such sociological wisdom, that they derive theoretical guidance and inspiration from Marxism in effecting the most profound revolutionary transformations?

I am reminded of a curious phenomenon in my trial (along with thirteen codefendants) on charges under the Smith Act of conspiring to teach and advocate the violent overthrow of the government. On several occasions the federal prosecutor harped on Lenin's line that Marxism is not dogma, but a guide to action. This, thundered the prosecutor, is what makes these people dangerous. It is as if the punitive might of the United States government — the prosecution mechanism, the judiciary, and the prisons — were all marshaled to impress upon us the discretionary wisdom of embracing Marxism purely as dogma, rather than as guide to action. The prosecutor, to be sure, was concerned with our imprisonment, not with Marxist explication, and yet implicit tolerance of Marxism as dogma is somehow associated in my mind with dogmatic predilections encountered among some who approach Marxism, not as criminal prosecutors, but as intellectual critics.

To me, for instance, the pedantic insistence on the rigidly exclusive consignment of Marx and Lenin to their respective time and place represents an incredibly obstinate, dogmatic rejection or dismissal of the empirical evidence of contemporary history. After all, the best witnesses, effective revolutionaries themselves, attest that components of the hyphenated ism do transcend the time and place of origin, precisely as a guide to action, and in the most diverse circumstances.

Of course, Marx and Lenin must be understood in the context of their time and place. Not to do so is to violate their fundamental precept that all social phenomena can be comprehended only in their concrete historical context, both as prod-

ucts of specific historical circumstance and as responses to it.
Nothing is more alien to the thought and spirit of either man
than to transmogrify him into a suprahistorical superman, time-
less and placeless. This has been done and it is dogma. It is not
remedied, however, by the inverse prejudice that employs time
and place as if they were the binding that once was used to
constrain the feet of Chinese girls. This, too, has been done and
it is also dogma. This static, rigid construction of their work is
also alien to the thought and spirit of both men, for their insistence on the comprehension of phenomena in the context of
historical time and place was accompanied by the corollary insistence that all things be perceived in their motion and development. From this latter vantage point the distinctive thing
about Marxism is not that it has been dogmatized, as it has
been at times by its professed exponents, but that it has displayed such amazing viability and flexibility. Not only in the
intellectual realm but in practice.

Consider Cuba. In the beginning it appeared that the Cuban
revolution was a triumph of pragmatism, a succession of im-
provisations, brilliant but extemporaneous, unrelated to any
theoretical framework. So marked was this appearance that a
school of American thought still holds that if only the United
States had behaved differently the revolution would have taken
another course. It is idle to argue about such might-have-
beens. In any event the Cuban revolutionaries had to contend
not just with how the United States might behave, but with
how it *did* behave and the endemic quality of this behavior was
illustrated by its most ignominious symbol, the Bay of Pigs.
That adventure was conceived by the more conservative Republican Eisenhower administration — and executed by the
more liberal Democratic Kennedy administration. Bureaucratic inertia is a frequent explanation for the continuum. I do
not dispute the power of bureaucratic inertia, but in this instance the inertia related, at most, to a particular tactical expedient. More fundamental were the implacable hostility toward
the Cuban revolutionary regime and the determination to
strangle it. This attitude and this policy, which gave birth to
the sortie of the Pigs, cut across party lines and the slender pin-

stripes between liberalism and conservatism in the United States Establishment, for they were reflex reactions of corporate interest and power.

The Cubans had to reckon with United States behavior not simply as it was manifested in one tactical blunder, but as it expressed a fundamental, systemic motivation. Simultaneously they had to take into account the behavior of the Socialist world and of the various classes and social strata in their own country. They had to estimate currents and conflicts in Latin America and throughout the economically underdeveloped world; it would have required incredible obtuseness for them not to recognize that heroic resistance of the Vietnamese, which engaged a major portion of United States military, economic, and political energy, had a material bearing on the survival of their own revolution. They had to assess the fissures among the advanced capitalist countries and the consequent holes in the United States blockade.

In short, they had to confront the intricate, changing global mosaic of class, national, social contraditions and conflicts; to determine as precisely as they could their place in this mosaic and their relationship to its multifarious details. They had to do it because the fate of their revolution was involved. And they had to do it even as they embarked upon the radical reconstruction of their own society, which was far more difficult and complicated than the conquest of power. Improvisation, no matter how brilliant or inspired, was no longer enough. It was not enough to say now as I had heard Cuban revolutionaries say repeatedly in Havana in the spring of 1960, "At each moment the revolution will do what has to be done." A longer-range perspective was needed. To discern some coherent patterns in the seeming global chaos a theoretical framework was necessary. To choose rationally between alternatives, economic and political, to make the decisions that determined the course of the revolution over a protracted period required a theoretical conception of ends and means and their interrelation.

The historic fact is that to fill this need the Cuban revolutionaries turned to the body of work that bears the name of Marx and Lenin. The choice was not fortuitous or compulsive, or as sudden as it seemed. To begin with Fidel and his comrades of the July 26 movement did not pop up in the Sierra Maestra out of an ideological vacuum. No one exists in such a vacuum. Certainly they did not, for their serious commitment to revolution was not only a reflection of ideological influences, but already represented a profound ideological choice, an embodiment of their view of the world and their relationship to it, which is ideology reduced to its simplest elements. Moreover, as serious revolutionaries they were acquainted with revolutionary thought, including, directly and indirectly, the ideas of Marx and Lenin. Assuming, as evidence indicates, that the ideological materiel they packed with them into the hills was an eclectic mix, it still is an open question as to what parts of this mix were Marxian. And if the mix deprived them of theoretical consistency, it also did not burden them with dogmatic preconceptions. Thus, through critical, concrete experience with the contending forces in the global arena, the primary leaders of the Cuban revolution arrived at Marxism-Leninism. By then they were not adolescents or novices first venturing onto the path of revolution. They were seasoned, combat-toughened veterans, who had tasted defeat, imprisonment, exile; who had narrowly escaped total disaster, had undergone the cruel test of guerrilla war, had conquered power and knew the burdens that came with its possession. They were mature revolutionaries who had displayed on more than one occasion great daring and courage in the exercise of options. They exercised their earned right to assert the autonomous integrity, the originality of their revolution.

Yet, recognizing the need for theory to chart their further course (and, indeed, to comprehend more precisely what they already had traversed), they sought for the most advanced synthesis of world revolutionary experience and, in their judgment, they found it in the work of Marx and Lenin. What a phenomenal testimonial to the genius of these men, to the viability and utility of their theoretical legacy.

To revert to an earlier frame of reference, the Cubans, too, lacked theoretical culture. They compensated for it by the immense richness of their time-compressed revolutionary experience. But the compensation was only partial, for some of their avoidable miscalculations and problems, as I think they recognize, may be traced to the theoretical lack. I doubt they concur in Regis Debray's celebration of their original innocence of theory as a supreme virtue, or in his implicit assumption that theoretical insight and dogmatic inhibition are inextricably joined.

I have concentrated on the Cuban revolution because it is closest to us in time and geography. And, I was about to add, because it is so original (a trait that fascinated Sartre), but then there never has been, nor can there be, a truly popular revolution that is unoriginal. An examination of the more complex, more tortuous, more protracted course of the Chinese revolution would adduce similar empirical testimony to the remarkable utility of Marx and Lenin in the most diverse settings.

Within the particular focus of this essay the Cuban experience affirms that creation of an indigenous revolutionary movement is not served by national isolationism, or by a kind of ideological protectionism that presumably shelters underdeveloped theoretical production at home from being inundated by the more sophisticated output abroad. On the contrary, a critical familiarity with all the "last words" is necessary, and a thorough knowledge of the most advanced theory is indispensable. If one looks at contemporary revolutions as they actually occurred (and not as they ought to have occurred according to anyone's preconceptions) then, on the historical record, the most advanced theory that served them all was the one bearing the names of Marx and Lenin.

The American Communist experience is used to fudge this reality and its relevance to the United States. Yet, a rounded, objective examination will reveal that American communism's international association, its ready access to an incomparable clearing-house of world revolutionary experience, were a primary source of the vitality, initiative, energy, and leadership capacity that won hegemony on the American Left for two decades. If this source of strength also became a source of weakness, it was due not only to monolithic excesses of the Communist International, but, as I have tried to show, it was also compounded by traditional weaknesses of American radicalism.

These weaknesses, a lack of theoretical culture and a consequent dependency on others (or its twin opposite, a supercilious national exclusiveness), antedate the Communist formation in 1919 and manifest themselves, sometimes as caricature, in the New Left proliferations of the present.

At this stage of world history, when the interconnection and interaction of the most dispersed and disparate global phenomena are so quickly manifest, it is, more than ever, an illusion to conceive of a serious American movement for revolutionary change that is unrelated to the world forces of revolution. To define this relationship is imperative. And in perfecting such a definition one must confront problems of American radicalism that are more deep-rooted and enduring than their specific manifestations in any single phase of its history.

VI. On the Waterfront—1

DEPARTING FROM PHILADELPHIA early in 1932, I exited from the strange corner of a children's world inhabited by the Young Pioneers. Returning to Philadelphia toward the end of 1932 I was plunged into the amphibian stretch of the adult world inhabited by the men who sail or load ships, for I was port secretary of the Marine Workers' Industrial Union. Even in a leap year this was a long leap. Young Communists prided themselves on their versatility.

The MWIU post also entailed versatility. With it came my first venture into journalism, my first experience with freedom of the press. A young seaman named Ted, an Indian from Oklahoma, was arrested in the Seamen's Church Institute for distributing the paper I was putting out, a mimeographed job that covered both sides of a legal-sized sheet of paper. The Seamen's Church Institute employed two private uniformed cops and the one who arrested Ted was also the chief witness.

"Your Honor," he testified, "they call me Pigface McGinty and they call my partner Slim McNasty [the man's name was McNulty], and — [here, playing his vocal cords like a pianist, the heavy note of indignation beaten out by the left hand was accompanied by a tremulo with the right] — and they call our Lord Jerusalem Slim!"

Guilty, your Honor, I am guilty. It was just before Christmas and I had the poor grace to refer to the holiday as Jerusalem Slim's Birthday. But they sent no gendarmes after me. Instead the dignity of Jesus and of Officers McGinty and McNulty was served by sending Ted to jail for ninety days.

Had Officer McGinty been more thorough he would have testified that "they" referred to the turkey, that most American of birds, as seagull, and to the Seamen's Church Institute, that missionary outpost to save the souls of sinners who sailed the seas, as the Scratchhouse. In fact, the sheet was called the *Scratchhouse News,* patterned in this as in its style after the *Doghouse News* of New York. Similar sheets appeared in other ports; all were organs of Waterfront Unemployed Councils. In latter-day jargon they were underground papers — proletarian style. Their scatology was social rather than biological, although the *Doghouse News,* referring to society matrons whose favorite charity was the Seamen's Church Institute, once contained this line: "how it tickles their titties to help the seamen." This, we thought, was very daring.

Instead of getting more involved in journalistic style and taste I should explain how I got to Philadelphia from Baltimore to assume my new role. Ordinarily, if you wanted to get to Philadelphia from Baltimore you would not go through New York. But I did. Having displayed an aptitude for work with seamen in Baltimore I was invited to come to New York in the late summer of 1932 to become youth organizer for the MWIU. One of my tasks was to guide the formulation of a youth program for the union, including special demands for young seamen. Efforts to sound out the more experienced union cadre elicited an amused cynicism with homosexual overtones. "Youth demands? Yeh, here's one. Tin pants for young seamen." Only the very top officers of the union did not repeat this standard joke but they were sufficiently entertained by it so I understood the idea of a youth organizer was not theirs, it was a concession to the Young Communist League. As my subsequent assignment to Philadelphia suggests I was integrated into the general activity of the union cadre and except for assembling a few seamen in a YCL unit I did what other union organizers did.

The MWIU was by its own definition a revolutionary union. Its purpose, as set forth in the preamble to the MWIU constitution, was "to unite all workers in the marine industry and lead them in their struggles against the employers for better working and living conditions and for ultimate freedom from wage slavery." The conflict between workers and employers in the marine industry was described as "only one front in the class

struggle which rages ceaselessly between the whole working
class and the whole class . . . of capitalists."

". . . this struggle can be won," the preamble went on, "only
by the most relentless, militant and revolutionary struggle of the
whole working class . . . The MWIU urges upon all its members the most active participation in the general struggles of the
working class, economic and political, directed toward the goal
of the establishment of a revolutionary workers' government."

True the MWIU only urged its members to fight for revolution and did not make this commitment a condition for membership, still the proviso created a problem for the worker who
wanted to join a union to improve his condition but was not
persuaded that "a revolutionary workers' government" ought to
be his goal. Some years later, when the maritime workers did
organize they flocked into unions with more modest objectives
and the MWIU was disbanded. Despite its revolutionary sectarianism, however, the MWIU assembled and trained a cadre
that was indispensable in formation of the large, powerful
unions to come. At its peak the MWIU claimed no more than
8000 members, but by 1932 it eclipsed its revolutionary rival,
the Marine Transport Workers of the IWW, and was a far more
dynamic force in the industry than its conservative competitor,
the moribund AFL International Seamen's Union.

In New York I served on the MWIU Port Organizing Committee (POC) whose members comprised the union's "labor
aristocracy" because they were paid seventy-five cents a day.
When the union's national office, in the person of a man named
George Mink, established a stewpot (or lunch counter) part of
the seventy-five cents was issued in meal tickets redeemable
only at Mink's stewpot. As I was to discover later in Philadelphia seventy-five cents — in legal tender or scrip — is much
better than no cents.

At the conclusion of the seven A.M. meetings of the POC,
where problems were discussed briefly and the day's assignments distributed, the daily stipend was doled out by Port Secretary Harry Jackson. He fished out the coins one by one from
an old-fashioned, worn-out, black leather woman's change purse.

Jackson, in his early thirties in 1932, was originally an iron-worker from South of Market in San Francisco, a one-time Wobbly, an early Communist, and before coming to the MWIU in New York he had been the party's organizer in Alabama. There were two legends about Jackson in Alabama. One arose from the expense accounts he submitted to the party's national center, which subsidized the operation in the South. Regularly the item appeared: "$2 . . . man is not made of wood." The other legend concerned the Scottsboro case.

A young white Southerner, a Communist, came upon Ruby Bates in Birmingham. She was one of the two white prostitutes allegedly raped by the nine young black defendants in this celebrated case. Miss Bates confessed to this young Communist that there had been no rape. He came to Jackson with the news and was told to produce Miss Bates. He did and she repeated her confession. Jackson then handed her a ten-dollar bill and said, "You go to this hotel and stay there until you hear from me." As an afterthought he added, ". . . and don't peddle your ass." She stayed at the hotel until Jackson made arrangements for her transportation and reception in New York. There her story blew the case wide open. This young white prostitute proved to be a woman of rare courage and integrity.

Jackson was a phenomenal soapboxer, speaking with the nasal twang and intonation of his native working-class district South of the Slot, which has an affinity with some variations of Brooklynese. One of his oratorical exploits came in a novel setting. In 1932 the list of intellectuals who endorsed the Communist presidential ticket, William Z. Foster and James W. Ford, resembled a who's who in American arts and letters. The committee of intellectuals for Foster and Ford staged a public meeting at Cooper Union, attracting 2000 persons who jammed the hall and an estimated 2500 who were turned away. The program was structured to present the viewpoints of several disciplines: Malcolm Cowley presented the viewpoint of the critic; James Rorty, of the poet; Hugo Gellert, of the graphic artist; John Herman, of the novelist; Eugene Gordon, of the black writer. Waldo Frank also spoke but I forget whether he doubled in some category or had one of his own. Sidney Hook performed a philosopher's chore; he was chairman.

In this glittering intellectual galaxy Jackson was chosen to present the viewpoint of the worker. His opening gambit was, "Capitalism is a great big dung heap. And the role of the intellectual is to sprinkle it with perfume . . ."

Under Jackson's command I was integrated into the POC and did essentially what the other members did: we soapboxed, distributed leaflets and the *Doghouse News,* organized demonstrations and other forms of direct action, but the staple chore was visiting ships. This meant sneaking past the watchman at the pier gate, boarding a ship, entering the crew's quarters and messroom to hawk the *Marine Workers' Voice,* the MWIU paper; to agitate for the union and recruit members; and, on encountering men who already were members, to collect dues and urge them to visit the union hall. In rare instances such ship visits produced organized action.

I was involved in one such action aboard the S.S. *West Kebar,* a ship of the Barber Line, which sailed to the Congo, up the Congo River, and other points on the West African coast. The company had its own variant of the checkerboard crew; the unlicensed men in the engine department were all Filipino, the sailors on deck were all white. When I visited the *West Kebar* the Filipinos had just been informed that wages for firemen would be cut five dollars below the scale for able-bodied seamen. The discrimination was flagrant because the common rule was wage parity between the two ratings, and the rare exceptions, especially on tropical runs, where the heat in the engine room was brutal, favored firemen. The Filipinos were so outraged they were ready to pile off the ship then and there, but I argued that simply quitting was futile. They remained on board and with the help of a more experienced MWIU organizer devised a strategy. They signed on for the voyage and just before the ship was to sail they walked off, demanding the wage cut be rescinded. Meanwhile MWIU men were deployed to points in the port where the Barber Line was most likely to seek replacements. Several of them were hired in the new engine crew; they, too, walked off just as the ship was to sail. The departure of the *West Kebar* was delayed for a day.

Given the state of organization among seamen we had not expected anything more. This was guerrilla warfare. In waging it we were guided by an old radical maxim: no strike is ever truly lost. At worst it keeps the spark of revolt alive and is part of a learning process; at the same time, as an overt reminder of the workers' latent capacity and power to revolt, it serves as a restraint upon employers. The logic of this maxim may be more subtle and complex when workers already have established strong unions that have won minimum conditions and rights, but in the merchant marine of 1932 the logic was simple and impeccable.

Ship visiting was my introduction to the human condition in the merchant marine; although later I made two brief trips to sea, the first impressions remain the more vivid. Monthly wages dipped in some instances as low as forty dollars and even thirty-five dollars for able-bodied seamen and firemen; frequently the eight-hour day was stretched to ten and twelve hours. In the self-contained universe of the ship at sea, however, companies set not only wages and conditions of work; they determined the conditions of life, what men ate, where and how they slept, and other amenities of living, including the elementary one of keeping yourself and your clothes clean.

If this last does not seem like much, try a steady regime of saltwater showers, try washing dirty dungarees in a tin bucket of saltwater, try working up a lather with saltwater soap. Try it and you will understand what happened on the passage through the Panama Canal, where fresh water was taken on board at one end and could be replenished at the other. Men spent much of the passage under freshwater showers, luxuriating in them, savoring the water's sweetness on their tongues, glorying in the feel of cleanliness without the sticky residue of salt.

Keeping clean was not only a matter of personal hygiene and self-respect, it was also a social compulsion in a crowded fo'c's'le — often literally a forecastle, jammed into the bow, where the ship meets the weather head-on, where for long stretches, even in the tropics, you cannot open a porthole because any kind of sea would have the fo'c's'le awash. Many companies did not supply sheets for the close-set double tiers of bunks, and denim mattress covers were not changed often. In crowded, unventilated quarters you could tell those covers had absorbed much sweat.

Board was on par with room. Aside from the initial cost of fresh fruits and vegetables, milk, and other perishables, there was also the cost of their refrigerated storage. To the companies a penny saved on the crew's food was another penny earned on a voyage, and earnings were hard to come by in 1932. I have served time in the U.S. army and some county jails, institutions that are not distinguished for the quality of their accommodations and fare. They did not match the dismal squalor of some ship crew's quarters; as for food, it was considerably better in the army and only slightly worse in jail.

Aboard ship the captain was not only boss, in the conventional meaning of employer-employee relations, he was the master, with all the connotations of the title that evolved through centuries of slavery and feudalism. Like the slave-plantation owner or the feudal lord he could dispense justice and impose punishment. Penalties ranged from logging (deductions from wages) to putting a man in irons and throwing him into the brig. Overt rebellion against the master's authority was the cardinal crime of the sea: mutiny. In the absence of organization the captain confronted no countervailing power; he could be as arbitrary as his whim dictated in the exercise of his absolute authority.

Conditions varied appreciably and I have indicated the worst. These were found on lines plying the Latin American trade, employing a large proportion of Latin American seamen. The two most notorious were the Bull and Munson Lines, although the banana navy, or the Great White Fleet of United Fruit, was not much better. It was the United States adaptation of colonial practice. The British, with their vast empire, employed many colonials to man their merchant fleet, arranging them in intricate checkerboard patterns, so that a British ship was a floating microcosm of the divide-and-rule principle.

United States companies had no comparable reservoir but some did their best with what they could get from Latin American protectorates. Relatively few blacks were employed, and those mostly in the stewards' department, and only a few ships in the coastal traffic also employed them in other departments in checkerboard patterns, all blacks on deck, all whites below, or the other way around.

Men aboard ship had at least the privilege of employment and such food and shelter as came with it. Almost half the seamen did not have even that; they were unemployed, on the beach, thousands of them in the small enclaves where seamen gathered in the port cities, scrambling for a flop or the next meal, hunting for a live one, hunting for work through the chaotic maze of companies and agencies that comprised the industry's hiring mechanism, preyed upon by shipping crimps (men who sold jobs) and an amazing variety of hustlers and parasites who somehow managed to feed off men who had so little to feed themselves. Unrestrained by shipboard discipline, not atomized into isolated shipboard units, goaded by desperate necessity, the men on the beach struck the first sparks of the rebellion that was to unionize the industry some years later.

In helping to fan this rebellion my motivation was profoundly political; this was the proletariat, in a basic and decisive industry. Yet there was fascination in it beyond politics. Conditions in the industry and its unique character created a subculture. The phrase — "running off to sea" — already conveyed an element of the seaman's alienation from the conventions and mores of shoreside society.

Not the least of the influences in shaping the subculture were the long voyages of men without women. Even on the beach, aside from visits to whorehouses, the same male isolation obtained for the most part. I say, aside from visits to whorehouses, but these visits, of course, accentuated the isolation. So the line about tin pants was repeated often and there was much relish in the telling of the Jacksonian legend of two dollars for the man not made of wood.

Long trips, without the diversions and the small time-consuming burdens of life ashore, also afforded time to read, to

think, to make conversation, to tell stories. Men with an aptitude for reading and thinking acquired a broad range of culture
and if most of these tended to be retiring and introspective,
others were great talkers and raconteurs. The transient, isolated existence, the residual influences of the old IWW, laced
rebellion among them with bravura; there were traces of nihi-
lism and anarchism, and much more than a trace of tough militancy. For me at nineteen it was a new world, a new dimension
of human behavior and human relations . . .

Jane Street Mission

This date I remember with certainty, November 17, 1932. It
was my nineteenth birthday.

There was a brief snow flurry in New York this day. Toward
evening a foretaste of winter was in the wind that swept South
Street. It was a north wind that attained a velocity of thirty
miles an hour and drove the thermometer below forty degrees.
South Street forms the upper jaw of the mouth of the East
River, and from the street, like teeth, piers jutted into the river's
mouth. Nearby and unobstructed by any buildings or natural
barriers was the Battery, where the North (or Hudson) River
also flows into Upper New York Bay. Behind South Street was
the New York skyline; in front of it were the waters of the harbor. When the wind was cold in Manhattan it blew coldest
along South Street.

This geography and weather are important because they had
a bearing on certain events this night. In the early evening several of us from the MWIU were scattered in the wind along
South Street, stopping men passing by and asking, "Hey, Mac,
you got a place to flop tonight?" In the migrant vernacular
"carrying the banner" was the phrase for not having a place to
flop, for sleeping out. We were looking for seamen "carrying the
banner."

(This, remember, was another age. You will find no seamen
on South Street nowadays. Gone are their former haunts; gone
the seedy restaurants that boasted of "pies like mother used to

make"; gone the old buildings that harked back to the days of "wooden ships and iron men," decaying buildings that in 1932 housed the MWIU, its New York headquarters on Broad Street, its national office on Whitehall; gone the Seamen's Church Institute; gone the musty, shabby quality of the old seaport. The one architectural landmark that remains is the Old Slip police station, an anachronism now, originally erected as a fortress of law and order in the waterfront brawl and hustle that are no more. All this has been replaced by steel-ribbed contemporary architectural monoliths — hives of clerks, secretaries, junior executives, and innumerable vice presidents, toilers in seas of paper, navigating through in and out baskets. The New York skyline, once well behind South Street, now encroaches upon it, almost to the water's edge.)

Our mission that autumn evening in 1932 had its origin in early summer when the Waterfront Unemployed Council, established by the MWIU, began an aggressive agitation centered on the Seamen's Church Institute. The SCI was a very visible target; its thirteen-story building at 25 South Street towered over its surroundings; at night the blue light in the lighthouse tower on top of the building, a memorial to the S.S. *Titanic*, could be seen throughout most of the harbor below Manhattan. Aside from its massive physical presence other attributes made it conspicuous. All relief to unemployed seamen at the time was doled out by private charity; the SCI was by far the biggest and richest quasicharitable institution on the waterfront. That quasicharitable institutions proliferated on the waterfront, some more than a century old (the SCI, founded in 1844, was not the oldest), said something about the condition of the seamen. As did a dubious distinction they shared with the Indians; they, too, were officially designated "wards" of the federal government.

The SCI building was a monument to its affluence, costing $1,225,000 to erect before World War I. Its scale of operations in the early 1930s was indicated by its boast that between 8000 and 12,000 seamen used its services daily. They paid for them — thirty-five cents for one of the 1614 regular beds, ten cents for a charity meal (121,286 ten-cent meals were served in

1931). During the winter of 1931–1932 the SCI made a modest
concession to the desperate condition of seamen who could not
afford a thirty-five-cent bed or a ten-cent meal; it transformed
its third-floor game room into a dormitory with 300 free beds
and gave their occupants a free meal.

The SCI's star public relations attraction was a house
mother, Mrs. Janet Roper, whose specialty was finding "missing
seamen." She found 330 of them in 1931, according to the annual SCI report. In a human interest newspaper story this cold
statistic frequently became the sentimental reunion between a
dying mother in Kansas or Iowa or North Carolina and her long-
lost son who had "run off to sea." This was good copy in soliciting donations. In the SCI–created waterfront legend the inter-
mediary in those reunions was Mother Roper; the *Doghouse
News* called her Mother Ropeyarns.

The agitational line of the Waterfront Unemployed Council
was nonsentimental: the SCI collected large sums of money in
the name of the seamen; as a charitable institution with a
chapel tucked away among its temporal service facilities it was
tax exempt; therefore it should provide free shelter, food, and
other services to thousands of unemployed and destitute seamen.

Such agitation was effective. In late July a group from the
Waterfront Unemployed Council staged an unauthorized rally
in the SCI assembly room where 1000 seamen or more were
milling about. A man just stood up on a chair and began to
address the crowd, setting forth the council's indictment and
program. The *New York Times* account of the incident reported, "His listeners supported the speaker to such an extent
that J. J. Kelly, inspector of the building's private force, feared
trouble and sent for police aid." Twenty policemen and detectives did arrive from the nearby Old Slip station. The meeting
was adjourned and the men were driven from the building.
(The *Daily Worker* story said, "The police made no arrests,
fearing the militancy of the crowd of 4,000 seamen . . .")

The focal point of the action was a petty but specially
chafing irritant. When a seaman, who checked his bag in the
SCI baggage room (as 56,347 did in 1931), finally got a ship he

could not retrieve his bag unless he paid the storage charge. If
he did not have the money, a likely circumstance after a long
stretch on the beach, he suffered two penalties: he had to sail
"schooner-rigged" (without his gear except that on his back)
and when he returned from his trip he had to pay for all the
additional storage time. At the hub of the July demonstration
was a delegation that had come with one seaman in a vain effort
to reclaim his baggage without payment.

The same issue served as the fuse for the big blowup that
came in August, one month later. This time, when the baggage
clerks refused to release a seaman's bag without payment, the
delegation that escorted him did not confine itself to verbal
protest. One seaman tore an emergency fire hose from the wall
and played its spray into the chapel. Some overturned tables,
chairs, and other pieces of furniture. There was bedlam and
shambles. The SCI's private cops panicked; two drew their
guns and one fired several shots before some seamen disarmed
him. Luckily no one was killed by the gunfire and only one
seaman was wounded, slightly as it turned out. The gun-toting
cops also required emergency hospital treatment, the one who
fired the shots, for lacerations of the scalp and injured ribs, and
his partner, for a scalp wound. Although only twenty-five seamen were on the organized delegation how were the cops to
distinguish between them and the big crowd that soon swelled
to several thousand in the assembly room? Seamen flocked in
from the cafeteria and other places, and they were generally
sympathetic to the purposes of the delegation, many of them
joining happily in the riotous manifestations of anger. Once
more city police were summoned from the Old Slip station and
this time they were rougher than in July; some seamen were
clubbed, several were arrested.

As thousands of seamen came streaming out of the building,
cursing and shouting, speeded on by police clubs, still animated
by the excitement of the fighting, the shooting, the purposeful
disorder, one man sat on a bench in Jeanette Park across Coen-
ties Slip from the SCI, unperturbed by the chaos, by the violence that came so close to major bloodshed. He was from uptown, a leader of the New York Unemployed Councils. He had

perched himself in Jeanette Park to await the outcome of the action. As men streamed past him he finally recognized someone he knew as an officer of the Waterfront Unemployed Council. The only question the uptown leader asked was, "Did the man get his baggage?"

No, the man did not get his baggage. But the months of prior agitation and the dress rehearsal in July had created mass sympathy and support for the outbreak in August that dramatically articulated the depths of discontent on the nation's waterfronts. More, the action propelled into the limelight a militant and resourceful force — the MWIU and its Communist cadre — to challenge the existing conditions. The splendid riot in the Institute was a mass coming-out party for Communist leadership among seamen.

It was an important antecedent of what we were up to on the evening of November 17. There was another element in the background: the seasonal prejudice of waterfront charity. The operative assumption was that in the summertime living is easy and destitute men can somehow find a place to sleep and something to eat. Charity was a winter grace. So the SCI made its token offering of 300 free beds in the winter of 1931–1932. So, too, in that same winter the financial captains of the shipping industry launched the Joint Emergency Committee of Seamen's Agencies in the Port of New York, and after being laid up for the summer the same committee was to be commissioned for the winter of 1932–1933. The committee was popularly known as the Haight Committee, after its chairman, Charles S. Haight, an admiralty lawyer who represented major steamship lines, domestic and foreign, decorated by France, Norway, Denmark, and Sweden for his labors in admiralty law. The committee's treasurer was Kermit Roosevelt, son of Theodore and distant cousin of Franklin, but more modestly indulging the family penchant for presidential office; he was president only of the Roosevelt Steamship Company, which owned no ships, operating vessels leased from the United States Shipping Board. When his own line was merged with the International Mercantile Marine Company, a giant shipping combine that operated, among other things, the United States Line, prime United

States entry in transatlantic passenger traffic, Roosevelt accepted a reduction in rank; he became an IMM vice president.

Closer to commercial calculation than to Christian charity the Haight-Roosevelt committee's worldly outlook was expressed by Haight. "The maintenance of our idle seamen," he said, "is quite as important as the upkeep of our idle tonnage." A businesslike sentiment that conjured up a perplexing image: in the language of the trade, idle tonnage was "mothballed," and how do you mothball men?

"Last year," the committee said in the autumn of 1932, "the conditions were bad enough when 10,000,000 tons of ships were laid up, but this year the laid-up tonnage amounts to 15,000,000 tons and the seamen have exhausted their savings . . ." To the maritime corporate mind the problem was best reckoned in tons; it was easier to compute tonnage because idle ships did not move, and they were less troublesome for, unlike men, they needed little upkeep aside from occasional scraping and painting. The 15,000,000 idle tons represented a bit more than one fifth of the world's merchant tonnage; the American ratio was roughly the same, 3,425,000 idle tons out of a total of 15,838,655. Since seafaring employment is casual, even in normal times there were men on the beach and we reckoned, therefore, that in 1932 somewhere between a fourth and a third of the seagoing labor force was unemployed, as many as 40,000 or 50,000.

"It is necessary," the Haight committee said, "to find some new source of income if the men are to be saved from absolute want." This necessity gave birth to a charge of ten cents for every visitor to a passenger liner in port. "Ten cents per person may seem like an insignificant sum," the committee explained, "but if collected from all visitors the total will save hundreds from hunger and want." Unhappily the reference to hundreds also seemed insignificant in the prevailing proportions of hunger and want; the SCI estimate that its clientele ranged between 8000 and 12,000 a day came closer to indicating the magnitude of unemployment among seamen in New York. Many, of course, managed to be unemployed without recourse to this Christian sanctuary on South Street.

Still, the Haight committee's charitable enterprise was geared to a scale of hundreds; its financial goal was $150,000, its major establishment was the Jane Street Mission, which contained 270 beds. Seamen called it the Jane Street Mission although the American Seamen's Friend Society, builder of the sturdy, six-story, red brick structure, had christened it the Sailors' Home and Institute of New York City. The Seamen's Friend Society antedated the Seamen's Church Institute, having conceived a Sailors' Home in New York in 1830 and given birth to it twelve years later. Its first home, at 190 Cherry Street on the Lower East Side, gave way to progress in 1903 when the site was preempted for an anchorage to the Manhattan Bridge. In 1908 the new home was opened at 507 West Street, just where this traffic artery along the North River is joined by the Greenwich Village street called Jane. The Women's Christian Temperance Union of New York State contributed "a beautiful Italian marble drinking fountain" to the appointments. By 1932 the mission had been converted into an annex of Seamen's House, an installation of the Young Men's Christian Association farther up West Street. The bureaucratic arrangements meant little to us; what mattered was the provision of free shelter, which was to be financed by the Haight committee.

When the committee announced its fund-raising campaign in late September, word on the waterfront was the mission would be opened October 1, but it wasn't. Nor was it opened October 15, the next rumored date. It finally opened November 1, admitting about twenty men a week, and at that rate most of the winter would be past before its 270 beds were filled.

Those empty beds on Jane Street were on our minds as we patrolled South Street on the evening of November 17 when the wind was a chilling witness that the season for "carrying the banner" was gone. Bedless men were invited to the MWIU hall with the promise that a practical solution for their problem would be presented. At the meeting finally assembled it was proposed to "pull a Gandhi" at the Jane Street Mission. That was the phrase we used; today it would be called a sleep-in or a lie-in. Some twenty men agreed to go to the mission, bed down there, and refuse to leave. Invocation of Gandhi's name defined the tactic; in contrast to the violence at the SCI in August, this time resistance was to be passive. Thinking back upon it, it would have seemed absurd to us to enter into a philosophical argument about violence and nonviolence. There was a time for overt force in August to crystallize the prevalent mass anger and no need was felt to embellish it with rhetoric about "disrupting the system" or progressing "from protest to resistance"; now, for our purpose this November night, a Gandhi seemed handy.

A steering committee of three was chosen, and I was designated its chairman. It was a long walk up West Street, time to think of possible alternatives we faced. Our intentions were peaceful but we had no way of knowing how the mission management would respond, and if it did call the cops, how would they behave? Badly, of course; this was the assumption of experience and training, but how badly, and then how would we behave? Not just we, but I, for at that point the question would be personal, especially with the responsibility of leadership. It being my birthday the awareness of age was acute, and with it a sense of honor at being chosen to lead this expedition up West Street, a street I knew well in the daytime, its broad expanse jammed with traffic, with taxis and autos, with trucks of every dimension and style, especially the caravans of green trucks when a white United Fruit ship was in port with a cargo of bananas. But at this time of evening West Street was still and empty; on the other side of it shadowy masts, booms, and ships' superstructures were magnified in the dim glow of night lights. It was a huge, darkened corridor to our uncertainty, and I moved through it with a buoyant mix of elation and suspense, feeling very close to the other men, most of whom were strangers to me. It was a curious birthday party that could wind up in jail — or in a hospital.

We got to the mission after ten and the only representative of authority on the premises was a clerk in a wired cage, visibly frightened by the sudden invasion of twenty men ("a YMCA punk," one seaman said). His nerves got no better when he was told we had come to stay and he had better get Captain Page, the mission's manager, down there in a hurry. We trooped into the reading room, grabbed newspapers lying about, spread them on the floor, and bedded down on them to wait for Captain Page — or the police. It was E. M. Page who came.

Page was an Englishman (a Scotch seaman, Alexander "Ding Dong" Bell, who claimed to know him, said Page was not truly a ship's captain, but a holder of a "red ink" ticket that British authorities doled out during World War I when the need for ships exceeded the supply of bona-fide captains). I retain no distinct impression of Page, possibly because of the circumstances of our encounter. The regular occupants of the mission were asleep and the place was in semidarkness. In the darkened surroundings, aware of the sleeping men, the brief meeting of our steering committee with Page was conducted in hushed tones; I remember him as a disembodied whisper with an English accent. After a glance at the bodies sprawled on the reading room floor, Page offered us mattresses. When these were secured and distributed, he said we would be registered in the morning and assigned beds. Then he left. It took a while to get to sleep, as there was a whispered celebration of our triumph, time to reflect on it; then it was a good sleep.

The occupation of Jane Street only began a period of guerrilla warfare. Men who were there before our incursion had received two meals a day; after our arrival it was one meal for everybody. With the unplanned expansion of the roll the administration claimed it could afford no more. We saw the one-meal edict as a devious maneuver to incite hostility among the older tenants against the new arrivals. To consider this issue and others a half dozen of us trooped down to South Street for a session with George Mink, one of the two men in national MWIU headquarters (the other was Roy B. Hudson).

Mink was one of those men who create an aura of mystery about themselves. It's intangible and yet unmistakable. In Communist history his name popped up occasionally in the context of the "George-Hardy-Mink group," which came out of the IWW into the new-born Communist party. So I knew he was an old Wobbly. I learned something else from the occasional grumble of a seaman about a Jewish taxi driver from

Philadelphia heading up a seamen's union, but in this manifestation of craft prejudice, flavored with anti-Semitism, there often was an undercurrent of grudging respect. Mink was brash, tough, shrewd, and he must have possessed ability as well as tenacity, for in the formative years of the MWIU he was its guiding spirit. I say he must have possessed ability because he lacked the attributes of a popular leader and the grumbles about his background were symptomatic of prejudicial obstacles he encountered; yet, despite these disabilities he steered a viable, turbulent movement.

Mink was short, stocky, with small eyes, gleaming and quick; the configuration of his nostrils and mouth suggested, to me, a predatory quality. He sported a shiny black leather jacket and on one occasion, when there was a threat of rough stuff on the waterfront, I saw him slip a revolver into a jacket pocket. His "carrying the heat" made him seem more intrepid to me, heightening the romanticism in the aura of mystery. There was ambivalence because, at the same time, I was repelled by what struck me as his utter cynicism, an impression shared by many others; yet when I mentioned it in later years to a sophisticated man, who knew him far better than I did, a lawyer named Leon Josephson, he argued it was not so. Maybe Mink just blurred the boundaries between hard realism and cynicism, as he blurred the line between revolutionary decisiveness and bureaucracy. To one MWIU convention a delegation arrived from San Pedro, armed with a long list of demands and proposals, mostly a compendium of old Wobbly notions about organization (or disorganization). Whatever its merits the list represented many hours of thought and labor by the MWIU branch in the Southern California port. Mink received the delegation and he did not wait for it to leave before depositing its detailed mandate in the wastebasket, doing it casually, without any dramatic flourish that might have attached importance either to his action or to the document.

Our delegation from Jane Street fared better. Mink was attentive and finally delivered this counsel: The first thing you do is fight for two meals and when you get two meals you fight for three meals and when you get three meals you fight about the menu; if they give you stew you want roast beef and if you get roast beef you want steak and if you get steak you want a choice on the menu. Remember, you cannot demand too much because the workers created it all and until the workers take it all they are not demanding enough.

This, I thought, was sage revolutionary counsel, but first there was this problem of a second meal. The campaign for it was launched by dispatching a dozen seamen to serve our demand on Haight in his law offices, a mild overture that proved more effective than we had anticipated. Haight would not see the seamen, presumably because he was not prepared to say yes and he was unsure about what they might do when he said no. Nor could he have them ejected; that would be bad public relations. Told that regrettably Mr. Haight could not see them, the men just sat in his waiting room.

Haight's offices were in the financial district, at 80 Broad Street, only several hundred paces south of the New York Stock Exchange at the intersection with Wall Street. In keeping with the locale and his own status the offices were furnished with the sedate elegance appropriate for the reception of executives from Standard Oil or the French Line. It clashed with the décor to have seamen in dungarees and peacoats and other casual gear draped over the waiting room chairs, several of them squatting on the floor. The atmosphere, which invited the rich aroma of Havana leaf and, indeed, was often scented with it, now reeked with the acrid smell of Bull Durham. The ashtrays were loaded with the stain and staleness of roll-your-own butts, and much passing and handling of Bull Durham sacks and cigarette papers had scattered yellow grains on the gray carpet. The first delegation remained there all day until the offices closed; the next morning another was there to continue the vigil. It was a war of nerves, a tacit class confrontation, and barring a call to the police, with all its unpleasant repercussions, Haight's options were limited: either he produced meal number two or his aristocratic office would be transformed into the replica of a fo'c's'le. We got our meal.

Meanwhile, back at Jane Street, there were constant skirmishes. Our rooms were monklike cells of stone or masonry,

most of them with slits for windows, no more than two feet
wide. They were very cold at night because the furnaces were
banked so low as to barely keep the water from freezing in the
pipes and radiators. One night several of us roamed through
the halls shouting, "Is there a coal-burning fireman in the
house?" In a few minutes a half-dozen coal-burning firemen
turned up. We descended to the furnaces in the basement and
there they were told, "Get the steam up and don't spare the
coal." This they enjoyed. They opened the drafts wide and
with the exception that the men were not stripped to the waist,
soon the scene could have been from the hairy ape school of
Hollywood sea pictures, the flames leaping as coal was shov-
eled into the furnace. Seamen were entertained by such Hollywood flamboyance; they knew that if you ever wasted coal like
that on a ship the engineers would be all over your back. They
wasted enough coal that night to keep the place warm for a
week or more, enough to persuade the management it would be
much more economical for it to keep steam up than to have our
fellows do it.

One morning, on approaching the cage from which our meal
tickets were issued daily, I saw Hamlet there. Hamlet was not
his real name, but he was a Dane and it humored him to use the
name. He was more utilitarian than the Prince was in "enterprises of great pith and moment." A good sailor, who learned
his craft aboard sailing ships, he was handy with canvas and, of
course, with a knife; he had employed these seafaring skills the
previous summer on an overland voyage through New England.
Heading north he entered towns only at night, using his knife
to rend the awnings of randomly selected shops. Retracing his
course he was a daytime voyager, carrying his sail-mending kit,
offering to repair damaged awnings. His enterprise nourished
him through the summer and left a small stake to tide him
through the autumn.

Now this same Hamlet was at the cage, tearing "a passion to
tatters," pushing a cup of coffee at the clerk and snapping
through clenched teeth, "Drink it." From Hamlet's manner and
tone the clerk could infer that he either took a swallow or he
might be treated to a bath. He took his potion without a grim-

ace. "It's slop!" Hamlet screamed. "It's swill! It's piss! Tell that goddam belly-robber down below to give us coffee fit to drink." Our meal tickets were good at a public lunch counter in the basement of the Jane Street building, where breakfast was a bowl of mush, a roll, a cup of coffee. The proprietor had established a double coffee standard: one urn for his cash customers, another for holders of the mission's meal tickets. We were persuaded that after fresh coffee grounds had served their purpose in the public urn they were transferred to ours; we never saw this actually done but the taste of what we got was convincing circumstantial evidence. After Hamlet's improvisation the coffee was better.

At about this time I left Jane Street for my assignment in Philadelphia, but the style had been set; the place was to be well organized, agitated, and propagandized. It was shipshape and before the winter was out even in Philadelphia I heard occasional references to the "Jane Street Soviet." When spring came there were barricades in Jane Street. In May the seamen learned that, in conformity with the seasonal rhythm of waterfront charity, the place was to be shut down by mid-June, and the first step would be the eviction of seventy men lodged in the second-floor auditorium that had been converted under organized insistence into a dormitory to supplement the 270 regular beds. When Captain Page summoned police to evict the seventy auditorium lodgers they and some of their mates in the single cells barricaded themselves on the inside. A swarm of police and detectives — as many as fifty, according to some accounts — battered their way through the barricades with fire axes and a pitched battle ensued. It lasted for twenty minutes and ended with the arrest of fifty-seven seamen. (The *Daily Worker* story reported that Gus Nelson, also known as "Wing Ding" Nelson, a sailor on the house committee, was "blackjacked into unconsciousness." The *New York Times* reported that Nelson "was identified as the man who had hit Detective Stephen Devine, one of the raiders, with a chair.")

By then Kermit Roosevelt's distant cousin, Franklin, was in the White House. Within a year government relief supplanted private charity for unemployed seamen. Battles did not cease, notably in Baltimore, where seamen demanded and, for a time, won the right to administer their own relief. It is a pardonable pride to attribute the assumption of government responsibility for the elementary needs of the jobless and destitute to the battles we waged and to note that with the revival of shipping in 1934 the veterans of Jane Street, the SCI, and the conflicts in other ports were among the shock troops of the great union offensive in the maritime industry.

Philadelphia

A little after six A.M. on a December day a half-dozen seamen and I assembled at the MWIU hall at 211 South Second Street in Philadelphia. We were dressed against the winter and armed against other contingencies. Hidden in our winter clothing were lengths of pipe or chain that were, along with a folded speakers' platform, standard equipment for a street meeting at the point where the port's longshoremen, some 6000 of them, gathered for the morning shapeup, a daily open-air market for the sale and purchase of labor power to load and unload the ships in port.

Our pipes and chains were not for protection against the longshoremen, they were tolerant and friendly. But a man called Polly Baker was not. He was Philadelphia chieftain of the AFL International Longshoremen's Association, the established union on East Coast docks. As an alumnus of the IWW, once dominant in the port, Polly retained a faith in direct action, only now it was not directed against the employers; occasionally he and his muscle men ventured forth to "dump" MWIU agitators on the waterfront. Polly had enough trouble controlling the longshoremen, especially black longshoremen, when the scarcity of work made the favoritism and corruption in its distribution more conspicuous and galling. Looking at it from his vantage point you could understand why Polly objected to outside agitators who exhorted the men to revolt against the shapeup hiring system, with its kickbacks and discrimination, and against union officers who sanctioned such abuses. In Philadelphia the ILA officialdom never attained the notoriety it did in New York for professional thuggery and thievery; no corpses encased in concrete were ever fished out of the Delaware River. But Polly was no pacifist.

Early in 1931 the MWIU had given him serious trouble when several hundred longshoremen signified their intention to switch unions. Polly handled that difficulty. Over the dissident longshoremen he wielded the power of job control; he did it with buttons that denoted up-to-date payment of ILA dues. No buttons, no work. Against MWIU agitators he employed muscle and there were several bloody clashes on the waterfront.

On the particular December morning of which I write the street meeting passed without incident. Longshoremen did not crowd around the speakers' platform, they kept a discreet distance, but since some were within earshot we assumed they listened and heard. During the time I was in Philadelphia we never had occasion to resort to the pipes and chains. Polly, I suppose, had concluded it was not necessary to sic his heavies against us. His ability to crush the abortive revolt of 1931 — or our inability to sustain and expand it — tightened his control. At the time, however, I did not know Polly's disposition, and the half dozen of us escorting the speakers' platform seemed like a fragile band in the vast array of men toughened by hard work. Our chains and pipes did not allay our uncertainty for we never knew when we might be attacked or by what numbers.

In Philadelphia, although the MWIU was composed of seamen, its focus was on longshoremen. This schizophrenia was induced in part by the economics of the port. Philadelphia was a port of call for many ships and home port for very few, which meant that very few seamen signed on or paid off here but a large force of longshoremen was needed. To further our effort among longshoremen I was accompanied to Philadelphia by a Pacific Coast sailor named George Clark who was to seek work on the docks, secure membership in the ILA, and "bore from within." Blond, with turquoise eyes, Clark was a big man, standing a couple of inches taller than I and as many inches wider from shoulder to shoulder. I became acutely aware of these comparative dimensions because once, when invited to address a hotel luncheon of the Women's International League for Peace and Freedom, I borrowed his blue serge suit.

Clark had tried his hand at art. He said he had served as handyman helper to José Clemente Orozco when the great Mexican painter did his Prometheus mural at Pomona College in California. Clark was seriously interested in writing; some years later he wrote a long novel based on the Denmark Vesey slave insurrection. Clark also had a passion for long spells of solitude. When he sailed from the Pacific Coast he would stay on a ship long enough to save up a stake and then, a pack on his back, he would wander for months all alone through the High Sierra. One winter he spent as the manager of a silver fox farm in the Sierra, snowed in and totally isolated from any human contact.

His long stretches of communion with himself, when he had to serve as his own alter ego, were responsible, I suspect, for some of his idiosyncrasies. One was the disconcerting habit of suddenly launching into the middle of a story as if you were acquainted with the principals and what had gone on before, and then, as you were beginning to identify the characters and to get some sense of the narrative thread, the story just as suddenly trailed off . . .   I had the feeling he acquired this story-telling style in the Sierra, where he could begin the tale anywhere because as the sole listener he knew as much about it as he did as narrator. He talked softly and slowly. What was the point of shouting at yourself, and in the Sierra there was no need to hurry. On occasion, when he was unusually animated or excited, he tried to talk more rapidly, but being unaccustomed to it he would emit a brief burst of very rapid speech, stumble, make several false starts, then emit another burst. In contrast to his soft speech was his booming, wall-trembling guffaw of a laugh, only it was evoked by things that never struck me as quite that funny.

When we came to Philadelphia I did not know about Clark's creative interests and personal idiosyncrasies. I knew and respected him as the author of *The Point Gorda Strike*, a twenty-four-page pamphlet. Publication of such a pamphlet already tells how microcosmic union organization and struggle were among seamen at that time.

The S.S. *Point Gorda*, aboard which Clark shipped as an able-bodied seaman (and MWIU ship's delegate), was a small freighter, about 3600 gross tons, carrying a crew of twenty-eight men from captain to messboy. Only the unlicensed men on deck, eight in all, were actively engaged in the strike. Attesting to prevailing conditions the strike demands were: an eight-hour day (the deck crew worked twelve hours), grade-A food including fresh greens, compensation for all personal gear damaged because of unseaworthy storm doors and portholes, new mattresses and pillows to replace those ruined when the fo'c's'les were awash, clean linen weekly, and new buckets. The conflict between the sailors and the Swayne & Hoyt Steamship Company, owner of the *Point Gorda*, began when the ship was docked in Oakland, was resumed in San Pedro, and was climaxed in New Orleans where the men finally walked off the ship and wound up in jail after a picket-line scuffle that sent the chief mate to the hospital.

Just eight men on a rusty tub rebelled in unison and for the MWIU active it was Lexington and Concord. We spread the news on the beaches and on the ships. Clark's detailed recital of the several skirmishes and final encounter on his long voyage was published as a practical manual in seafaring unionism, as the story of the first sustained and organized union action aboard an American ship since the early 1920s. For me, as for other MWIU activists, this was the class struggle in embryo. Most of us did not question the logic of the MWIU preamble that bracketed the fight for new mattresses and buckets with schooling for the struggle to establish "a revolutionary workers' government."

Clark certainly didn't. His pamphlet may have served as a manual for others, but in writing it and in organizing aboard the *Point Gorda* he was guided by another handbook, *The Strike of the Dredging Fleet*, written by a Russian Bolshevik who was sent by his party as an agitator-organizer to a Black Sea port. The old Bolshevik related how he assembled the first small group of dredging fleet workers to discuss petty economic grievances, how the group expanded and the struggle was "raised to a higher level," advancing from economic to political issues, all of this reaching a grand climax with the pivotal role of the dredging fleet in a general strike and the Revolution of 1905. To Clark this was the revolutionary success story, a true life model, and his enthusiasm was infectious.

When he was dispatched from Philadelphia to Norfolk where there was an insurgency of black longshoremen, led by a lay preacher who worked on the docks, Clark decided to try the Bolshevik pamphlet on the Norfolk longshoremen, thinking he would read the first few pages at the end of a meeting, and if the men displayed an interest he would propose to read it in installments at the end of subsequent meetings. But after he read the first few pages the men were captivated by the narrative (or maybe it was Clark's fervor), and they would not let him stop. Secondhand, still the scene is vivid to me: the very Nordic-looking sailor, sitting in the glow of a kerosene lamp, straining his blue eyes to read an old tale from a Black Sea port by a Russian Bolshevik to black men, half-hidden in the shadows of the dimly lit "parlor" of a longshoreman's shack in Norfolk, Virginia, reading all through the night until the predawn hours. I met the lay preacher from the Norfolk docks at an MWIU conference in New York. He had the body of a longshoreman and the eloquence of an evangelist. "In this struggle, brethren," he said at the conference, "we must be as brave as the lion and as wily as the serpent." Amen.

Shortly after our arrival in Philadelphia Clark mentioned the University of Pennsylvania, "They have a museum out there with a fabulous collection of ancient art." Clark kept on reverting to it in the weeks that followed; from his persistence, from his assumption that it would be an abnormality of reason and sensibility not to visit the museum, I knew we would go there. We finally went on a Sunday in February, trudging on foot from the waterfront, which is the city's eastern boundary, to the university campus in West Philadelphia, getting there in the early part of a sunny afternoon. There I was treated to a

Marxist tour of the art of antiquity, dug up by many university-sponsored archeological expeditions to Egypt and Persia, to Babylonia and Phoenicia, to other locales of long-gone civilizations that once straddled the juncture of Africa and Asia.

Somehow, because of the antiquity of their exhibits the museum chambers seemed more tomblike than galleries displaying the creations of man's only-yesterdays, from the Renaissance and on. Or maybe they seemed tomblike because so many of their prizes were, in fact, excavated from tombs. Whatever the reason for the atmosphere Clark talked in a very low whisper, very intense, his eyes aglow with excitement when he spotted the artistic representation of an implement, a fabric, or something else that afforded a clue to the productive means and processes of the time. In stone relief carvings he studied the placement and juxtaposition of human figures, the raiment they wore, the artifacts and other tangible symbols of wealth for the signs of class position, social status, and social relations. With these fragments, in his low, intense whisper he transmitted his vision of these ancient societies. My own ignorance of antiquity was such that I could not judge his expertise, but never having had reason to doubt his integrity, I believed his whispered, spasmodic lecture was authentically informed.

Clark's materialist interpretation of ancient history, as reflected in art, contended unhappily with a more urgent confirmation of the primacy of material need over aesthetic gratification. I was hungry. We had not eaten lunch and did not know if or how supper would materialize. Clark was totally absorbed in his discoveries and interpretations but I, more Philistine than he, was torn, torn between this socioaesthetic feast and my famished stomach. The succession of chambers began to seem endless as we traversed the southeastern rim of the Mediterranean and the Fertile Crescent to the East, up through time and down the diminishing numerical scale of the centuries before the Christian era. I got hungrier.

It was late afternoon when we emerged from Babylon, 1900 B.C., into Philadelphia, 1933 A.D. The question before us was how to get something to eat and we discussed it on the long

walk back to the waterfront, across the bridge over the Schuylkill River and into South Street, the main artery through the old
black ghetto, past a showcase of the black performing arts, the
Standard Theater, which was Philadelphia's edition of the
Apollo in Harlem, through the unique mixture of congested human life, vitality, tawdriness, and poverty that is a ghetto main
street.

A short way east of the Standard Theater we were attracted
to a crowd forming a semicircle on the sidewalk in front of a
building. From the talk in the crowd we gathered that a
woman had just jumped or fallen from a window several floors
up. We white folks were not about to push and elbow our way
through the tight, black human mass to get a ringside view.
We stood on our toes and craned our necks. The fall and the
terminal impact had disarranged the clothes; no one had re-
dressed the body's modesty, it didn't matter now. Her head
had hit on the pavement, the ooze of blood from it forming a
patch on the sidewalk, the shattered skull revealing and oozing
other matter, too. It was just a fleeting glance, enough to hit
you with the morbidity of your curiosity, with the indignity of
your intrusion into the awful privacy of death. Clark must
have felt this, too, for we both withdrew at the same time and
we did not talk about it. Death on South Street was the ultimate farewell this day to the ancient dead, the harlots of Babylon, the good mariners and merchants of Tyre and Sidon.

I do not know the reason, physiological or psychological,
why an empty stomach is queasier than the full. But it's so,
and after the queasiness subsided I was even more acutely
aware of my hunger than before. Although the problem of food
dominated our conversation on the long walk from the university, this did not mean we had many options. By the time we
got back to the MWIU hall we settled on one option, the Communist party's district organizer, who lived only a few blocks
away. We rang the bell, knocked on the door, but there was no
answer until a head popped out of a neighboring apartment
and said, "You lookin' for the couple that lived there? They
moved."

Clark said, "That dirty son of a bitch!" He was convinced the organizer had moved with his wife just to elude us, for on two prior occasions, when we were desperate, we had come knocking on his door. I did not dispute Clark's conclusion. According to waterfront legend, the organizer had once referred to seamen as "those unruly people" just because of an unfortunate incident during his tenure as party leader in Buffalo. A couple of seamen, who were organizing on the Great Lakes, came to him and tried to impress upon him the urgent necessity of raising the money to pay the rent for the MWIU hall. They threatened to throw him out of his office window if he didn't.

Faced with a locked door and empty apartment, that precedent was of no use to us. There was a Christian mission nearby where the temporal reward for enduring a sermon and a stretch of gospel hymns was a cup of coffee and some doughnuts. We considered it, but we had not fallen that low, partly because Clark remembered a sympathetic butcher in South Philadelphia. It being Sunday evening his shop would be closed, but he lived in a flat behind the shop and we could rouse him. We also thought of another sympathizer in West Philadelphia; he was hospitable and generous, but he was a vegetarian and our hunger was beyond carrots and nuts.

We walked a couple of miles to the butcher's, knocked on the door loudly and insistently until a ray of light pierced the darkened shop as a door opened in the rear. A woman came to the front door, peered suspiciously at us through the window, and then, apparently recognizing us as people she had seen at Left-Wing meetings, opened the door slightly to ask what we wanted. Clark told her. She began to explain that her husband was out but Clark cut off her explanation.

There was very little flesh in Clark's face. When he was hungry and tired the skeletal concavities between the cheekbone and the jawbone, and in the bone sockets of the eyes, became awesomely distinct. This evening Clark was very hungry and very tired. The woman flinched at the abruptness and intensity of his interruption, "We're hungry." She looked at this tall man, towering above her, at the skeletal face, at the deep-set eyes staring at her with desperate insistence. There was compassion in her invitation to come in, and also fear. She picked out a couple of steaks and fried them for us. It was the end of another day with Clark in Philadelphia, different from other days, but not in the elemental struggle to get by.

VII. On the Waterfront—2

The Passion of Joe Bianca

IN AN INSURRECTIONARY VISION of the future there are special measures of a man. Of Joe Bianca it was said, "When the great day comes and Bianca is sent to take the telephone exchange you can forget about the telephone exchange. You may worry about the post office or the railroad depot or some other vital installation but you do not have to worry about the telephone exchange."

Something of the man's temper was revealed in a theatrical episode. It happened during a performance of *Sailors of Cattaro*, a play by Friedrich Wolf, produced by the Theater Union at the theater on West 14th Street that for many prior years had been the home of Eva Le Gallienne's Civic Repertory Company. In one scene of this drama about a World War I naval mutiny the leaders of the revolt, having seized the ship, debate what to do with the officers. The argument was too long and involved for Bianca; from his seat in the orchestra his bass whisper resounded through the house, "Shoot the bastards and throw them over the side."

Having seen Bianca on a soapbox, Rodin's thinker seems listlessly becalmed, his muscularity synthetic. Bianca on the box was the dynamic thinker; you could see, almost feel this physically strong workingman cerebrate up there, grappling with ideas, struggling to give them verbal form, and when the words issued in his deep bass they were sealed with the integrity of his intelligent effort. Of all the soapboxers I heard, most more fluent than he, Bianca was the least likely to be heckled.

I first got to know Bianca in Baltimore, which was before anyone called him the Corsican Cutthroat because it was before he acquired the scar that ran the length of his left cheek, a memento of an encounter with Polly Baker and his boys during a stopover in Philadelphia en route to a meeting in New York. That scar was set in a swarthy face dominated by an aquiline nose over a large, firm mouth, and when Bianca scowled you understood why his best friend, Blackie Kaufman (or Kid Everett, as I knew him in Baltimore), referred to him affectionately as the Corsican Cutthroat. Registration of mood was not tentative or dubious on Bianca's face; he scowled very well, and so he smiled, and about as often. He was fond of the phrase, "fanning the flames of discontent"; he had a gift for agitation and took pleasure in it. "Aha," he would smile, rubbing his chin with his hand, "so you're fanning the flames of discontent."

Drinking was a common waterfront indulgence and I early noticed that Bianca was uncommonly restrained about it. I sometimes wondered about this quirk until one evening in the late summer of 1934 when I learned the reason for it, or at least I saw what drink could do to Bianca. We were at some cause party in Greenwich Village when Bianca cast off his restraint. At the critical moment when the liquor gave out and the dwindled party was to do the same a sculptor came to the rescue. He invited the survivors for gin at his studio nearby. There was gin, all right, but nothing to mix it with, so we drank it straight. Ordinarily Bianca was no party lion but here he decided to entertain the guests. He borrowed needles from the sculptor and pushed them through his cheek, piercing the flesh from the outside and pulling the needle out through his mouth. For a moment it occurred to me that perhaps the knife slash, which left the scar, had severed the nerves, but I dismissed this suspicion as unworthy; if Bianca wanted to amuse the company with this particular parlor trick he would have done so, with or without a live nerve in his cheek.

No one else would try it and the entertainment petered out. So did the gin. And we found ourselves in the street, Bianca, I, and another companion, William Coulter McCuistion of Paris, Texas.

McCuistion, like Bianca, was a prime MWIU cadre; both were in their early thirties then, about a dozen critical years older than I, appearing to me as much more experienced proletarian veterans of the class wars than I was, as more knowing

men of the particular world that still was new to me. But they
were very different men. When the great day came and Mc-
Cuistion was sent to take the telephone exchange you would
worry about it. Especially if there were barrooms on the way.
To mention barrooms is to seize upon the most obvious. It
does not do justice to McCuistion's capacity for diversion. If
there were a rich mansion on the way, for instance, he might
have been inspired then and there to expropriate it and transform it into a seamen's club. The sight of a luxury shop could
have produced an impromptu resolution that the time had
come, by all true standards of justice and morality, for the
workers with him to make up for all their years of deprivation.
Or, he simply might have remembered a long-standing grudge
against a steamship company and taken off for its offices or the
residence of its owner; the telephone exchange could wait
while he settled this old score.

Even such hypothetical diversions may not give the full
measure of McCuistion's imagination. He also had a fabulous
memory. Like some other self-taught seamen he could recite
for hours passages from famous orations or verse that ranged
from Keats and Poe to doggerel, either of Wobbly vintage or of
his own improvisation. He was a wonderful raconteur; for the
fullest enjoyment of his tales, however, it helped to stop wondering whether they were true.

A small incident is typical. Later that year the MWIU
staged an abortive strike. In Baltimore the secretary of the
strike committee was a young seaman named Bill Bailey; in the
performance of his office he had to affix his signature to strike
cards that would be issued to the seamen. McCuistion urged
Bailey to hurry, but Bailey, no facile penman, took his time. At
a strike meeting later McCuistion orated, "This is a rank and
file strike, fellow workers. Why, one of our strike leaders is a
young seaman who never even learned to read and write. In
fact, today was the first time he ever wrote out his name. He
did it to sign the cards that are being passed out to you . . ."

Once I brought McCuistion home to meet my mother, probably out of pride in his friendship and a desire to show him off.
She was cordial for I introduced him as a fine comrade and a

good friend. Afterward she revealed her disturbance. "This friend of yours, McCuistion, he makes a strange impression," she said. "He has the face of a killer."

So that was it. Often in his company, especially when he was drunk, I felt the excitement of danger, but without my mother's perception. I did not read his face as she did. It was a big face perched on a big body and capped by a huge, bulking, knotted forehead that was generously extended by the patch of skull cleared of thinning, disordered hair. His nose was broad, fleshy, his mouth large and full-lipped. All of this rested on the foundation of a strong jaw. You could not tell about his eyes because they were distorted by thick lenses. When he was drunk, the lower lip, protruded belligerently, was flecked with tobacco particles and bits of cigarette paper, and sometimes you could hear the breathing through his nostrils. He had other faces, too; I suppose there is prejudice in remembering this one vividly and not the others. Contradiction as well as prejudice, for I was fond of him once.

McCuistion went to Spain and there was a small impromptu farewell party; being for him, it was a drinking party. Although other Spain-bound men were there, the conversation centered on him. Someone suggested he was going to Spain to escape his creditors. He protested the accusation was unjust; there were just as many people he knew to whom he did not owe money as he owed money to, therefore he was even. Someone else essayed a variation on the theme; the accumulation of debt was a kind of life insurance, for fate could not be so cruel to so many creditors as to allow him to die in Spain.

With such drunken wit the talk turned to death; even before it was talked about there was a consciousness of it, as was inevitable at a party for men going to war. Somebody said the only way McCuistion would die in Spain was if he got drunk and accidentally slashed his throat on a broken bottle. A Spanish volunteer from Chicago, a big fellow from a packinghouse or a steel mill, had joined often in the light banter and heavy drinking; at this point he roared with laughter, "Won't it be funny if nobody else came back, only Mac?" Then he realized what he had said and he acted as if he had sealed his own death warrant. He did not talk anymore. His brooding silence depressed the party, and it soon broke up.

McCuistion did come back from Spain, and aside from the possible hazard of a broken bottle (he was on the booze much of the time) the closest he came to death, according to the stories that followed him, was before a firing squad of his own side. Nominally his side, for his behavior created a doubt about which side was his; he was dissolute, demoralized and demoralizing, disruptive, generally obnoxious, and he did not choose to fight, not against the fascists. Saved from the firing squad by the intervention of other American volunteers, he deserted. One of several stories about his desertion relates that he killed two young Spanish frontier guards on his flight into France.

Having deserted as a soldier of conviction he became a soldier of fortune in 1938, enlisting in a corps of freebooters commanded by Ray Carlucci and Jerome (Jerry Madeiros) King, who were trying to capture the National Maritime Union. His name cropped up in association with a "goon squad" that cut a bloody swath with guns, blackjacks, and chains through the Gulf ports, especially in his native state of Texas. During this foray an NMU Gulf District official, Phil Carey, was killed, several union members and officers were beaten with chains and blackjacks, among them Adrian Duffy, NMU agent in Corpus Christi, Texas, once McCuistion's home port. In 1939 he was expelled from the NMU as a labor spy, provocateur, and terrorist. He became a witness, first for the House Un-American Activities Committee, chaired by his fellow Texan, Martin Dies, and then in a deportation proceeding against Harry Bridges.

Of all this that was to come I had no premonition on that summer night in 1934 as McCuistion, Bianca, and I stood on a Greenwich Village street, several sheets to the breeze, still thirsty and plagued by a familiar disability: no money. On McCuistion's initiative we wandered into a bar and there, choosing forthright candor as the most effective tactic, McCuistion addressed the bartender: we are honest seamen, thirsty but broke, and would the good man stand us to a beer? It was near closing time, maybe it had been a good night, or maybe it was McCuistion's gift for persuasion; the bartender set three glasses of beer before us.

Next to Bianca one of two drinking companions, strangers to us, shuffled off to the toilet, leaving his drink and some change on the bar. Very deliberately, making no effort to conceal what he was doing, Bianca reached for the change and put in his pocket. When the stranger returned he said, "Hey, what happened to my money?"

"He took it," his partner said, pointing at Bianca.

"Gimme my money," the stranger said.

"I haven't got your goddamn money."

"Yeh, he got it. I saw him take it," the partner said.

"Gimme my money."

This bar was on the western outskirts of the Village where Bohemia yields to teamsters, longshoremen, and other members of the working class; it was a neighborhood saloon where regular patrons are at least acquainted with one another. As they became aware of the argument they manifested an ominous unity against the interlopers.

The bartender, fearing for his stock and accessories, so much of both in fragile glass, exercised some restraint upon his regular clientele as the three of us backed out through the door, but the restraint did not last. For that matter the bartender might not have cared about what happened off his premises. They came at us where we stood on the sidewalk, facing them, braced for the charge. Luckily they did not come all at once, but were formed into an irregular file by their exit through the barroom door.

Just as the first man and Bianca traded inconclusive punches suddenly, seemingly out of nowhere, a woman appeared, crying, "Stop! Don't!" and planted herself between us and the men from the bar. I had seen her earlier in the evening and knew her by sight as McCuistion's companion of the moment. Whether it was alcohol or chivalry or a bit of both the brawl was ended before it began. The men trooped back into the bar and we, four of us now, headed east, walking in pairs, Bianca and I in front, the woman and McCuistion several paces behind us.

To make conversation I mumbled something about how lucky it was that McCuistion's companion came along when she did.

"That cunt," Bianca growled.

The vehemence of it shook me and seemed unfair. "Aw come on, Joe," I protested, and again mumbled something about her having saved us from a beating.

"That cunt," Bianca repeated. "She's no good. She's no good for Mac. I'm gonna carve her up."

He showed me a knife with a long blade, then slipped it back into his pocket. If only Bianca were one of those waterfront blowhards or braggarts, but he wasn't. I had to believe he meant it. It was now some hours and many drinks beyond that point of alcoholic intake when you feel your mind is sharp and your speech is eloquent. My mind was diffused in an alcoholic haze; driven by fear I tried to pull it together, to focus it for the desperate argument with Bianca. It would do no good, I sensed, to argue abstractly the ethic or equity of Bianca's intention, or its propriety; but Joe, you don't go around cutting women with a knife. It would be no use to attempt ideological persuasion; we were far adrift from such moorings. I searched for tangible points and alcohol was not my only handicap. I did not know the woman, I could not cite one virtue, one redeeming feature, or any extenuating circumstance in her behalf except the one I again repeated: she had done us a good turn that ought to count in her favor. Then with a flash of alcoholic cunning I added one new theme: she was Mac's woman, Mac was no fool, he could take care of himself, it would be unfriendly, an uncalled-for display of no confidence in him, to cut her up.

As I talked I kept wondering what I would do if my argument failed and Bianca made his move, knowing I would have to try to stop him, knowing also he was strong and tough. Bianca said nothing. And I was running out of things to say. After my one inspired argument no other inspiration came. I dreaded a lapse into silence and I was afraid of lapsing into unreasoned chatter, without logic or cunning, dimly aware of peril in the ill-chosen word. As we walked I did not look directly at Bianca, occasionally trying to scan his face out of the corner of my eye; in the profile toward me I could discern nothing except the long, ugly scar. My resources for monologue about spent I glanced furtively back over my shoulder. The woman was gone.

McCuistion joined us and Bianca said nothing to him about the woman. Nor did McCuistion say anything about her. If she had vanished because she had overheard the conversation — or monologue — ahead of her, McCuistion did not allude to it. We walked a short way, then stopped to consider what else we might do for excitement. Bars were closed, we had no money, except for the change Bianca had picked up, and we had no ideas. It seemed the long party was to break up when Bianca whirled around and struck an enormous restaurant window with his first. It is a neat trick, this glancing blow that shatters a huge expanse of plate glass, yet leaves your fist unscathed. Bianca may have learned the trick from organizers for the cafeteria workers' union. His technique was good but not his choice of time and place. We were at the southeast corner of Fifth Avenue and 13th Street. Two cops were on the northeast corner. They were on us before the tinkle of breaking glass had ceased.

Escorted by the cops on foot toward a police station in the vicinity of Cooper Union we had walked several blocks when Bianca suddenly broke and ran. One cop drew his revolver and fired a warning shot over Bianca's head. The other cop covered McCuistion and me with his revolver. Looking into the muzzle of the gun, waiting for the report of the next shot, this was the moment of terror; at that moment all else that night was a mild excitement, even the long walk with Bianca, the knife, and the woman. Before a second shot was fired a police patrol car drew up. There was no more shooting as the car took off after Bianca to overtake him quickly.

The party was over. Bianca was booked on a charge of malicious mischief, McCuistion and I were charged with "acting in concert." In the morning, along with most occupants of the Saturday-night drunk tank, McCuistion and I were let go, but Bianca was held. Released later on modest bail, he skipped. In confidence I was told he chose not to face trial on the misdemeanor charge because of a prior police record (in jailhouse shorthand he faced "a petty with a prior").

I never found out what was in the prior police record, but something I learned later suggests it was serious. In 1933, the year before the Greenwich Village party, Bianca had been sent to school in Moscow, only to be refused admission when the responsible authorities were informed of his record. It was a hard blow to him, not just the exclusion from the school, but the implications of it: in the Communist movement to which he had committed himself unreservedly there was this cloud over him and it would not go away; whatever it was he had done in his youth would continue to haunt him. Before the ill-fated mission to Moscow he assumed leadership posts in the MWIU; afterward he did not. Then, as in a progression of classical tragedy, came the bail-jumping episode that cast him as a semi-fugitive.

Bianca turned up in San Francisco where he joined the Sailors Union of the Pacific (after the 1934 maritime strike on the West Coast the MWIU was dissolved, its members going into the resurgent AFL seafaring unions). He was an active militant in the Sailors Union, always at the rank and file level, inconspicuous, the agitator in the rear of the meeting hall, fanning the flames of discontent in his bass whisper, egging on others to make the open challenge.

Considering his temperament, his absolute dedication, it was inevitable, I suppose, that Bianca would wind up in Spain. But surely that fatal flaw in his past, the consequent incidents in Moscow and Greenwich Village, might have been subsidiary factors; aside from their psychological effects, they released him from such encumbrances of organizational and political responsibility as could have stood in his way or delayed his decision. He went to Spain with his inseparable friend, Blackie Kaufman.

Bianca became a machine gunner. He tended his machine

gun, and he also cultivated and tended a luxuriant black mustache, a Budenny mustache, long, thick, curled. In the recollection of men who knew him he still was the agitator, grumbling against bureaucracy. This was in the rear. In battle his machine gun spoke with authority, for chronicles of the Abraham Lincoln Battalion, the primary formation of Americans in the Spanish Republican army, refer to him as "legendary" and "indestructible." He was not indestructible. It only seemed so in the several campaigns and battles, in the costly attacks and harrowing retreats, before the early spring of 1938. That's when he was among the first lucky members of the battalion to get a forty-eight-hour pass to Barcelona, close to 100 miles up the Mediterranean coast from the front.

His partner on the short furlough, Bill Bailey, a seaman who had known Bianca on both coasts back in the States, recalls two scenes in Barcelona.

They were sitting at a sidewalk café table. A hurdy-gurdy street musician moved slowly up the line of tables, grinding out tunes, pausing to pass a hat around for coins. When he reached their table, Bianca asked, "Can you play the *Internationale?*" The man could. "Play it," Bianca said, slipping him some money.

"It was ten pesetas," Bailey recalls, "a lot of money, about two dollars."

It could have been the money, or maybe the hurdy-gurdy man truly liked the *Internationale;* he stood at their table for a full hour, playing the anthem of World Revolution. Ta-ta ta-ta-ta-ta-ta-ta-ta, ta-ta ta-ta-ta-ta-ta-ta . . . over and over again.

"The people all around us were going out of their minds," Bailey says. "But not Joe. He just sat there, sipping his wine, a satisfied smile on his face, nodding his head in time with the music."

Second scene. They picked up a couple of whores and took them up to their hotel room. Food was scarce in Barcelona and provident soldiers on leave brought food packets with them. They offered the food to the women. The women ate it with the relish of the very hungry. Bianca looked on with the beatific smile he had worn for the *Internationale*. "What sur-

prised me though," Bailey says, "was how shy he was with
those women."

It is not possible to synchronize the exact time but coincident
with some point of Bianca's gentle pleasures in Barcelona,
Blackie Kaufman was killed in combat. Not by a bullet or by
shrapnel, Kaufman was hacked to death with the sabers of fascist cavalry. Bringing up the rear of a retreating column, somewhere between Corbera and Gandesa in the great bend of the
Ebro River, Kaufman and several gun crews under his command were cut off from the main body of the battalion by a
cavalry charge from the flanks. They were butchered by the
saber-slashing horsemen.

Bianca mourned his friend's death, obsessed by the manner
of it. He brooded on it, the living flesh riven by cold steel. He
was burdened with guilt. If only he had been there, he kept
repeating, he could have done something. Four months later
he still had not shaken off the grief, the horror, the guilt. It was
mid-August now and the Lincoln Battalion was ordered to relieve Spanish troops on Hill 666, a strategically vital height in
the Sierra Pandolls.

To men who were on Hill 666 and have memories of it because they had the luck to live through it, hell may not be a pit.
It could be a hill. Number 666 was a high, desolate mound of
rock. It afforded no cover, no concealment. Men could not dig
into the rock for foxholes or serviceable trenches. There were
few bags for sand and it would not have been much good if
there were more bags because there was no sand. Men fashioned small parapets from the loose rock and other debris they
could find, including chunks of shrapnel. These afforded some
concealment, shielding faces and weapons from enemy eyes,
but they were no good as cover. From commanding heights,
overlooking Number 666, the Fascists directed a torrent of artillery fire at the men, exposed and vulnerable on the barren
hill. The Fascists had much artillery, supplied from Germany
and Italy, and they had a clear target. They pulverized the
rock and the flimsy parapets (one survivor recorded that as
many men were killed by shell-blasted rock fragments as by
shrapnel). The barrages were sustained, hour after hour, day

after day, methodical, relentless, combing the hill, so that it seemed nothing and no one could survive. In the Spanish mid-summer the men hugged the stony earth, sweltering between the hot rock and the burning sun. No water or other supplies could be brought up during the day, and the days were unbearably long.

What men see or believe they see in the heat of battle, what they remember or think they remember afterward, is often contradictory. Joe Bianca's fatal wound may have been in the groin, or the abdomen, or the neck. He died before a medic got to him, so there was no expert location of the wound, and there was no time for post-mortems.

Of the several accounts I have heard and read of Bianca's death I believe Bill Bailey's is the most authentic.

Bailey and another man carried Bianca on a stretcher, blood flowing from his neck where shrapnel had hit. They carried him along a goat path down the relatively sheltered side of the hill, the side that did not directly face the Fascist guns, toward the first-aid station at the bottom. There was a spasm, then Bianca lay still. "He's dead," Bailey said as they put down the stretcher. "But you better get a medic to check it out." The man got a medic. Bianca was dead.

To bury Bianca men took half-hour turns to hack away at the rock with a pick. Grunting and sweating, man after man swung the pick at the hard rock. They worked for a long time but they did not carve a grave out of the stubborn rock. It was a niche, barely big and deep enough to accept Bianca's body. Then they gathered up the stone chips and other loose rock to make a covering mound. Bailey found two sticks, which he fashioned into a cross with the help of a shoelace. On one stick he wrote: "Joe Bianca" — the date of death (which he has forgotten) — "Norte Americano." He added one decoration: a hammer and sickle.

The man who first tried to wedge the cross into the mound of rock was not thinking. He chose a spot over Bianca's face. Someone stopped him in time. The marker was driven into the loose rock just above Bianca's head.

In the first chronicle of the Abraham Lincoln Battalion, writ-

ten by the poet Edwin Rolfe, an epitaph is suggested. Rolfe
wrote that men of the battalion called Bianca "the best soldier
in Spain." Good and brave men from Spain and many lands
fought on Spanish soil. It may be American conceit to call Joe
Bianca the best soldier of them all. It also could be true.

Internationalism

When Lawrence Simpson, an American seaman sailing on
the United States Lines, was picked up by Nazi police in Hamburg for possession of "Communist literature" in the summer of
1935, waterfront Communists were not surprised. No more
than we were upon learning at about the same time that George
Mink had been arrested in Copenhagen where he was involved
in a clandestine depot of the anti-Nazi underground in Germany. Our response to these events, especially the announced
Nazi intention to confine Simpson in a concentration camp, was
to supply the backbone of a demonstration by several thousand
persons at the North German Lloyd berth for the prize passenger liner, the S.S. *Bremen*. In the climactic act of the demonstration a seamen's boarding party stormed aboard the vessel
and my friend Bill Bailey fought his way to the bowsprit to cut
down the swastika.

Because they were clustered and dramatic, because anti-Nazi
feeling was on the rise in the summer of 1935, these incidents
attracted public notice. But even before, without the benefit of
an interested audience, internationalism was a more practical
proposition on the waterfront than it was uptown. Seamen
were human links with other lands; the waterfront was the
gateway to the world. This still is true, but it seemed more true
then, for it was a time before jet sets, when ships were still regarded as the normal conveyances for crossing the ocean. The
men who sailed them could perform useful services.

For example, a brilliant young intellectual named Arnold
Reid, sailing out of Brooklyn as a cadet on the old Red D Line
and guided by revolutionary exiles from Latin America, was instrumental in reestablishing the Venezuelan Communist party,

which had been shattered by the dictatorship of Juan Vicente
Gómez. As wicked as any dictator in Latin American history
Gómez ruled longer than most, twenty-seven years of blood and
sperm, for he was distinguished for sexual fertility as well as
cruelty. It was said of him that when he murdered a man he
estimated the procreative potential lost to the nation and compensated for it by siring an equivalent number of bastards. Secrecy shrouded both patriotic pastimes, so it is not known
whether he practiced murder or fornication more often, or
which gave him greater pleasure. His indulgence of other car-
nal appetites was also immoderate; money was no problem, he
was compensated well for having opened Venezuela to exploitation by Standard Oil.

Much of the functional internationalism on the waterfront
was related to revolutionary movements in countries governed
by dictatorships, such as Venezuela and Germany. Of necessity
it was clandestine. I learned of Reid's mission only by chance.
I was aware of other missions, perhaps not so special as his, but
only vaguely because a responsible discretion precluded prying.

One internationalist chore, however, was more freely shared;
bales of printed matter, in Chinese and Japanese, came from
the Pan-Pacific Secretariat of the Red International of Labor
Unions. We could not do much with the Japanese material, not
on the East Coast; Japanese ships were few, their security was
tight. At best we sometimes managed to scatter Japanese matter in the holds of Japan-bound ships, hoping it would be found
by Japanese longshoremen when they unloaded the cargo.

We did much better with the Chinese literature because
there were Chinese seamen on American ships. The old Dollar
Line manned its stewards' departments with contract laborers,
most of them Cantonese, hired out of Hong Kong. The con-
tracts, as elaborate as any unequal treaty, required each man to
post a $500 bond, which, among other things, was supposed to
be a guarantee against his jumping ship in the United States.
At the time the Chinese Exclusion Act was still in force, afford-
ing a rationale not only for the bond, but also for denial of
shore leave to Chinese crews in United States ports.

The man posted $500, the company posted a coffin, a by-product of the company's contractual obligation to return the man to his home port, alive or dead. That is, if he died aboard ship he was not to be buried at sea, as is the Western custom, but his body was to be returned to Hong Kong for burial alongside his ancestors. As tokens of good faith some Dollar Line ships carried one or two roughhewn coffins. I was told of one Chinese seaman who became seriously ill on a Dollar Line ship; to reassure him the captain had a coffin moved into the sick bay near his bunk.

On visits to Dollar Line ships we took the Chinese literature and collection lists with the appeal inscribed in Chinese characters. I could read neither the literature nor the appeal, but the response was phenomenal, especially when the crew spokesman or leader, who could speak English because he had to represent the men in dealings with ship's officers or other company representatives, was sympathetic, as he often was. It seems incredible to me now but at the time, in searching for the crew leader, we used the old British colonialism, number-one boy. Where is the number-one boy?

Sometimes you came off the ship with as much as thirty dollars from a Chinese crew that may have numbered no more than thirty men whose monthly wage was twenty-five dollars in Mexican money or twelve-fifty in United States exchange. Reference to dollars, to the pitiful number of them paid Chinese seamen, recalls a choice bit of symbolism. The dollar sign served as the insignia of the Dollar Line. You could see the company's ships, the most modern of them, the S.S. *President Coolidge* and the S.S. *President Hoover*, big and sleek, and on the smokestacks, big and ugly, was the dollar sign. As often as I saw the sign the brazenness of it never wore off. When the Dollar Line was reorganized by the government and rechristened the American President Line the sign of the dollar also underwent a metamorphosis; it became a stylized American eagle.

In the summer of 1932, having laid up three ships in New York, the *Presidents Pierce, Jackson,* and *Johnson,* the Dollar Line calculated it would be cheaper to hold the Chinese crews

prisoner aboard the *Johnson* than to supply their passage back
to Hong Kong. An MWIU delegate came upon the ninety-five
Chinese seamen after they had been herded aboard the *Johnson*
for a month in dry dock, kept on a bare subsistence diet, and
denied permission to go ashore. There is no way of telling how
long the company intended to hold the men prisoner; presumably it was until their ships were ready to sail again, an uncertain prospect in the economic chaos in 1932. We raised a minor
storm about it — a demonstration at the company's home
offices in San Francisco, the threat of a lawsuit in New York,
other forms of protest. Enough to persuade the company to
ship the men home.

The MWIU received a letter from the homewardbound men.
"Friends: Thanks to your help, we are returning to China on
the *President McKinley*. We are all very grateful and shall
never forget it." The Dollar Line, however, bore its white
man's burden with poor grace. Three days out at sea the ship's
chief steward ordered the Chinese seamen to paint C Deck on
the *McKinley*. "We all know this is not our duty," they wrote.
"This act on his part is mistreatment. Therefore, we all acted
as one man, resisted."

The steward called the captain. The captain called twenty
officers and sailors to intimidate the Chinese, but they stood
firm. "The chief officer saw that we were determined and sol-
idly united, suddenly changed to savage tactics," the letter said,
"brandishing his blackjack and revolver, threatening to im-
prison us." They were also threatened with fines, with cancellation of their work books, which meant exclusion from the industry. "We all stood at iron solidarity and refused to yield."

The most fascinating story of the Dollar Line and international solidarity was told to me by a man named Steve, a sailor
of Croatian origin. This was Steve's story:

"Early in nineteen twenty-seven I was sailing quartermaster
on the Dollar Line. We were about a day out of Shanghai and
during my turn at the wheel up on the bridge I overheard a
conversation between the captain and the mate about a wire-
less message from the company shoreside. Seems there was a

general strike in Shanghai. All the coolies, longshoremen included, were out. So the company wanted the sailors to work
cargo. That's what the captain was telling the mate, telling him
to get the sailors to work cargo when we docked in Shanghai.

"I was not a Communist then. Hell, I wasn't even class-
conscious. I'd never heard of international solidarity, for all I
knew it could have been the name of a race horse. But that
message went against my grain. As soon as I was relieved at
the wheel I dashed down to the sailors' fo'c's'le and told them
what I heard. Hell, I said, they want us to scab on coolies who
make fifty cents a day, and I'd be damned if I would do it, and I
didn't think anybody who would do it was much of a man. The
sailors agreed they wouldn't work cargo in Shanghai, and they
didn't.

"Going ashore in Shanghai I just stepped outside the dock
when a gang of coolies mobbed me, screaming rickshaw, rickshaw. I didn't want no rickshaw. I never liked 'em and anyway
I didn't even know where I was going. I was going to mosey
around, drop in at a bar or two, maybe find a restaurant and
have a meal, you get tired of ship's grub. So I said no, no, no
rickshaw. But they insisted and before I knew it I was in a
rickshaw. As we went along more and more coolies gathered,
seems like there was thousands of 'em, all excited and chattering. I didn't know what the hell it was all about, and then a
Chinese who talked English came along.

"Seems like the Chinese crew aboard ship overheard me agitating the sailors not to work cargo and they passed the word
ashore. I was a hero in Shanghai. Hell, I looked around and
there wasn't another rickshaw in sight. I don't believe the British governor general could have got a rickshaw in Shanghai
that day. The town was down. And there I was riding this
rickshaw and everywhere there was this excitement.

"So the fellow who talked English asked me where I wanted
to go. And I said I didn't know, I had no particular place I
wanted to go. Then they talked among themselves and I felt
they were taking me some place. You know where they took
me? To a Chinese whorehouse."

The Legend of Harry Hynes

Wait till you meet Harry Hynes . . . Really, you don't know Harry Hynes?

Several men said such things to me on the New York waterfront and always in a tone I never heard in reference to anyone else. The confinement and closeness of life aboard ship, sharing sleeping quarters and eating facilities, inhabiting the same tiny, metallic, floating island for weeks on end (ships were slower and trips were longer in those days) left seamen with few illusions about their mates, least of all illusions that make for idolization or hero worship. Some men were more respected or admired than others, but in the references to Hynes there were always traces of something beyond respect or admiration. One cynic, involved it was said in small-time waterfront rackets (a little smuggling, a little pilfering), shed his cynicism in talking about Hynes. Even George Mink, whose judgment of men tended to be hard-boiled or derisive, spoke of Hynes with gentleness and affection.

Hynes was on the Pacific Coast when I came to New York and I did not meet him until he returned to the East in 1933. During the next three years I saw him off and on; the acquaintance was social, conversational — we never worked together, never shared any revealing experience. I did not really get to know him, yet felt he was very special. I was young then, romantically inclined perhaps to overly generous judgments of people I liked and called comrade. Many years have passed, each adding to an awareness of human vanities, and I still think of Hynes as the best man I ever met, which is to say, given my scale of human values, that of all the people I encountered he came closest to being a pure revolutionary.

Regretting I did not know him better I have turned to others who spent more time with him, in closer and more functional association than I, seeking significant details, intimate insights to fill in the portrait that in my own mind was impressionistic, almost intuitive.

I sought out a Liverpool Irishman; as loquacious as Hynes was taciturn, he had wit and the worldly wisdom a man with quick intelligence can acquire by sailing the seas as a coal-burning fireman and getting by on the beach in Capetown, New York, and other ports. Among his childhood memories was arrest for stealing potatoes to get something to eat and a fondness for tinned corned beef, which was the rare meat dish for the Liverpool working class during World War I. He was not one of life's novitiates when he met Hynes in the shipping office of the British Consulate in New York in 1933.

A consular clerk came into the office, really a barren room, and ordered men who were smoking to put out their cigarettes. The Liverpool Irishman defied the order with a stream of the profanity he had learned in the Liverpool slums and in his years at sea. At this point a man he had noticed before in the shipping office, a man he had tagged "the Australian cowboy" because he wore a broad-rimmed hat and a tweed suit, intervened. The Australian told the clerk the waiting men should be supplied with benches; the men should be treated as men, he said, not as animals forced to stand and mill about. The other men in the office, sensing trouble, moved away from the two rebels. ("They were sheep," the Liverpool Irishman said.) The clerk, facing mutiny, called for the police. The Australian said to the Irishman it was time to leave, and they did.

In this moment of mutual rebellion, tempered with discretion, the Liverpool man's friendship with Hynes began. Almost four decades later he still paid homage to Hynes as his teacher. "The thing about Harry," he said, "he took sheep and turned them into men, he gave them a reason for living." The Liverpool man did not think of himself as a sheep when he met Hynes for he already was a rebel. If he were to pick a likeness in the animal kingdom it would probably be the mule; in his own estimation he was not yet a man with a reason for living. His entry into the estate of purposeful humanity he attributed to Hynes.

In the three years after their meeting the Liverpool man and Hynes were shipmates, partners on the beach, they shared a New York flat for the better part of a year. In all that time Hynes conveyed no intimate confidences; he kept his hurts and disappointments to himself, the Liverpool man said; he was too modest to talk about himself or go in for personal reminiscences.

From my own observations I thought Hynes was closest to a Maine Yankee named Tom Ray who possessed probably the most astute and toughest mind among the seamen who played any part in the formation and growth of the National Maritime Union. "Yes," Ray agreed. "You are right. Harry was a very good man. I've known several good ones and Harry was one of them . . ." This was a rare tribute, for in his more than sixty years the human trait that has impressed (and distressed) the Maine Yankee most is corruptibility. But his recollections of Hynes were sparse. Things like: "I don't know what his formal education consisted of but I had the highest respect for his intellect and his honesty and integrity. We spent some happy hours in the New York Public Library." Their association, he said, did not include the confidences that serve to round out the portrait of a man.

Among other men, too, the homage was categorical, the human personality elusive. If Hynes's purpose was self-effacement (and he was the most self-effacing of men) then his success was phenomenal. What remains is part legend, part mystery, and I have only a few impressions of my own and the miscellaneous remembrances of others to recreate a human form.

Hynes was a tall, slender, handsome man with long arms and the strong utilitarian hands of a ship's carpenter and sailor. The hands were used to work and when they were idle he did not quite know what to do with them; this physical dilemma fitted in with a reticence that was almost shy. In his early thirties when I met him, he had been going to sea since he was nineteen, he had been an organizer on all United States seacoasts and on the international level, and yet in his unassuming reserve, as in his smile, there was a youthful innocence. He had not acquired behavioral barnacles common to his craft, even to such minor matters as smoke or drink. He did neither. Sometimes in a restaurant, when he was festive and had some money (a rare conjunction), he would toss his head, attempt a debonair wave of the hand, and declare, "Let's have some vino!"

Having played the bon vivant he went on to nurse one glass of wine through the evening. One custom of the sea he observed: he was a patron of brothels, on occasion a prodigious patron. He was attractive to women and liked their companionship but his several noncommercial liaisons with them never progressed beyond a casual relationship.

For a time Hynes was employed at the Marine Hospital in Staten Island as a carpenter for room, board, and seventy-five dollars a month. He donated seventy dollars of his wage to the MWIU. Five dollars a month was enough for incidentals, he said, for he did not smoke and he had food and lodging. This selflessness, which was equally indifferent to petty luxuries and physical discomforts, contributed to the man's serenity. Men who had shared quarters with him in a Lower East Side tenement flat, rented to shelter the MWIU Port Organizing Committee, marveled at one display of his inner calm. In this POC shack there was recurrent debate about one question: after the revolution what will it take to rid the Lower East Side of bedbugs? The radicals argued the whole district would have to be burned to the ground. The moderates insisted systematic fumigation, tenement by tenement, block by block, would do the job. Schooled in shipboard arguments that can go on for days and weeks the men had no difficulty in prolonging the debate. Its hypothetical after-the-revolution frame of reference confounded any conclusive resolution and the nonhypothetical presence of bedbugs kept the issue alive. The POC shack crawled with the bugs. Men slept with flit guns at their sides. All except Hynes. He slept all through the night, his face in repose, his body still and relaxed, not tossing or scratching in his sleep. This man was at peace with himself.

I was often struck by Hynes's fine sensitivity, and it sticks most in my mind as it informed a tale he told me after a trip aboard a British ship to Hamburg in 1935. Hynes had been on the beach in Hamburg for six weeks in the fall of 1931, working out of the headquarters of the red International of Seamen and Harbor Workers. He had become intimately acquainted with the Hamburg waterfront when it was a Communist stronghold in pre-Hitler Germany, when the post-World War I general strike and armed uprising were vivid memories, when water-front workers were proud that one of their own, Ernst Thäl-mann, was the national leader of the powerful German Communist party.

Returning two and a half years after Hitler's seizure of power Hynes went ashore to search for some sign of the Hamburg he had known. He searched in cafés and bars where acquaintances had gathered, only to encounter strangers, impassive and uncommunicative. He passed by buildings he remembered as busy union or Communist headquarters; now they were quiescent except for one. It was Nazi party headquarters. He walked through streets where walls and fences were once plastered with Communist posters and proclamations, looking now for some telltale shred of paper, for a surreptitious inscription or a trace of one. In these streets he had known people and he scanned passers-by for a familiar face. Everywhere nothing. What he had known only five years earlier as a vibrant movement, its face and clenched fist ever present in these working-class quarters, had vanished without a trace. Tired, dejected, he came upon one divertissement of the new order, an out-of-doors anti-Semitic puppet show, to mock his depression.

Sailing from the port he was at the wheel, his mind and spirit burdened with his melancholy quest, mechanically following instructions of the German pilot guiding the ship through the channel. In his meditation Hynes suddenly became aware of a familiar tune. The pilot was whistling *Stenka Razin,* an old Russian folk song about a Cossack rebel. Hynes looked at the pilot, signifying he knew the song, and thought he detected a responsive sign. Just then the pilot had to leave the ship. It was so little and so tenuous — the tune of *Stenka Razin,* for instance, is also used in a very bawdy Finnish song. With a wry smile Hynes asked: but was it a vestige of the Hamburg he had known?

Hynes's acquaintance with Hamburg was a detail in a larger familiarity. He knew the whole world. And not as most seamen know it, which is much about its geography and a little more through chance glimpses and encounters in the ports to which they sailed. He knew the world's economics and politics, its contemporary history. I never met anyone who knew as much about the colonial world and this was at a time when United States ignorance of that vast human majority was not disturbed by revolutions and wars (to be sure, both were present even then, notably in China, but they only touched the periphery of the United States popular consciousness). What he saw firsthand as a seaman was blended finely with the voluminous reading of a self-educated and highly cultured man. On the beach the public library was his second home and it is part of the Hynes legend that on the New Year's Eve that ushered in 1935, when the rest of us were zealously conforming to the alcoholic rites, he was reading in the library on Fifth Avenue until closing time. In his broad reading range the specialized interest in colonialism may have been influenced by his origins to which he alluded rarely and never in detail.

He was born in Rawalpindi, now in Pakistan, but in 1900, the year of his birth, it was in British India, site of a military base, one in a chain that stretched through Kipling country to Peshawar and the Khyber Pass, where British imperial might confronted the Czarist empire across Afghanistan. His Irish father was a sergeant major in the Fourth Dragoon Guards, an Irish regiment. His mother was an English seamstress from Aldershot.

When he was two and a half the Fourth Dragoon Guards were transferred to Hexham in Northumberland, the northernmost English county. The proximate frontier now was the Scotch, not the Afghan. In Hexham he received his only formal education, which was cut short at thirteen when the sergeant major, mustered out of the armed forces and the father of five children, could not make it in English civilian life. The ex-soldier and his family sailed in steerage to Australia, their passage partially subsidized by an Australian government program to encourage agricultural settlement. They settled at Tongala in the state of Victoria to raise cows and lucerne (Australian for alfalfa). Conditions were primitive, the work hard, and the thirteen-year-old boy became a hand on the farm.

After World War I broke out a former sergeant major could make more money at the lighter work of training troops in Mel-

bourne. The family migrated again and the country boy of sixteen was transplanted to the big city, a lonely stranger at loose
ends. He escaped by enlisting in the army, lying about his age,
an easy deception because he was tall and strong. He also was
intelligent, educated beyond his formal schooling because of
his avid reading. His qualities — physical and mental — must
have been apparent for even the Australian military bureaucracy discerned them; he was shipped off to an officers' training
school in England, graduating at seventeen (with the rank of
captain in the artillery, according to a sister). Just as he was to
be sent to the front his mother intervened, revealing to the military authorities that he was underage. Back he came to Mel-
bourne, transformed from a military officer into an unskilled
and unemployed worker.

After odd jobs in the construction trades he went to sea in
1919 as a ship's carpenter. From his infrequent allusions to his
past life, it seems he joined the IWW in Australia and was active in a militant minority movement in the Australian seamen's
union. By 1927, when he decided to make the United States his
home, he was a confirmed revolutionary.

His birth on a military post in India, the arch colony, his
childhood in the "mother country," his youth in a British Commonwealth (much more closely integrated in the imperial system then than it is now), his subsequent experiences aboard
Australian and British ships, where the empire was a many-
faceted presence (in cargoes, routes, crew patterns, and relationships) — all this past, I believe, encouraged his intense interest in the struggles to overthrow the colonial system once he
arrived at his revolutionary convictions.

Certainly at twenty-seven, when he chose the United States
as his home base, he was uniquely a citizen of the world. This
world citizenship imparts a historical logic to a tombstone capsule: Born 1900 in Rawalpindi, India, son of a sergeant major in
the Fourth Dragoon Guards. Died 1937 in Spain, political
commissar, Third Company, Washington Battalion.

Spain was to come later; in 1934 we talked about Cuba. He
had just returned from a trip to Puerto Tarafa, the port for
Nuevitas, on the north coast of Camagüey Province. This is

when I was first intrigued by one of the mysteries about Hynes. How did this quiet, unassuming man do what he did in Puerto Tarafa?

He sailed into the port in late January aboard a British freighter, the S.S. *Gypsum King,* which was to take on sugar. But the sugar-mill workers were on strike, the workers on railroad feeder lines from the sugar centrals to the port were on strike, and the longshoremen were on strike. The strike was symptomatic of that moment in Cuban history. Several months earlier the dictatorship of Gerardo (The Butcher) Machado had been overthrown and the short-lived radical reform administration of Grau San Martín was in power. Having been the decisive force in the overthrow of the dictator, and released now from the restraints of Machado's murderous terror, Cuban workers were on the offensive. They had been caught in the vise between the domestic dictatorship and the world economic crisis, which played havoc with the sugar market; their wages and conditions had plummeted below the deplorable levels that obtained even in the best of economic times. Now, with the dictator gone and the world economy slightly recovered, they were battling for economic redress.

For Hynes sympathy was not enough; the obvious challenge was to secure solidarity action by the ships' crews in port with the Cuban strikers ashore. Aside from the *Gypsum King,* five ships flying four different flags were in the harbor: the *Munlisto* (U.S.), *Teraloy* (British), *Asbec* (German), and two Norwegian freighters, *Helle* and *Lyngholm.* To begin with, Hynes and his shipmate, the coal-burning fireman from Liverpool, went to the Cuban longshoremen's union. On Hynes's initiative a committee consisting of himself and his partner and representatives from the Cuban longshore and railroad unions visited all the crews in port with a strike bulletin and an invitation to send representatives to a meeting. At the meeting a resolution drafted by Hynes was adopted unanimously.

"We seamen, members of the crews of ships of various nationalities in the Port of Tarafa, Nuevitas, Cuba, declare our international solidarity with the longshoremen, railroad men, and sugar-mill workers now on strike; and will do everything in our power to stop the loading of scab cargo, by firemen refusing to give steam and sailors refusing to handle winches."

The resolution took effect January 26 and all cargo-loading ceased. Hynes was coopted on the Cuban strike committee in which Communist leadership predominated although there also was a strong syndicalist faction. He was toured through the province to address strike meetings. A young nurse, who worked in the pharmacy of her father, a Communist leader in Camagüey, was his translator. His direct involvement in the Cuban class conflict was cut short when the *Gypsum King* sailed back to New York — without a cargo of sugar.

I never saw Hynes so exuberant as he was on his return from Cuba. He was aglow with the Cuban experience, in love with the island, with its workers. He talked with rare animation about their militancy and understanding, but his sensibility also extended to the climate (it was a cold February in New York), the natural beauty, the social hospitality, the charms of Cuban women. (About himself he did not speak; the Liverpool Irishman told of Hynes's feat in bringing together seamen of four nations for a common action of fraternity with the Cuban workers, of the natural ease with which he won the trust and respect of the Cubans.)

In his quiet way Hynes converted about a half dozen of us and we came to share a romantic dream. Hynes would lead us all to Cuba to establish an outpost of the International Seamen and Harbor Workers to conduct agitation on foreign ships in Cuban ports. We talked ourselves into taking this far-fetched venture seriously. Ray, the Maine Yankee, as I recall it, was commissioned to look into the possibility of a small boat we could sail to Cuba. Hynes even secured an appointment with William Z. Foster to outline the proposition. It was a beautiful dream while it lasted.

That Hynes could get caught up in it testifies to how footloose he was at the time. When he came east from the Pacific Coast he was given no organizational responsibility. Whether this was his own choice or the calculated decision of Communist leaders who dispensed such assignments I do not know. As the Liverpool Irishman said, Hynes kept to himself his hurts and disappointments, which figure nonetheless in Left-Wing waterfront lore.

One of a handful of pioneer Communist organizers in the United States maritime industry in the late 1920s Hynes was a founder of the MWIU, editor of the *Marine Workers' Voice,* and, for a time, the union's national secretary. At one point, however, the national Communist center vetoed him for the top union post as insufficiently aggressive and voluble. This is when he was assigned to the Pacific Coast and ran into troubles that involved a Communist conflict of interest between agriculture and the maritime industry.

In the early 1930s conditions in California's farm valleys were flammable. Even a mediocre organizer could get quick, spectacular results in dramatic strikes and mass confrontations. On the waterfront, particularly on the docks, the going was slow and imperceptible. The first tiny group of longshoremen had just been brought together in San Francisco; because of a company union and the blacklist, its activity had to be clandestine. Waterfront organization looked like a long, painstaking job with uncertain results in an indefinite future. To California's Communist leader at the time, a man named Sam Darcy, the agricultural valleys, where intense class conflicts ripened so swiftly and abundantly, were the places to concentrate all the resources he could command. These resources were mostly human, money was scarce, and all the people available were deployed to the fields. Disagreeing with these priorities Hynes was firmly convinced that the maritime industry was the more decisive, that potentially it was the firmer and more durable base for trade-union organization and revolutionary politics, which could influence the entire working class in California. To sharpen this clash over policy Darcy and Hynes were opposites in personality and temperament. Darcy was anything but quiet and unassuming.

Hynes could not prevail over Darcy in California, and he was unable to secure the requisite support at the national level to offset his local disadvantage. The relationship became so strained that he requested to be released from his post and came east.

It would appear that his mission to the West was a failure. But it was not. In San Francisco he was the founder and first editor of the *Waterfront Worker,* a modest mimeographed paper that was the genesis of the great revival of waterfront unionism on the Pacific Coast. The paper's germinant role is acknowledged in the official historiography of the Pacific Coast longshoremen's union. Launched in December 1932 and appearing monthly (more or less), the *Waterfront Worker* assembled the nucleus of rank and file longshoremen who supplied the primary initiative and leadership for union organization on the docks in 1933 and for the maritime strike of 1934, which ranks among the "top ten" strikes of American labor history. In time sequence the 1934 strike assumed historic importance as precursor of the later working-class revolt in the steel, auto, and other industries that are the primary motors and levers of the American economy. Regionally the strike directly stimulated unionization of hundreds of thousands of workers in the varied industries of the West.

In a social movement of such scope and force as the industrial rebellion of the 1930s it is not possible to designate any one origin with certainty, to say: here it all began. But to the significant extent that the *Waterfront Worker* was in the beginning so was Hynes.

This may be said in the perspective of history. In 1933 the *Waterfront Worker* was not yet history and Hynes was one more seaman on the beach in New York, worse off than most because he did not have United States citizenship and had to buck the shipping office at the British Consulate to sail on British ships with their inferior wages and conditions. Not a gregarious man, he exerted his influence then over a small circle of acquaintances. His class identity and his utter commitment to the revolutionary cause were reflected in his unique success at Puerto Tarafa and in his lonely, futile search in Hamburg. Between ships he spent much time at the public library; he discovered a Slavic room and read his way through the Russian literature he had missed, pre- and postrevolution.

After almost three years of this existence, he was asked in December 1935 to assume editorship of the *ISU Pilot,* the organ of an insurgent rank and file movement in the AFL International Seamen's Union. This was different from his journalistic enterprise in San Francisco; this paper was already established and the movement it represented was well under way. Still, to confuse martime metaphors, he was at the helm of the *Pilot* through 1936, the critical year that molded the character and style of the movement that attained its final form in 1937 as the CIO National Maritime Union. In the embryonic phase of a labor insurgency a paper exerts much greater influence than it does in an established union with a codified structure and a legitimatized bureaucracy. It may be assumed that through the *Pilot* Hynes left his mark on the NMU in its early days when its democracy and militancy, its range of social and political concerns, made it one of the more admirable American unions.

To argue this assumption, to buttress it with citations from the *Pilot,* would entail a more detailed examination of the NMU's prenatal year than is appropriate here. Certainly men who were associated with him at the time do not doubt that his was among the more important influences in that formative period. One of his innovations was a page in Spanish to reach the most exploited seamen aboard United States ships. Simultaneously, for introduction of the Spanish page coincided with the outbreak of the Spanish Civil War, the paper reflected a growing concern with Spain. Less than a month after the fascist rebellion against the Republican government the first item appeared: a letter from a United States seaman who was caught in a clash between workers and fascist police in Tenerife in the Canary Islands off the African coast. Subsequently photographs (including one of seamen and longshoremen manning barricades in Valencia) and items on the Spanish war became staples.

When recruitment of United States volunteers for the International Brigade began Hynes told a friend, "In Spain they're fighting the fascists with guns. That's where I ought to be." So we come to a parting scene. "The last time I saw Harry," Ray recalls, "was just prior to his departure for Spain. Harry was darning his socks at the time. I made a passing reference to his

going to Spain to die but he ignored the remark and went on
darning his socks. That was the last time I saw him."

It was characteristic of Ray to say something like that (he
believed it and he did not want good men to die). It was also
characteristic of Hynes to go on darning his socks. The sailor
was getting his gear shipshape for one more voyage. Once he
got to Spain Hynes did something else that was in character, he
did not reveal he once graduated from a military training
school with an officer's commission. He preferred to begin in
the ranks. By the time he went into action in the Brunete offensive of July 1937 with the Third Company, Washington Battalion, he was the company's political commissar. His unit faced
the deadly marksmanship of Moorish riflemen deployed along a
height called Mosquito Ridge. A bullet pierced Hynes's neck.
He was carried on a stretcher to the aid station. There some
officer barked, "All right, all you guys that can walk, get off
those stretchers." Hynes got off, collapsed, and died.

The essential detail, that mortally wounded he got off the
stretcher to make way for someone else, is verified by several
witnesses. It is also authenticated by the kind of man Hynes
was. As Ray said, "Harry would have done that."

My life's vocation, as it turned out, was to be journalism,
Communist journalism. The waterfront, if I may borrow
Gorky's phrase, was my university. Those years (1932–1934)
marked the beginnings of a transition from elemental outbreaks
among the unemployed against hunger and destitution to the
industrial wars in which workers successfully stormed the open-
shop fortresses of General Motors, United States Steel, Ford,
and other corporate giants that rule the country.

By chance my involvement in that incipient transition was on
the waterfront, but it afforded the insight to comprehend the
similar process everywhere, then and later, from coast to coast,
and in the country's industrial heartland. To have taken part in
that process, even in a minor way and for a brief time, was to
have glimpsed something of the initiative and creative energy
exhibited by the American working class in that transformative

period. Without that glimpse it would have been difficult to understand much that happened in that decade.

On a more intimate plane were the personal associations. For me the free fraternity of those associations has rarely been equaled since. The more bizarre escapades might seem diversionary; yet these, too, are essential to a true portrayal of that distinct environment and its inhabitants. I like to think that from those associations I derived a broader range of human understanding and sympathy, and in some instances a more critical human discernment. I do not say this with greater certainty because in such matters we all are inclined to flatter ourselves. But if what I like to think is also true, it is not least in value among the things I learned on the waterfront.

VIII. Notes on the Revolution and the 1930s

WHAT ABOUT REVOLUTION in the 1930s? To display a revolution not begun may be more hazardous than to show an unfinished picture. A preliminary look at finished revolutions can be helpful.

Like humdrum human events, revolutions do not end where they begin. Revolutions are distinguished by the degree to which their ultimate attainments transcend the modesty of their initial impulses and objectives.

In the revolutions of the eighteenth century — the American and French — the progression from the beginning was impelled more by the logic of events than by the informed foresight of human consciousness. When the shots were fired at Concord and Lexington the American colonists did not realize that in little more than a year's time they would be waging war for independence instead of fighting for the redress of grievances as loyal subjects of the British Crown. And when the Bastille was stormed neither the mass of Parisians who joined the assault on the prison-fortress nor the nominal leaders of the incipient revolution anticipated that in less than four years the revolution would lop off a king's head at the top of the social pyramid and destroy the foundations of feudalism at the bottom.

Even then the appearance of pure spontaneity was deceptive. The thinkers of the Enlightenment had undermined the ideological rationales for feudal society and supplied the ideas and rhetoric for the emerging bourgeois order. And in the course of the revolutionary conflicts some participants perceived their nature more quickly and pushed with greater determination to the limits of the historically possible. So in the British colonies

Tom Paine helped create the popular consciousness that was given formal expression in the Declaration of Independence, and in France the Jacobins were most relentless in the insistence upon the most thorough demolition of feudal power.

Ideological make-ready and the appearance of vanguard elements in the eighteenth century were not of the same order as in the major popular revolutions of the twentieth century — the Russian, Chinese, and Cuban; the latter were distinguished by the qualitatively different prior consciousness of ultimate destinations among organized revolutionaries. Their awareness of revolution as a process did not dispense with the process, but it certainly enabled them to accelerate it, to act with greater purpose in projecting new objectives and more revolutionary means for their attainment.

In Russia the revolutionary progression was remarkably swift and clear: from the overthrow of the Czar (i.e., the rule of the feudal nobility) and the establishment of a bourgeois democratic republic in March 1917 to the overthrow of the bourgeois regime by the working class and its allies in November and the proclamation of the Soviet Socialist Republic. Although actual events, as Lenin noted, were "more original, more peculiar, more variegated than anyone could have expected," the development "on the whole" confirmed the Bolshevik perspective. In the Bolshevik program the overthrow of Czarism by a bourgeois democratic revolution was the indispensable precondition for subsequent advance to Socialist revolution. And if a unique constellation of circumstances made it possible to traverse an entire historical epoch in the brief span of eight months, undoubtedly Lenin's revolutionary genius and will were decisive in the leap from possibility to actuality.

In China the revolution was more protracted and its nodal points were not delineated so sharply, but throughout its course its most consistent exponents drew a distinct line between intermediate objectives and ultimate destination. In the quarter of a century before the establishment of the People's Republic one central idea was constantly reiterated (as it was, for example, by Mao in 1928): "At present China certainly remains in the stage of bourgeois democratic revolution . . . We must go through such a revolution before we can lay a real foundation for passing on to socialism."

In April 1945, four months before the Japanese surrender, Mao outlined a "general program . . . for the present stage and for the entire course of the bourgeois democratic revolution," spelling it out in basic economic terms affecting property relations.

In agriculture, to further national unity in the war against Japan, the Communists had substituted for their revolutionary program of "land to the tillers" the moderate reform of reducing rent and interest. This policy was justified by the exigencies of war. But Mao went further. "If no particular obstacles turn up," he said, "we are ready to continue this policy after the war; we shall first enforce reduction of rent and interest throughout the country and then adopt proper measures to attain gradually the aim of 'land to the tillers.'"

In industry "measures will be adopted to adjust the interests of labor and capital." To protect labor he proposed "a workday from eight to ten hours . . . unemployment relief and social insurance . . . safeguarding the rights of trade unions." For "properly managed" private capital "reasonable profit will be guaranteed."

The instrument for effecting the moderate program of economic reforms was to be "a coalition government," then the principal political slogan of the Chinese Communists. And this "bourgeois democratic revolution," Mao anticipated, "may last for several decades."

In China, as in Russia (and later in Cuba), the confluence of historical circumstances speeded the pace of development. Kuomintang-Communist negotiations for a coalition government broke down after World War II. Chiang Kai-shek (egged on by powerful United States interests) forced the issue to civil war. When the Communist armies were victorious and the People's Republic was proclaimed in 1949, the Socialist transformations that followed were far more rapid and thorough than Mao had indicated in 1945.

In Cuba Fidel Castro and his colleagues in the July 26th

Movement did not produce the prior theoretical elaborations that the Russian and Chinese revolutionaries did. True, early in 1957 the word "Socialist" was used as a self-descriptive term by Castro in an interview with Herbert Matthews of the *New York Times*, and it also appeared in a July 26 statement. But its usage was vague and enveloped in ambiguities so that the distinction between an a priori conscious purpose and "spontaneous" response to events is not easily discerned.

However, the initial goals proclaimed by the July 26th Movement came under the heading of what the Russians and Chinese called bourgeois democratic revolution. These goals included restoration of the Cuban Constitution of 1940 and realization of Cuban independence, political and economic. Proposed radical reforms in agriculture, industry, education, and social welfare did not transgress the essentially bourgeois democratic limits of the 1940 Constitution. Not until two years after the conquest of power was the revolution formally designated as Socialist; by then the label came after the fact.

Indeed, the contrast between the relative moderation of the original July 26 program and the Socialist course of the revolutionary government has been cited in accusations that Castro betrayed the Cuban revolution. But that is something like reproaching Lincoln for betraying his election promises of 1860 by signing the Emancipation Proclamation in 1863. Exigencies of revolution in Cuba (not least of which was Washington's hostility) were no less compelling than the exigencies of civil war in the United States. It is Castro's merit that his revolutionary consistency subsumed an apparent inconsistency in political program. And in a fundamental respect the inconsistency was more apparent than real; to realize the original objectives (most notably Cuban economic independence from the United States), it was necessary to transcend them. At this stage of history it is a patent illusion to conceive of a Cuban capitalism that would not inexorably become dependent, economically and politically, upon the capitalist colossus to the north. Therefore the elementary bourgeois democratic right, national independence, required a Socialist regime for its substantiation.

The preceding capsules of several revolutions are not novel. And the point they illustrate is not original. Still it is worth repeating that a key issue in any strategy for Socialist revolution is discernment of the transition to it, the delineation of intermediate objectives en route to the ultimate destination. In the contemporary revolutions mentioned, the transition could be defined with relative ease. Russia, China, and Cuba were burdened with problems that in the advanced capitalist countries were solved essentially (if not completely) in the eighteenth and nineteenth centuries, such problems as economic retardation rooted in an agrarian economy hobbled by feudal or semifeudal institutions and relations, national independence and unification, despotic rule. These problems provided the initial impetus in the transition, for in the twentieth century they could not be solved in the same way as they were in preceding centuries. And so Socialist revolutionaries undertook to perform historical services that in times past were performed by revolutionary bourgeois democrats, but being Socialists they did it differently and always with the awareness that such chores (eliminating feudal backwardness and oppression, consolidating national independence) were preconditions for realizing their ultimate goal: Socialist reconstruction of society.

In the advanced capitalist countries there is not the accumulation of the same problems to provide the flammable material for revolution. Transition to Socialist conquest has proved to be more elusive, more complex. For more than a century the best, most consistent, and dedicated revolutionary minds have contended with this problem, and their efforts have not been crowned with empirical success. These efforts represent a staggering expenditure of human thought, energy, devotion, courage, and sacrifice from the generation of Marx and Engels to the two generations since the emergence of the modern Communist movement in 1917–1919. With this background anyone who approaches the problem of revolutionary transition in an advanced capitalist country would do well, it seems to me, to do so with modesty (and this is so irrespective of seniority or the lack of it).

Without peremptory judgments and a priori assumptions it

would be most useful to study thoroughly and thoughtfully the very rich accumulation of experience, contending ideas, varied tactics, trials and errors, failures and successes (although for a revolutionary movement any success short of its ultimate goal is of necessity tentative and qualified).

In the United States the 1930s warrant special attention, for in many respects that decade marked the most advanced and sophisticated attempts to cope with problems of revolutionary transition. Unfortunately, however, many younger radicals view that decade as one big mess of blunder and opportunism that is best skipped. And even those who are not prone to such sweeping dismissal, who believe something may be learned from that decade, most often fail to approach it with the objectivity and concreteness that would be truly productive.

One might begin with the origins of the overall Left strategy of "United Front" and "People's Front" that took shape in the mid-1930s. This strategy was two years in the making, from Hitler's seizure of power in January 1933 to Georgi Dimitrov's report to the Seventh Congress of the Communist International in August 1935. The tragic debacle in Germany confronted the Left with questions. Why did it happen? How can similar catastrophes be averted? I remember how compelling these questions were for me and my immediate associates, how we welcomed the "People's Front" as the appropriate answer. To us it seemed the strategy of marshaling in one common front all forces opposed to fascism grew out of the anxious search in which we, along with millions of others, were engaged for two long years.

All this was brought back to me recently by the curt characterization of the People's Front as a Kremlin manipulation in a book by one of the more thoughtful and scholarly younger radicals, David Horowitz. His treatment was not original, of course, nor was my response. How different, I thought, is history as living experience.

My subjective reactions at the time might have little bearing on the origins of the People's Front, but there is also objective evidence. In France the Communists began to apply the

United Front policy in municipal elections in 1934. In fact, they were called up on the carpet for it before committees of the Communist International. In the same year the Communist youth organizations in the United States and France pursued what was, in effect, a Popular Front policy. (In the United States this policy guided Communist participation in the American Youth Congress, initially sponsored by such figures as Eleanor Roosevelt and New York's Mayor La Guardia; the young Communists sought to transform the congress into a formation that would unite the younger generation against fascism and war.) The American and French Communist youth leaders were under intense pressure in the Young Communist International to abandon their course and to acknowledge it was mistaken.

Such initiatives, undertaken when they still were at variance with official positions of the Communist International, demonstrate that the United Front and People's Front were sprouting at the grassroots before the Soviet Communists exerted their hegemonic influence in the final, authoritative formulation of the program that embraced these tactics. Indeed, in his concluding address to the Seventh World Congress Dimitrov acknowledged the importance of the French initiative in the decision-making process.

"We have not invented this task [creation of the People's Front]," he said. "It has been prompted by the experience of the world labor movement itself, above all, the experience of the proletariat in France." He added that by their pioneer united front "the French workers, both Communists and Socialists, have once more advanced the French labor movement to . . . a leading position in capitalist Europe . . . It is the great service of the French Communist Party and the French proletariat that by their fighting against fascism in a united proletarian front they helped to prepare the decisions of our Congress."

That, I believe, was no pro forma tribute. I was persuaded then (and still am) that Dimitrov's report articulated thoughts and conclusions of millions on the Left, Communists and non-Communists, all over the world. Certainly the energy and enthusiasm generated by the People's Front policy would indicate it was no externally imposed manipulation, that it accorded with Left assessment of political realities and needs in the respective countries. Of course the Popular Front dovetailed with the Soviet diplomatic pursuit of a collective security arrangement with the capitalist democracies to isolate and constrict the Nazi regime, either to strangle it in peace or defeat it swiftly and decisively if it resorted to war. But if one is opposed to dogma, one also should reject the dogma that anything conforming with Soviet interest automatically contradicts interests of the Left in the rest of the world.

With the passage of time and no little obfuscation, a definition of terms might be useful. As initially formulated United Front and People's Front described precise class alignments. United Front meant united action of the working class, and in the first instance of its political parties, Communist and Socialist. The People's Front was originally defined by Dimitrov as "a fighting alliance between the proletariat on the one hand, and the toiling peasantry and the basic mass of the urban petty bourgeoisie, who together form the majority of the population even in industrially developed countries, on the other." (In other renditions he included intellectuals in this formation.) In the United States the Dimitrov formula was modified to read: "a coalition of the working class, the toiling farmers, Negroes, and middle classes against capitalist reaction, fascism, and war." This was the constant formula and it should be noted it did not include capitalists, liberal or otherwise.

As projected the political platform of these fronts, United and People's, called for defeat of the Fascist threat and prevention of the world war then in the making. From the beginning, however, those formations were related to a transition to Socialist revolution.

In his report Dimitrov remarked, "Fifteen years ago Lenin called upon us to focus all our attention on 'searching out forms of *transition* or *approach* to the proletarian revolution.'" It may be that in a number of countries the *united front government* will prove to be *one* of the most important transitional forms." (The italics are Lenin's and Dimitrov's.)

In the United States a couple of years later Earl Browder discussed transition in more general terms. "Certainly," he said, "we are not indifferent to the problem of 'transition' from a victory over fascism to victory over the whole capitalist system, 'transition' to socialism. But the transition does not come from empty slogans, disconnected from everyday life. This transition arises upon the basis of the growing strength, organization, discipline, fighting power, and understanding of the working class, which gathers around itself as allies all other oppressed strata of the population — a working class which has learned how to meet in battle its worst enemies, today the Fascists and the monopoly capitalists, and to defeat them on the immediate issues of the day. It is not a discouraged, defeated, and demoralized working class that will take up and realize the great program of socialism; it is the enthusiastic, victorious, and organized workers who will move forward from victories in the defensive struggle to the offensive, and finally to socialism. Every strong defense passes insensibly to the offensive. To stop the retreat means already to prepare the advance. The defeat of fascism is the first precondition for the victory of socialism."

The mischief in the conception of an *insensible* passage from defense to offense will be dealt with later on. Here my concern still is with the larger transition. It was only touched upon in the above citations, speculatively by Dimitrov, and by Browder with generalities. Such treatment was symptomatic of the tentative and limited approach to the issue of transition in the formative phase of the People's Front strategy. What was consciously said about transition, it seems to me, is less than what was objectively inherent in the People's Front. Inherent was the kernel of an idea that, in my opinion, is indispensable to any fruitful search for forms of transition to revolution in the advanced capitalist countries. I would outline this idea as follows:

Bourgeois democracy arose as the political extension and reflection of free economic competition, suggested in the commercial imagery of the phrase, "a free marketplace for ideas." The operative term is "marketplace": a free marketplace for commodities, a free marketplace for ideas. In the beginning, property qualifications for holding office and voting officially stamped existing political institutions as arenas in which propertied interests freely competed. Popular struggle and movements expanded the franchise and modified this arrangement; without minimizing the significance of these modifications, still the power of property was sufficient to retain the essential character of the arrangement, to validate the characterization of the democracy as bourgeois.

With the advent and growth of monopoly, however, economic competition became and becomes increasingly restricted. Inevitably this economic reality finds its extension and reflection in the political realm, just as the former reality did in capitalism's salad days. The old rhetoric and the old forms are retained where possible because they are hallowed by tradition and invested with legitimacy, but the content is different. Increasing centralization of power (paralleling the increasing concentration of economic power) is characteristic of advanced capitalist countries. Occasionally, as with the Pentagon Papers, a glimpse is afforded of the clandestine, manipulative exercise of power by a tiny clique. Also prevalent are two significant tendencies: imposition of controls upon the working class to restrict the right to strike and to depress wages, and mounting subsidies for "technological renovation," which are, in fact, subsidies to cultivate and strengthen monopoly. (The economic logic is simple: "technological renovation," especially with contemporary technology, means machines and enterprises producing and marketing on an ever vaster scale. This, in turn, inevitably means bigger and fewer giants in each branch of industry.)

In a sense, the economic-political development has a cyclical character. Capitalism, in its advanced age, reverts to attributes of its childhood. In the beginning such vices as political despotism and economic constraint were embodied in feudal institutions; today similar vices, but in different forms necessarily, are embodied in the financial and industrial oligarchies. If in the economically backward countries of our century the initial impulse to Socialist revolution originated in the assault on feudal despotism and constraint, is it not possible that, in the industrially advanced countries, a similar impulse is to be found in assault on the comparable impositions of monopoly?

Recognizing vital differences in the two sets of circumstances, I still believe the answer is affirmative. Historically the People's Front was a pioneering effort to cope with the complexities implicit in the above question. It was a beginning, characterized by the trial and error that marks all beginnings. Mistakes and opportunistic compromises that attended implementation of a People's Front policy in the United States ought to be analyzed, criticized, and even condemned, if you will, but for maximum usefulness such exercises ought to confront the vital kernel in the People's Front concept.

In the spate of criticism heaped upon the People's Front there is much nonsense and a serious argument. Typical of the nonsense is a historical hallucination in which the working classes of the advanced capitalist countries (including the United States) were straining to make a Socialist revolution but were inhibited and diverted by People's Front projection of fascism, not capitalism, as the immediate target. Only two things are missing from this vision: (1) any serious conception of what makes revolution and (2) any serious comprehension of the relevant realities in the United States. As to the first point no one has improved on Lenin's observation that revolution is possible "only when the *'lower classes' do not want* to live in the old way and the *'upper classes' cannot carry on in the old way.*" Certainly President Roosevelt, utilizing the considerable economic reserves of United States capitalism, displayed the flexibility and skill to go on ruling in the old way (his reforms did not change the essence of rule). And his massive support among those sectors of the population that presumably should have been most ready for revolution (i.e., the working class, the black people, the unemployed) showed they had not concluded it was impossible to go on living in the old way.

The sophisticated critique of the People's Front began with an absolute truth: capitalism breeds fascism; only destruction of the source can irrevocably eliminate the consequence. Appended to this impeccable logic was a dubious addendum: by focusing on effect (fascism) rather than cause (capitalism) the

People's Front did not effectively come to grips with either. Most directly this argument centered on priorities of sequence in a given historical moment but it also joined more enduring issues: the relationship between the specific and the general, between the immediate and the ultimate, between beginning and end. And all these are essential issues of transition to revolution.

To me it seems the argument inverts beginning and end; it contravenes the historical experience of revolutions, all of which progressed from intermediate to ultimate objectives, and it also is at odds with what occurred in the 1930s. The call to an anti-Fascist front evoked a powerful response; it generated enormous political energy and motion. It represented a politics in which the Left moved, influenced, and led millions. It stimulated new levels of organization and alignment, new levels of consciousness, activating large numbers of people previously apathetic or, at best, on the periphery of political and social conflict. It provided the framework for rich and varied practical Left experience in mass organization, tactics, relationships between different classes and social groups. And this initial People's Front period, it must be remembered, lasted for only four years, 1935–1939, a brief moment in the historical time scale. Aside from periods of actual revolution I know of no other in which such vast political experience for such vast numbers was compressed in so short a time.

By all those signs in that particular time the People's Front proved to be an effective and viable *beginning* in the search for forms of transition or approach to revolution. If, however, the Left critics are mistaken, as I believe they are, in projecting the end (Socialist revolution) before the beginning (searching out forms of transition), there is also the hazard of confusing the beginning for the end, or more exactly perhaps of becoming so preoccupied with the beginning as to obscure the end.

This, too, can result in an absence of conscious confrontation with problems of transition. Instead it can produce Browder's thesis of the insensible passage from defense to offense. Insensible passages, being insensible, have no sense of direction. Insensibly, defense can pass to accommodation just as easily as to

offense, or it can insensibly oscillate between advance and retreat. Both accommodation and oscillation were manifested in
the United States. Horrible examples have been amply cited in
radical literature. Frequently these examples have been presented as inevitable consequences of Left engagement in coali-
tions with moderates for relatively moderate objectives. And
the conclusion was drawn that Left integrity is best guaranteed
by abstention from coalition politics. Instead of solving the
problem, such an approach only evades it.

In the two most significant popular revolutions since the
1930s, variations of the People's Front were very prominent.
Patently coalition was not a quicksand of opportunist compromise because the revolutions succeeded. The experience suggests that the problem is not, to coalesce or not to coalesce, but
the character of coalition, and how the Left retains independence and integrity and exerts influence in a coalition.

Undoubtedly the most remarkable example of united front
and coalition is presented by the Chinese revolution. The Chinese Communists learned about coalition the hard way. In
1924–1927 they were joined in a united front with the Kuomintang. The united front armies marched and fought from Canton
to Shanghai in a spectacular military campaign to overcome
feudal warlords and unify the country. When they reached
Shanghai in 1927 the Kuomintang and its leader, Chiang Kai-
shek, representing propertied interests and reaching an agreement with imperialist powers, suddenly ruptured the united
front, turned on their allies, and slaughtered thousands of
Communists or alleged Communists. In a mass slaughter political identification tends to be sloppy. Subsequently Chiang
launched campaign after campaign to encircle and annihilate
Communist forces that regrouped after the 1927 debacle and
established base areas.

Less than a decade later, applying the People's Front strategy, the Chinese Communists made the most energetic and persistent attempts to establish and maintain a united front with
the Kuomintang and Chiang, with those who had butchered
their comrades and tenaciously sought their total annihilation.
The emphasis of repetition is warranted: the Chinese revolu-

tionaries deliberately sought a united front with their executioners. They did so without any illusions about the ethics of the Kuomintang leaders, without any naivete about their past, about their behavior at the time or in the future.

In China, faced with aggression by Japan, the People's Front assumed the form of an "Anti-Japanese National United Front," a coalition that was proposed a few months after the Seventh World Congress of the Communist International. That the Chinese approach fitted in with the strategy outlined by Dimitrov was made clear by Mao when he said, "Not only in China but in the whole world it is necessary as well as possible to establish an anti-Fascist united front for a joint fight against fascism. Therefore we propose to establish a national and democratic united front in China."

That the united front entailed compromises was also made clear. In sum, as Mao put it, "to subordinate the class struggle to the present national struggle to resist Japan — that is the fundamental principle of the United Front." Subordinating the class struggle in agrarian China meant, first of all, muting the agrarian revolution, substituting reduction of feudal rent and interest for the distribution of land to those who tilled it. But it also meant moderating the demands of workers, necessarily so, because a united front between the Communists, the party of workers and peasants, and the Kuomintang, heterogeneous in its following but dominated by capitalist and landlord interests, was inconceivable without a mediation of contending class interests in the common objective of saving the country from Japanese conquest.

Communist persistence, pressure, argument, tactical flexibility, and selective concessions succeeded in creating an uneasy, contradictory united front with the Kuomintang. This policy extended from 1935 to the outbreak of civil war in 1946. Without going into all the twists in the eleven-year period, certain principal features may be noted.

First is the almost incredible persistence in the united front despite all obstacles, including occasional bloody armed clashes between its principals. The most notorious perhaps occurred in Southern Anhwei province in January 1941, when Kuomintang troops, attacking suddenly, killed 9000 soldiers of the Communist New Fourth army. After this incident and several related provocations by the Kuomintang, a Communist Central Committee directive to the party cautioned, "Throughout the country . . . we must oppose the erroneous appraisal of the situation to the effect that there is already a final split or will soon be a split between the Kuomintang and the Communist party, together with the many incorrect views arising from it."

Alongside the tenacious adherence to the united front was a constant remembrance of the 1927 experience. Thus, after the Anhwei episode, a public Communist statement emphasized, "The Chinese Communist party is no longer to be so easily deceived and destroyed as it was in 1927." Indeed, except for individual lapses as in Anhwei, the party kept its guard up, was always candid in recognizing the contradiction between cooperation and antagonism in its relationship with the Kuomintang. Two themes were recurrent: the absolute necessity of retaining autonomy and independence within the united front, and what Mao termed the unity of "solidarity" and "struggle," or the principle that the united front is maintained by struggle within it. The complex duality of that last principle was illustrated in Mao's advocacy of "a revolutionary dual policy towards the anti-Communist die-hards, i.e., a policy of uniting with them insofar as they are still willing to resist Japan and of isolating them in so far as they are determined to oppose communism.

"In their resistance to Japan the die-hards are again of a dual character; we adopt a policy of uniting with them insofar as they are still willing to resist Japan, and a policy of struggling against them . . . insofar as they vacillate. In their anti-communism the die-hards also reveal their dual character and our policy should be one of a dual character, too, i.e., insofar as they are still unwilling to bring about a final breakup of the Kuomintang-Communist cooperation, we adopt a policy of uniting with them and, insofar as they pursue a highhanded policy and make military offensives against our party and the people, we adopt a policy of struggling against them . . ."

In implementing so flexible a tactic, emphases constantly

shifted. In 1935, when the endeavor for a national united front was just begun, Mao said, "The present situation demands that we boldly give up closed-door sectarianism, form a broad united front and curb adventurism." Two years later, after the first formal announcement of Kuomintang-Communist cooperation, he said, ". . . the main danger . . . is no longer . . . closed-door sectarianism but . . . capitulationism." In the first instance the fire was aimed at obstacles to creating the united front, but once the united front came into being there was a new target: the danger of impermissible compromises that surrendered autonomy. Still later, in 1939–1940, when severe strains in the united front produced anticipations of its imminent rupture, Mao again shifted emphasis, "The main danger in the party at present is the mischief done by a 'Left' stand." Throughout, however, autonomy was retained, independent power was consciously reinforced, "a policy which integrates alliance and struggle" was followed.

When the united front was finally ruptured in 1946 the consequences were the exact opposite of what they had been in 1927. Instead of Chiang slaughtering the Communists, the Communists drove him from the mainland.

Even so brief a sketch of this political virtuosity, this superb blend of principled positions and tactical flexibility, shows how sterile are general admonitions against coalition, or against compromises, either with liberals or even corrupt reactionaries (you would have to look hard to find greater corruption and reaction than that of Chiang and his clique).

A similar observation is prompted by Cuba. In their fascination with guerrilla warfare many radicals totally ignore the revolution's politics. Not only was the original political platform of the July 26th Movement relatively restrained, but some five months before the revolution's military triumph the July 26th Movement signed a formal political agreement with nine other groups, which ranged from traditionally liberal to mildly radical. Both the participants and program of this coalition were of a People's Front character. Indeed, the single most conspicuous distinction from other People's Fronts was exclusion of the Communists.

No momentary aberration, this broad coalition policy stamped the provisional government installed after Batista fled and the rebel army commanded effective power in the country. The provisional President was Manuel Urrutia, a moderate judge who was distinguishable from other judges by his retention of judicial integrity during the Batista regime. The Prime Minister, José Miro Cardona, was Cuba's most successful criminal lawyer and president of the Havana Bar Association, professional distinctions that were hardly revolutionary. In its make-up the regime dramatized Castro's politics of the united front embracing all who had opposed Batista's tyranny. (Once again exclusion of Communists was conspicuous.) This regime was short-lived; as the revolution advanced, class and political differentiations emerged in the anti-Batista front, and corresponding alterations were made in the make-up of the government. But the all-inclusive nature of the anti-Batista front initially and its reflection in the first revolutionary government were salient features defining a distinct phase of the Cuban revolution.

I know the United States is not China or Cuba. I know the Chinese and Cuban revolutionaries waged armed struggle, carved out base areas, established what was, in effect, a dual power. I know that guerrilla warfare helped shape the political character, the ethics and relationships of the armed revolutionaries. But they represented only a minuscule fraction of the population. Beyond them were vast millions, who did not take up arms, but whose active support, or sympathetic neutrality at the very least, was decisive. To influence and activate those millions there was a politics that in its immediate, unifying objective — overthrow of the Batista tyranny or defeat of Japanese aggression — may be termed the politics of the lowest common denominator.

Yes, the United States is different, but for a serious Left the difference makes even more mandatory a politics that activates and unites millions. As has often been noted in radical literature, in the industrially advanced capitalist democracies ideological hegemony or persuasion is, for the present, more important than coercion in maintaining the authority of the existing regime. One may deplore manipulation, illusion, deception, but just the same millions participate, or think they participate in the political process. Here, consequently, the battle to change the consciousness of millions assumes even greater importance than in countries where coercion eclipses any pretense that government rests upon the freely given consent of the governed.

Changing the consciousness of millions requires a politics that *is*, rather than ought to be, relevant to them. It requires a politics that overcomes apathy and a sense of helplessness, that stimulates a self-realization that what people think is important and what they do can be effective. In a sense it requires the creation of an environment in which issues, events, conflicts are conducive to ideological mobility. Such an environment is created by objective circumstances (the economic crisis of the 1930s or the Vietnam war of the 1960s) and specific responses to these circumstances (the radical initiatives in the two decades). A distinction may be usefully drawn between the creation of the environment and Left behavior in it. The Left's ability to determine its own behavior is qualitatively different from its ability to shape the environment, which is decisively influenced by factors beyond its control. But the usefulness of the distinction goes beyond this basic fact. In the 1930s, for example, the Left indisputably contributed to creating an environment in which it could influence the minds of millions; controversy centers on what it did in the milieu it helped to make. Once a Left that numbers in the thousands aspires to a politics that is relevant to millions, and without this it is idle to talk of an environment for substantial ideological transformation, it inevitably confronts problems of alliance with those outside its ranks, and intermediate objectives that are the basis for alliance.

In such a confrontation, after making all the allowances for different circumstances, the Chinese and Cuban experiences may be useful. Although specific answers will differ, some of the essential questions are the same. These concern independence within an alliance, the freedom for the contest of ideas, retention and projection of a Left perspective that goes beyond the common objectives of the alliance, the exertion of ideological influence, and reinforcement of the Left. In considering these matters it is illuminating to relate their treatment abroad to what occurred in the United States in the 1930s.

Significantly, Chinese Communist assessment of their own history does not regard the united front with the Kuomintang in 1924–1927 as a mistake despite its catastrophic finale. On the contrary they refer to the period as the "First Great Revolution." What they do regard as a tragic mistake is that toward the end of that period their policy, as Mao put it, "was one of all alliance and no struggle."

I find this thought very helpful in assessing alliances made by the American Left in the 1930s, and most particularly the "Left-Center bloc" in the CIO, which was perhaps the most significant of all. Because the Left was an important factor in the CIO, this alliance, directly or indirectly, affected millions of workers in that era and the present-day American labor movement bears the residual traces.

An episode at the 1939 United Auto Workers convention may serve as an introduction to the complications of this united front. A delegation of national Communist leaders, headed by Earl Browder, descended on that convention to persuade Communist delegates to support R. J. Thomas, an incompetent opportunist, for the union presidency against George Addes, a militant who was associated with the Left in internal union poltics.

This episode was once cited as a horrible example of "Old Left" opportunism by Staughton Lynd, historian and radical activist who believes "it is desperately important" for the "New Left" to "come to grips" with the experience of the 1930s. But his own grip of this episode was not quite firm. He posed the question: Why did the Communist leaders do that? "The argument of the Left," Lynd replied, "was always labor unity." He went on with a long list of invidious questions: why did the Left do this and that? After each question came the refrain, "Because of labor unity."

Placed in this way "labor unity" has little relation to reality.

There was no labor unity. Two rival labor federations existed, the more militant CIO and the conservative AFL. True, as a general desideratum Communists advanced the slogan of "labor unity," but in the everyday conflict between the two federations they unequivocally supported the CIO. The general slogan of "labor unity" had nothing to do with the tactic in the auto union that insured election of Thomas. At stake was the Left-Center bloc. In this formula the Center was personified by such CIO leaders as Sidney Hillman of the Clothing Workers and Philip Murray of the Steelworkers. Thomas was the Hillman-Murray choice and the national Communist leaders acquiesced to it to safeguard the alliance. To learn anything from this incident it is no help to talk of "labor unity" in the abstract; it is necessary to examine a particular relationship, its origin, rationale, evolution, and consequences.

Loose and informal, the Left-Center bloc originated in a common endeavor to organize millions of workers in the country's basic industries in industrial unions. Was this a valid Left objective? Undoubtedly. And in the circumstances it could be achieved only by Left-Center cooperation. The Left could not do it alone, nor could the Center. A mutual recognition of this fact and a common commitment to getting the job done created the bloc. And, in the main, the alliance achieved its initial objective.

It is difficult to convey to young radicals, who only know the present-day labor movement and even this superficially, what organization of the unorganized meant to the Left of the 1930s. It meant creation of an elementary sense of power among the workers, manifested tangibly at first in their capacity, through united action and halting the productive process, to win some voice in setting the terms of their employment and labor. After generations in which unilateral settlement of these terms was regarded by the employers as an exclusive management prerogative, such a change represented a startling awareness and exercise of workers' power.

Unionization meant, in the historical evolution of the working class, the first great leap in consciousness, from unbridled competition among the workers to cooperation and solidarity.

It also provided more favorable conditions for expanding consciousness. When corporate despotism governed in the workplace it also embraced the culture and politics of the industrial communities. Free speech was a utopian notion. Any manifestation of radicalism or any other challenge to corporate domination was ruthlessly suppressed. In the classical remark by the mayor of Duquesne, even Jesus Christ could not speak for unions in that Western Pennsylvania steel town. Once union power curbed economic terrorism in industry workers also won a measure of democracy in the community, a degree of freedom to express and disseminate hitherto forbidden ideas.

Corporate resistance magnified the issue in the battle for unionization. According to the La Follette Senate Committee, employers were spending $80 million per year for spies, private armies and arsenals, and other devices to thwart unionism. Private instruments of violence were augmented by public means. Use of police and troops, state and federal, to break strikes and crush unions was a commonplace of American industrial history. For the Left capitalist behavior was irrefutable confirmation of the value it placed on union organization in the vital sectors of the American economy. Even without the social vision of the Left, John L. Lewis and others of the CIO Center couched their appeals in radical and militant terms, for they understood that a moderate summons could not arouse millions of workers from submission into battle against the odds they faced, to brave violence, hunger, and the loss of their livelihood if they did not prevail.

Did the adversaries in those industrial battles, frequently bitter and occasionally bloody, totally misjudge the issue between them? Was it all a response to a false alarm, the upheaval and conflict that swept industrial America? I think not. An end to corporate absolutism in relation to the workers and the formation of unions to shield and advance the economic interests of the workers — these, in themselves, were stakes sufficient for the magnitude and intensity of the conflict. But the march of the CIO also signaled the emergence of the working class as a vital, organized power on the American scene, not yet autonomous and not conscious of distinct class character and purpose, although the potential of such consciousness seemed near the surface. This potential inspired Left hopes and corporate fears, serving to sharpen the conflict.

Its own vision contributed to the idealism, energy, and devotion with which the Left threw itself into the CIO organizing drives. It may have been too sanguine in its expectations. Browder, for example, said, "The CIO marks the emerging of a conscious working class in American life." This larger vision did not materialize. Nonetheless the CIO's success remains the biggest single advance yet made by the American working class, a peak of creative initiative and militant solidarity, and a durable achievement.

If it had not been done then, the organization of the millions in the basic trustified industries would still be at the top of any serious radical agenda (without the benefit of hindsight), as it was for preceding generations of radicals. And if the Left today can focus much attention on problems of consciousness, on political and social issues transcending narrow economic interest, this is largely because the primary economic organizations of the workers were fashioned a generation ago and still provide the framework for dealing with immediate economic needs. (This, however, does not justify supercilious attitudes that have cropped up in some "New Left" quarters toward the workers' economic concerns or the assumption that economic issues have lost their potency as a source of class confrontation. I feel uneasy about theoretical profundities that boil down to something that was stated long ago much more lucidly and succinctly in the bromide, "Money can't buy happiness!")

Any new advance of the American working class, whatever forms it takes and however it reflects the changed composition of the laboring force, will proceed from plateaus attained by the CIO. Without understanding what the CIO meant in its time it is not possible to understand the commitment of the Left to the bloc with the Center or the internal evolution of the alliance.

A portent of things to come was revealed in June 1937 during the CIO's best days. Some Michigan Communists had criticized a Chrysler strike settlement by auto union leaders. They were severely rebuked by Browder in a report to the Communist Central Committee. There were no "intolerable compromises" in the settlement, he said, "there was merely a secondary problem of the impatience of certain leaders in dealing with the rank and file."

"But," he went on, "even if their fears had more solid foundations, it was necessary to proceed with much more tact, foresight, and consideration . . ." Consideration of what? He made this clear: "We are a fully responsible party, and our subdivisions and fractions do not independently take actions which threaten to change our whole national relationship with a great and growing mass movement . . . We do not attempt to estimate such difficult and complicated trade union problems [as the Chrysler settlement] by ourselves . . . but only on the basis of . . . discussion with our comrades-in-arms of the general trade union activities . . ."

Two points in the message were implicit. Even if a contract was bad the Left should refrain from criticism if the criticism threatened to disturb the Left-Center bloc at the top. And the Left should estimate such agreements, not independently, but only in consultation (and, implicitly, agreement) with the Center.

Here a Chinese treatment of a variation of this position is pertinent. In roughly the same period one Communist leader advanced the slogan, "Everything through the united front." Both Liu Shao-chi (subsequently the number-one scapegoat in the Cultural Revolution of the mid-1960s) and Mao said that in practice this meant securing prior agreement of Chiang Kai-shek before doing anything. "As the policy of the Kuomintang is to restrict our development," Mao said, "there is no reason whatever for us to put forward such a slogan, which merely binds us hand and foot."

Very definitely the policy of Hillman and Murray, like the Kuomintang's, was to restrict the development of the Left. And "everything through the united front" within the CIO also had the effect of binding the Left hand and foot. The injunction to the Left after the Chrysler settlement controversy contained strong elements of "everything through the united front." Just as the Left-supported election of R. J. Thomas to the auto union presidency entailed some hand-and-foot binding.

The Thomas choice was also revealing in its methodology. From the testimony of Wyndham Mortimer, who was intimately associated with the Communists as a founder and early militant leader of the auto union, it is clear the Communist decision was made at the top after consultation with the Hillman-Murray combination. But there was no prior consultation with the Communist auto workers, who were most intimately acquainted with conditions in the union and the industry. They did not participate in making the decision although the burden for implementing it would be theirs, they would have to live with its direct consequences and would be held accountable for them by their fellow workers. The governing consideration was the Left-Center bloc at the top, or more specifically the relationship with Hillman and Murray, and this same consideration inevitably produced the same methodology in other situations. The bureaucratic method was poorly designed to cultivate Left independence or build Left strength in the respective unions.

From Chrysler and Thomas it was no great leap to Left self-abnegation at the 1940 CIO convention where Communists and their close associates voted for a resolution that declared: "We neither accept or desire — and we firmly reject consideration of any policies emanating from totalitarianism, dictatorships, and foreign ideologies such as nazism, communism, and fascism. They have no place in this great modern labor movement. The Congress of Industrial Organizations condemns the dictatorships and totalitarianism of nazism, communism, and fascism as inimical to the welfare of labor, and destructive of our form of government."

To accentuate the humiliating irony Lee Pressman, a lawyer whose Communist affiliation was an open secret, had to perform the formal chore, as secretary of the convention's resolutions committee, of moving adoption of this anti-Communist declaration.

Having swallowed that bucket of castor oil in 1940 the Left could not very well gag at a pill in the 1946 CIO convention.

Here the Left (including Communists) participated in drafting a unanimously adopted resolution that said: "We resent and reject efforts of the Communist party or other political parties and their adherents to interfere in the affairs of the CIO. This convention serves notice that we will not tolerate such interference." (The reference to "other political parties" was demagogy. The convention stage swarmed with Democratic party dignitaries wearing the mantle of government office, and the intervention of the Roosevelt and Truman Democratic administrations in CIO affairs was notorious.)

When the Left-Center rupture finally came in 1947 and Murray turned on his erstwhile allies to flay and slay them, it was, if a Chinese parallel may be invoked again, 1927 for the Left and not 1946. The Left was decimated and depleted. It did not even have the will to regroup. For the next quarter of a century (up to this writing) the Left in labor was a scattering of tiny fragments, isolated islands. Not since the formation of the AFL in the 1880s was there ever so long a period when the Left was so impotent in the American labor movement.

At each point of the CIO story there was, of course, a credible tactical argument, hinged on preservation of the Left-Center bloc, for the position taken. Viewing it all in historical perspective, however, it is difficult not to conclude that in their sum those positions represented a rape of principle by tactic. And in the end what profit was there in the shrewdness of the tactic? The question concerns more than narrow self-interest. Patently surrender of independent positions and compromises of principle eroded Left strength and moral authority, but did not these concessions also vitiate the character of the CIO as a militant, progressive movement? The more the Left conceded, it might be said, the less it contributed to the CIO and the less it got for itself. True, it retained nominal leadership in several unions that claimed a total of 900,000 members, but fundamentally it was weaker at the termination of the alliance than it was at the beginning.

I am intrigued by a coincidence. At just about the time that the Left engaged in self-flagellation at the 1940 CIO convention the Chinese produced this previously cited formula: "Insofar as they [Kuomintang leaders] are still unwilling to bring about a final breakup of the Kuomintang-Communist cooperation, we adopt a policy of uniting with them and, insofar as they pursue a highhanded policy and make military offensives against our party and the people, we adopt a policy of struggling against them." As intriguing as the coincidence is the question it suggests: was it feasible to devise an effective American variant of this delicate duality, this flexible combination of alliance and struggle, in the CIO Left-Center relationship?

It is a tragedy of the American Left that the CIO experience has fallen between two stools. The "Old Left" (with some exceptions), prone to nostalgic revels in the glories of the CIO's heyday and understandably bent on insuring the historical credits that are its due, has not come to grips, critically or analytically, with its experience. And the "New Left," for the most part, has been too obsessed with negative aspects of the experience to confront it with critical objectivity. Scattered efforts made by the "New Left" have not avoided the pitfall of hindsight, which may be described as a failure of historical empathy, an inability to apprehend people and events in their historical context with its particular imperatives.

A generic condemnation of the Left for entering into a bloc with the CIO Center, it seems to me, misses the whole point; it substitutes the illusion of an easy solution (abstention from such a bloc) for the reality of a difficult problem (how to behave in such a bloc). Historically, I believe, the bloc, especially in 1936–1939, was as valid, in American terms, as the Communist-Kuomintang alliance in 1924–1927. And if the latter has been called the First Great Revolution, the former may be more modestly called the First Great Upsurge. The fatal flaw of Left policy, as I see it, was that it became "all alliance and no struggle."

Like any generalization this one only approximates the truth. Given the contradictions between the Left and Center, conflicts arose. The generalization is valid only to the extent that conflicts were inconsistent and at the top were subsumed by the alliance. Thus, it is not altogether true to say as Staughton Lynd said: "The Left sought to salve its ideological conscience by passing resolutions. Little was done about these resolutions, but 'one took a position!' and that was felt to be significant." This picture does not encompass the long, intense, wearying battles in countless local unions and councils throughout the country. Many of these battles related to both action and a more heightened consciousness among the workers.

Certainly this was true in battles against racist prejudices and barriers. The National Maritime Union was an example, a very striking example because racist prejudice exploited the uniqueness of the seafaring crafts in which men not only worked together but lived together. Drawing on personal experience I encountered the racist argument, "On a shoreside job I wouldn't mind working with them, but on a ship you got to sleep and eat with them." To think that a breakthrough against such prejudice was achieved without the most intense struggle is un-American fantasy. And to belittle this breakthrough and others in their time is to misconstrue totally the presence and effects of racism in American life. One cannot come to grips with this experience by patronizing references to ideological conscience-salving.

(I might interject here that, in general, Left exploration of what then was called "the Negro question" represented the most important single contribution to American radical theory yet made. The perception of the national character of the black liberation struggle was a great leap from prior radical approaches, which were crudely racist at worst, and at best humanist or marked by the simplistic class analysis that the condition of blacks was just part of the overall working-class condition. True, black nationalist leaders had overtly expressed aspirations of black people as a people, but being nationalists they did not relate black liberation to any total conception of Socialist revolution. On this last score the Left of the 1930s pioneered; recognizing the autonomy of the black liberation struggle, it simultaneously comprehended the struggle as a dynamic, integral element in any general strategy of Socialist revolution. Despite rigidity and errors this Left initiative blazed a new trail for radical theory and set new standards for radical practice.)

A common complaint against the Left was that it constantly injected "extraneous" political issues into union affairs, such issues as the war in Spain, the Japanese aggression against China and the Italian aggression against Ethiopia, and more generally the issues of war and fascism. The frequency and irritability of the complaints suggest that to argue for union concern with such issues, and not only with "porkchops," was already to fight for a higher level of consciousness than was prevalent at the time. By joining these issues the Left was not salving its conscience, it was articulating its true consciousness. And these thousands of small deeds ought to be taken into account along with such big phenomena as the mortification at the 1940 CIO convention. The valid overall generalization of "all alliance and no struggle" was modified by contradiction in actual life.

Contradiction also beset such Left efforts as were made to project a Socialist alternative. These were handicapped by the rigid contours of the Left's own vision. Typically, a 1936 national Communist convention resolution contained these formulations: "for a socialist revolution and Soviet power — the only road to socialism" and "for a Soviet America." This position can only be understood in the context of its time. Initially in the revolution and later on in the contrast with the cataclysmic economic crisis in the capitalist world the Soviet example possessed an enormous power of attraction. Moreover, the substance of Soviet power, as distinct from the particular form that gave it its name, contained features (e.g., dual power) that are indispensable to revolution. Millions throughout the world were, in fact, won for a Socialist vision under that slogan. Just the same the insistence that the only existing model of Socialism is also the only possible model was theoretically wrong and tactically alienating. The enormous damage done by the model fixation defies precise measure.

After 1936 the "for a Soviet America" slogan was dropped. It vanished without a trace of thoughtful theoretical explanation. Nor was there a theoretical elaboration of an alternative at the time. What existed was a vacuum — or the lively ghost of the old slogan. The resultant ambiguity impaired the communication of a Socialist vision. And for those who had it the relevancy of it was obscured, for the ambiguity obstructed a systematic, consistent exposition of the relationship between the earnest pursuit of immediate objectives and an ultimate destination. The transition became nebulous. Undoubtedly this state of affairs intensified the powerful and ever-present pressures for total immersion in the issues of the moment with the Socialist vision relegated to the back of the mind or the tail of an omnibus resolution.

A theoretical gap existed, and coupled with the tactical accommodations exemplified in the CIO Left-Center bloc, it contributed to an inability to create a larger, more durable and viable Socialist constituency. The relative weight of these lapses is incalculable among all the other factors that were heaped on the scales, including the momentous events that soon followed: World War II, the postwar economic boom, the cold war, McCarthyism. To consider just one of these, the effects of the war upon internal politics in the United States and on the European continent were diametrically opposite. In continental Europe the governing classes led their respective nations to the disaster of defeat and subjugation by the Nazis. The Left inspired and led the resistance to the Nazis and their collaborators. In the United States the governing class was in command during the war and people of the Left were loyal troops in the ranks. To accentuate this relationship the Left, in the name of its valid commitment to defeat of the Nazis, was subordinated so completely to the Commander-in-Chief, President Roosevelt, that its independent identity was increasingly smothered. Indeed, the reason for its existence as a political entity was compromised. The extent to which these things occurred was symbolized by the dissolution of the Communist Party, still the hegemonic influence in the American Left.

Opposite circumstances, opposite consequences. In several European countries the Left emerged from the war as a major or dominant force; in the United States it was compromised and weakened in its most important constituencies, the working class and the black community, and beset by an internal crisis.

Origins of Left wartime policy can be traced, of course, in

the prewar trends. I have chosen to concentrate on the Left-Center bloc in the CIO because it was the most tangible and vital in the complex of united front relationships. I believe, for example, that subordination of the Left to the Center within the bloc exerted a major, probably a decisive, influence on the Left attitude toward the Roosevelt administration. But any serious treatment of that relationship, culminating in Left dependency upon Roosevelt, would require a separate examination.

In the CIO bloc the validity and the perils of a united front were strikingly illuminated. Because I believe that comprehension of the united front is indispensable in the search for a transition to Socialist revolution, I think the experience warrants thoughtful study. The important point is not to arrive at retroactive judgments of what the Left should have done. The point is to arrive at a better understanding of what needs to be done now. As the contemporary Left attempts to engage in a politics of the millions, it will encounter opportunities and difficulties comparable to those of the 1930s. If this is true, what was and was not done then has relevance.

IX. Journalism

NEITHER THE MANNER OF MY ENTRY into journalism nor the nature of my apprenticeship is anything you will find in conventional newspaper memoirs.

In the autumn of 1934 the Communist party's Political Bureau, conducting a perennial review of the *Daily Worker*, was disturbed by what it saw as an imbalance in the paper's personnel. Several very bright young men had recently been added to the staff (I can recall Edward Newhouse, who did sports for the *Worker* and later did other things for *The New Yorker*; David Ramsey, a competent economist; Theodore Draper, who came on as assistant to Foreign Editor Harry Gannes and later became an academic historian of American communism). That the paper had new, young talent was good, in the bureau's judgment, but that these acquisitions were all intellectuals straight out of the university was bad. They had to be leavened with young people who had, in the bureau's terminology, mass experience in working-class struggle. To fill this need Gil Green, leader of the Young Communist League, nominated a fellow named Leo Thompson, who had organized automobile workers in the Midwest, and me.

My first job on the paper was editing workers' correspondence. Each day almost a full page (standard, not tabloid) was filled with correspondence from workers in industry. Different days of the week were regularly devoted to specific industries or related industrial groups; it could have been mining (metal, as well as coal) and oil extraction on Monday, transportation and communication on Tuesday, and so on.

If a piece of correspondence included a name and address these were entered on an index card. I had some 600 such cards, filed alphabetically, and when the correspondent was in an important industry a metal tab was clamped to the card, the color of the tab denoting the industry; it might have been, for instance, red for transportation, or blue for steel. When a major development occurred in an industry I pulled the appropriate cards and sent a query to the correspondents on effects and reactions in their locale.

Some correspondence exposed an exceptionally noxious condition or practice. On rare occasions just the exposure brought a remedy. I remember a complaint by women in a Kentucky tobacco plant about being frisked by male guards when they left work. The guards were supposedly looking for stolen cigarettes, but the eagerness with which they pawed the women, their anatomical range and selected emphases, suggested sins other than pilferage or smoking. Publication of the correspondence halted this orgiastic protection of private property.

The end of 1934 and most of 1935, the time I presided over workers' correspondence, also marked its heyday. The source of supply was vastly expanded as, with the economic pickup of those years, workers who had come under Communist influence in unemployed battles returned to industry. By 1936 such correspondence was virtually dead, for these militants were swept up in the great wave of union organization; by then, if they had a grievance they were not prone to write about it to the *Daily Worker*, having more effective means for its redress, either through direct action at the point of production or through their union machinery.

My first tutor in journalism was an erudite leprechaun I knew as "Trick" Lewis (later on he used the by-line Ben Levine). Trick worked nearby for Fairchild Publications, publisher of *Women's Wear Daily* and other apparel trade journals. On several late afternoons of the week, when he finished his stint with cloaks and suits, he transposed himself into the editorial citadel of social revolution to instruct me in the rudiments of copy reading, headline writing, typography, and layout. He was a journeyman.

I've since thought it fortunate to have broken into editing with workers' correspondence. This may evoke the old medical practice of breaking in surgeons at hospitals for the poor, and possibly, wielding my pencil like a scalpel, but clumsily, I occasionally did butcher the correspondence of some unfortunate worker. I refer to good fortune in another sense. Regardless of editing that had to be done (for conciseness, word usage, construction, or spelling) a prime value of the correspondence was its authenticity, making it essential to retain its flavor and originality, its genuine emotion, for the workers often illustrated the rule that is supposed to govern writers of letters to newspapers: they do not take pen in hand except in anger. And the workers had much to be angry about.

If I had begun on the copy desk, armed with delegated authority and a pencil, I would have made certain that all copy I handled conformed with the paper's editorial policies and rules of style. With workers' correspondence the demand for conformity was not so rigid, there was more flexibility and latitude in style and policy.

I was consequently helped in avoiding the great temptation of an editor, which is to exaggerate God's conceit by recreating everything in his own image, so all that passes through his hands sounds as if he had written it (or, if he cannot write, as he would have written it if he could). Indeed, publications that make the greatest claim to divine omniscience exhibit the most extreme uniformity in style, an observable phenomenon that cuts across national and ideological boundaries. I escaped this magnetic lure, and I also was given more opportunity to cultivate an essential element of the editorial art, which is to help people say best what *they* want to say in the mode most natural to them.

At the time I did not fully appreciate this fortuitous advantage in my education, but I did appreciate other benefits. The correspondence, in the aggregate, afforded a kaleidoscopic view of the American working class at a vivifying moment in its history. The rebellion of the workers was on the rise, and so the correspondence not only depicted the abysmal condition in American industry, which reached a nadir in the Great Depression, it also articulated the aggressive discontent, the new militancy, the discovery of power. Moreover, whereas much of the paper served as a conduit for the top, the Communist leadership, I was in the position to channel the flow from the opposite direction, from the bottom, from the American industrial vastness. Having just come off the waterfront, where the influences of "rank-and-filism" were pervasive, I was particularly impressed with the importance of this position.

About an incidental sideline of my job I was ambivalent. Every newspaper, I suppose, attracts its quota of the disturbed and unbalanced. Whenever someone turned up who seemed to fall into one of those categories and did not have a story that readily fitted into the paper's definition of news, he (or she) was shunted off on me. The rationale was that maybe I could extract something suitable for workers' correspondence. Sometimes I did manage to dig out a squib for publication; mostly I had to listen to long, involved tales of personal misfortunes, of persecutions and humiliations that afforded insights into the inhumanity of our social order or may have served as raw material for a creative writer, but did not fit into the restricted norms of what's fit to print in a newspaper. Sometimes these interviews ended with my doling out some coins, maybe for carfare to the offices of an organization or agency that could help with a given problem, or just for food. My wages did not really allow for the luxury of philanthropy.

Because workers' correspondence was an autonomous department and my tutor was not employed by the *Worker* I was functionally isolated from the rest of the staff. Even physically I was as far removed as I could be from the newsroom, the hub of any paper, and still remain on the editorial premises, placed at a desk in a corner of a large room that also housed the receptionist. In the line of duty my one daily encounter with the editorial mechanism came when I presented the proof of my page to James Casey, the managing editor, a gray-haired, near-sighted little man who squinted at the page through thick lenses to ascertain, among other things, that "tool" appeared in no headline. In party agitation the word was used often as a variety of people were designated tools of the bosses, economic and political, and it cropped up in workers' correspondence.

But on the *New York Times,* from which Casey transferred to the *Worker* with much fanfare as a portent of greater professional excellence, "tool" was banished from headlines (except in its narrowest meaning: a hammer, for instance, or a machine tool) because of its earthier colloquial usage. Casey impressed upon me the tool taboo — and nothing else.

For almost a year my relationship with other staff members resembled the kind that is common among tenants in a New York apartment house, a nodding acquaintance at most. About mid-1935 I began to get reportorial assignments, which brought me within the staff ambit. My social life was still spent largely with waterfront friends, but during working hours I was drawn into the staff environment, different from any I had known, one in which there was a vocational preoccupation with ideas and intellectual trends.

The big event of 1935 in our lives was the Seventh World Congress of the Communist International. Among the congress mandates was one that Communists display sensitivity to national feeling, project their identification with progressive national tradition and culture, expose the posture of Fascists as champions of the nation's heritage and interests. Earl Browder's pursuit of this vein culminated in the immodest motto, "Communism Is Twentieth-Century Americanism," which was subsequently withdrawn because it obliterated seamier sides of national history (slavery, for instance) and represented "Americanism" as a classless epitome of good. Despite such excesses, Browder's initiative provided a greater stimulus for exploration of America, its past, its institutions and traditions, its culture, its people, the sources and influences that molded them.

Not that all this began from point zero; we were, after all, products of this country, enveloped by its culture, but there was an unprecedented ferment about it, a new sense of purpose. I felt the excitement of a fresh voyage of discovery. Even men I had read before and much admired — Twain and Whitman, for example — could be read anew to divine fresh meaning in search for clues to the American character, for psychological insights into the national amalgam. I found then Vernon Parrington's history of the main currents in American thought, uncovering intellectual vistas I had not known were there. By a happy coincidence I also first read at that time the classics of the economic determinist school, Gustavus Myers' *History of the Great American Fortunes* and Charles A. Beard's *An Economic Interpretation of the Constitution,* and read them with a more critical intelligence than I would have earlier. In part, the atmosphere on the paper, the conversational themes and incidental references, provided a greater incentive than I otherwise might have had for such intellectual pursuits. That they took the turn they did was due to the influence of the Seventh World Congress and its effects in the United States.

The primary thrust of the Congress was, of course, the popular front strategy. An offshoot of that was the *Sunday Worker,* our boldest venture into popular journalism. I became the paper's news editor immediately after its first edition, January 12, 1936. As conceived this Sunday paper was to reach for the mass audience created by independent Communist influence, and by the network of cooperative relations with others, foremost in the tidal wave of union organizing campaigns and strike battles, but also in the Workers Alliance, the still-formidable organization of the unemployed, and in a variety of other vital movements in the black community, among the youth, in the cultural realm, in politics. This audience was estimated in the hundreds of thousands. The *Daily Worker's* circulation was in the 30,000 range.

The weekday paper, it was tacitly agreed, would continue to serve as the explicit, comprehensive, and authoritative exponent of the party's policy, aiming primarily at party activists and cadre in related movements. The Sunday paper was to reach into the great beyond, to the vast number of those others who were sympathetic, responsive, and peripherally involved. For me, then twenty-two and fascinated by the craft I was still learning, the new paper was a challenging adventure. It is a recurrent dream of most journalists with a cause to break the frustrating barrier between what is and what they fervently believe could be, to attract the audience they sense is there but somehow remains just beyond their grasp. We were going to do it.

Named editor of the new paper was Joseph North, brought in from the *New Masses* with a reputation for editorial talent and skill, for under his direction that magazine had gained prestige and influence in the American intellectual sphere. Although I had not known North I saw his appointment as an earnest of the serious determination behind the vision for the new paper. He turned out to be a friendly bear of a man, not an overwhelming grizzly but a more modest specimen of the family *Ursidae*. He had engaging simplicity and good humor, an apparent naiveté frequently dispelled by a knowing, quizzical expression and by his perceptions of irony and paradox. More important for the task at hand he had much enthusiasm and energy. I had been on the *Daily Worker* for more than a year, but not until my association with him did I feel the intimate camaraderie of men joined together in a great undertaking.

He was older, more experienced and knowledgeable, and I looked to him as a mentor. I derived something from him about the exercise of imagination in searching for the angle, the added dimension, the dramatic fillip that transcends the conventional limits of a story. He was fond of repeating a variation of an old maxim, "Genius is an infinite patience for detail," which is not an adequate definition, and in the absence of genius it just means much drudgery. We worked very hard.

A weekly publication falls into a rhythm of its own. The first couple of days are relaxed, contemplative, and conversational; at midweek the pace picks up; by the last day it is a mad race to the deadline. With Joe's infinite patience for detail there was much reading and rereading of proofs, which was fair enough, but not so fair were last-minute changes in the text or layout of completed pages. Sometimes the final day stretched into twelve or more grueling hours. When it was over we retired to an Italian restaurant and the opening toast always was, "Food is good and life is beautiful."

This is how we felt. We drank the red wine to life as it was just then, to that era, to its portents and hopes, sure of our responses to the rhythm of this time, for in it we heard our own beat. We drank to the industrial rebellion that erupted in 1934 and was still gathering strength. By early 1936, the time of our toasts, the elemental working-class revolt, hitherto scattered and sporadic, had created its central command post, the CIO, and found its most articulate tribune, John L. Lewis. Launched only a few months earlier, in November 1935, as an alliance of eight AFL unions, with Lewis' United Mine Workers supplying the backbone, the CIO was dedicated to organization of the workers in the country's basic production enterprises along industrial union lines.

The Lewis-led formation was born as the Committee for Industrial Organizations; later on, after the committee's component unions were suspended by the AFL, they (except for David Dubinsky's International Ladies' Garment Workers' Union, which returned to the AFL manger) and additional adherents retained the original initials in a metamorphosis into the Congress of Industrial Organizations, an independent labor center with a structure of state and local councils that paralleled and rivaled the AFL's. At the beginning CIO's primary target was steel, kingpin of American industry. To generations of labor militants steel was the key to a general union offensive, and for them the timid deference of the reigning AFL hierarchy to the steel trust's "No Trespassing" signs was a prime symbol of prostration before the industrial status quo. CIO's first major initiative was formation of the Steel Workers Organizing Committee with Philip Murray in command and a front-line staff that soon numbered 200 organizers.

Having determined to do battle with the corporate giants in their industrial domains, Lewis was realist enough to know that the power represented by the eight-union alliance, the money and organizers at its command, was not enough to prevail. He would need all the effectives he could enlist with the commitment and capacity for this sort of battle. Under his direction the new CIO headquarters in Washington opened its doors to all volunteers for the industrial wars without political or ideological screening tests; the sole qualification was fitness for the combat at hand. Old antagonisms and recriminations were forgotten. As his adjutant, titled CIO director of organization, Lewis installed John Brophy, a man who had opposed him for the mine union presidency a decade earlier as the standard bearer of an insurgent coalition that conspicuously included Communists. The CIO public relations post went to Len De Caux, a veteran labor journalist whose sympathies and associations with Communists were no secret.

With his uncanny sense of drama and timing Lewis signaled in these first appointments the burial of old enmities, a readiness to cooperate with all who would join in doing what had never been done before, unionization of the country's major industries controlled by the oligopolies that dominated the national economy. At the time it seemed like a miraculous transfiguration. No figure in the American labor movement had been more detested by Communists than Lewis; he was the supreme autocrat, a conservative Republican in politics, a compromising moderate in the economics of the coal industry, the misleader who presided over the near-disintegration of the once mighty miners' union. So we regarded him, and we did not keep our portrait private, it was disseminated in vitriolic tracts. And Lewis responded in kind. Ruthless, unscrupulous, he employed his rare oratorical gifts, his impressive public presence, his tactical skills, the powers of his office, and the muscle at his disposal to crush Communists and all other opponents, to drive them out of the miners' union.

All those acrimonies of the 1920s were interred by the fraternity of common endeavor in the mid-1930s. Lewis' stature at that historic moment is not diminished, nor is his breadth of vision or generosity of spirit, by noting that Communists brought something of inestimable value to the informal compact. They offered more than dedicated and competent personnel for the CIO organizing staffs. In the steel mills and auto plants, the principal fortresses the CIO proposed to storm, on the waterfronts, in the woods and mills of the Pacific Northwest, in enterprises as different as electrical machinery plants and newspaper offices, Communist initiative and leadership had been instrumental in creating such union organizations as existed, embryonic or full-blown, when the CIO came upon the scene. If Communists supplied much of the sinew and intelligence, particularly at the base and also at varied levels of leadership, at the apex Lewis' magnificent eloquence articulated the aspirations and militancy of the millions drawn to the CIO standard. His captaincy directed and inspired the assaults upon the citadels of industrial serfdom.

A simple, traditional toast should not require so involved an explanation, but all this was very much part of the life to which we drank. And it was related to the paper Joe and I had just put to bed. In the unprecedented upsurge of millions of workers, with Communists as a dynamic force, it seemed that by striking the right popular chord it was surely possible to create, for the first time since the old *Appeal to Reason*, an American Socialist paper with a mass circulation.

Although I yielded to no one in zeal and effort I was the fourth wheel of our editorial vehicle. The others, aside from Joe, were James Allen, a scholarly, serene man who did the serious political commentary and analysis, and Edwin Seaver, a novelist with an air of wistful preoccupation, who was our literary critic, and also the resident dilettante. One morning, when there was much work for all, he did not show. Arriving in the afternoon to be greeted with, "Where the hell were you, Eddie?" he replied he had been strolling in Central Park and it was not time altogether wasted; he had dropped in at the zoo and seeing the lions he was struck with the sudden revelation that good prose should not be constructed brick upon brick, it should move with the sinewy grace of a lion. How can you scold a man like that?

Two other men were essential to production: Sam Shaw, a mercurial bundle who flitted over from the art department of the *Brooklyn Eagle* to design our magazine pages, and Lew Levinson, the all-purpose house writer. Shaw, later on, turned out to be a collector. Other people collect stamps, butterflies, or even match covers, but Shaw's hobby was more exotic: he collected geniuses. Levinson wrote.

Prolific, versatile, indefatigable, Levinson wrote. Once, I was told, he wrote for Street & Smith, premier publisher of pulp magazines, and books. On occasion he kept four serials going in as many Street & Smith magazines, and his output peaked to 90,000 words in a week. Watching him work I believed it. He used at least four by-lines, each for a different genre, ranging from Benjamin Cardozo for punditry to Annette Castle for what the trade calls the sob-sister story.

In the beginning we had a rotogravure section that wrapped around a magazine and a news section. Our circulation peak, in excess of 100,000, was attained in mid-February with a full-page rotogravure cover photo of Joe Louis, bearing the legend: *The Battle of the Century: Joe Louis vs. Jim Crow.* A month later it was a winsome, dimpled, white child on the cover, and underneath: *The Truth About Shirley Temple.*

"I know it is difficult to make outsiders believe that there is anything tragic in a child whose earning capacity is as high as $30,000 a week," wrote "Annette Castle" about the film prodigy. "But to me . . . no greater tragedy exists than the lost childhood of Shirley Temple."

Little did Levinson (or Joe, or I) realize how difficult it would be to make the Temple tragedy credible to the special group of "outsiders" who occupied the floor above us. In our nine-story building the paper's offices were on the eighth floor, and above, in the rooms at the top, was national Communist headquarters. Down came Jack Stachel, who served as political overseer for the *Worker,* daily and Sunday. Stachel had a sophisticated, complex mind, some even called it devious, but he also could exhibit dogged passion in belaboring the obvious.

With all the children slaving in the agricultural fields, he thundered, how could you shed these tears for Shirley Temple, how could you make this pampered doll a symbol of child labor? He knew he had us dead to rights there and he didn't let up; embroidering this theme, contriving variations upon it, he played it, relentlessly, in brass. Levinson, a mild-mannered man and no political heavy, went limp. The rest of us were silent. Only Gerhart Eisler, the German Communist who accompanied Stachel, partially meliorated the crushing atmosphere. Eisler was an anti-Nazi exile and a Communist International representative. "You can write about anything," Eisler said. "There are no forbidden subjects. Only write about them from a Marxist standpoint."

(Incidentally, from several encounters with him that year Eisler certainly did not warrant the sinister aura created around Communist International representatives. His function, as I observed it, was consultative, not commanding. He was a man with vast culture and a greater breadth of spirit than many of his American colleagues. In one talk to the staff he projected two needs: the need for passion and the need for study, research, thought. You must read, he said, and then to underscore the point he searched for the English equivalent of what in German is "sitting flesh," or flesh you sit on, finally blurting out, "Half of genius is the ass!")

From the references to Joe Louis and Shirley Temple do not conclude that this is what the paper was about. Mostly the paper was about the industrial uprising, and the big political and social issues of the time, although the Temple affair suggests bypaths in the search for the popular chord.

The first damper on our great expectations came early. The Sunday paper was a semiautonomous branch of the daily, but because it aimed at a different audience and essayed a different style, Joe concluded it could best serve its purpose as an independent enterprise, separate from the daily paper. Agreeing with him, the rest of us on the Sunday staff joined in a petition for independence, addressed to the national party leadership.

Clarence Hathaway, editor in chief of the *Worker*, daily and Sunday, adamantly opposed our proposal and he commanded the political authority (and, perhaps, the valid political arguments) to prevail. Having won, he intervened more overtly, at times capriciously, in the operation of the Sunday paper.

A second damper came with Earl Browder's nomination for President on the Communist ticket as "a new John Brown from Osawatomie." (He did come from Kansas.) The pressure was inexorable for turning the paper into a personal campaign organ, and his election speeches became staples for the magazine.

To refer to these dampers is only to record a subjective reaction, and not to offer an analysis of why our expectations were not realized, or of their soundness to begin with, or even of the paper's merits. It attracted a circle of talented contributors (more so in the graphic arts than the literary for reasons I can't explain); it had a vital spark that somehow never blazed.

By the time Browder was nominated I was into other things, which also related to that bizarre political summer. For a brief spell I was writing mammoth editorials for the daily paper. Well, not exactly writing them. If they carried a by-line it could have been: by Alexander Bittelman as told to Al Richmond. Except that even this was not exactly so. Bittelman never told it to me. The arrangement was more complicated.

It all grew out of Hathaway's absence; he spent most of the summer meeting with assorted progressive groupings in the Communist effort to encourage a coalescence for a Farmer-Labor party. With Hathaway gone Foreign Editor Harry Gannes assumed nominal command as the senior editor, but apparently he was not entrusted with editorial expression of specific subtleties and nuances in that political season. This responsibility was given to Bittelman, a veteran party leader and theoretician, who was encamped at the Albert Hotel, two blocks down University Place from the paper's offices. On appointed mornings off went Gannes, with unique technical skills, for a seance with Bittelman. Gannes once made his living as a court reporter (not a newspaperman covering trials, but a skilled worker hired by the court to record its proceedings), and he was, therefore, a topnotch stenographer and typist. At the hotel room Bittelman thought out loud as Gannes took it all down in shorthand. Returning to the office, Gannes transcribed his notes on a typewriter. Then, handing this long stream of political consciousness to me, he said, "Turn it into an editorial."

I confess I liked Bittelman's reasoning process, which is to say I found it coherent and consistent. He did tend to be schematic but then, unlike some other schemata I have encountered, his at least possessed an inner logic. Anyway, in the matters to which he addressed himself that summer the schematicism was unobtrusive. I did not like his feeling for the English language; this, I assumed, is where I came in.

Most memorable of the Bittelman-to-Gannes-to-Richmond productions were long manifestoes to panacea movements of that era. One, the Townsend movement (named after its founder, Dr. Francis E. Townsend), had a mass following among the elderly as it offered a plan for generous pensions that would, simultaneously, heal all of the country's economic ills. Another, its origin suspect, its purpose sinister, was the National Union for Social Justice, the creation of Father Charles E. Coughlin, a pro-Fascist radio orator who influenced millions. The problem was that the Townsendites were being seduced by Coughlin and Gerald L. K. Smith, a Protestant accomplice (it was an ecumenical pro-fascism), into supporting a newly formed Union party with Congressman William Lemke as its presidential candidate. This party, like the George Wallace party eight presidential campaigns later, had a patina of populism over its ultrareactionary substance.

Our principal salvos, one covering more than half of the paper's front page, were directed to the Townsendites, who met in convention at Cleveland in mid-July. We regarded their motivation as authentically progressive, and presumably, therefore, they would be responsive to arguments centered on their movement's tangible reason for being, the quest for economic security. The essence of our appeal to them may be summarized in two words, which were in fact used, "Townsendites, beware!" — beware of Coughlin and Smith, beware of being dragooned behind the Lemke misadventure.

Our message to followers of both Townsend and Coughlin contained two major themes: the Lemke candidacy was a stalking horse for the Republican nominee, Alfred M. Landon, whose victory would be the most calamitous election outcome for their hopes; if they wanted a new party to advance their aspirations for economic security and social justice they should join with progressive forces "to create a true people's party, a Farmer-Labor party."

Those were, indeed, the two primary notes in Communist politics that year: defeat Landon, build a Farmer-Labor party. Without any text from Bittelman I wrote two commentaries on the Democratic National convention, the first an acid survey of the more unsavory characters assembled in Philadelphia, the second a discussion of the platform, of forces and considerations in "the taffy-pulling party" that produced it. The conclusion was:

"For labor and the farmers to reap any fruits from the planks sown, it will be necessary to organize a powerful political center to the left of Roosevelt and carry on a consistent attack against his vacillation in face of the Wall Street attack.

"That center is the Farmer-Labor party!"

An element of contradiction may be discerned between our two principal political thrusts. To the ordinary person "defeat Landon" meant vote for Roosevelt, and how did this square with building a Farmer-Labor party? More of this later. In 1936 we pursued both objectives with great energy, in public agitation and in more tangible enterprises, such as Hathaway's political reconnaissance missions.

Between that summer and the next I was shifted about, even spending three weeks as a Washington correspondent, this in the summer doldrums when little happened in Washington, especially before everything was air-conditioned, and winding up at the *Sunday Worker* as managing editor.

One day in midsummer 1937, Jack Stachel sauntered over to my desk, wearing a straw hat, a jaunty air, and a broad smile, which habits, especially the last two, were not usual with him. Something was up.

"How would you like to go to San Francisco?" he said.

"I'd love it."

I answered before he made any explanations. He teased, I bantered. Then he explained and I became seriously excited. Two weeks later I went west to direct the editorial creation of a new daily paper, a relatively rare venture in radical history that is strewn with the corpses of weeklies and monthlies. I had little time (less than five months before the scheduled publication date) and little experience (less than three years in the newspaper trade), but I had enthusiasm and the audacity of youth. Doing the spadework for the new paper I also served as the last executive editor of its predecessor, the semiweekly *Western Worker*.

To begin these labors, on a Sunday morning in August I arrived at the Oakland Mole, then the transcontinental rail terminal. When I stepped off the train one hand gripped a suitcase with all my belongings and the other was prepared to grasp the whole world. On the ferry trip across the bay I saw San Francisco in the early morning sunlight, saw its hills and the rows of little houses stretched across them; constantly bathed in fog and dried by the bright sun, those houses looked like bleached, fresh laundry on the line. I had just left the enervating, sultry, August heat of New York; here the air was pure and bracing, and all about were the blue waters framed by rolling hills. From my mother's occasional recollections of our transit through it in 1917, San Francisco was an enchanting apparition. That morning was one of these rare moments when the reality is more resplendent than the dream.

The rest of that first day was discordant. I spoke at a picnic (to raise money for the new paper); it was dust-blown and wind-chilled, as August afternoons sometimes are in the San Francisco region. Returning to the city from the picnic ground on the peninsula to the south I witnessed a shrill, abusive family quarrel. That evening, when I went to get my bag at Communist party headquarters at 121 Haight Street I was met by a surly man with a gun and a monstrous dog (in 1934 party offices had been wrecked and vandalized by vigilante gangs and it was still considered prudent to have a night watchman on the premises). Despite the day the buoyancy of that morning did not leave me. In days that followed it grew. The physical beauty of the city was not embraced with one glance; it had many moods and miens, changing with the time of day, the weather, the vantage point, so that those first days were filled with a constant excitement of discovery. And the city did have a greater talent for living than the cities I had known, a grace, an openness, a flair, all those gifts that have been fashioned into a San Francisco legend by those who were young and knew her then. For me, a very political young man, there were also other attractions.

About a fortnight after my arrival I witnessed the Labor Day parade, 80,000 strong, in it the longshoremen, row after row of them, thousands of them, in their parade uniforms, white caps, hickory shirts, black jeans, sturdy men marching proudly, conveying by their bearing their awareness that they were the crack battalions of San Francisco's working class. The centerpiece of their contingent was a giant float, mounted on a flatbed truck; three cardboard worker figures, labeled "Seaman," "Longshoreman," and "Teamster," and in big, bold letters the message: "Lords of the docks, Unite!"

Oh, Lord! Ideological lookouts immediately spotted the fallacy in that float: the workers were not lords of the docks, the shipowners were. It occasioned a minor furor in ideologically oriented circles. Despite its theoretical vagary, however, the float did capture the marvelous élan among San Francisco waterfront workers in those days.

The memory of the 1934 maritime strike was fresh. A longshoreman who fought in the Battle of Rincon Hill above the Embarcadero, the city's waterfront artery, still marveled at the instinct that prompted the strikers to throw up barricades against the charging police. Barricades and rocks were not enough against the gunfire and a tear gas barrage; the workers retreated, some were wounded, but miraculously none was killed on Rincon Hill. The two pickets dead that day, which was christened Bloody Thursday, were shot down on level ground near the longshore union hall on Steuart Street. Workers remembered the dark stain on the sidewalk, large and thick where the blood oozed from a dying man, thinning out at its jagged extremities. They still talked with awe and pride of the procession up Market Street, 40,000 mourners behind the coffins of their two slain comrades. And later these waterfront workers were the shock troops of the sympathy general strike that brought the city's economy to a standstill for four days, asserting the power of labor, and in administering vital functions of a strikebound city they caught a glimmer of a greater power that was latent in them. Such memories do not fade in three years; their mark was on the Labor Day parade I saw.

On Friday evenings I went to meetings of the San Francisco

Labor Council (one of the rare labor councils that provided, not only a press table, but a small spectator gallery). I went to the first meeting to become familiar with personalities and currents in the city's labor movement. Afterward nothing could have kept me from the Labor Temple on Friday evening. If conflict is the essence of drama no theater in San Francisco offered anything comparable. I have a distaste for the word parliament, it connotes so much humbug and empty rhetoric; in American usage the word council is insipid (as distinct from its Russian usage circa 1917). Call it an assembly of the working class.

In this assembly Left and Right were almost evenly matched, the antagonism was naked (outside the council it was on occasion expressed with baseball bats). Debate was free-swinging, vigorous, sometimes cutting, generally well reasoned. These were real men clashing over real issues, attaching real importance to what was resolved. I have heard debates in legislative bodies, state and city, and have waded through the *Congressional Record;* those proceedings are vapid compared with what went on in that labor assembly. The assembly bore the mark of 1934, for that year helped to illuminate and define conflicting currents in the labor movement.

It did not last long. This was shortly after the national cleavage between the AFL and CIO, and I was there when the CIO unions were expelled from the council. Harry Bridges delivered the valedictory in behalf of the longshoremen and warehousemen and their CIO allies. It was the first time I heard that sharp blend of Australian accent and intense assertiveness, free of rhetorical flourish but not devoid of argumentative device. I have since heard him speak at formal public meetings where he was meandering and disjointed, so that people asked: what's he got? Anyone who has heard him as the rough-and-tumble debater in a labor setting does not ask that question. To me, at the time, he was the articulate protagonist of working-class consciousness and militancy, of the power and the promise revealed in the general strike. That evening he was at his best, reciting experiences in the AFL, grievances, injustices, reasons that led the longshoremen and warehousemen to cast their lot with the CIO, presenting his catalogue in precise detail, going on for forty minutes in an assembly that usually began to fidget when a speaker neared the five-minute mark. Not even his antagonists (except for Council Secretary John O'Connell, a compulsive mutterer) displayed impatience. There was a sense of history in that assembly and Bridges measured up to it.

To heighten the drama a rumor had spread that some council elements intended to kick out the CIO delegates, not only figuratively, but physically. In response some longshoremen were in the spectator section and one thousand more of them milled outside the Labor Temple to preserve the peace. There was no violence that evening. Afterward I dropped in on the council only once. It was listless.

In the beginning was 1934 — in California then this also meant EPIC (End Poverty in California), brainchild of Upton Sinclair, Socialist, novelist, muckraker. Sinclair had launched EPIC in 1934 with a quasi-Socialist program that so captured the imagination of an economically distressed and troubled people that he not only swept the Democratic primary but came close enough to winning it all to have some moments of genuine panic at the prospect of becoming governor of California.

Panic among the state's corporate interests was not momentary, nor were they ambivalent at the prospect of an EPIC victory. Not even in the days when the Southern Pacific Railroad was called the Octopus did corporate wealth intervene so flagrantly in California's electoral process. Big employers tried to sow hysteria among their workers with predictions of an economic doomsday if Sinclair won, and since these seers owned the state's major enterprises they communicated the threat of a self-fulfilling prophecy. They also made a more direct threat: discharge of any employee who voted for Sinclair. Film magnates produced faked newsreel interviews with heavies cast as "bums en route to California," and extorted from their employees contributions for the incumbent Republican, Governor Frank Merriam. More than $10,000,000, a fabulous sum in those days, was spent to beat Sinclair, much of it used to shower the electorate with visions of anarchy, chaos, revolution. Considering that Sinclair began with little more than an idea and a flair for propaganda, his 879,000 votes (as against 1,138,000 for Merriam) told much about the popular frame of mind.

By 1937 Sinclair was gone from politics, so was EPIC, but its residue formed a potent Left bloc within the Democratic party. A combination of this bloc with the Left and generally progressive labor groundswell, we Communists (and others) believed, could supply the driving energy in the 1938 election to end forty-four years of Republican rule in the state.

So it turned out, and in the first week of January 1939 I was in Sacramento to cover Governor-elect Culbert L. Olson's pardon of Thomas J. Mooney and to make preliminary arrangements for a regular correspondent in the state capital. In the excitement, exultation, and (most of all) chaos preceding Olson's inaugural I found myself in a hotel room (I am not altogether sure now how I got there) with Phil Gibson, a key man in the Olson entourage (later Chief Justice of the California State Supreme Court), and the ranking labor figures in the Olson campaign: Bridges, H. C. Carrasco of the railroad brotherhoods, George Kidwell, whose stature overshadowed his home base in the San Francisco Bakery Wagon Drivers' Union, and others.

It was not a celebrant gathering. Some of the labor leaders had been to see the governor-elect and he tried to beg off from the Mooney pardon hearing scheduled for the first Saturday after his inaugural. He was so busy, Olson pleaded, with the inaugural, his maiden message to the legislature, the unfinished organization of his administrative team. Couldn't this Mooney thing be put off? The labor leaders held fast: if he never did anything else he was going to honor his commitment to free Mooney on the appointed Saturday. The governor yielded. Still the labor leaders were disturbed by the vacillation.

My reportorial duties took me into lobbies of better hotels, but my twelve-dollar (or was it fifteen-dollar?)-a-week wage did not permit me to stay in them. I was so broke I accepted the assurance of the Communist organizer in Sacramento that he

could sneak me into his hotel room, seventy-five cents a night
on Skid Road, down near the river, as foul a Skid Road as any in
the West. In the middle of the night we were awakened by
excited chattering in the hallway — and the smell of smoke.
Clarence opened the door a little and the smoke came billow-
ing in. The hall carpet was so old, so saturated with dust —
only a small fire made thick smoke. When we dashed out into
the hallway we saw a flock of women running down the stairs;
the hotel, we learned, also did business as a brothel. I gave
Clarence the benefit of the doubt; I concluded he was naive.
The next night I spent at the private residence of a local Communist. So I did not have to go directly from a Skid Road
whorehouse to the state assembly chamber for the Mooney
pardon ceremony.

Like others in that chamber I could not count how many
times I had heard or read "Free Tom Mooney!", or how many
times I had shouted it, nor could I remember exactly for how
many years that was. By then it seemed as if it had been always. Constant repetition over so long a time made it seem
that the free-Mooney refrain would go on and on, if not for
eternity, then until a millennial day. I had heard orators say that
some day the workers will march on San Quentin in a second
storming of the Bastille and then Mooney would be free. I was
not yet three when he was imprisoned and here I was, twenty-
two and a half years later, to witness and record the event that
had assumed such large symbolical meaning for an entire generation. Didn't my Lord deliver Daniel, and why not every
man?

That was the spirit the next day when Mooney came home to
San Francisco to be welcomed by a procession up Market
Street, assembling in the same locale and following the same
route as the Preparedness Day parade of 1916, when the fatal
bomb exploded and his long ordeal began. This time it was no
parade, it was a surging, irrepressible mass of jubilant humanity,
filling the street from sidewalk to sidewalk, without rank or
order, exercising one restraint by permitting Mooney to remain
in the van. The *Daily People's World* celebrated with the only
extra and the only Sunday edition in its history, and ever after

the 144-point type, the biggest we had, which blazoned, "Welcome Mooney!" was referred to in our shop as the Mooney type.

I have played loose with chronology to leap from 1937 into the Mooney pardon hearing because I have been trying to convey, as I felt it, the texture of the times into which the *Daily People's World* was born. It appeared on the crest of a wave. Call it democratic, progressive, reform, or whatever, but it was a wave of enormous popular energy and it was at its flood in California on January 1, 1938, when the paper's first edition issued from an ancient flatbed press that groaned and creaked with its natal labor.

Two years later would have been different, by then the Nazi-Soviet pact and the first phase of the war had created a new political temper, or distemper. It would not have been the same two years earlier, for then the wounds were still fresh from the lacerating Communist attacks against Sinclair and EPIC as demagogic, even social-Fascist, excrescences (a self-critical apology came fairly soon; the healing process took longer). Allowing for a period of gestation this daily paper would not have been conceived in the earlier time, and it could not have been born in the later.

A daily paper, as the mortality rate of the species attests, is a difficult and hazardous venture. When it is a political paper without money or an angel, it either has a political base or it dies. Even at that time, according to Harold Ickes (a member of the Roosevelt Cabinet), to launch a metropolitan daily one needed at least $15 million. Our initial capital, aside from the old equipment and subscription list of the *Western Worker*, was $37,500. True, we did not pretend to the grand scale of a metropolitan daily, but the discrepancy was nowhere near the gulf between 15 million and 37,500. We were completely dependent upon resources in our region. Occasionally I encounter the notion that we must have been well kept because opulent Hollywood was in our sphere of interest and the film colony, as a dispenser of gold to communism, was a kind of Moscow of the West. This, alas, is just another illusion about Hollywood. The paper received more help from ships' fo'c's'les than it got from dream castles. It did not suckle at the golden teats of Hollywood. It was a daring enterprise made possible only by the brief conjunction of an idea and its time.

The unique circumstances attending the paper's birth stamped its character and also introduced elements of spontaneity and improvisation into its formative period. When I arrived in San Francisco, for instance, it was tacitly assumed the name would be *Daily Western Worker,* and this was little more than four months before the scheduled publication date. Only later was it decided to have a different name. A bona-fide contest was hurriedly organized, cash prizes were offered, and out of that came *Daily People's World* to denote a new departure, not merely a change in frequency. But what sort of a departure?

This was determined by Communist politics as they related to objective circumstances. When I engaged in the curious collaboration with Bittelman in 1936 the Farmer-Labor party was projected as the distinct American form of a popular front. By 1938, gradually and almost imperceptibly, a change had occurred. "Popular front" was supplanted by "democratic front" (party resolutions called the latter "the beginning of the development of a real people's front against reaction and fascism"). In practice this meant shelving the Farmer-Labor party slogan and placing the emphasis on other independent political formations. These were real. Labor's Non-Partisan League certainly was, as I know from my observation of it in California. In the 1938 California elections we took the initiative to bring together former EPIC's and others of the Left into a "Federation for Political Unity." Elsewhere there were the American Labor party in New York, the Farmer-Labor party in Minnesota, the Washington Commonwealth Federation. As varied as these and other formations were they had one thing in common: they operated within the national ambit of the Democratic party as parts of a "Roosevelt coalition." Thus the apparent contradiction of 1936 between "defeat Landon" and "build a Farmer-Labor party" was resolved.

Patently this "democratic front," a generalized abstraction of political realities, was amorphous, as compared with a Farmer-Labor party. The problem of the paper was how to relate to it.

Or, more specifically, how to relate to the Left current within it, which included a great deal more than Communists. Should the paper simply reflect or address this Left current, or could it be an articulate expression of what was, in effect, a loose, un-structured united front? In California this united front had vitality. The CIO was a dynamic force, the EPIC remnants and their accretions were a political factor, and these were but the brightest stars in a larger galaxy. Now, it was no secret that the Communists launched the paper, supplied its principal resources, and retained control over it. Nonetheless, was it possible to get others to accept it as a serviceable medium to assert their particular interests within a larger community of interest they then shared with Communists? To a degree it proved possible.

I recall unions that bought subscriptions for their entire executive board, and these ranged from a mine local in New Mexico to a railroad lodge in Stockton, which had no Communist in its ranks. The longshoremen's local threw a Labor Day ball for the paper's benefit, the warehousemen's local sponsored a raffle, a conference on the paper attracted official delegates from a score of unions. Some of these locals had Communist leaders, others did not, but in no union was support for the paper conceived as a philanthropic gesture for a Communist enterprise. It was a *quid pro quo*, a recognition of services rendered. And this with awareness of who was principally behind the paper, who was putting it out. The same phenomenon was observable in other fields and forms: endorsement of the paper by a variety of public figures, their identification with events it sponsored.

With all that has happened since, it may seem incredible that such association with Communists in a tangible enterprise was once possible. The description and explication of it may even sound archaic. To me, at the time, these relationships posed an intriguing test of political and journalistic creativity. At the very least they indicated a range of coverage, a breadth of approach, a quality of style that were consonant with this mixed constituency. Such efforts imparted a distinct flavor to the paper.

They also created complications of identity, which may be

illuminated by a small incident. On election night 1938, I was
at a social gathering to listen to the results. This was before
television with its election-night spectaculars, starring imper-
turbable computers and harried men. The radio broadcasts
took longer to arrive at the outcome, but when it finally became
certain that Olson, the Democrat we had supported, was the
winner in the gubernatorial contest, a young woman came
dashing over to where I was standing with William Schneiderman, the state Communist leader. "We won!" she gushed. "We
won!" Ordinarily courteous, Schneiderman replied with cutting formality: "We did not win, comrade. The Democratic
party won."

That I have remembered this chance remark for more than
three decades already attests to the impression registered by
the distinction he drew. That the distinction so impressed me
also suggests that, at the moment, I was swept up by the same
exuberance as the young woman, and was jolted, therefore, by
the sudden confrontation with what I knew, of course, was the
reality. To recall the lapse is also to recall the indelible recognition of what it was.

On the paper, awareness of the Schneiderman distinction was
a constant necessity. There was a duality in representing a
united front platform and simultaneously articulating the distinct Communist viewpoint within the wider political configuration. In the first two years of the paper's existence the reconciliation of those roles was relatively easy because the united
front and the Communist position within it had authenticity.

Those were not idyllic years. In the first year of publication
the paper reacted to the agony of Spain and the shame of Munich. We perceived in these events the portents of World War
II. The Japanese invasion of China was gathering strength, and
on the Pacific Coast, particularly in San Francisco ("gateway to
the Orient"), it was far more ominous than somewhere east of
the Donner Pass. Domestically the New Deal had palliated the
most acute distress, but the problems of mass unemployment
and poverty were no nearer solution. The presentiment of impending catastrophe, especially in the tide of world affairs, be-

came more compelling with the defeat of the Spanish Republic, a scant six months after the pact at Munich.

There was foreboding and there also was in the paper's staff the temper of engagement in battles that were not dubious, battles in which we were one with masses of the people. We were animated by the conviction that what we wrote, what we published, our editorial judgments, would influence the course of these battles. We were, in our self-image, not objective recorders of history but partisan participants in its making. Most of the staff was relatively young, and with the passion and energy of our youth we entered into the union organizing drives, the tough strikes, into the interminable resistance to the assaults on the jobless and the poor in the name of governmental economy, into the then prevailing forms of the Negro liberation struggle. I have referred to Spain, Munich, the war on China; we exhorted, we warned, we encouraged the demonstrative acts that brought about a temporary, symbolical halt in the shipment of supplies to militarist Japan. We were preoccupied with all these things that in their sum we sloganized as the struggle against war and fascism, and for economic security and democracy. We were preoccupied with what we conceived as instrumentalities for joining these issues — democratic front, popular front. In their juxtaposition the foreboding of catastrophe and the temper of engagement endowed many moments, especially in the months after Munich, with a desperate urgency. So we focused on these moments, but always in the picture, in the background, hazier, was our vision of the new and better world, and the encounters of the moment, we were convinced, blazed the long road to that destination.

I digress now from politics to people, to my associates at the time. Only many years after the fact did I learn that when I was proposed from New York as the last editor of the *Western Worker* and the advance man for its daily successor, the California Communist leaders expressed great qualms upon learning my age, only twenty-three. Oh, he's unusually mature for his years, they were told. I do not know how reassuring that was, not much, I suspect, knowing how skeptical some of those Western leaders could be. At any rate, by the time the daily paper appeared, so had two more mature men from New York: Harrison George, executive editor; Vern Smith, labor editor. I was designated managing editor.

I had met Harrison only casually in New York but I knew a great deal about him. He was an old Wobbly, one of the 165, among them Bill Haywood and other major figures of the IWW, who were tried under the World War I Espionage Act before Judge Kenesaw Mountain Landis in Chicago in 1918. I remembered a line in John Reed's account of the Chicago trial — "There goes . . . Harrison George, whose forehead is lined with hard thinking." He was the author of "Red Dawn," the first American pamphlet on the Russian Revolution, written in jail and published under the IWW imprint in February 1918, on the eve of the Chicago trial. He translated the Russian lyrics of the Workers' Funeral March, Lenin's favorite song, it was said ("Dying as soldiers, fighting for freedom, so did you fall . . .").

After the Chicago trial he served five years in Leavenworth prison, and as if to compensate for this long confinement he later traveled widely — he was a worker for the Communist International and the Red International of Labor Unions, more particularly its Pan-Pacific Trade Union Secretariat.

I had read the column he used to write for the *Daily Worker*, "Red Sparks by Jorge," which exhibited an astringent wit and occasionally was the scourge of bureaucracy (not on the national party level, to be sure, but several district bureaucrats were well flayed). I had been deeply moved by his published outcry of grief and anger when his foster son was murdered (after being tortured, the circumstances indicated) by the secret police of Brazilian dictator Getulio Vargas.

Knowing all this I looked forward to working with him. Upon closer acquaintance Harrison turned out to be a perky, somewhat eccentric fellow, his frequent excursions into humor accompanied by his own chuckles. In a description of him at the time I noted, "His face is weatherbeaten and his complexion looks like the side of an old barn which has undergone many

coats of paint." In harmony with his facial hide were the strong
traces in his speech of his native Kansas prairie, a corncob pipe,
his taste in clothes (which may have dated back to his youthful
vocation of tailor in Cody, Wyoming) — he easily could have
been taken for a Kansas farmer.

He had several eccentricities, or so they seemed to me, such
as a zeal for health food and colonic irrigation. (That last habit
made credible an anecdote about him. As cover for a Pan-
Pacific Trade Union Secretariat operation in Manila, it was
said, he set up a colonic irrigation dispensary.) Despite these
foibles and a generation gap — he turned fifty when I was
twenty-four — we fell into a very amicable, functional, live and
let live relation. He was content to write the editorials and his
column, conduct a voluminous correspondence, and otherwise
leave editorial direction of the paper to me. I think it was his
genuine appreciation of this arrangement, which freed him
from administrative responsibility and the many day-to-day decisions in the production of a paper, that accounted for my im-
munity from his proselytizing forays. Other staff members, detected in a grievous fall from dietetic grace, such as eating
hamburger or pie, were in for a lecture. Although my dietetic
habits were, from his viewpoint, abominable, he never mentioned them. Also, I constantly had a vague feeling that he was
engaged in some political intrigue, but he did not try to involve
me. (Not until later did I fully realize his penchant for faction-
alism, a trait that cropped up among those of my elders who
had been through the acrimonious schisms in the Socialist
party or the IWW, and through the marathon factional struggle
in the Communist party's first decade. I was dismayed by the
resort to the most malicious personal gossip and innuendo in a
factional tract he wrote.)

If Harrison appreciated our arrangement, so did I. It gave
me rare latitude.

Vern Smith, like Harrison, was also an old Wobbly, a former
editor of *Industrial Solidarity*, but in physical appearance and
temperament they were opposites. Smith was a tall, large
Westerner, with thick white hair and placid blue eyes that
peered through thin-rimmed spectacles. He had equanimity

and this, in his writing, crossed the line into blandness. He sat very straight at his typewriter, pecking away at an even pace, and out came page after page of copy, each page workmanlike and each undistinguishable in tone or feeling from any other. Vern reminded me of a character described by Egon Erwin Kisch, one of the great journalists in the era between the two world wars. In his memoirs Kisch relates that when he, as a cub reporter in his native Prague, was filled with excitement about a big fire or a grisly murder one old man in his office was sure to recall a bigger fire or a grislier murder.

Vern possessed a remarkable range of knowledge. It was unwise to ask him a question if you did not have a lot of time to listen to the answer. Once someone asked him for the spelling of a Civil War general's name, and got, not only the correct spelling, but a lecture on every battle in which the general participated, including a detailed exposition of strategy and tactics.

Vern's equanimity was manifested in a staff crisis occasioned by Ernest Hemingway's *For Whom the Bell Tolls.* Our volunteer critic was Steve Nelson, a veteran of the Abraham Lincoln Battalion and by a consensus of the ranks the most popular officer in the battalion. Nelson, who did not write easily, chose as his collaborator a young staff member named Ralph Robinson, very bright, very literate, and also an ardent Hemingway devotee. Their collaboration produced a panegyric for Hemingway's Spanish Civil War novel.

On the other side of the continent the *Daily Worker* and *New Masses* lanced and gored the novel as if it were a bull in the ring. Other Lincoln Battalion veterans reacted to the book with the special anger of men who felt they were betrayed by someone they thought was their friend.

A pivotal point at issue was Hemingway's portrayal of André Marty, French Communist leader and chief of the International Brigade, as an arbitrary and capricious megalomaniac (a characterization corroborated in large measure by his own party when it expelled him some years later). The severe critics contended the treatment of Marty was symptomatic of a more pervasive denigration of the brigade and the Spanish Republic.

When Nelson read all this (which appeared after his review) he was shaken. He was an honest man without any literary conceit. Moreover, aside from sex in a sleeping bag and some other interludes, the novel was largely political, and the sharp difference was about its politics, not its aesthetics. A clash about politics was much more serious than a dispute about aesthetics. Urged on by fellow veterans and prodded by others, Nelson agreed to write a critique of his review. In this difficult endeavor I was his collaborator.

The staff was so agitated by this sequence of events you might have thought the bell tolled for it, but not Vern. Only time can tell the true impact of a book, he said; look at *Uncle Tom's Cabin*, it could have been subjected to devastating criticism when it was published, but on the historic balance it turned out for the good.

You may have properly inferred that Vern was even less inclined than Harrison to be involved in the direction of a paper's daily operation. Still, both of them brought something of value to the paper. Indigenous men of the West, old Wobbly propagandists and agitators, they had a feeling for the native idiom, for the regional lore, they retained something of the popular touch that was a hallmark of IWW agitation (the Wobblies were much better agitators than organizers). They had roots in a native radicalism that antedated their entrance into the Communist party. I do not mean to romanticize all this, and certainly they were not altogether free of political contradictions between their past and present, but they did contribute this intangible quality, call it style or even spirit, that was important to this particular paper trying to relate to a particular movement. As a tangible matter, in California's labor radicalism and dissident politics of the time were many others with a Wobbly background; Harrison and Vern had the benefit of shared tradition in communicating with them.

We also had two gifted columnists, one a chance pickup, like a thumb-waver on the road or a congenial drinker in a bar, only this one was picked up in a Los Angeles radio station, which broadcast a *Daily People's World* news program by Ed Robbin, our Los Angeles bureau chief. Robbin ran into this young hillbilly singer from Oklahoma, who turned out to be socially conscious (in a favorite phrase of that era), and accepted an invitation to perform at several Left events. As their acquaintance blossomed into friendship the hillbilly became more interested in the paper Robbin worked for and finally offered to do a column for it. Since the man asked for no money I advised Robbin, when informed of the offer, to get some samples. They were good. We had a column: brief text, primitive drawings. Being suspicious of folksiness and words misspelled for comic effect, I wondered at first: is this columnist phony or genuine? I soon met him when he came to perform in San Francisco, a man in his late twenties, slender and wiry, a wild mop of hair and a beard. He might have been called a hippie in later years, except that his Oklahoma speech was authentic and so was his familiarity with the folkways of the open road as it was traveled by uprooted farmers and migratory workers. He was genuine.

If one were to emulate the conceit of Columbus it could be said that with publication of "Woody Sez" the *Daily People's World* "discovered" Woody (Woodrow Wilson) Guthrie, balladeer, composer, folk-music legend unto the second generation. For me the episode is expressive of the paper's free and easy style in that time. We took on this unknown hillbilly as a regular columnist, without pay, to be sure, but with some front-page fanfare, and also without serious examination of his political credentials or antecedents, let alone an ideological screening test.

The other columnist was much the most talented writer associated with the paper. He went through three cycles and three names in his creative life. In the first, as Paul Ryan (his given name), he achieved such distinction as attaches to inclusion in an O'Brien collection of *Best Short Stories*. In the second cycle, as Mike Quin, which is where his heart was and also the overwhelming bulk of his prodigious literary output, he was a columnist for the *Western Worker* and *People's World*, radio news script writer for the CIO, pamphleteer, author of a well-researched and vivid book about the 1934 strike (published posthumously as *The Big Strike*). In the final cycle, as Robert

Finnegan, he published three better than average mystery novels and created a credible central character, a newspaper-man-sleuth, who could have gone on and on. Except that his creator did not. What Mike wanted most to write then was a novel or play about Karl Marx, and he calculated that by turning out a mystery novel in six months he would have the financial security for the rest of the year to pursue his favored project. It did not work out that way. In 1947 his life was cut short by cancer of the liver at age forty-one.

In Mike a superb craftsmanship was combined with imagination and a gift for fantasy that poured forth fables, allegories, poems, dialogues, along with the more conventional forms of the column, informed with wit, satire, humor, wisdom, passion, with the rare knack for explaining complex problems in simple terms, or, where appropriate, reducing apparent complexity to its essental absurdity. Theodore Dreiser perceived in Mike's columns "the type of concentrated essence of social logic and philosophy and irony to be found in Finley Peter Dunne (*Philosopher Dooley*) and George Ade (*Fables in Slang*)" and "in spots" was "reminded of Rabelais, Voltaire and Thomas Paine."

Mike probably reached his largest audience with a column, originally published in the *Western Worker*, that was transformed into a stage skit in *Meet the People*, a successful Hollywood musical review of social significance circa 1940. Subsequently a routine, bearing a remarkable resemblance to Mike's creation, popped up in a British two-man song-and-comedy show (Michael Flanders and Donald Swan). In recent years I have heard a BBC version of it on radio. The original dialogue between Wowsy, the worldly-wise, tolerant cannibal, and his young idealistic friend, Bongo, is a fair sample of Mike's satirical gift.

> BONGO: Human beings should not eat each other.
> WOWSY: Good Gooey Gow! You can't dictate to people what they're going to eat and what they're not going to eat. Men have always eaten each other and always will. It's natural. You can't change human nature.
> BONGO: I love my fellow men.
> WOWSY: So do I — with gravy on them.

I had read some of Mike's columns and poems before I came west and greatly admired them. When I arrived in San Francisco he was not writing for the *Western Worker;* there had been an inner staff struggle, he was on the losing side, and he was off. It seemed incredible to me that this rare talent was not being employed. One of the first and most useful things I did was to get him back on.

Somehow, maybe it was a provincial eastern conception of the West or something in the few things of his I had read, I imagined him as an old Wobbly type. Instead I encountered a young, short, slender, high-strung, black-haired Irishman with big, horn-rimmed glasses. In the personal relationship I felt more strongly the qualities in his writing that transcended craft or imagination. These were the essence of the man: the compassion, the anger at injustice and sham, the preoccupation with the *fundamental* ills of contemporary society and the human condition within it, the almost tactile quality the Socialist ideal had for him. It is also a mark of the man that after hearing he had two months to live he composed only one public farewell message to be released after he was gone; it was addressed "to my brothers, the longshoremen and warehousemen."

Among Mike's many creations was a slogan to which considerable notoriety has been attached, and I had a modest hand in it. One day in 1940 he came to me with the manuscript of a pamphlet he had written for the Northern California council of the Maritime (labor) Federation of the Pacific. He did not have a title and was looking for one. Reading the text I came across one brief sentence and said to him, maybe this might do for a title, why don't you try it? He did. It was "The Yanks Are Not Coming."

Considering all the malice and derision with which it has since been repeated, the oddity of it is that just about every major political figure and grouping was saying the same thing at the time, only not with the flair and lilt of Mike's slogan. President Roosevelt said it: "And while I am talking to you mothers and fathers, I give you one more assurance . . .   Your boys are not going to be sent to any foreign wars." Wendell Willkie, his Republican opponent in the 1940 campaign, echoed: "I give you the pledge. No American soldier boy will be sent to the shambles of any European trench." The available citations are voluminous.

Still, I suppose, it is a tribute to Mike's slogan as slogan (quickly grasped and long remembered) that it has been used as a generic symbol of Communist behavior in the tortuous twenty-two months between the Nazi-Soviet nonaggression treaty in August 1939 and the Nazi invasion of the Soviet Union in June 1941.

It is not easy now to disentangle one's immediate responses, intellectual and emotional, to those events from subsequent layers of thought and feeling about them. The treaty came as a megaton shock, stunning, sudden, wrenching. The Russians said later, with justice, that they had uttered some warnings that should have reduced the element of surprise. The Western powers chose to ignore those warnings for their own bad reasons, but that they did not fully register with us, if I am a fair exemplar, was due not only to a political absorption in building an anti-Fascist front, nationally and internationally, with Hitler as the primary enemy on the global scale. There was also a powerful emotional factor: an authentic hatred for the Nazis as the supreme embodiment of political criminality and moral malignancy.

Unprepared, knocked off balance by this abrupt turn, our reflex defense of the treaty had elements of the frenetic. Scanning the *People's World* of those days one can find much that is reasonable and stands the test of time, and much folly and confusion. I will speak for myself: I was confused. One argument for the treaty was that it created a zone of peace. From this I deduced that surely Hitler would not strike eastward, and so thoroughly persuaded myself that even when the Nazis threatened Poland I gave my personal assurance to the liberal publisher of a modest Beverly Hills newspaper that they would not attack. (This publisher's name was Will Rogers, Jr., and I used to run into him on his infrequent visits to San Francisco, mostly

at a bohemian bar operated by a man named Izzy Gomez.)
Despite my personal assurance Hitler invaded Poland two days
later.

This might have been my private confusion but from my recollection refreshed by the printed record, confusions were
ample and well distributed. Uncertainties, explanations to
one's self that did not fully explain, and with all that one solid
rock of faith. *They*, I said, know what they are doing. And
even though my comprehension floundered in the rapid whirlpool of world politics I could still grasp some empirical data to
reinforce the faith.

In historical retrospect *they* did, indeed, know what they
were doing, far better than we American Communists did. Our
troubles essentially stemmed from a compulsion to turn Soviet
diplomatic necessity into an American political virtue. I will
not recite here the mass of historical evidence and expert testimony by competent historians that the treaty was, in fact, a
diplomatic necessity, made so by the refusal of the Western
powers to enter into any effective collective security arrangement, impelling the Soviets into unilateral action to make certain they were not the first target of Nazi attack, with the corollary prospect of the Western powers then acting as honest
brokers, or worse, as Hitler's accomplices, tacit or formal. Objectively, reflex justification of the treaty stands the test of history far better than the more popular interpretations of it as
Moscow's Machiavellian compact with the anti-Christ. If our
defenses were tainted with the frenetic, denunciations were
saturated with it.

As diplomatic necessity it was justifiable and this did not preclude the addendum that because the first and only Socialist
state was involved its necessity had special implications for the
rest of the world. As American political virtue the matter took
on other hues. In its first, "phony" phase we said it was an imperialist war, they were all imperialists — except that in our
emphases some were more imperialistic than others. We redis-
covered "perfidious Albion" with a resurgent vehemence. With
rare exceptions, there was a moratorium on anti-Nazi criticism.

Soviet diplomatic necessity also determined certain norms of diplomatic behavior toward the other treaty power, which precluded hostile manifestations or imputations of bad faith (whether they overdid it is a collateral question and does not alter the requisites of protocol). But we had signed no treaty with the German state; diplomatic considerations need not have constrained us from recognizing even then a dichotomy in the war, a tension between popular aspiration and ruling-class maneuver. In Western ruling circles the calculation persisted that somehow they could clear up Hitler's unfortunate confusion about political geography that pointed him toward the West; it was still possible, they thought, to remind him that he was supposed to go east, not west. Alongside this, however, was the genuine fear of European peoples of Nazi enslavement and a resistance impelled by this fear. By the summer of 1940, after Nazi troops had overrun Western Europe, it was an open question as to which side of the war was up.

I realize, of course, that all this is easier said in the perspective of subsequent history, especially the epic Soviet resistance that destroyed the Nazi power. Conceding that the wisdom of hindsight is second rate it is still permissible to suggest that an autonomous compehension and expression of the dual elements even in the war's first phase would have removed (or tempered) the flip-flop appearance of responses to the abrupt turns in the events of those years. We would have been battered just the same, but we would have emerged with fewer lacerations and more credit.

Thinking back upon my reaction to Hitler's invasion of the Soviet Union, among all its complex facets there was an enormous sense of release. Not just from the station of pariah in the period of the Nazi-Soviet treaty. And not only in the identification with the Soviet resistance. Those were factors, but there was another. Within me (as within others, of course) the anti-Nazi passion had not been extinguished, it had smoldered, and now it burst forth, all the more fervently for having been restrained so long; at last, I believed, the historical juncture had been reached for crushing this supreme evil. Without recognizing this elemental motivation one cannot understand the heroism and energy exhibited by so many Communists during the war, for men do not scale such heights as automatons.

After Soviet involvement in the war, after the Japanese attack on Pearl Harbor, all else on the paper was subordinated to one goal: victory. And no one pursued this end with greater zeal than Mike (The Yanks Are Not Coming) Quin. His very earnestness gave birth to a comic episode that might be titled "The Quin Plan for Victory Through Chastity." He would not have minded my relating it for, as he wrote in a manuscript he was working on at the time of his death, he "never fully trusted either the friendship or humanity of anyone who did not make a damn fool of himself on occasion." By this sensitive standard you could truly trust Mike's friendship and humanity (as, indeed, you could by any other).

The episode had its origin in disturbing, if unconfirmed, reports we began to receive shortly after our first troop convoys sailed across the Pacific. By the time some ships reached Hawaii as many as 25 percent of the troops aboard exhibited mementos of their last fling in San Francisco: symptoms of gonorrhea or syphilis. The sulfa drugs and penicillin were still too scarce for routine army treatment of VD. In hard military logistics the reports meant then that one fourth of the effectives were partially incapacitated before they got within 4000 miles of the enemy.

The VD rate also soared in San Francisco, up 75 percent before the war's first year was out, according to official statistics. In a display of the police mentality at work, San Francisco Police Chief Charles Dullea proposed an ordinance to outlaw all sexual intercourse out of wedlock, with maximum penalties of six months in jail and a $500 fine. Mike considered the chief's proposal extreme and impractical, but being concerned with the casualty rate among the troops he put his own logical and radical mind to getting at the root of the problem. When Mike arrived at a thought-out conclusion it was seldom tentative.

"There is only one way to halt the spread of the disease," he wrote, "and that is to apprehend the carriers, prevent them from having intercourse with others, and cure them as rapidly as possible.

"This can be done and I'll tell you how to do it."

And he did. He proposed "a light harness or belt next to the skin around waist or hips, which is locked or sealed onto [each diseased person] . . . And it should be so fashioned that it cannot be moved without breaking a seal or otherwise betraying the deed." There followed an outline for administrative rules, medical examinations, certificates of clearance, and extreme penalties to guarantee that those who should wear the chastity belt did, in fact, wear it.

I published the column, partially because I shared Mike's tolerance for human folly (after all a man could not make a damn fool of himself if all his chances were foreclosed), and anyway, I thought, this is a single shot. The next column he submitted expounded the same cause with even greater zeal and I realized Mike was embarked on a crusade. He had to be dissuaded. Heavy is the cross of an editor who has to contend with genius bent on making a damn fool of itself.

If you wanted to exchange a few words with Mike you could do so in the office, but if it was to be a serious talk you had to repair to a bar, and unless you had a strong contrary preference in beverages you tended to drink what he drank, a sickly green ale. It is difficult to argue with a strong mind that is captivated by the inner logic of its own scheme. You are compelled to fall back on the practicalities and the feasibilities, and thereby invite a healthy scorn for expediency and opportunism, or the lack of guts to do what you really know should be done. An awful amount of the sickly green ale was consumed before Mike was persuaded that he might do more to win the war by turning to other subjects.

In a few months I, too, turned to other subjects to help win the war. Early in 1943 I was inducted into the army and was glad to go. In May 1946, I returned to San Francisco with my honorable discharge, a good conduct ribbon, and three years of undistinguished service in the medical corps, fourteen months of it in the south of England, which is the closest I came to the action.

In the army I had turned thirty, even then considered a milestone of sorts, although not as the mystical passage into the age of the damned that it was to become in the culture of certain circles later on. My first marriage was broken up (by me, and not well). I came back to the *Daily People's World* and the paper had changed. The staff had changed. The world had changed.

I learned about one change in the world aboard the SS *Queen Elizabeth,* somewhere in mid-Atlantic, homeward bound from Europe, along with 12,000 other enlisted men, 3000 officers and nurses, and a regiment of Dutch Marines en route to the East Indies to save the empire. You could tell they were Dutch by their language; their uniforms and equipment were American. It was August, the evenings were balmy, a young slender moon made its brief appearance beyond the foremast. On one such evening a soldier in my outfit told me he had heard from somebody else that a big bomb, a superbomb unlike any other bomb, made out of atoms or something, had been dropped on Japan. In the happy bedlam of a large troopship sailing home from the wars even the announcement of doomsday would have difficulty in registering. I heard more talk about the bomb but I learned no more about it aboard that ship.

The paper had a new address. It was now housed in expanded quarters, with fluorescent lighting, a real copy desk with a slot and a rim, and a new, shiny rotary press in place of the antique flatbed I had left behind. All these physical appointments were, in a sense, ironical, material monuments to Teheran. That's Communist shorthand for the Browder program. He used the agreement Stalin concluded with Roosevelt and Churchill at Teheran as the point of departure for his thesis that the wartime collaboration would extend into the postwar world, which collaboration could be and should be reinforced with class harmony on the domestic scene. Flushed with this vision of the world to be, basking in such spirit of unity as did exist during the war, the paper's directorate made these capital investments so that it would better harmonize with the anticipated ambience. (In the world as it actually turned out to be the rotary press had to be sold a few years later and the better half of the quarters surrendered.)

Teheran and its consequences also wrought changes in the staff. Harrison George was out, Vern Smith was on his way; they were involved in a grouping that wanted a sharper veer to the Left in the party's course and called for cleaning all the rascals out, meaning most of the leaders associated with Browder's policy.

I was designated executive editor, a post that had been filled in the interim by John Pittman, a black man from Atlanta, one of the paper's founding fathers who had served previously as foreign editor. Pittman was off to Europe for a tour of duty as foreign correspondent, an ambition he had harbored for some time. My associate editor was Adam Lapin, for many years Washington correspondent for the *Daily Worker*, an able, experienced journalist with a broad knowledge of American politics and the people in it. For all his sophistication he retained an air of apple-cheeked ingenuousness, which was not a put-on. He did have apple cheeks. He also had integrity.

Coming back I felt a bit of an outsider for I had not gone through all the convulsions of the Teheran cycle. When Browder presided at the metamorphosis of the Communist party into the Communist Political Association in May 1944, I was at Fort McClellan, Alabama, caught up in the final frenzy of a military preparation for a movement overseas. A later year, when the condemnation of Browder's program by Jacques Duclos, French Communist leader, precipitated a quick, agonizing reappraisal in the American ranks that led to prompt reconstitution of the American party, I was in Dorset, England. As readers of English literature, from Thomas Hardy to John Fowles, well know Dorset is for brooding and backwardness. Even in Dorset, however, I received bits and pieces of news, through the British press and personal correspondence, of the American Communist development. It aroused puzzlement, questions, which I tried to sort out in my mind, but not having the relevant documents or an opportunity for informed discussion, it seemed best to refrain from definitive conclusions until I got back home.

When I did get back the Cold War was well under way, so was the postwar strike wave, and it was evident to me that Browder had been wrong in his projection of postwar class harmony, international and domestic. Thus I shared the conclusion of my associates, but not the experience through which they arrived at it, and it was not an experience well shared vicariously. I could not truly empathize with those among them who had been agitated by the question: why did they do it? Why did they acquiesce in Browder's policy, despite instincts and deeply rooted tenets to the contrary, despite misgivings, doubts, reservations?

Not everyone acquiesced. Among the few who had balked at the Browder line was Mike Quin, and he had been given a bad time for it on the paper and in party circles. As a result one thing was the same as it had been when I came to San Francisco in 1937: Mike was off the paper and I set out to bring him back. He had been deeply disturbed and still was — by developments in the party, by ominous trends in world affairs, by the shadow of atomic war. As yet unaware of the malignant growth within him, he already was feeling its effects and these may have colored his mood. His sense of the appropriate setting for serious talk had not changed, only this was not an absurd crisis like the chastity belt interlude, one pub was not enough and often the drink was stronger than the sickly green ale. We both lived in North Beach. This was before the Beach became a garish showcase of naked breasts and buttocks, it was still mostly a mix of Italian colony and bohemia, with a generous quota of quiet pubs. Through these we crawled and talked, mostly Mike talked, and out of the torrent of words came his very elementary conclusion: back to Socialist fundamentals, back to communicating his vision of what he once described as "a collective, friendly society in which human beings would cooperate with each other for their mutual welfare . . . a decent, good-natured society where a man can work and laugh and have friends." He finally agreed to resume his column, telling me that this is what he was going to write about, fundamentals, and so he did, in his clear, simple style, in an almost didactic vein, until his fatal illness compelled him to stop.

My outsider sensation vanished quickly as the paper became immersed in the politics that culminated in creation of the Progressive party with Henry A. Wallace as its presidential candidate. A quarter of a century has since gone by and one hears congratulatory declarations of statesmen on having traversed this passage without a global war and that this already is some years more than the interval between the first two world wars. But 1946 was the Year I. The Cold War had just broken out, the atomic bomb had just been used by the United States, not once but twice, and the second time in an even more insensate slaughter than the first, for the "demonstration" over Hiroshima had been an unqualified success, the ruins and the corpses proving conclusively that the bomb would devastate a large city and kill or maim most of its people. Nagasaki was an exercise in redundant murder, as if someone had casually said to the amateur piano player in the White House, play it again, Harry.

Living with the fresh memory of these horrors, living with the Cold War and the bomb was an unprecedented and uncertain existence. Political reality and human imagination joined to make credible the peril of a world war with all its incalculable ravage. To be sure, there was the revolutionary surge in the wake of World War II, which kindled hope — and also sharpened the question: will the men who command American power resort to its ultimate use in their manifest efforts to check and turn the revolutionary tide?

Out of this soil of uncertainty and apprehension, which I shared with so many others, sprouted the Progressive party and the Wallace candidacy as the concentrated political resistance to the Cold War drift toward disaster. It acquired the fervor of a crusade. In California 275,970 valid signatures of registered voters were needed to place the new party on the ballot, which meant that perhaps ten times that number of persons had to be solicited, indicating the scale of mobilization and work. Here it was called the Independent Progressive party because the name "Progressive party" was preempted by a paper ghost of the Hiram Johnson–Bull Moose era. (This produced the initials IPP with their unfortunate urinary evocation.) Getting those signatures seemed like a superhuman undertaking, and such journalistic skill and imagination as the paper's staff possessed were dedicated to stimulation and organization of the effort.

In effect the *Daily People's World* was the voice of the Wallace movement in the West and the paper was very lucky in its living links with the campaign: Lapin, whose acquaintance with national principals of the new party was intimate, and Steve Murdock, our very competent reporter of state politics. The paper reflected the vitality of the movement and was invigorated by it. The afterglow of the New Deal was still bright and Wallace appeared as its credible revivalist for he had been, after all, a Roosevelt cabinet officer and vice president (one of three, Roosevelt was hard on vice presidents). If the hope of a revived New Deal had overtones of political regression, the actual thrust of the campaign was directed at the central contemporary issue: the Cold War and its domestic consequences. And the vehicle, a new party, was definitely a radical departure.

As the political pros say the campaign peaked early, some time in the first half of 1948. Its base, resources, and initial momentum were not enough to withstand what was thrown against it. Truman campaigned effectively, the reigning labor officialdom exerted its muscle, liberals supplied the ideological whetstone for the edge of "anti-Communism," and on top of all this was the enormous, imponderable weight of the two-party tradition. The Wallace vote was a disappointing 1,157,172, almost two thirds of it in New York and California.

The movement proved to be what its quixotic standard bearer once called it, a Gideon's army, but only in the sense of being select and small. I still believe that a radical, clear-cut alternative to the bipartisan Cold War consensus was obligatory and useful, although I cannot gauge its precise effect at that historic moment. What was not necessary, let alone obligatory, was the corollary illusion that the Wallace party fulfilled the dream of generations of American radicals and progressives, that it was the new, viable, mass party. So strong was this illusion that even after the vote was counted one authoritative

Communist comment (by Eugene Dennis) compared it with the showing of the new-born Republican party in 1856. Taken literally this parallel anticipated that in 1952 the Progressive party would be contesting for power (its presidential vote in New York and California dropped to 87,000 in 1952, from 700,-000 in 1948). An illusion is not regrettable; it can even be pleasant, if one does not have to pay for it. This one exacted its payment. If you truly believe that you are creating the new, major party that will compel a complete realignment in American politics, then you go for broke. You are not too concerned about severing old ties and associations, believing it will be only temporary, for you think you are riding the popular wave of the immediate future and those other people will soon be swept along.

Even if we exhibited greater concern and pressed the Wallace campaign without the illusion that it represented a major realignment in American politics many old ties would have been cut. The illusion made it worse. And after the revelation of weakness at the polls the offensive against Communists and those aligned with them was waged with greater fury in certain quarters, most notably the CIO. The Left unions, which had been associated with the Wallace campaign in varying degrees, were expelled. Speaking from his position of strength CIO President Philip Murray poured on the scorn and vitriol, resorting again and again to a chosen word in his Catholic vocabulary — diabolic — infusing the assault against the Left with the temper of a holy war. To invoke a more charitable expression from that vocabulary, perhaps they knew not what they did, but they were heralding the entrance of Senator McCarthy.

For me as editor this increasing political ostracism of Communists presented distinct problems. The duality that arose from the circumstances attending the paper's birth became less credible. In the halcyon days of the united front it was more feasible to reconcile the dual roles: expression of a united front and articulate Communist voice within it. But as each real united front relationship was destroyed the old balance became

294 A Long View from the Left

less tenable. You cannot express what does not exist. Politically the paper became ever more constricted to its Communist core.

Still tradition, habit, style are tenacious, and the retention of old appearances was also induced by a practical consideration. As the danger and reality of suppression increased so did the incentive to provide the paper with the maximum protective coloration for its legal existence. In the popular mind the suppression of a newspaper is envisioned as a dramatic descent by police and a padlock on the premises. But, as we learned, there are many less spectacular devices for destroying a newspaper: intimidating visits by FBI agents to its subscribers, threats of boycott and violence by Rightist groups against news vendors who sell the paper and small businessmen who advertise in it, use of association with the paper (reading or supporting it) as evidence to blacklist workers (as was done most extensively in the maritime industry). Faced with these techniques for slow strangulation and the threat of sudden death, either through arbitrary use of existing laws or several bills pending in Congress, it seemed prudent to maintain elements of style, approach, and self-image that had reflected, and responded to, the wider constituency of the paper's formative years.

A certain ambiguity was created, especially with the decline of the Wallace movement, which had provided a credible framework for the paper's natal duality. This made for problems of editorial tone, selection, treatment, balance, involving essentially the discrepancy between the content, which ever more exclusively projected the distinctive and pressing needs of the Communist core, and the form, which was shaped by a system of relationships that no longer obtained.

Soon, however, I was beset by more pressing problems.

X. The Arrest

IN THOSE DAYS I rode to work on the California Street cable car, past Old St. Mary's Church in San Francisco's Chinatown. As in former days I usually glanced up at the church clock to check whether I was on time, but in those days, which were in the first half of 1951, I also looked at the inscription beneath the clock:

> Son, observe the time
> And fly from evil
> Ecc. IV. 23

Recitation of those lines became a morning rite. I looked for their scriptural context, first in Ecclesiastes, only to discover that Chapter IV contained no more than sixteen verses, then in Ecclesiasticus, which the Protestants, unlike the Catholics, relegate to the Apocrypha; all I could find in my Protestant Apocrypha to approximate the Catholic text was in Chapter IV, Verse 20:

> Observe the opportunity,
> And beware of evil

Damn, I thought, now here is a transfiguration in the mercantile spirit of Protestantism: instead of watching the clock, look for the main chance; instead of fleeing evil, be prudent. My fascination with those lines had nothing to do, of course, with any passion for comparative theology; it was political. In 1951 we Communists had a greater affinity with the Catholic text than with the Protestant; it was not opportunity we observed. As a rule, when I looked up at the church clock it read about a quarter to eight, but on our political clock it was five minutes to midnight.

How did it get to be so late? Not suddenly. We watched the hand moving in the five years after World War II, heard the seconds ticking away. *Tick* — one more loyalty checked. *Tick* — one more security risk screened. *Tick* — one more worker fired from a job, blacklisted from an industry or trade. *Tick* — one more career blasted in the arts, professions, or civil service. *Tick* — one more arrest, prosecution, prison sentence. *Tick* — one more suicide (a few physical and countable; many spiritual, their number defying count). *Tick . . . tick . . . tick . . . tick . . .* one more fear, one more silence, one more betrayal of a friend, one more exile . . . *Tick* — an acquaintance of mine visited a doctor, catering mostly to the assorted mix of liberals, progressives, radicals, who made up the amorphous Left Wing of the New Deal. "You'd be surprised," the doctor smiled, "if I told you how many people you know have sat in that same chair and recited the same symptoms." *Tick . . .*

Some events, more ponderous, marched to larger measures of time, to the chime of the hour perhaps, or the flutter of calendar leaves. One million workers expelled from the CIO, ostensibly because their leaders followed the "Communist Party line"; a Paul Robeson concert at Peekskill, New York, attacked by gangs of toughs; ten Hollywood film creators sent to prison for contempt of Congress, hundreds more Red-listed in the mass media. These last were victims of the Committee, a strange spectacle, something old, something new, a ritualistic atavism in modern dress, the Roman circus under klieg lights, the Spanish Inquisition before television cameras.

The Committee epitomized the spirit of the age; so a new word was coined as tribute to the man who was shrewd, most ruthless, and cynical in conjuring up the powers of the Committee. McCarthyism.

The universality of McCarthyism's effects upon national life is widely acknowledged, but it also had a particularity as it affected Communists. Much confirmation has since been offered of what we said then: we were the primary targets only in the sense of being first, others were more important. The McCarthyites were bidding for political power, and to get it they had to wrest it from those who had it, which most certainly did not mean us. They were happy, however, to mangle us in order to intimidate and paralyze more highly placed personages; to give them their due they not only perceived the tactical utility in this, they also derived ideological gratification. They were living the wild dream of Babbittry: the combination of business and pleasure.

I don't suppose it would much console a minnow to know it was being scooped up in a net only to be used as bait for bigger fish. Our circumstances were even worse, for liberals and moderates were not only content to see us caught in the McCarthyite dragnet, hoping their adverseries would be partially appeased by such a catch, they also joined in the sport to demonstrate they could fish for Communists as well as anyone, albeit more discriminately. In short we were being clobbered from both sides. Our time also marched in calendar years.

1947: Secretary of Labor Lewis B. Schwellenbach declared the Communist party should be outlawed. A trial balloon?

1948: If it had been a trial balloon, it was no longer: twelve national committeemen of the party (the entire committee except its one woman member, Elizabeth Gurley Flynn) were indicted under the Smith Act. The indictment charged they "unlawfully, willfully and knowingly, did conspire with each other, and with divers persons to the Grand Jury unknown, to organize as the Communist party of the United States of America a society, group, and assembly of persons who teach and advocate the overthrow and destruction of the Government of the United States by force and violence."

1949: A nine-month trial concluded with a guilty verdict against eleven (the twelfth, William Z. Foster, was severed from the case because of poor health). Ten defendants received maximum five-year prison terms; in deference to a Distinguished Service Cross for valor in World War II, Robert Thompson drew three years.

1950: After outbreak of the Korean War, Congress passed the McCarran (Internal Security) Act. Similar measures had been pushed in 1948–1949, notably by Senator Karl E. Mundt of South Dakota and Representative Richard M. Nixon of California. Fumbling with a sticky legal technicality — how to achieve an unconstitutional purpose through constitutional means — Congress hit upon the McCarran Act formula: by requiring registration of the party and its members, by imposing a host of sanctions against both, legal existence of the party would be rendered impossible, although the act contained a devious disclaimer: party membership *per se* was not unlawful.

1951: The Supreme Court, in a six to two decision, upheld constitutionality of the Smith Act's antisedition sections, confirming the conviction of the eleven national Communist leaders.

That was on June 4. On June 14 a Communist national committee statement said, "This decision makes a fundamental change in the 'American way of life.' The process of creeping fascism . . . has gathered new speed . . . Our country now stands on the edge of the precipice . . ." Ostensible escape clauses only magnified the sense of impending catastrophe. "Only a new tempo . . . of popular resistance can save us from full-fledged fascism and a third world war . . . Disaster can even now be averted . . . but only if . . ."

Five minutes to midnight. And the hand kept moving. On June 20 a federal grand jury in New York returned Smith Act conspiracy indictments against twenty-one more Communist leaders; seventeen were arrested. Press stories referred to these as "the second string." On June 24 a *New York Times* dope story said, "The United States Government last week made plain the strategy of its legal assault on the Communist party in America. That strategy is to cut off the party's head, so to speak, by jailing its leaders as criminal conspirators and repeating the process each time the party installs new leaders. In practical effect, if not technically, the operation of a national Communist party would be outlawed."

The story reported the twenty-one indictments "caused much speculation over how far the Government intends to carry its drive against the Communist party. There was talk that prosecutions might eventually mount into the 'thousands.'" The *Times* man was dubious about the government's going that far. "One federal prosecutor said last week that the total of indictments now envisioned," he reported, "probably will not go over 100." Even if the anonymous prosecutor's projection were accepted at face value, it referred only to what was "now envisioned"; assuming plausibly that dragnet arrests gather a momentum of their own, what will be envisioned tomorrow, or the day after? Dope stories in other papers were less restrained; some talked of 2000 arrests, some of 20,000, some soared into six figures.

Son, observe the time, and fly from evil . . . On July 2, when the eleven "first-string" leaders were to surrender for imprisonment, only seven appeared. The other four vanished. Their disappearance signified the meaning of the national committee's June 14 statement more forcefully than its words. In preceding months and weeks colleagues of mine in the California Communist leadership also vanished. They were "unavailable," you said; unavailable, that is, for arrest, although most often you did not verbalize it. Oh, so-and-so, you said, and then you described a sweeping downward arc with your hand, as if to indicate some vast subterranean region. Since those who remained available were prone to arrest, the operative organizational leadership was vested in the unavailable.

I was then executive editor of the *Daily People's World*. Two colleagues, Associate Editor Adam Lapin and Foreign Editor George Lohr, and I comprised the paper's editorial board. Lapin became unavailable; Lohr suffered a nervous breakdown, so severe it was thought best to arrange for his departure from the country. (Arrangements for his reception on the other side, in Eastern Europe, were flubbed, so he went through a long, harrowing ordeal before matters were finally straightened out.)

And what about the children? This was a topic of earnest conversation. Suppose both parents were clapped into jail, what happens then to young children? People worried about it. They made private arrangements with kin or friends, who were thought to be less vulnerable. Perhaps the questions about children, which seemed so real, so urgent, convey in personal terms the political ambience in those June and July days of 1951. Perhaps, and yet the questions about the children were only symptomatic, remembrance of them, abstracted from the political spirit of the times, might even seem like sentimentality, and this would be a bad mistake. The main thing was the political ambience, which was described with big, abstract generalizations — a period of repression, a time of social retreat.

It seemed an exposed and beleaguered post, editorship of the *People's World*. Here the big generalizations — repression, retreat — registered in minute detail on the sensitive instrument that is a newspaper. Sources, which are the sustenance of the working newspaperman, shriveled. People, who had talked to you with cordiality and candor, now were not in or had no comment. Some were brazen about it, parading the hysterics of the time as their own cherished convictions. Others, shame-faced, apologetic, asked you to understand their prudence, to forgive their fears. Petty things, petty in both senses of the word, trivial and mean, but parts of a large design, which was to isolate you, to hem you into an ever more constricted circle, the more easily to destroy you. This was only one tangible manifestation among many of repression. There was also retreat. Inexorably, year by year, circulation declined, from a peak average of 15,411 in 1947 to 9427 in 1951. The corollary of losses in circulation and support was steady retrenchment, from publication six days a week in 1947 to five days in 1951, with a concurrent shrinkage of the daily paper's size by more than one-third, from six standard pages to eight tabloid. I became a perennial master of ceremonies at office farewell parties for staff members let go in our economic retrenchment.

I could salve professional vanity with the recognition that the paper's decline was induced by powers more formidable than journalistic skills, but this was small solace. It only accentuated the sense of being in a war of attrition with the overwhelming odds against you; for the time being, to be sure (there still was the long view), but you did not know how long this time would last, except that the five-to-midnight reading assumed it would get worse and the night might be long. Still you fought, conceiving of editorials and headlines as salvos in a desperate battle.

What did I write about? I recall particularly one editorial, spread across the front page under the question, "Is war inevitable?" Such display was exceedingly rare; as a rule we conformed to the newspaper convention that the proper place for editorials is the editorial page. The moment was also exceedingly rare, November 27, 1950. A week earlier advance elements of General Douglas MacArthur's armies in Korea had reached the Chinese frontier, despite prior warnings of Chinese countermeasures. The day before Chinese units counterattacked in force on the Korean side of the Yalu River. The world was on the brink and people asked, is world war inevitable? Our answer that it wasn't had always been greeted with skepticism by some readers; that chill November the skepticism became more vocal and widespread. The editorial was addressed to this skepticism. I do not propose to reproduce the body of the editorial, which essentially was an itemization of powerful forces and factors against global war, and an argument against "one mischievous misconception," which "holds that a belief that war is *not* inevitable means support for the inverse proposition that peace *is* inevitable." I wish to convey its tenor:

". . . But the last die has not been cast . . . We believe there is a fighting chance to avert the catastrophe of World War III . . .

"We are not bookies. We do not quote odds . . . While there is a fighting chance, it is the supreme duty of every thinking worker, every human being that has no vested interest he thinks can be enlarged or salvaged through a world carnage, to grasp that chance with both hands, and fight for peace."

Scanning editorials and headlines of those days I am struck by their tenor. They were not fanning the flames of discontent, with the offensive élan attached to that phrase. They fanned the sparks of resistance. The mood then was charged with urgency, with crisis; often, it seemed, I worked with fevered intensity, the more so because of something else: as I wrote and edited I also wondered when I would be picked off, ever aware of being watched. The young men sat in a car all day long outside of the paper's offices. Across the street from my home was a top-floor flat that had an odd air of being occupied, but not lived in; no matter how late I came home at night there was a light in it. When I looked out of the window before climbing into bed the light was out.

I was thirty-seven then, married, two sons, aged four and three (yes, my wife, Nancy, and I discussed the question: what about the children?). It was a long time since I had accepted arrest and imprisonment as occupational hazards, as general possibilities. Now they were not mere possibilities, no longer general.

Son, observe the time, and fly from evil. The clock on Old St. Mary's read twenty-five to eight on the morning of July 26, earlier than on other days, it being a Thursday, bloody Thursday we called it in our office because this was the day our enlarged weekend edition went to press. By the time the San Francisco Ferry Building siren wailed its eight A.M. wail I was in shirt-sleeves at my typewriter, pecking out an editorial. The siren was the signal for the FBI agents, at least ten of them, who burst into our office, and before I extricated my editorial mind from the Korean War stalemate one agent was upon me, saying I was under arrest. The next morning's San Francisco *Chronicle* reported, "The 37-year-old editor put on his brown corduroy jacket and was handcuffed." What I had been expecting, when it finally came, was that casual. Not for the FBI agents, however. Only one other *People's World* staff member was on the premises; ten agents (with I know not how many outside) did seem redundant. They came on like gangbusters, their tension and excitement communicated by the trembling hands of the agent who slipped the handcuffs on me.

In the car, en route to FBI headquarters, I had a terrible feeling of aloneness; the three athletic young men with me were armed, I assumed, and my implacable enemies; I was handcuffed. It was momentary, this feeling of being so totally in their power, for mostly my thoughts ran in an opposite direction, concerned not with my solitude but with how much company I had. I took it for granted others had been arrested and I wondered who and how many.

The answer came soon. I was one of twelve. Six more had been picked up in the San Francisco area: Bernadette Doyle,

Ernest Fox, Carl Rude Lambert, Albert J. (Mickie) Lima, Loretta Starvus Stack, and Oleta O'Connor Yates. Four in Los Angeles: Philip M. (Slim) Connelly, Dorothy Healey, Rose Chernin Kusnitz, and Henry Steinberg. One in New York: William Schneiderman. The FBI agents, their watches synchronized, moved everywhere at the stroke of eight A.M., Pacific Daylight Time (which was, of course, eleven A.M. for the solitary arrest in New York). We had not been indicted, no warrants were secured for our arrest; we were picked up on telegraphed FBI complaints charging conspiracy to violate the Smith Act.

Afterward I was grateful my schedule brought me to work before eight A.M. Almost all my codefendants were seized at home, some still in bed, others in the midst of the morning rituals that prepare one to face another day. When the knock on the door comes, it is better for it not to be a knock on the bathroom door. In at least two instances the FBI agents barged into homes with young children, and the scenes were traumatic. It seemed more appropriate to have them break into a newspaper office to seize the editor in the criminal act of composing an editorial. This is only half irony, in the overt acts subsequently charged against us, what I was doing that morning was as criminal as any of the others.

On the afternoon of our arrest the seven of us in San Francisco were taken before the United States Commissioner, a small, white-haired, courtly gentleman of the old West, looking as if he had been molded to fit his name, Francis St.J. Fox. The government demanded no less than $75,000 bail for each of us. Commissioner Fox accepted that figure for the four men, but in a gesture of Western chivalry set $7,500 for Oleta Yates, and $2500 for the other two women (Loretta Stack was a mother of small children, Bernadette Doyle was in poor health). The women were released on bail, the men were deposited in the San Francisco county jail.

San Francisco enjoys a worldwide reputation for its cuisine and its scenic accommodations, but these distinctions never extended to its jails. Certainly not to the old county jail on Kearney Street, which harked back to the nineteenth-century "durance vile" tradition and has since been mercifully torn down.

The food was worse than in the Los Angeles county jail (a grudging admission from a true San Franciscan); the bread had an odd chemical flavor that recalled the perennial question in the army: do they really put saltpeter in the food?

After a night in this jail we experienced our first formal court hearing on a motion to reduce bail for the men. Maybe it was not a surrealistic scene, but this is how I saw it and remember it (all except the words, which I did not trust to memory alone). United States District Judge Louis E. Goodman, short, thin, pinch-faced, sharp-nosed, the rich summer tan setting off a mad gleam in his eyes, perched on the bench in his black robe, was a witch. Assistant United States Attorney Joseph Karesh, large, beefy, pumpkin-faced, was a mobile jack-o'-lantern. In the hysterical climax of the scene the jack-o'-lantern dashed toward the witch, waving four freshly printed WANTED circulars with the wicked mug shots of the four national Communist leaders who had vanished twenty-five days earlier. These men fled, he screamed, these people will flee. Make the bail high, he exhorted, so high they will not be able to flee because they will be locked up in jail.

Now it was the turn of our attorneys, curiously detached from this scene (they seemed sane, so what were they doing there?), but very much in it, of course. But, Your Honor, they argued, the maximum penalty for the charged offense is five years, the same as for taking a stolen car across a state line. If Your Honor please, the court should follow the established rule of reasonably relating bail to the gravity of the offense as measured by the penalty prescribed.

The witch had the last word (don't they often?). ". . . the most serious offense that can be charged . . . *more serious than treason* . . . By virtue of that fact and irrespective of the penalty involved, the bail should be substantial. Still $75,000 is a little high [this with a maniacal smile] . . . Fifty thousand dollars for all of them!"

One immediate consequence of his ruling was the return of the three women to jail. No sexist chivalry for the witch. I was the only Jew in this group of seven, so the little pang at the ethnic identity of judge and prosecutor was mine alone.

Five days later, August 1, we were transferred to the Los Angeles county jail, the four men handcuffed en route, except when the plane was aloft. The move was a surprise. Our adversary, the government, possessing the prerogative to choose the locale of the trial, preferred the Los Angeles political climate, so it had us indicted the day before in a fifteen-minute session of the federal grand jury in Los Angeles. We were to be jailed and tried in Los Angeles although the fountainhead of our conspiracy, according to the government's theory of the case, was in San Francisco, at the Communist party's state headquarters. This caprice of venue seems trivial now; it didn't then. Being forcibly transported somewhere you do not wish to go strengthens the feeling of captivity; perhaps it is because movement is ordinarily associated with freedom.

Serving "dead time" in the Los Angeles jail, the most irksome of times to serve, we began the battle for bail. Just getting out of jail was incentive enough, but as we saw it more was at issue. The government had gone through a tense, ugly, wearying, costly nine-months trial to convict the first batch of eleven Communist leaders. Having secured Supreme Court validation of the law and the convictions, the government wanted no more long, messy trials, no more extensive appeals. The Communists had their days and months in court. The Dennis case (as the prosecution of the first eleven was christened in legal annals) was a test case that disposed of all legal and constitutional issues; what was there left to litigate, once the accused was proven to be a knowledgeable Communist? With such assumptions the government sought a political and psychological atmosphere in which subsequent Smith Act trials would be pro forma, belt-line productions.

By imposing prohibitive bail to keep us locked up, the government was exerting enormous pressure for our acquiescence in its streamlined haste. After all, the purpose of prosecution is to put you in jail, but when you already are there the psychological impulse is to "get it over with." Aside from psychology, there is practicality: jail impairs serious preparation for a long, involved political trial. A no-bail precedent before trial all but precludes bail after conviction, effectively prejudicing the right to appeal. A full-dress appeal may take anywhere from three to five years for final disposition in the Supreme Court; in purely personal terms, therefore, the ultimate decision, even if favorable, would be moot for by then you would have served all, or almost all, of your prison sentence.

This, in effect, was preventive detention. Putting and keeping Communists in jail was to be made routine. By extension the same formula could then be applied to others, whose politics distressed the government. In retrospect, two decades later, such a diagnosis of the government's intentions seems as valid now as it seemed then.

Mounting the battle against the government's design we were enveloped in two environmental layers, first jail, and beyond it that which on the inside is sometimes called "the free world." The Los Angeles county jail, like most local jails, ostensibly intended for relatively brief confinement and making no pretense at rehabilitation, had no provisions for exercise, for work (except for minimal housekeeping chores), or for entertainment (unless you found the succession of Sunday gospel singers entertaining, which most prisoners did not. The washed, eupeptic Christians, shining with the virtue of being among sinners, planted themselves in front of the cell tier and blasted the fervor of their hymns at the captive audience that could not shut them out or elude them. One black choir had the spirit and beat to make the hymns attractive, except that the hymn it sang with the most verve was "Every Day Will Be Sunday By and By," which was a mistake. The dreariest of jail days, one Sunday a week was more than enough.)

The jail had its own hierarchical system, which worked curiously to our advantage; it being a society of criminals, real or alleged, the greater the crime, the higher the social status, and we were treated as important felons indeed — important enough to be lodged in "high power," the maximum security section on the tenth floor of the Los Angeles Hall of Justice. In other tiers lesser criminals were terribly overcrowded, some compelled to sleep in corridors, which meant they had no bunks of their own, and there was a jam-up for toilet facilities.

No such congestion was permitted in maximum security, showers were more frequent and regular (no small amenity in the heat and smog of a Los Angeles summer), access was easier to a peddler's cart that came by with milk, pies, magazines, and other incidentals. The maximum security tier consisted of two adjacent corridors; ten or twelve double-bunk cells strung along one side of each corridor, the other side consisting of heavy bars, beyond which was an alleyway for guards — or gospel singers. The corridor adjacent to ours housed Mickey Cohen, a pudgy baron in the kingdom of organized crime, who occasionally dispensed his largess to us in the form of used pinochle decks. To give Mickey his due, he must have been fastidious, or suspicious, or simply a conspicuous consumer; the cards were almost new.

As a jail it was not the worst, not the best, but it was a jail, and this was the worst thing about it. Creature discomforts, denial of the most advertised American freedom, the consumer's freedom to choose in the free marketplace were small irritants. The onerous, oppressive essence of the place was being imprisoned in it. Nothing special, no specially brutal guards or depraved inmates, no specially vile food or quarters, nothing sufficiently abnormal to be described as horror, just normal, routine captivity in an urban county jail with its measured, cumulative cruelty and human indignity ingeniously expressed in the phrase "serving time." Judges used to say thirty lashes, now they say thirty days; this denotes penal progress, it also says something about the quality of penal days.

(I do not offer my casual jail experience as typical, being well aware of cruelties and humiliations in our prison system that go far beyond the primary punishment of confinement and are aptly described as horror. We did not encounter these. One cruelty we shared with California's prison population is the indeterminate sentence; we had not been tried, let alone sentenced, we had no terminal date for our confinement. We did not know if or when we would get out on bail.)

In jail the days dragged; in "the free world" outside the clock moved on, perhaps a little more quickly. On the day we were arrested, United States Attorney Ernest Tolin said in Los Angeles, "This is the first move in a program to destroy the Communist party in the west." Similar programs unfolded elsewhere. We read about more Smith Act arrests in jail: August 7 — six in Maryland, August 17 — six in Pittsburgh, August 28 — seven in Honolulu. On August 31 three more of our colleagues — Frank Carlson, Ben Dobbs, Frank Spector — were arrested in Los Angeles, so that our California conspiracy now embraced fifteen indicted suspects and numerous co-conspirators "to the Grand Jury unknown." On October 8 Gus Hall, one of the four national Communist leaders who vanished July 2, was seized in Mexico City and abducted back across the border without the formality of an extradition hearing. This was seventy-four days after our arrest; we still were in the Los Angeles county jail.

When there was no news of arrests we could always read about Senator Joseph R. McCarthy. It was a vintage year for McCarthyism. The once obscure freshman senator from Wisconsin had staked his first claim to national attention in February 1950, with a declaration in Wheeling, West Virginia, that he had a list of 205 Communists in the State Department. By the summer of 1951 he was the man of the year, dominating the news media, exercising the powers that soon led William S. White, *New York Times* correspondent, to report: "Highly placed and sophisticated men arriving in Washington from abroad — not excepting cabinet ministers — often ask anxiously about McCarthy before inquiring about the President of the United States."

From the tenth-floor cell tier of the Los Angeles Hall of Justice we had a distinct view of McCarthyism. Here it was not a miasma, or a face on a TV screen. Here it was more tangible, something like the metal bars and the heavy metal doors. Here the man, his id and his ism, epitomized the constellation of forces, prejudices, fears, passions, and political calculations that put us in jail and were bent on keeping us in jail. It was not absolutely necessary to be in jail in those days to know McCarthyism, for its spell was pervasive and worked in many ways, but sitting in jail gave me a sense of greater intimacy with its ultimate logic.

My mood, in those August days, was not good. I was possessed with the five-to-midnight mentality, made more compelling by the continued arrests outside, by the accelerating, unimpeded ascent of McCarthyism. In this mood legal due process was an empty charade, a futility that did not warrant the expenditure of much energy, money, time. I recalled that in the World War I era, when the Industrial Workers of the World was the target of dragnet arrests and mass trials, one group of Wobblies resorted to "standing silent" in court. Their absolute silence was their protest, their demonstrative refusal to participate in the mock rituals of a "kangaroo court." I leaned to this tactic, or something like it. I did not think it through; this inclination was more emotional than calculated. I was never pressed to argue for it; if I had been, I suppose my argument would have been that after the protracted Dennis trial, after the Supreme Court decision in that case, a repetition of all that would be a grotesque farce; the revolutionary alternative was a dramatic protest against the legal sham by refusal to take part in it. The rhetoric would have been revolutionary, but thinking back upon it the motivation was an underlying pessimism.

Not all was that grim in our cell tier. Some of us played pinochle with other inmates. One transient pinochle player had been brought down from San Quentin to be a witness in a trial. I suspect the con from Q was a state's witness, as he was nervous and jumpy. He drew as his pinochle partner one of my codefendants, Mickie Lima, a very deliberate, calm, unhurried man. The ordinary pinochle player picks up the cards dealt to him, studies them a while, and decides what his maximum bid will be. This decision is subject to modification by the bidding of the other players, but this does not necessitate a reappraisal of the cards in his hand when the bid gets around to him again. Lima, however, was no ordinary pinochle player. Each time the bid came around to him he carefully studied his cards anew, as if he saw them for the first time. In one hand, when Lima went through this meditation for a third time, the nervous con from Q exploded, "Goddamn it, Mickie! How did a man as cautious as you ever get in a place like this?"

How did we get into a place like this? A comic relief of sorts

was afforded by our attempts to explain the legalities of it to
the prisoners (the politics was easier). They had picked up the
evocative words . . . conspiracy . . . overthrowing the government by force and violence. So that's what you're in for,
trying to overthrow the government by force and violence? No,
that's not the charge. Conspiracy? Yes, but not conspiracy to
overthrow the government by force and violence. Then what's
the conspiracy? Well, they say we conspired to teach and advocate the overthrow of the government by force and violence.

The normal, pragmatic American mind can comprehend the
deed, the action, but in our case the crime alleged was thrice
removed from the substantive action. We were not charged
with attempting to do it, or even conspiring to do it, or even
teaching and advocating the necessity and desirability of doing
it, but with *conspiring* to teach and advocate that it ought to be
done. To compound the complexity, human intent — elusive,
intangible — was an essential element of the alleged crime.
Conspiring alone was not quite enough; it had to be done with
a specific intent, which was, in the prosecution phrase, to bring
about the violent overthrow as speedily as circumstances permit. Just when such permissive circumstances might arise, or
just what their character would be, was immaterial in the government's correlation of intangible intent and hypothetical future.

As we later discovered, explaining the legal intricacies of
conspiracy law, as applied in our case, wasn't any easier outside
of jail. In jail, having had experience in trials, some prisoners
asked: what's the evidence? Mostly, the physical evidence, the
exhibits, will be books. Books? Yes, books.

On a primitive level some of our fellow-prisoners considered
themselves skilled practitioners of force and violence: they
were familiar with small firearms, knives, clubs, comprehending these as instruments of violence. But books? One young
fellow, taciturn and tough, spent the better part of one afternoon filing the end of a toothbrush handle on the cell floor into
a sharp, murderous point; he had the imagination to conceive
of a toothbrush as a lethal weapon. But not a book.

In my own imagination I played with books as instruments

of violence. Marx's *Capital,* especially the bulky Kerr edition; now this was a missile or clumsy bludgeon that might do some damage, but the "Communist Manifesto" or "State and Revolution," skinny pamphlets, weighing only a few ounces and usually paperbound, how could you hurt anybody with them?

We never did explain our indictment to the satisfaction of our fellow-prisoners. Aside from one old man, who was in for a crime of passion, virtually all the others (between a dozen and a score came through our cell cluster while we were there) were young men, who began their careers as outlaws and prisoners in adolescence, climbing up the penal ladder, which is as rigidly structured as the academic: juvenile detention, county jail, state penitentiary (minimum, medium, maximum security). One man, who was with us only briefly, had achieved the penal equivalent of the Institute for Advanced Studies: he had been to Alcatraz. They were well acquainted with the prison population but they were too young to have encountered the last wave of organized radicals in California's prisons in the 1930s. We were something new in their experience; although almost all were friendly, a few very friendly, they could not quite make us out. This led to a game. To break the monotony of jail routine people play games. This particular game was inspired by an item in a weekly news magazine about a new clue in the million-dollar Brink's robbery in Boston the year before. Hell, one con said, this bit about overthrowing the government is just a shuck, you guys pulled the Brink's robbery. The game caught on. We were the gang that pulled the Brink's job and our mastermind was William Schneiderman, the defendant arrested in New York. As California state chairman of the Communist party Schneiderman was billed in the press as chief of our conspiracy.

Extradition proceedings in New York took a little time, and so did Schneiderman's manacled trip cross the country. We awaited the man who had been our political leader for many years; our fellow-prisoners awaited the big brain of the Brink's job. This waiting period was only a fortnight but in the drag of jail time it was enough to build up much suspense. On the day Schneiderman arrived the prisoner issuing jail uniforms in the

admission section might have been once a costumer of burlesque comedians. Schneiderman's short, slender figure, with
slightly sloping shoulders, was draped with an enormously out-
sized jacket. The pants were at least six inches too big at the
waist. As he shuffled into our cell corridor the only prop missing was the hot-water bag burlesque comedians pulled out of
their pants. I do not know what sort of an image of the Brink's
robbery mastermind our fellow prisoners had created in their
minds but what they saw was not it. This much was clear in
their faces. When Schneiderman came in the Brink's game
went out.

His physical presence was not impressive; his mind was,
lucid, methodical, purposeful, stubborn, and, more than most,
insistent upon confrontation with reality. Aside from his mind
he also possessed the experience and authority of leadership.
With his arrival our preparations for trial began in earnest. To
cope with the many problems of policy, big and small, political,
legal, administrative, a trial committee of five was established,
consisting of the arrested members of the party's state board,
thus deriving its legitimacy from the inner-party electoral process.

In the first meeting of the trial committee there was a revelation, an astounding political self-recognition; a consensus
emerged that it was not five to midnight after all, that this reading of the political time and all the practical decisions that
flowed from it were erroneous. The initiative in this was not
mine certainly, for I had succumbed to the zero-hour syn-
drome, and if I now shook it off quickly, this was still without
any special merit of perception. An element of contradiction in
my political existence facilitated a reappraisal of the time: a
newspaper is a public institution, my editorial function was
both assertion and defense of legal right by its practical exercise. Almost all my energy was consumed in affirming the
party's legal existence, restricted and conditioned as it was,
whereas the zero-hour estimate dictated contrary priorities of
adjustment to illegal existence, of preparations to survive in this
imminent extremity.

The lead in a critical look at the political time was taken by the two very able women on the trial committee, the party's leaders in California's major population centers, Oleta O'Connor Yates of San Francisco and Dorothy Healey of Los Angeles. Schneiderman circumspectly refrained from joining in our political consensus, for he was the representative of the national center, and therefore bound by its policy. Not until five years later was it revealed that in the party's national councils he had fought doggedly against adoption of the five to midnight political line. Not knowing this in the late summer of 1951, I assumed his failure to challenge our consensus was prompted by a realization such an endeavor would likely be futile and would create an enormous strain at a time when we were trying to shape a common strategy in the difficult battle forced upon us.

Inexorably interrelated, like the hands on the clock, two political estimates went into the five-to-midnight line. First, the American ruling class was actively preparing for war to secure world hegemony, and although this global war was not inevitable its likelihood was such that the country's rulers were bent on creating all the conditions — military, strategic, political — for the swift exercise of the war option. Second, the political precondition for war was a Fascist regime that suppressed all dissent and opposition. In disagreeing with the official party estimate of the rate of Fascist development we differed implicitly with a comprehensive analysis of world and domestic politics. However, in a letter we sent to the California underground center for transmission through channels to the national party leadership, we focused on domestic reaction and the resistance to it. We drafted no elaborate political theses.

The reply from our California associates told us, in effect, to mind our own business. Responsibility for the operative leadership, they assumed, also vested the underground centers with authority to formulate, interpret, and execute policy. We did not plunge into an extended polemic. Situated as we were, behind prison bars, preoccupied with the fight to get out, physically cut off from the party organization, we were not inclined to press a battle for a full-scale critical review of the party's course.

Even if we were so inclined the obstacles were formidable, probably insurmountable. The entire national leadership was either in prison, in hiding, or awaiting trial. The network of underground leadership centers was new; the personnel, much of it inexperienced, inept, and clumsy in the operation of a clandestine system of organization, was snarled in the technical details of exercising leadership and yet eluding police detection and surveillance. Defects in technical finesse only compounded the underlying problem, which was the validity of the political rationale for devising an organizational structure patterned after that of some Western European Communist parties during the Nazi occupation. In the party ranks the strains of existence "on the edge of the precipice" (to employ the phrase of the party's national statement of June 14), of preparation for the plunge into the abyss, were incalculable.

Sensing all that, our trial committee consensus in the Los Angeles county jail, for all its dramatic divergence from national party policy, manifested its sole practical effect in the approach to our trial and defense. Our premise that we were not five minutes from fascism, that the possibilities of fighting for legal existence were not near exhaustion, that, indeed, our primary energies ought to be thrown into this fight, rather than into adjustment to its foredoomed failure, dictated a maximum defense, in the courtroom and out. This meant lawyers, a full-dress public campaign, money.

A contrary course was indicated in the drumfire of criticism from our colleagues in the underground leadership centers. The California center reproached us for too many lawyers, too much money, and charged these excesses reflected "legalistic illusions." The same accusation accompanied a testy question from the national center: how come so many of the party's principal leaders in California were available for arrest?

The accusation of "legalistic illusions" was ironically gratuitous. Sitting in jail, kept there by arbitrary judicial caprice in exercising discretion to set bail, it would have taken an inordinate attachment to illusion to cherish any about the intrinsic equity and justice of the legal system. If jail were insufficient antidote to such illusions, there was also United States District Judge William C. Mathes.

Mathes allowed no illusions. It is said that psychiatric patients are prone to fall in love with the psychiatrist; in political trials defendants are prone to develop a pure (and reciprocal) hate for their judge. Hate, like love, tends to possessiveness and conceit; defendants in some other trials will claim their hate is purer because their judge was more deserving of it, but I will stick with my judge.

He and I shared the same courtroom for almost a year, and during half that time he had the satisfaction of keeping me in jail. He was short, squat, broad-faced but sharp-featured, fifty-three years old when I encountered him and six years on the federal bench. He came into the courtroom with a flourish, wheeling around to face the flag, preening his small stature to its full martinet height in reverent attention (he was a member of the American Legion). When he was angry his Harvard Law School veneer rubbed off and he reverted to his native Texan drawl. "Mis-tah Ma-a-hrgolis," he would then growl at our counsel, Ben Margolis, "ah wan' a law-'er-lahk argument . . ."

One of his memorable performances was a soliloquy on what is reasonable, as employed in "reasonable bail." Reasonable, he intoned, was anything within the outer bounds of reason. In our case, $5000 would be within the bounds of reason — and so would $100,000. The difference between $5000 and $100,000 was a difference in degree, not in kind; he savored this formulation of the dialectical distinction between quantity and quality. It was eminently reasonable, therefore, to set bail at $50,000 each (or $750,000 for fifteen of us). Yes, I thought then, within the bounds of his reason — and beyond the limits of our resources.

To the argument that $50,000 was far in excess of bail usually set in cases involving a maximum prison sentence of five years, he had a ready reply. He just could not understand how Congress could prescribe the same penalty in the Smith Act as it did in the Dyer Act, which concerned no more than transportation of stolen automobiles across the state line. The sincerity of his regret that ultimately he would be able to impose no greater sentence upon us pierced the mask of judicial dispassion. Meanwhile, unencumbered by congressional vagary, he kept us in jail.

To support our contention that $50,000 was beyond our means we submitted affidavits on our weekly earnings, which were in the forty-to-fifty-dollar-a-week range. Looking at these affidavits he shook his head in disbelief. It was inconceivable to him, he said, that people would engage in so hazardous an occupation as overthrowing the government for so little money. He did not believe us.

He had a single-minded belief: we should be behind bars. There we remained while the bail issue dragged through appellate due process, all the way up to the Supreme Court. On November 5 — 104 days after our arrest — the Supreme Court decided in our favor. Free at last, we exulted, not reckoning with Judge Mathes. This may have been "legalistic illusion," this notion that a Supreme Court decision would shake his determination to keep us locked up.

On November 7 Mathes convened court to hear our motion for reduction of bail, the remedy suggested by the Supreme Court. But he did not act on the motion. He said he could not understand the Supreme Court's decision. A practiced lawyer, a judge, presumably trained in deciphering the most recondite legalese, he claimed to be baffled by the Supreme Court, although in this instance its opinions seemed clear enough to be comprehended by the layman.

"It is not denied that bail for each petitioner has been fixed in a sum much higher than that usually imposed for offenses with like penalties," wrote Chief Justice Fred Vinson for the court, "and yet there has been no factual showing to justify such action in this case . . . In the absence of such a showing, we are of the opinion that the fixing of bail before trial in these cases cannot be squared with the statutory and constitutional standards for admission to bail."

More blunt was a concurring opinion by Justice Robert Jackson (joined in by Justice Felix Frankfurter). ". . . the defect in the proceedings below," Jackson wrote, "appears to be, that, provoked by the flight of certain Communists after conviction, the Government demands . . . a use of the bail power to keep Communist defendants in jail before conviction. Thus, the amount is said to have been fixed not as a reasonable assurance of their presence at the trial, but also as an assurance they would remain in jail. There seems reason to believe that this may have been the spirit to which the courts below have yielded, and it is contrary to the whole policy and philosophy of bail . . ."

All this, said Mathes, was so elusive he needed at least six more days to meditate upon it. The bail reduction hearing was put off until November 13, and then in extravagant excess of due process the hearing dragged on four days, essentially regurgitating the evidence and arguments offered in prior hearings. Upon termination of the hearing on Friday, November 16, Mathes announced he still was not ready to rule, he would have to ponder his decision. The next day, November 17, was my thirty-eighth birthday and it passed in the Los Angeles county jail without celebration. I recalled another birthday, spent in "pulling a Gandhi" on the floor of the Jane Street Mission on the New York waterfront, with its tense exhilaration at the prospect it might wind up in jail. I was now exactly twice as old.

The weekend passed and Monday brought no decision from Judge Mathes. Now the drag of days was more excruciating. A week went by; he still pondered, we still chafed. On November 28 — 12 days after the hearing, 23 days after the Supreme Court decision, 127 days, more than four months, after our arrest — Mathes finally ruled. He still could not understand the Supreme Court's opinion; it did not alter his judgment that $50,000 was reasonable bail.

Oh, the son of a bitch, I thought, and he's going to be our trial judge. By then we had been in the same courtroom many times, for bail hearings and pretrial proceedings, and we were yet to face each other day after day during six long months of trial. But on no day, before or after, did I feel more strongly the quintessence of our relationship than I did on November

28. We sat together all those days, almost within spitting distance, each knowing the enmity and hatred of the other. Court decorum, judicial form, these were less than a G-string on the nakedness of the confrontation. In his flamboyant homage to the flag, in many comments and asides from the bench he signified to us that he was the avenging defender of his social order, his status quo; we were its enemies, and he would inflict upon us the maximum punishment within his powers. His sole regret was that it could not be more; Congress had been flippant in the punitive sections of the law, the Supreme Court was obtuse in its deference to the constitutional injunction against "excessive bail." On November 28 he still had the whip hand; the Supreme Court opinion to the contrary, he could still inflict a few more lashes, and he did.

Once more we started up the appellate ladder. Judges of the United States Circuit Court of Appeals had no difficulty in understanding the Supreme Court; with relative speed they set bail at $10,000 each for seven of us, and $5000 for the other five who had been arrested July 26 (the three jailed August 31 were involved in separate bail proceedings).

Mathes retained one power: acceptance of the bail, ordinarily an administrative detail delegated to a clerk. He transformed it into a formal hearing in open court. With a great show of devotion to duty and solicitude for our rights he set the hearing for a Saturday, December 8. The persons posting bond were compelled to take the witness stand to be grilled by Mathes. Did they truly have the authority to dispose of the bond they posted? Did they truly realize the enormous responsibility they assumed (he threw in the ancient common law that made the bondsman responsible for producing the defendant in court)? Were they truly aware of their risks if we fled?

While we were prisoners, for all pretrial proceedings we were placed in the jury box, which kept us isolated from the courtroom audience and presumably made it easier for the responsible officers to retain custody over us. From my vantage point in the jury box I saw Nancy in the spectator section. My arrest had left her alone suddenly to cope with our toddler sons, to explain to them the disappearance of their father. A skilled legal secretary, she was also called upon to organize and manage the office set up for our legal counsel. This entailed transplantation of the household from San Francisco to Los Angeles, adjustment of the children to a new environment. The strain and fatigue of it all showed on her face. So did something else. Pain. She had been to the dentist that morning. Not having much time for dentists she subjected herself to about three times as many extractions as any normal human being would permit at any one time. In court the anaesthetic wore off, and I could see her pain. Yet, when my bond was posted and Mathes signed the release papers we managed to exchange a smile. It did not occur to us that Mathes could contrive one more turn of the screw. But he did. He ascertained somehow that the man who posted my bond, an attorney named George Andersen, was a partner of Norman Leonard, a defense counsel. Dredging up an obscure procedural technicality about counsel not posting bail for their clients, he interpreted it liberally to blanket members of a law firm. The bail was invalid, he said, deliberately tearing up the release order he had just signed. My wife and I exchanged another look. We did not smile.

I was remanded to jail for yet another Sunday. I forget whether it was a stew Sunday or a meatball Sunday. The weekly specialty on the jail menu on alternate Sundays was either a thin stew or a heavy, soggy meatball. On the women's side, where they were less delicate about it and more imaginative, the ground meat offerings were called horse balls. Whatever the menu was it was my last jail dinner for 1951. On Monday, December 10, I was out on the street, well in time for Christmas.

We had spent Thanksgiving in jail, and the more experienced cons said Thanksgiving was not so bad, wait until Christmas, that's the hardest time in prison. About a half dozen of them, all in their early or middle twenties, joined in this conversation about holidays. They began to compare notes on when they last spent Christmas on the streets. Among the lot there were few such Christmases in the preceding five years. It was a melancholy reckoning, and I wondered again about their vocation.

Not about the morality of it, I was not going to get moral about petty larceny and small-time violence in an endemically corrupt society that could perpetrate the violence of Hiroshima. It wasn't the ethics, it was the odds; why would anyone gamble with such bad odds?

Assuming they exercised an option, which is sociologically a questionable or much qualified assumption. As for my calculating *their* odds, my jail mates would have been amused; to them what I was doing was a crazier long shot than any caper they attempted.

One peripheral insight into motivation was afforded by a young black prisoner, handsome and very personable, who did not simply tell a story, he recreated situations with an actor's flair. What is commonly called honest labor, he referred to as the "lunch-bucket route." He was the only black man in our cell corridor in all the time we were there; I've wondered whether this was by chance or by some deliberate policy to keep black men from political contamination. This fellow, call him Harold, had served time in Q and when he was green he got into trouble often enough to be well acquainted with the interior of the associate warden's office. On one wall was a painting of the Western school: an old gold prospector, pan in hand, squatting by a mountain stream. His face was weatherbeaten and wrinkled, his hands gnarled, his clothes as old and worn as he was. While the associate warden lectured him, Harold stared at the picture on the wall. "I kept looking at that face, I kept looking at those hands," he recalled, "and I thought, if that's what the lunch-bucket route gets you, it's not for me."

The odds were poor and mostly the game was solitaire. Few of our jail mates had visitors, few received mail. The long years in stir, broken by brief, intermittent spells on the streets, had severed, for most of them, their ties with the "free world." Their sense of loneliness was impressed upon me ten days after our arrival in the Los Angeles jail. Some 500 pickets marched in front of the building to demand bail for the Smith Act prisoners. We could not see them, of course, and ten floors above the street we barely heard them, only infrequently when they were uncommonly united and loud in some chant or song. I can recall the faint strains of "Solidarity Forever." The demonstration created a stir of excitement in our cell corridor, certainly among the Smith Act prisoners, but also among the others. One young con said to me, "You're lucky, I wish there was somebody on the streets hollerin' for me." He said it wistfully, which surprised me even more than what he said, because he was a very hard young man.

Those people on the streets, bless them. Jail, Judge Mathes, the jangling pressures of political crosscurrents, the bad dream that is a long political trial — through all this and against all this was the vibrant solidarity of those people; comradeship, devotion, generosity, affection. This was one human element of the Communist movement at its finest. In the dehydrating politicization to which the movement is most often subjected this human quality is evaporated, and yet without this it is not possible to comprehend the movement's capacity for heroism and self-sacrifice.

In our case the devotions of comradeship found some unusual outlets, which may not have been heroic, but were very practical. One of these was the creation of Judge Mathes. He was willing to make fringe concessions — as long as he could keep us in jail. Responding to our complaint that imprisonment impeded serious preparation for trial, he directed the United States marshal to provide us with a place each weekday, between nine A.M. and five P.M., where we could confer among ourselves, with attorneys, prospective witnesses, investigators; read and keep books and documents. We were to have breakfast in jail, and for the other two meals we could have either jail fare or make our own arrangements for food from the outside.

We chose the second option. Each weekday two meals were brought in for the fifteen of us; by rough reckoning, over the three and a half months of this arrangement more than 2000 individual meals were served. Never have I eaten so well. Our political catering service drew on the culinary resources of the Left community in Los Angeles; each meal was a voluntary labor of love and political conviction. There was, I understood,

a competition for the honor of preparing a meal for the comrades in jail. On one occasion there was also a politico-ethnic
scandal. A group of Chicanos offered to prepare a meal but
someone in command decreed, with a mix of bureaucracy, good
intentions, and insensitivity to national feeling, that confinement and lack of exercise made Mexican food "too heavy" for
us.

Later on, during the trial, there was another miracle of voluntary labor. On the evening of each court day a half-dozen
volunteer typists turned up at our legal office to copy the transcript of the day's proceedings on stencils designed for offset
reproduction. The court reporters' transcript was usually available between six and seven P.M.; the letter-perfect stenciled
copies had to be finished in time for delivery by midnight, so
that they could be reproduced, bound, and presented to each
defense counsel before court convened the next morning. The
trial went on for six months, some days the transcript ran as
many as 100 pages, and our pool of thirty volunteers, a couple
of housewives among them and the rest office employees who
came in after a day's work, never missed a deadline. Their
labor proved to be more than a trial convenience. On appeal
the higher courts accepted the trial record as it had been reproduced from night to night, which saved us $25,000 or $30,000
in printing costs.

I cherish the cooks and the typists, their constancy and care,
with a particular warmth, but there were other manifestations
of bracing support: bodies and souls on picket lines, at the several mass rallies, and in the courtroom, where the benches were
filled with our silent witnesses. All this was in 1951–1952,
when McCarthyism was at its zenith, when our partisans, dismayed by the Supreme Court decision in the Dennis case,
might well have said: what's the use? We were not deluded
about the extent of our support; it was limited, yet animated by
a morale that reinforced our political conviction a full-dress
battle could and ought to be mounted. In part, I suspect, Judge
Mathes helped to gather the resistance around our case. For
reasons that remain a mystery to me we in Los Angeles were
chosen for the experiment in preventive detention through ex-

orbitant bail. In the thirty-six other Smith Act arrests that summer — in New York, Baltimore, Honolulu, Pittsburgh — neither the courts nor the Justice Department were so intransigent in insisting on prohibitive bail, which made our confinement more outrageous. The battle for bail dragged on four and a half months, time to marshal people and resources.

We began to chart strategy in the place provided us by the United States marshal at the direction of Judge Mathes. This turned out to be a cage, eighteen by sixteen feet, in which fifteen defendants, occasionally joined by several lawyers, were supposed to prepare for trial. Here, too, defendants received personal visitors, the visitor sitting outside the cage, the prisoner inside. At least they could see each other between the bars, which they could not do easily through the double thickness of meshed wire screens in the visiting facility of the county jail.

A typical scene in the cage: in one corner the trial committee of five is in session. Nearby lawyers are interviewing clients. Over to one side a prisoner is talking with a visitor through the bars. Of the remaining defendants, one or two are reading, the others, having exhausted their reading attention span in this bedlam, are engaged in conversation. All this in a space sixteen by eighteen feet. We called it the Snake Pit.

The trial committee proceeded slowly, hesitantly, cautiously. Its pace was not helped by the common-sense assumption the place was bugged. To confound the buggers certain names, words, phrases were unspoken, they were written down on sheets of paper and thereafter discussion of these unmentionables was conducted with finger-pointing references. My reaction to our proceedings was reflected in a bit of doggerel that began:

Procrastination is the thief of unkept minutes at meetings ad
 infinitum
Where the insolubles and the imponderables are left unsaid because you write 'em.
To do or not? To decide — but what? From here to yonder five
 sit and ponder . . .

Despite the irony the broad outlines of a policy emerged, a legal team took shape. Our legal battery in court finally consisted of two attorneys long and intimately associated with the Left in California, and three others who symbolically represented links with sections of the population that we deemed important. I say symbolically because there was little evidence their participation in the case had much practical effect upon their client constituencies in the trade union movement, in the black community, in liberal middle-class circles.

These three (in alphabetical order) were:

Leo Branton, black, young, bright, quick. This was his first big case. Later on he achieved success and prominence. The high point of his career was his distinguished triumph as defense counsel in the murder-kidnap trial of Angela Davis in 1972.

Alexander Schullman, counsel for several American Federation of Labor local unions.

A. L. (for Abraham Lincoln) Wirin, chief counsel for the American Civil Liberties Union in Southern California, a strict civil libertarian, who loved nothing more than an argument about constitutional law before the United States Supreme Court. He was my trial lawyer.

Our two Left attorneys afforded an interesting contrast. Ben Margolis of Los Angeles was a dramatic courtroom presence; dynamic, eloquent, with flashes of brilliance. Norman Leonard of San Francisco was low-keyed, dispassionate, his meticulous craftsmanship free of thespian flourishes.

Schneiderman served as his own counsel. He could present the defendants' political position in the first person. In his role as counsel he could also serve as operative liaison between defendants and attorneys.

A legal battery in court, I learned, is like a front-line army; it is helpless without the supporting troops. In our rear echelons two men were very important. Sam Rosenwein, a lawyers' lawyer, did the legal research, wrote the drafts of motions, briefs, memoranda. Attorney Benjamin Dreyfus directed investigations (mostly about prosecution witnesses) and administered the legal operation with cool efficiency and an incredible amount of work. It has nothing to do with the case, but Dreyfus was one of the most gracious men I have ever known. He also had irony. When his investigations turned up something particularly foolish done by a defendant, which was more frequent than we would have liked, he exclaimed, "Oi, what a conspiracy!" This became a refrain.

One passing glance at the defendants. A striking thing about the ten men and five women as a composite group was their average age at the time of arrest: forty-three. This was also the median. Turn the clock back two decades, to the Great Depression year of 1931, and the average was then twenty-three. Most of us came of age in the crisis years and even the others, those older, except for three, came of age politically during the Depression and its recession aftermath prior to World War II. As a group those were our formative years. In this we were representative of the Communist cadre. The 1930s had been a great cadre-molding experience and there had been nothing comparable since.

In charting a trial strategy we confronted the nature of our case. Among varied cases called political some are more political than others. Ours was almost pure politics. In some prior, more celebrated prosecutions a specific, tangible crime was involved; politics entered as an issue of motivation and/or prejudice. In the case of Tom Mooney and Warren Billings, for example, it was alleged they planted the bomb that killed ten persons at the San Francisco Preparedness Day parade, conceived in 1916 as a flag-waving brass band prelude to the march of the country into World War I. Their political credo, revolutionary and antiwar, supplied the motive, according to the prosecution theory. Mooney and Billings countered they were framed, that the frame-up was instigated by powerful corporate interests to punish and eliminate them as effective labor organizers. In similar guises politics entered the trial of the Haymarket defendants in the wake of the bomb explosion that killed seven Chicago policemen in 1886.

There was also a bomb in the case of Julius and Ethel Rosenberg, but they were not charged with its detonation; President Truman assumed responsibility for that and the consequences at Hiroshima and Nagasaki, which made the earlier bombs at

Chicago and San Francisco seem like overcharged July Fourth firecrackers. This was legally all right. The President did it. The Rosenbergs were accused of conspiring to steal the "secret" of this bomb, prompted, so the prosecution claimed, by their political loyalties. In their prosecution the Cold War atmosphere, the atomic bomb mythology, did, indeed, create "a kind of hydraulic pressure," in Justice Holmes's phrase, which is the essence of a political case. Their death sentence, incidentally, was pronounced four months before our arrests; they were on Sing Sing's death row when we were dividing our time between the Los Angeles county jail and the Snake Pit. This coincidence helps to place in perspective the relative pettiness of our inconvenience. Still the coincidence also suggests the "hydraulic pressure" of those times.

A variation on the theme was afforded by Nicola Sacco and Bartolomeo Vanzetti, accused of killing two men in a payroll holdup, an act not readily ascribed to political motivation, and yet the case became political because their anarchist credo, as well as their foreign identity, was used to fan prejudice against them.

In all those cases, however, dominated by political passion, conflict, prejudice, there was a clearly probative issue. Who planted or threw the bomb? Who committed the payroll murders? Was there, in fact, an attempt at espionage? Although the defense was compelled to meet the political challenge, to probe and expose the political motivation of the prosecution, there yet remained the clash of evidence as it related to a specific act, which is at the hub of the ordinary criminal trial.

In our case there was no specific, clearly defined act. We faced a trial of doctrine. We were charged with conspiring to teach and advocate a political doctrine and, in purely judicial terms, the outcome hinged on the interpretation of that doctrine. In the New York trial that preceded ours, defense counsel reduced the prosecution's case to a formula: M-L (Marxism-Leninism) equals F & V (force and violence).

This was, indeed, the foundation of the prosecution's theory, constructed as follows: the doctrines of Marx and Lenin, on their face, advocated the violent overthrow of the government;

the defendants, by organizing the Communist party on principles enunciated by Marx and Lenin, by employing the party as a vehicle for disseminating those principles, entered into a criminal conspiracy.

The crux of the case was the meaning of Marx and Lenin. Anyone even slightly acquainted with schisms among self-professed followers of Marx over many decades, and in more recent times the sharp disagreements among avowed adherents of Lenin, will appreciate the hazard of reducing their work to a single, simple, pat formula. Thoughtful, able people, who devoted much of their lives to serious study of Marx and Lenin, have disagreed about the meaning and application of their work in the contemporary world. By this I do not mean their thoughts were so ambiguous or elliptical as to baffle human comprehension. What seems self-evident to me, however, is that such comprehension demands a kind of interest, study, and capacity as are not likely to be found among Federal prosecutors, paid FBI informers, and randomly selected jurors.

If our trial record proved anything at all, it proved conclusively that our principal prosecutors (United States Attorney Walter S. Binns and his assistant, Norman Neukom) had no notion of what Marx and Lenin were about, and not the slightest inclination to learn. A typical colloquy may convey the flavor of the prosecution. Prosecutor Binns had just read an excerpt from Government Exhibit 606 (*Foundations of Leninism* by Joseph Stalin) when defense attorney Schullman rose to his feet.

MR. SCHULLMAN: May I inquire the date of that book, please?

MR. BINNS: (After looking at the flyleaf) Copyrighted 1939.

MR. SCHULLMAN: Your Honor, may I inquire now the date when it was written, not when it was copyrighted?

MR. BINNS: Your Honor, I am not familiar with this literature enough to know when it was written. All I know is it bears the copyright 1939.

Binns's eye for the obvious was again revealed when he attempted to introduce the same Stalin booklet as two separate government exhibits. Defense attorney Margolis protested it would confuse the record "to have the same book introduced as Government's Exhibit 1 and 606 and maybe four or five other copies, which may create the impression it is six books instead of just one." At this point Judge Mathes intervened.

> THE COURT: Is there any point in duplicating any of the record?
> MR. BINNS: Just the fact, your Honor, that they are manifestly different books. One is red and stiff-bound, and the other is green and paper-bound.

Most of the prosecution witnesses happily, even proudly, acknowledged a pristine ignorance of Marxist-Leninist theory. David (Butch) Saunders, brash, garrulous mariner, was cross-examined about his attendance at a party school.

> Q. Did you read some books on dialectical materialism?
> A. I tried to read on it. It was over my head.

Saunders at least tried, for he did not enter the party as a spy for the FBI. The FBI plants, more than half of the prosecution witnesses, did not even try. Lloyd N. Hamlin, a deadpan graduate from Naval Intelligence to the FBI, was cross-examined by defense attorney Branton about his attendance at a school shortly after his infiltration into the party.

> Q. You were, of course, interested in learning everything that you could about the Communist party in order that you could report on your learning to the Federal Bureau of Investigation, isn't that correct?
> A. Not necessarily from the standpoint of theory, no, sir.
> Q. I beg your pardon?
> A. Not necessarily from the standpoint of theory.

I do not dispute the American right of prosecutors and FBI informers to ignorance of Marxist theory. What I felt then, and still feel, however, is a profound indignation at casting them as exponents in a trial that was supposed to arrive at so definitive a judgment of the theory as to clap its advocates into prison.

What is sometimes billed as courtroom drama became a theater of the absurd. But we were not given the luxury of existential detachment to savor it as spectacle. We were deadly serious; not only was our freedom at stake, but our beliefs, and what we perceived as the meaning of our lives.

Trial strategy hinged on two interrelated, yet distinct, elements: defense of our right to advocate what we did and defense of what we advocated, its probity and rationality. The first defense involved the broad, fundamental constitutional issue, going to the core of American democratic tradition and practice. Its wider compass encircled the right to teach biological evolution in Tennessee, which was contested in the Scopes "monkey" trial in Dayton in 1925, along with our right to advocate social revolution in 1951. As an incidental irony, what we advocated has much deeper roots in the American tradition than what John T. Scopes taught; the Founding Fathers had no inkling of biological evolution (Charles Darwin was still unborn), but entering upon revolution, they were impelled to proclaim recourse to it as a human right. As it concerned the country at large, the overriding issue in our trial was the right to advocacy.

Of much narrower concern, but supremely important to us, was the substance of what we advocated. This was being traduced; an elementary sense of honor and dignity dictated an aggressive rejoinder. And we were political people, representatives of a party; our prosecutors (not just their legal instruments in court) were our political enemies. If they chose the courtroom as an arena for joining the issues between us, then all our instinct and training impelled acceptance of the challenge. The court was a political stage, the audience was beyond its walls. In any event, except as pure abstraction the right of advocacy cannot be severed from matters advocated.

Because the two elements of our defense were interwoven it required some subtlety and much conscious persistence to place and keep the emphasis where you thought it ought to be. In preparing for our trial I read the record of the nine-month trial in New York. There, it seemed to me, the heavy accent was on the validity of what had been advocated, so much so that at times it appeared the defense was demanding the jury corroborate the correctness of the Communist party's policies and tactics, with all their turns, abrupt or gradual. At the time

I explained it to myself. As the party's national leaders, as the principal architects of its policies and tactics, the eleven New York defendants bore a special burden, which was not lightened by their awareness of the spotlight upon them, international as well as national.

We charted a somewhat different course. We would place the heavy accent on the right to advocacy, and within that context would attempt the most comprehensive, most effective presentation of our beliefs, principles, activities. We would exercise greater restraint. We made our choice without entering into a critique of the New York precedent; it was enough for us that our status and circumstances were different.

I was convinced our general approach was appropriate, and still am. It corresponded to an appraisal of the political realities. We were on the defensive, we were in retreat; at the same time, the fight for our democratic legality was not foredoomed. The telling gauge of our defense, in and out of court, would be its effect upon the existing possibilities for turning the repressive political tide.

On the eve of our trial the FBI put on a show of conspicuous surveillance, or overshadow, as in overkill. Two cars with two agents in each were assigned to shadow each defendant, a total of thirty cars and sixty agents on the day shift for the fifteen of us. After one defendants' meeting, six of us, all bound for the Eastside in Los Angeles, piled into one car; our shadows intrepidly formed a tail twelve cars long. In Los Angeles rush-hour traffic, thirteen cars make a very long caravan. For sport, our driver executed a variety of turns, the shadow cars following bumper to bumper in a grotesque, winding procession from the vicinity of Ninth and Spring Streets in downtown Los Angeles out to Broooklyn Avenue and beyond, two cars peeling off as each defendant was delivered to his destination. For the night shift the visible FBI complement was halved. Outside the house where I was staying with my family on the Eastside two men sat in a car, the motor running all night long.

XI. The Trial

THE NEXT MORNING, February 1, our trial began. Jury selection consumed less than a day. Of the thirty-six prospective jurors examined only four admitted to a fixed bias against communism; all the others said they had no opinions as to what the Communist party does and advocates, this in the sixth year of the Cold War and its domestic feedback, a relentless, pervasive "anti-Communist" crusade. All thirty-six said they had not read a series on the Communist party by Herbert ("I was a spy for the FBI") Philbrick, then being featured prominently in the *Los Angeles Times*. They had not even seen the series, except for one woman, who said she saw it but read none of it. On the surface, I suppose, this incredible insulation of my peers from the overt reach of the Establishment should have been heartening. Instead the proceeding seemed desultory. Perhaps it was too incredible.

A protracted political trial is, among other things, an endurance contest. Many years earlier I read about Art Young, the cartoonist and one of the old *Masses* editors prosecuted under the Espionage Act of 1917 during World War I, falling asleep at his trial. This impressed me enormously as drowsy "grace under pressure," cool disdain for the punitive Establishment. Not until my trial did it occur to me that Young's catnap might not have signified courage or sangfroid; it could have been sheer boredom. There just are long stretches of tedium; their soporific effects, especially in the stomach-filled sessions after lunch, can overwhelm the wakeful awareness that one's fate and much else is in the balance.

Political defendants tend to be very vocal, opinionated, unaccustomed to remaining silent in the midst of talk and controversy that concerns them. But in the courtroom, judges and attorneys strut in the stellar roles; defendants, for the most part, perform the function of the corpse in a mortuary or the patient in the operating theater. My colleagues, habituated to the public platform, the picket line, the demonstration, the intra-party debate, were maladjusted to their passive parts. Keeping still in court for six months was also a trial.

I was more fortunate than the others. I covered the trial for the *People's World.* Actually I covered half the trial; my co-defendant, Slim Connelly, Los Angeles bureau chief of the *People's World,* filed stories on alternate days. We sat at the defendants' table — and we performed the chores of working newspapermen. Such work was better for morale than doo-dling and occasionally jotting down a discrepancy or falsehood in prosecution testimony. Also more useful; our coverage of the trial served to sustain the interest and support of the *People's World* audience. Being a politically motivated audience, with a generous proportion of activists, it exerted an influence be-yond its own relatively small number.

Connelly had been for many years the secretary of the Los Angeles CIO Industrial Union Council. Before that he was a veteran newspaperman on the *Herald-Express,* the Hearst afternoon newspaper, and a founding father of the American Newspaper Guild in Los Angeles. Ten years my senior, Con-nelly was a towering man, weighing in at 240 pounds or more, even when he was not running to fat.

These bare facts affected our relationship; we were caught in the hostile cleavage between Northern California and Southern California. Much has been written about this antagonistic con-tradiction, and I shall not delve into it. However, one factor that entered into it confirmed Lenin's theory of "uneven devel-opment." Even after the balance of population and wealth shifted to the South the old California Establishment retained the seats of power in the North. In this respect the California Communist party was certainly indigenous. Like its corporate and ideological adversaries (e.g., Southern Pacific, Standard Oil, Bank of America, University of California), the party kept its state headquarters in the North, although a majority of its membership was in the South. There were reasonable arguments for this arrangement; vital centers of the labor movement, for instance, were situated in San Francisco, but this did not alter the peculiar dichotomy. The *People's World* conformed to this pattern. The bulk of its circulation and financial support was in the South, but the paper was edited and published in San Francisco.

Into this situation stepped Connelly, attaching great value to his newspaper professionalism, to his experience and status as leader of the CIO through its stormiest encounters and finest days in the Los Angeles area. He was not disposed to accept editorial decisions from San Francisco in matters ranging from journalistic style to political emphasis. His long tenure as CIO executive officer in Los Angeles had given him matchless training in North-South warfare; in few California institutions was San Francisco's authority as domineering as in the state CIO. At times, it seemed to me, even his seniority in age and his physical preponderance were thrown into the breach. I thought him irascible, contentious, stubborn, overbearing, and, on occasion, irrational and impossible. He never compiled an explicit catalogue of qualities he discerned in me, but from his complaints it is a fair inference that bureaucracy and incompetence were high on the list. It was a trying relationship.

Then we became jail mates, codefendants, working reporters covering the same story. Our relationship changed. In that mammoth bundle of distempers and idiosyncrasies I perceived other traits: incorruptible integrity, true gentleness, human compassion. I do not know what his judgments were of me, but his attitude changed. Not that our conciliation precluded subsequent frictions but the bond fashioned in jail and in court was unbroken.

The courtroom is a world of its own. In jail one refers to the outside world as free; in court one may refer to it as real. The courtroom itself is unreal. Especially in a political trial. In the highly stylized, formalistic conventions of judicial procedure, the real thoughts, emotions, conflicts, subtleties, elasticities of political life are reflected as in distorted mirrors. It is difficult, however, not to be mesmerized by this unreality, not to be caught up in its trivial triumphs, in calculations as to whether this or that evidence was damaging, in the compulsive game of jury-watching. You know these pastimes are irrelevant or futile, but you engage in them just the same.

I was the particular beneficiary of a trivial triumph in the testimony of John Lautner. By prior rank and experience in the party, by his testimony in other trials, Lautner qualified as the prosecution's star witness.

On direct examination by Lawrence K. Bailey, a special prosecutor from Washington, this colloquy occurred:

Q. You identified the defendant Richmond. Where did you meet him?
A. At the 1945 convention.

On cross-examination by Wirin, Lautner reiterated on six separate occasions that he saw me at the 1945 national Communist convention. The exchange went into whether I was a delegate, where I sat, what I wore ("there were a number of people there who were wearing Army uniforms," Lautner testified, "and he could have been one of them").

At the time, July 26–28, 1945, I was indeed in army uniform but not in New York City where the convention was held. I was with the 106th General Hospital on the outskirts of Wimborne Minster in Dorsetshire, England, a fact irrefutably established by my military service record.

In the overall design of the Smith Act prosecutions the 1945 convention was a seminal act. This convention reconstituted the Communist party after its self-dissolution and transfiguration into the Communist Political Association the year before under Earl Browder's leadership. In the New York trial this convention was the hub of the indictment; the reconstitution of the party was the birth of the conspiracy. I had been placed at the major scene of the crime by the principal prosecution witness — and I had an ironclad alibi. In the ordinary criminal trial it might have been good for sensational headlines. In ours what did it matter? What difference did it make if a star witness was mistaken or perjurious? In a case resting on inferences to be drawn from a sociopolitical theory, material facts were immaterial.

I knew all that, but in the unreality of courtroom gamesmanship it was a point for me. Just as I scored again in the flustered performance of Margaret Louise Ames, a small-time FBI informer. Bailey again was the luckless prosecutor.

Q. Do you know Al Richmond?
A. Yes.
Q. Do you see him in the courtroom?
A. Yes.
Q. Will you point him out, please, describe him?

After some fumbling and exchanges between counsel, the record continued:

THE WITNESS: It *should be* the man in the brown suit . . . the man standing up there now.
MR. SCHULLMAN: May the record show the witness has identified Norman Leonard?
MR. BAILEY: So stipulated.

From the telltale "should be" and her brown-suit fixation it was apparent she had been given this helpful sartorial hint for the purposes of identification. I was wearing a brown suit — but so was defense attorney Leonard, a contingency for which she had not been prepared by her prompters. Confronted with the unexpected choice of two men in brown suits at the defense tables she pointed at the wrong one. She was unstrung by the blunder.

THE WITNESS: I am sorry. My mind is going blank on me.
Q. Just take your time, if you will, Mrs. Ames.
MR. NEUKOM: May we have a brief recess?
THE COURT: Would you like that?
THE WITNESS: I have got the shakes so bad, I can't think.
THE COURT: No one is going to hurt you.
THE WITNESS: I know. It's just nerves. Everyone has it.
THE COURT: You are doing well. At least you are making yourself heard, which is more than some of the witnesses have been able to do here. Do you feel like proceeding?

THE WITNESS: I would like to have a few minutes, if I may.

THE COURT: We will take a brief recess.

THE WITNESS: I'd like to have a cigarette, if I could. Is it possible?

THE COURT: Not in here, but at recess.

Whereupon a recess was taken to give Mrs. Ames time to regain her composure. My copy-desk mind saw headlines: PROSECUTION WITNESS COLLAPSES. That was play. Mrs. Ames's peccadillo rated no more than brief mention in the middle of my own story of the day's proceedings. Lautner's more serious lapse from fact was treated with similar restraint. In my schizophrenic existence the relative detachment of the reporter balanced the involvement of the defendant.

Unreal, frequently trivial, occasionally tedious; these were only attributes of form. Ever present in the court was the substantive reality of what they were trying to do to us, and not just us, not even primarily us, for we were persuaded that our trial was a significant detail in a larger pattern of means toward ends with vast, incalculable consequences for the country. Ever present, too, was the feeling of danger, of combat, heightening senses and faculties, generating nervous energy, more than could be released through my journalistic chores. I volunteered to help with the drafting of position papers on critical issues of theory and politics (e.g., force and violence, war) that might be of value to our counsel and prospective defense witnesses.

I was busy. On alternate days, during the lunch break, I wired a comprehensive lead for the body of the story that had been mailed the evening before. On the late afternoons and early evenings that were not taken up with journalism there were the position papers, the research and the writing. By late evening all this busyness produced physical fatigue, but no slack in the taut nerves. Tired, tense, there was a great need for relaxation, a need I shared with my associate in the position-paper project, Frank Carlson. He had a quick, keen, restless, imaginative mind, and a very sharp tongue. In a feature story I described him as the gadfly among the defendants. "Some people are irritated by a gadfly," I wrote, "and this includes some of his friends and co-workers at times." It did not include me.

He was a neighbor of mine on the Eastside; frequently I wound up at his home in the late evening in the quest for diversion. There was not much for that. Television was not so common then as it became later; neither he nor I owned a set, partly because we had no money, partly out of a cultural snobbery at this opiate of the people. But when a friendly neighbor occasionally invited us in to watch his set we were pleased to accept. Aside from such infrequent dips into the "Dragnet" era of television, there were even more infrequent penny-ante poker games, or a few drinks and light talk, or entertainment afforded by Carlson's distinct outlet for nervous energy; he composed lyrics, set to popular tunes, about personalities and incidents at the trial. Small divertissements, yet they served as prelude to exhausted sleep and then still another day of trial and work. This went on for six months.

The distinction between unreality in court and reality outside became blurred; that half year was a phantasm, but in all the mix of emotion and attitude what remains uppermost is the quickening sensation of combat. And not just combat, for also inspiriting was the certainty that in this encounter we were fighting for the right. Living intensely, all the time I felt I also was living on borrowed time. I was not sanguine about the outcome of the trial, nor were my codefendants. There was no cause for sanguineness in 1952, not with the stalemated Korean War dragging on, not with the presidential election campaign, dominated by McCarthy's strident refrain (echoed by Nixon), "Twenty years of treason." If this is what they did to Democratic sheep, what will they do to Communist goats?

In court the relationship with my lawyer was casual, occasional banter about our political differences serving to gloss over an underlying respect and even a measure of affection. Once, returning to the defense tables after a particularly effective bit of cross-examination, Wirin whispered to me, "Pretty good for a dirty old social democrat, eh?" Later on he caught cold and was excused from court. When his absence extended for several days other defense counsel suggested that I, as his client, call him to ascertain when he would return, and to prod him to make it sooner. I called his home during a recess; there was no answer. When I got through to him in the evening I made a pointed reference to his earlier absence from home.

"Yes," he said, "I'm not so sick as to be confined at home, but I'm not well enough to come to court."

"That's wonderful, Al," I said. "That sounds like a classical liberal dilemma."

Another courtroom relationship was not bantering or casual. Like Wirin, other counsel, defense and prosecution, were occasionally excused from trial sessions. Some lawyers could be missing, but indispensable to a quorum were judge, jurors, defendants, all of them all of the time. One other participant in the trial was as constant as they, so faithful I almost felt that if she were absent the trial would have to be recessed. This was my mother.

She was then a woman of sixty-eight, a white mane over a wide, tall forehead; a broad, open face, a peasant face, she used to say, with a potato nose, which was not quite accurate and omitted an important feature: large, gray-brown, intelligent eyes. Physically, the most striking thing about her was her carriage. She was a tall, large-boned woman, and she walked erect, head high, shoulders back, a figure of imposing dignity and calm.

After my arrest we first met in the visiting facility of the Los Angeles county jail. I described that encounter when it was fresher in my mind. "I could only see her blurred silhouette through a double thickness of meshed wire, and she couldn't see any more of me. If we both stepped back from the screen at a particular angle in relation to the light we could make out human features, but then we couldn't hear one another. It is difficult to talk at a shadow through two wired screens. Especially is it difficult to convey a deep-felt emotion, which is not an easy thing to do even under more favored circumstances. We talked small talk . . ."

I can surmise the anxiety with which she came, only to be appalled by the barrier of finely spun metal that separated us, that so effectively screened human communication. I tried to reassure her about the physical appointments at the jail: I slept well, the food was tolerable, the showers good. It did no good. Her depression was too great to be so easily dispelled, and it was not concealed. It was a bad visit.

That was on a Friday; on Tuesday I wrote to Nancy, "My mother visited me again yesterday afternoon. She had sensed the effect of her mood on Friday and told me she came yesterday especially to dispel the former impression. She did well with her mission, was cheerful and brave, almost buoyant. I was very proud of her . . ."

Later, when she came to visit me at the Snake Pit, we could see and hear one another at the same time through the steel bars and had some sense of being together. During our conversations it became evident she was reliving the six years she spent in Czarist prisons. She did not say so, and perhaps was not consciously aware of it, but things she now saw revived long-dormant memories of her prison life.

One morning she saw us being led from the county jail across the street to the federal building, the men in single handcuffs hooked to one chain. This chained procession recalled the final and most cruel leg of the long journey to a Siberian prison. The prison was several hundred miles from the Trans-Siberian Railroad; this distance from the point of detrainment was traversed on foot. This was the *etap*, a physical ordeal, and more, for the sense of remoteness from civilization in the Siberian wilderness loosened the small restraints upon the brutality of the guards. In her convoy there was a Chinese prisoner with the traditional pigtail. He became the primary object of abuse and humiliation by the guards. He did not make it to the prison. He committed suicide en route.

She did not simply relate such episodes, she relived them. Not that she saw our chain-gang shuffle across Spring Street as the equivalent of the *etap*. The chain gang was a memory trigger, not a parallel. She was very aware of the contrasts.

One contrast was afforded by our custodian. To shepherd us to and from the Snake Pit and to maintain surveillance over us while we were there, an elderly United States marshal, a big, hearty Irishman, was brought out of retirement. The work was easy and I assume he welcomed the extra money. Perhaps it was just appreciation of the job, or perhaps it was something about my mother, but he treated her with great courtesy and consideration. She marveled at it, for of all the wardens and guards she had known she could remember only one whose attitude toward prisoners or their kin approached civility.

My description of our jail tier brought on remembrance of cells she had occupied, especially one invaded by rats, who made their entrance through holes they gnawed in the wooden floor. After repeated complaints by the several women in the cell the warden took a countermeasure; the gnawed-through boards were replaced with thick, wooden planks. The next morning the rats were back, having gnawed their way through the new floor. More protests by the women, and the warden placed his own cat in their cell as their protector. Three rats darted out of the floor, fell upon the cat, and when the brief, savage struggle was over the mutilated animal was dead . . .

Such recollections, it might seem, highlighted the distinctions between penology in backward Czarist Russia and in advanced, democratic America, but she did not celebrate American democratic virtue. Not in the face of meshed wire and crisscrossed bars, for her own experience enhanced her comprehension of these enclosures; not with the likelihood that her son would be punished with five years in prison for beliefs she shared. To her this community of conviction was not fortuitous, she assumed some responsibility for it, and also for its consequences. I do not know how painfully she relived her own imprisonment, or how it colored her empathy with me; after the first visit in the county jail she never again bared her own vulnerability.

After jail came the trial. No one was more deeply involved in the trial than she was. To understand her involvement it is again necessary to revert to her origins. The old ghetto village of the Czarist Russian empire has been romanticized and sentimentalized. As with other legends this one, too, has its rational kernel; the community of poverty, oppression, ostracism cultivated human compassion. Along with this there was a veneration for wisdom and learning, strained as these were by Talmudic scholasticism. But overlaying the mean squalor of the Jewish Pale, the mire of its village streets in the spring thaw, were medievalism and superstition, and a bigotry that decreed that women were unclean, were not communicants with God, and could aspire to heaven only as footstools for their husbands.

She was born into the Middle Ages. In the two decades of her childhood and youth the ghetto village was shaken from its torpor by a remarkable compression of intellectual influences that, in Western Europe, evolved over two centuries. The eighteenth-century Enlightenment and nineteenth-century socialism entered the ghetto village in tandem. Something comparable, of course, transpired in the vaster Eastern European environment of the Jewish Pale, but it was not so compressed and concentrated. To her, as to the best representatives of her generation, socialism was the materialization of the human reason and human hope that were heralded by the Enlightenment.

Her exaltation of human reason did not wane with youth. Only a few years before the trial, regretting she had never undertaken a systematic, comprehensive study of philosophy, she decided to fill this void. She lived then with her husband in Stelton. Behind the house they occupied was a small cabin; this they let to a retired professor and in lieu of rent she accepted tutorial lessons in philosophy. Then in her sixties, she immersed herself in Hegel and Kant, in the philosophical schools that came before and after, in the intricate relationship between philosophy and science.

And now, in Los Angeles, she observed, not the philosophers, but the prosecutors, Binns and Neukom.

Here is Binns, a porcine fellow, looking like a one-time college athlete gone to pot. He hands a booklet to Lloyd Hamlin, impassive FBI informer on the witness stand.

"I show you government's 39 for identification," says Binns, "and I ask you if you have ever seen a copy of this before?"

"Yes, sir," says Hamlin. "This is *The Communist Manifesto* and at one time I had a copy of this, as it was sold to me at the Communist bookstore in San Diego."

"I offer government's 39 into evidence at this time, Your Honor," says Binns.

To my mother this is incredible. *The Manifesto*, one of those very rare products of the human mind that has had a truly profound effect upon human thought and action, upon the course of history, is thus transformed into a piece of evidence in a criminal trial. Her indignation is the greater because it is apparent to her that neither Binns nor Hamlin knows what *The Manifesto* is about. For them it is, indeed, nothing more than Government's Exhibit No. 39. Binns reads a few lines from it to the jury, lines that had been selected and underscored by some research expert at the Department of Justice. Nothing in the record suggests even remotely that Binns had read anything in *The Manifesto*, except those few lines in the peroration.

"The Communists disdain to conceal their views and aims," he reads. "They openly declare that their end can be attained only by the forcible overthrow of all existing social conditions. Let the ruling classes tremble at a Communist revolution. The proletarians have nothing to lose but their chains. They have a world to win.

"Workingmen of all countries, unite!"

His reading is absolutely expressionless; it is informed with the intelligence and feeling of a school child self-consciously negotiating a second-grade reader. The jurors wear their masks. It is a surgical tour de force, a simultaneous performance of lobotomy and castration, totally excising the magnificent audacity from that passage, leaving no trace of its imprint upon successive generations in the century since it first made ruling classes tremble.

After such Kafkaesque scenes my mother was beside herself, deeply, personally offended by such affront to human reason, such debasement of human aspiration. At such times she was not a mother at the trial of her son; all that she so passionately believed in was being traduced; she was the proponent of her own life and faith, a kind of transcendent human conscience at the trial.

Busy, preoccupied, I spent very little time with her during the trial. Imbedded in my memory of it, along with all else, is an undercurrent of filial guilt. But what remains most indelible from our brief encounters was her scorn and fury at the prosecution. My own indignation paled beside hers, which was the purer and more intense. I tried, especially in two feature stories, and in part influenced by her, to convey something of the quality of this trial of books, and I have drawn upon those stories in the present account.

The prosecution case consumed four months, covering more than 8000 pages of the record. The trial had begun February 1; it was not until June 11 that Oleta O'Connor Yates took the witness stand for the defense. We were lucky to have her as our protagonist; lucid, articulate, and, as events were to prove, possessed of great courage and stamina. She also was a handsome woman, then forty-two, very poised and dignified, and extraordinarily precise in her diction. Communists are fond of saying this or that did not happen in a vacuum. I've heard the word many times, but no one has ever given to vac-u-um the full measure of its three syllables with such distinctness as Oleta did.

For two weeks she was on direct examination by Ben Margolis. For the first time in the trial a competent human intelligence attempted a reasoned exposition of what was in those books, marked as government exhibits and lodged in metal cabinets. As personal introduction she briefly sketched her background: born into an Irish-American working class family "south of Market" in San Francisco; on the maternal side the family came to San Francisco in 1850, sailing around the Horn from Ireland; unionism was endemic, a grandfather was a charter member of Teamsters Local 85. More elaborately she recited observations, experiences, intellectual influences that brought her, as a graduate student at the University of California at Berkeley, into the Socialist party in the Great Depression year of 1932, and a year later into the Communist party. The bulk of her testimony centered on four major themes: a general outline of Marxism-Leninism as a scientific theory; a more specific treatment of the Marxist-Leninist theory of revolution, including the issue of force and violence; a presentation of the contemporary American Communist party program and practice; an affirmation of the democratic element in American tradition with a spirited defense of the right to revolution as the most fundamental of democratic rights, as the ultimate assertion of the people's sovereignty, which is hollow if it does not encompass the right to abolish and institute forms of government. Much of this was on a high intellectual plane, unavoidably so, given the subject matter and her probity, which eschewed vulgarization.

I do not attempt to recapitulate her testimony that, in itself, would fill a book. To treat only with portions that directly and explicitly met the prosecution's charge is to do some violence to the testimony for it was an integral whole. Still I will do so, touching on the central ideas, rather than offering a comprehensive summary.

The first line of rebuttal embraced two classical principles of Marxism. The essence of one was stated in response to a question. "No, I do not think that a revolution ever can result purely from the subjective will or intent or desires of any one person or even any group of people. It can only result from certain objective changes in society, in the material conditions of society, and I believe that both Marx and Engels were very specific on this point." The other principle was referred to in an exchange about violence in the American Revolution, the American Civil War, the Russian Revolution of 1917. "I believe that the violence developed because the old ruling groups refused to accept the will of the majority and initiated violence; and this situation was further complicated, as in the Russian revolution, by the closing of the democratic avenues through which the people could express their will."

The second line of rebuttal involved the strategic perspective of the American party. Pivotal was the conception of a great popular alliance to defend and expand democracy. Such an alliance, the argument went, especially as it combated Fascist encroachment and the domination of corporate monopoly over

American society, could both marshal the forces and create the conditions that enhanced the possibilities of a peaceful passage to socialism. Not that this eliminated the possibility of violence because ruling-class resort to violence and to its ultimate institutionalized form, fascism, was not excluded. The urgent emphasis of Communust advocacy, however, was to prevent such an eventuality — to keep democratic channels open, to enlarge them, so that a popular majority could, when it so chose, exercise its option for Socialist revolution.

None of this was original, but then she was not engaged in a seminar for innovative theoretical exploration; she was a witness at a trial with the burden of relating what she and her party actually advocated. This she did with admirable competence and clarity, and in the theoretical explication with dispassionate restraint. It did not make for what normally passes as courtroom drama; yet, in its very departure from the courtroom norm, in its flight into the rarefied realm of theoretical precepts, it exerted a fascination. I do not think it is just my partisan identification with her; by any decent standard of human reason and dignity hers was a redemptive presence after the prosecution's performance. Now when I encountered my mother she beamed.

The drama came during cross-examination, which was conducted by Neukom. The choice of Neukom signified it would be a dirty job; Binns, as chief prosecutor, assigned the dirtier chores to his assistant. What else are assistants for? Neukom was not going to engage in a duel of wits or a disputation about Marxist theory with the witness. What he was going to do was revealed in the first minutes of cross-examination. He asked her to name persons with whom she met in Los Angeles in pursuit of her duties as state organizational secretary of the Communist party.

"I am quite prepared to discuss anything that I did," she replied, "but I am not willing to provide names and identities of people . . . I think that would be becoming a government informer and I cannot do that."

After several exchanges and intervention by defense counsel, Judge Mathes took a hand.

THE COURT: You will answer the questions which the court directs you to answer; the court directs you to answer that question.

THE WITNESS: I am sorry, Your Honor. I cannot be an informer.

THE COURT: You understand the possible consequences of your refusal to answer, I take it?

THE WITNESS: I am afraid I do, but the possible consequences, grim as they may be, are not as bad as going around hanging your head in shame for the rest of your life.

MR. NEUKOM: Your Honor, may I take up another subject at this present moment, then?

Neukom did go on to other subjects for several hours and all that time everyone in the courtroom waited for him to do what he finally did in midafternoon.

Did she know a "Mr. Harry Glickson" as a member of the Communist party?

"Well," she replied, "that is a question which, if I were to answer, could only lead to a situation in which a person could be caused to suffer the loss of his job, his income, and perhaps be subjected to further harassment, and in a period of this character, where there is so much witchhunting, so much hysteria, so much anti-communism — I am sorry, I cannot bring myself to contribute to that."

THE COURT: You are instructed by the court to answer the question.

THE WITNESS: Well, my answer is the same.

THE COURT: Do you decline to answer the question?

THE WITNESS: I do, Your Honor.

THE COURT: The court holds you in contempt, Mrs. Yates. Put your next question.

Neukom's next question was whether Harry Glickson was a Communist club chairman in San Francisco in 1945–1946. The question after that was whether she knew Harry Glickson as an active member of the Communist party in 1950. With such persistence, Glickson's name alone was good for three contempt citations. She was also cited a fourth time by the end of the session when Judge Mathes pronounced:

"It is the judgment of the court, Oleta O'Connor Yates, as to each contempt of which you have been found guilty, that you be committed to the custody of the marshal to be by him imprisoned in a jail-type institution until you have purged yourself of your contempt by answering the questions ordered to be answered."

When she was taken to the Los Angeles county jail it was late afternoon; there were no vacancies. She spent the night on a cot in a crowded hallway, a light glaring overhead, people coming and going. She did not sleep. Next morning she again faced cross-examination.

The conditions in jail were brought to Judge Mathes' attention by Margolis with a request that execution of the contempt sentence be stayed until Oleta completed her testimony, so that she would not be compelled to undergo the rigors of cross-examination after sleepless nights in a crowded corridor. Denying the request, the judge entered upon a gratuitous soliloquy that suggested he may have lain awake part of the previous night. He was not content with punishing Oleta, he wished also to demean her. To this end he gave vent to his nocturnal musings.

"I find it very difficult to reconcile her readiness to testify as to William Z. Foster and her unreadiness to testify as to persons concerning whom she refused to answer, as a matter of principle," the judge said.

"There may be some difference in degree, but principle does not deal with differences of degree; it deals with differences of kind, as I understand it."

This was a preface to a strange colloquy.

MATHES: If she is to be a martyr, if that is her desire to be a martyr, she should be a martyr in the best sense of the word, not one of these present-day martyrs who wants all the glory and is unwilling to stand the pain, but a martyr of old who is willing to take the glory and the pain with it.

MARGOLIS: If Your Honor please, I had hoped that we were living in an era where martyrdom was not required of people.

MATHES: Some people choose to be martyrs.

MARGOLIS: And I had hoped particularly, Your Honor, in an American court that would not be required of any defendant.

Margolis persisted in his argument that Oleta's position was consistently principled, that there was, in fact, a difference in kind, not degree, between identification of William Z. Foster as a Communist and her refusal to testify about others.

"I say, not only is it a principled position, but it is a courageous position," Margolis concluded.

"Be careful, Mr. Margolis," Mathes snapped, his anger visible, "I would not want to catch you in contempt for advising contempt."

MARGOLIS: I am not advising, Your Honor —

MATHES: I do not need to caution you that one who solicits or counsels or advises contempt is in contempt also.

MARGOLIS: I am advising —

MATHES: Are you suggesting, as an officer of this court, that you are advising contempt?

MARGOLIS: All I am suggesting is —

MATHES: Answer that question.

MARGOLIS: No, Your Honor.

Still Margolis repeated that Oleta's position was principled. The judge interrupted again, almost shouting this time.

"I will hear no more of it. Sit down! Call the jury!"

This was Friday morning; the rest of the day was uneventful. Oleta spent the weekend in jail. Subject to flare-ups of bursitis, she had a very bad one, probably brought on by the nervous tension in court and physical discomfort in jail. She was in great pain when she returned to the witness stand Monday morning. Pain may have been on Mathes' mind that weekend, the pain of old-fashioned martyrdom, for when he returned to the bench he virtually directed Neukom to give him the opportunity to inflict a little more of it on Oleta.

Neukom was questioning her about the 1934 maritime strike when Mathes abruptly intervened.

MATHES: Have you about concluded your cross-examination of this witness?

NEUKOM: No, I have not, Your Honor.

MATHES: Let's move on to something more important and up to date than 1934.

Neukom understood. Quickly he asked who attended Communist state board meetings in 1947 and 1948. He asked the question as if it were intended to elicit information. Mathes was too impatient for the pretense. He gave Neukom a helpful hint: "If you wish to ask the witness leading questions as to the names of persons previously mentioned in the testimony [not hers, but the prosecution's], you may do so."

"I intend to, Your Honor," Neukom said, and he did.

There were eleven separate questions about names, eleven refusals to answer, eleven citations for contempt. At the end of the session Mathes announced he would treat the new citations as "criminal contempt"; the prior citations were for "civil contempt." The distinction was significant; for "criminal contempt" he could impose a prison sentence, separate from and in addition to any punishment inflicted for the "civil contempt."

She remained on the witness stand for two more days of desultory, flea-hopping cross-examination. She also remained in jail for those two days and for five weeks more until the end of the trial in early August. At this point Mathes sentenced her to one year in prison on the eleven counts of criminal contempt; he also decreed that independent of that sentence she must remain in jail until she purged herself of the civil contempt by answering the unanswered questions.

Another month went by. Legally and logically it was untenable to hold a witness in jail in order to compel her to answer questions that had been rendered moot, that were as irrelevant and immaterial as any questions could conceivably be because they had been asked in a trial long since over, in which a verdict had been returned. But Oleta remained in jail. She had already served seventy-four days on the civil contempt counts when Judge Mathes had her brought into court on September 8 to mend the incongruity of her confinement before an appellate court said: enough. With a wave of his judicial wand Mathes transformed the civil contempt into criminal contempt and piled another three-year prison sentence on her. (It is pertinent to note that in other Smith Act trials refusal to answer similar questions on similar grounds drew thirty-day jail terms.)

After Oleta left the witness stand the defense rested. Then came lengthy legal arguments for a directed verdict of acquittal, which was of course denied, and then the summations to the jury. Those last days were marked by two unusual events: a minor earthquake and the release in Washington of a secret report by FBI Director J. Edgar Hoover about a Communist plot to seize the country. The Hoover report, treated as a sensation by the news media and released on the eve of the jury's retirement to deliberate a verdict, provoked heated arguments by defense counsel that probable and prejudicial influence upon the jurors warranted a mistrial. To no avail. The earthquake came during defense attorney Schullman's final argument to the jury. The courtroom shook, the glass of water trembled on the lectern before him, but Schullman was oblivious to the tremor, and when he became aware of the buzz in the courtroom he appeared to be startled, as if he was surprised that his eloquence could evoke such excitement. Why mention this trivia now? Only because at the end of a very long trial, with the verdict imminent, one was grateful even for such comic relief.

The jury retired four-thirty P.M., Thursday, July 31, and we began what turned out to be a long vigil. On Saturday morning, with the jury still out, somebody said we had set a new record; in the first New York trial the jury was out seven hours, in Baltimore it took only two hours to arrive at a guilty verdict.

As the second day passed, then the third, hope surged against the inner barriers I had erected with the pessimism of reason. Not that I dared to hope for acquittal in the prevailing political climate. But a deadlock? If there were not the possibility of a deadlock, then what were those jurors doing all those days? There must have been conflict in the jury to keep it out so long, but what it was I do not know, for Mathes announced he would hold in contempt of court any juror who divulged information about what transpired in the jury room, and any one else who attempted to elicit such information from a juror.

Because a jury may return at any moment defendants were commanded to stand by. A waiting room was provided and this is what you did in that room: wait. I tried to do other things: converse, read, play cards, write; I even wrote a story about how it feels to wait for a jury, but all the time, regardless of what else I did, I was waiting. It was hard to do anything else and it became harder as time went by.

Each morning I came to the Federal Building with my little jail packet, toilet articles and some odds and ends of clothing, not knowing whether I would be home that evening, and truly not expecting to be. At about nine P.M., when the jury recessed for the night, we were permitted to go home. A minor triumph, another day, our record was more impressive. The next day it was the same; except for the suspense, it was a little more taut than the day before.

Five mornings I lugged my little jail packet downtown (I did not expect a verdict on the day the jury retired, but I was prepared) and five evenings I brought it home again. On the sixth morning, at eleven-forty, five days and nineteen hours after it retired, the jury returned with a verdict. Some defendants discerned traces of tears on the face of one juror, a Mrs. Muriel Fitzsimmons, widow of a mystery fiction writer. I didn't. Whatever the qualms and conflicts in the jury, the foreman said "Guilty!" fourteen times, once for each defendant (the fifteenth defendant, Bernadette Doyle, had been severed from the case because of illness). Defense counsel asked the jurors be polled as to each defendant; so our guilt was reaffirmed 168 times. Mathes, as we expected, immediately revoked bail; that afternoon I and my packet were back in the Los Angeles county jail.

In anticipation of a guilty verdict I had drafted a statement that was now issued in behalf of the defendants. We had not prepared a victory statement in advance. Even in retrospect the statement reads well. If the Supreme Court decision in the Dennis case signified it was five to midnight then our conviction, coming after one in Baltimore, plausibly moved the minute hand a notch or two closer to the upright position. Certainly, from our vantage point, the political situation in the country had not gotten better between June 1951 and August 1952. But this was not the tenor of our statement.

"We do not minimize the consequences and implications of the verdict," the statement said. "But we do affirm once again that the stubborn year-long battle waged in this case has helped create the conditions that ultimately will reverse the infamous verdict."

The bulk of the statement argued for this estimate and the peroration reverted to the original theme: "We have not just begun to fight. For a long year the battle has raged. Building on the successes attained, learning from the failures, the sort of battle can be mounted now that can reverse the verdict.

"We summon our friends and supporters to this battle. Let them take heart . . ."

Back in jail we were busy preparing what we would say before sentence. Some defendants labored with written statements. I have an antipathy to written speeches. Look, he's not talking to me, he's reading to me — maybe it's a quirk to attach any importance to this distinction. For myself I prefer to risk a possible loss in precision to attain the special quality of direct human communication in the spoken word.

Those final words before sentence are, in spirit, the very opposite of a last will and testament; only the sense of gravity is comparable. This feeling is heightened by the knowledge that others were there before you, among them the noblest spirits born of the race. And the judge is going to ask you as other judges asked them: have you anything to say before sentence is pronounced? After a year in his court, after a lifetime of thought, passion, hope, action that brought you to this juncture, have you anything to say? Have you *anything* to say in a few minutes that can match what he is going to say — five years? There is so much to say. And of all the things there are to say you must choose that which you think and feel most needs to be said, for aside from all else this subtle blend of political declaration and personal testament should also be brief. I paced the jail corridor, searching, sorting, choosing, discarding. My choice is set down here just as it appears in the trial transcript, without explication, for it is the record of what I thought and felt it was most important for me to say in those circumstances at that time.

"Your Honor, I am, of course, mindful of the solemnity of this proceeding, but I would like to make one observation, prompted by the arguments of the past few days and the past several months.

"It seems that membership and officership in the Communist party of itself is not a crime, but you can be sent to jail for it.

"Now, as for myself, I distinctly remember the prosecutor standing at this very lectern making a summation to the jury, and when he came to my name, he said this man is an editor, and then he went on at some length.

"But the burden of what he added was that this was my crime: being an editor of a certain political persuasion made me an important element of this nebulous conspiracy that is strung together by the flimsy thread of conjecture which here is elevated to the dignity of inference.

"Now, editorship can be an honorable vocation, and I have tried to follow it with honor. I have tried to seek the truth. I have tried to tell the truth as I see it. It is rather late in this proceeding to go into details, but one thing should be said:

"What I have advocated during these past years with the greatest passion, the greatest devotion, is what I believe to be the most fundamental, the most profound and overriding truth of our day, and that is that peace is possible, that the American people can find a path to peace, not through big stick diplomacy, not through the staggering armaments, but through genuinely seeking friendship and understanding with all the nations, and this truth I have proclaimed.

"The prosecutors have chosen not to introduce here the products of my labor as an editor and in that vacuum I can draw the inference that the reason I am here is because anyone who seeks to obscure that truth, who seeks to detract from it in any way is wittingly or unwittingly helping to set the stage for the most unspeakable, most monstrous force and violence that the human mind can conceive, the force and violence of an atomic war.

"And I would rather be in jail than have upon my conscience even the taint, the suggestion that I bear any responsibility for bringing about such an eventuality.

"I have tried to live and work by the ancient maxim, 'Know the truth and it shall set you free.' But this prosecution, and the repressive hysteria of which it is a part, seeks to impose a different, contradictory dictum upon the American people: Seek the truth and you will land in jail.

"Well, I have landed there, but I don't think the quest will stop, and if the people in their search will be led to those books that used to be in those exhibit cabinets, they will go there and no power will stop them, and the quest will go on, as it has gone on through the centuries, despite crucifixion, despite inquisition, despite witch burning, and I am sure the people will find the truth and there will be my vindication."

After I spoke Mathes pronounced sentence, as he did after the others spoke. It was the maximum for all, as we knew it would be. In a jest that dated us we called them Woolworth sentences, five and ten, five years in prison and $10,000 fine. Afterward we were returned to jail. This time it took a month to have bail set by the U. S. Circuit Court of Appeals, $20,000 each.

I was free pending appeal, which is a tenuous sort of freedom. In intimate personal terms the appellate grind is a shared experience, much more so than jail or trial. I knew that my being in jail and in court imposed great hardship and strain upon Nancy, probably greater than mine; we tried to succor each other but those things we endured separately. In the suspenseful vigil of the appellate process there is family togetherness. She waited, I waited. We both looked at the calendar, we both lived with when and if. Meanwhile our sons grew. Aged four and three at the time of my arrest they could not comprehend it, but with each passing year David and Joe comprehended more. It was necessary to share with them, to explain our situation, gently enough so as not to disturb them overly and yet with sufficient force so they would understand, would have this to sustain them when and if.

Nancy and I said to ourselves and to each other that life goes on; it must be lived as one would live it in ordinary circumstances, it is folly to be constantly suspended on an if, as if there might be no tomorrow. We said this and in large part we lived by this counsel but not altogether, certainly not all the time, as the shadow was always there, sometimes distant and faint, sometimes close and ominous, because the appellate ladder is not a smooth climb to the ultimate rung. You can fall along the way.

There is precedent for revocation of bail upon denial of appeal by the Circuit Court. A rare occurrence, I did not expect it in our case, but still there was uneasiness about it. When we passed this mild hazard, the next was much more serious. Will the Supreme Court agree to review our case? The apparent odds were heavily against us. The court had refused to review the Baltimore case. The New York trial of the "second-string" leaders had overlapped ours, beginning later and extending several months past ours. In January 1955 the Supreme Court denied their petition for review. All those comrades of ours, in New York and Baltimore, arrested at about the same time we were, were tried at about the same time on the same charge based on the same prosecution theory. By the end of January 1955, when they were all lodged in federal prisons, we were still free, still awaiting the ultimate outcome of our appeal.

To employ a favorite phrase of Judge Mathes there might have been some slight difference in degree between us and those others, although I really do not know what it could have been, but there certainly was no difference in kind. From the Supreme Court's disposition of the companion cases, it could be inferred its position was that the issues in Smith Act prosecutions had been resolved in its Dennis case decision of 1951 and there was nothing left to review. It was so patently reasonable, this inference, that our chances seemed slim; why should we be treated differently from those others?

When the court denied the New York petition Nancy and I looked at the calendar. It was January. Then we began to calculate. What made these compulsive calculations more pathetic was our ignorance of judicial tempo, for a layman's conception of time is not necessarily that of the courts; for that matter, lawyers are baffled by the caprice of judicial pace. Our New York contemporaries, for example, embarked on the appellate voyage four months after we did and now they reached its end in federal penitentiaries, whereas we still awaited judgment in the Ninth U. S. Circuit Court of Appeals.

Assume, Nancy and I calculated, the Circuit Court had been sitting on our case to see how the New York appeal made out in the Supreme Court. Summary denial of the New York petition was bad for us, but how bad, or how quickly bad? Suppose the circuit judges did not care about appearances that they had been waiting for the word from Washington and rendered an unfavorable decision right away? In February, let's say, could the judicial pace suddenly be accelerated so as to reach a final determination before the Supreme Court recessed in June? I still do not know how well informed these speculations were (poorly informed, I suspect); as it turned out they did not matter. The Circuit Court ruled against us on Saint Patrick's Day (perhaps in a whimsical celebration of Oleta's Irish ancestry; the case bore her name). Our lawyers played another card, a petition for rehearing, which was denied on June 15. By then we were clearly reprieved for the summer. The shadow receded, although we knew it would be back with the Supreme Court's term in October, when it would surely rule on our petition and might deliver the final blow.

I reconstruct these tortuous calculations because they were an essential part of our lives, and of the lives of many other social dissenters, rebels, or revolutionaries who traversed the judicial gauntlet in those years.

That summer Nancy and I went on vacation, a farewell vacation, feeling it might be our last together for several years. We went to what was for us a plush Carmel Valley resort; yes, I confess, to make merry this summer because in the autumn I might be in prison. It was a stupid thing to do. I am no proletarian snob, and definitely not an ascetic (indeed, some fool of a psychiatrist I once met socially, not professionally, called me a hedonist), but the precious affluence of the place repelled and depressed me. We moved on.

If all this suggests a state of suspended animation I have misled you. I was actively animated. Since our trial, aside from editing a daily paper with a short staff I had produced three pamphlets. One, on "McCarthy — the Man and the Ism," under the pseudonym of Joseph Morton, circulated in excess of 100,000 copies, most through sizable bundle orders by local trade unions, scattered from Wisconsin to Hawaii. The others, on the economic recession of 1953–1954 and on yet another anti-Communist enactment of Congress, the Communist Control Act of 1954, did less well. Life did go on, political and personal, much of it gratifying, some of it tragic and disturbing. I will relate these things later on. Here I wished to make certain that in conveying the appellate experience I did not reduce those years to just one long vigil.

On October 17, 1955, the Supreme Court granted our petition for certiorari. Another reprieve, once more the jail packet was stored away. Back to the calendar: the court had just convened, its term was to run for some eight months, would it decide our fate before adjournment in June 1956?

On this note of suspense I turn to other matters. I was not involved in the legalities of appeal, except for a journalist's curiosity and one development that specifically concerned me. In touching on the legalities I lay no claim to expertise despite a standing joke during our trial, which was that by the end of a long political trial all the clients become legal experts and all the lawyers become authorities on political theory and tactics. There is an element of truth in this transference of roles, but not enough of it to make me a legal expert.

As I understood the legalities they afforded an x-ray glimpse into what lies behind the exterior pretenses of the judicial process. Our knowledgeable attorneys realized a decision in our case, it being political, would be determined in the final analysis by political factors: the political climate, the intricate mosaic of international and domestic politics. They also knew the court, ultimate interpreter of the law, guardian of its purity, never concedes it is influenced by anything so crass as politics. Furthermore, they knew the fundamental First Amendment issues posed by the Smith Act were adjudicated in the Dennis case; it was highly unlikely that the court, now the Warren court, would explicitly reverse the decision of the Vinson court only a few years earlier. But suppose the court, even with this brief passage of time, with some change in personnel and circumstances, were inclined to reverse our convictions, to impose some check on the repressive momentum it itself had helped set in motion. There had been, after all, some political backlash against McCarthyite excesses. Although politics are paramount, you cannot argue them, except by implication, indirection, incidental reference; and even with respect to the law you will argue the broad constitutional issues of free speech and association, which are the judicial core of the case, but you will do so as a matter of principle, not in the anticipation the justices will rule squarely on such grounds. What can you do then to facilitate a favorable decision that might be politically possible?

Here another guiding principle of the court is germane: a case should be decided on the narrowest grounds because the broader the basis of the decision the more broadly may it be invoked as precedent in subsequent cases, and that can create all sorts of complications. So the board is set for the legal game. You know the decision will be political, but the skill of legal gamesmanship lies in devising a splendid variety of technical pegs upon which the court can hang its decision.

Ben Margolis, whip of our legal team, turned his prodigious energy and ingenuity to the production of pegs, from semantics (a favorite judicial preoccupation) to the sufficiency of the evidence, the most substantive legal point, for the Supreme Court had not considered it in the Dennis case and there were no judicial standards of evidence sufficient to convict under the Smith Act. Irrespective of its substance, the point may have been fortuitously decisive in our appeal. Of necessity it required examination of the long trial record as to each defendant, and this consumed time at each stage of the appellate ascent. Thus the point may have been instrumental in delaying the ultimate decision until times got better.

The legality that specifically affected me was the acquisition of Augustin Donovan as counsel in the Supreme Court phase of appeal for Connelly and myself. Donovan was a former vice president of the California State Bar, a prominent lay Catholic, an impeccable Republican. His one conspicuous vagary was the composition of doggerel, which appeared in the letters column of the Oakland *Tribune*. Having read some of this verse I can only assume the Knowlands, who owned and edited the *Tribune*, published it as a courtesy to the foibles of a fellow-conservative. When Chief Justice Earl Warren was district attorney in Alameda County, Donovan played handball with him at the Athens Club. (This led me to say later that our case was really decided upon the handball courts of Oakland.)

Donovan read our trial transcript and found it incredible; he said he could not believe people can be sent to prison on such evidence, he was outraged by the violence this did to the constitutional fabric. I believe he meant it. I cannot say this with firsthand certainty because of a condition he attached to his entrance into the case: he absolutely would not see either Slim or me. He also would not accept any fee. To explain these odd provisos he said he anticipated flak in his social milieu for association with our case, and he wanted to say truthfully he had never even seen his clients, there was not a penny in it for him, nothing but pure principle was involved.

This was a greater eccentricity than doggerel. I think of Donovan as one of those attractive contradictions in American society, attesting to the mysterious and multifarious workings of the democratic tradition. I also cherish him for one more thing: the brevity of his brief in conjunction with the oral argument before the Supreme Court. It read: "The evidence is insufficient to support the verdict against the petitioners." That was all. (Not to mislead the uninitiate, the more important brief accompanied the earlier petition for certiorari; that one, researched and written by the brightest Stanford Law School graduate Donovan could find, was considerably longer.)

When I left the calendar for these several digressions it was October 17, 1955, and the Supreme Court had just granted us certiorari. To the lay mind the time between October and June is ample for a decision. The lay mind tends to be egocentric, obsessed with the supreme importance of the case that is its concern, prone, therefore, to a different order of priorities than the court, which also has other cases to consider, and, insensitive as this might seem, may consider some of those more urgent. The congestion of the docket, the touchiness of a case, the range and intensity of division it may engender in the court — these and other factors determine how quickly it gets around to the case. In its unpredictable timetable there is one certainty: before the court decides it must hear oral arguments. This is the one tangible clue. When 1955 expired and the court still had not set a time for oral arguments, we relaxed; there would be no decision that term. One more summer of freedom, again possibly the last, and certainly the last, I thought, of waiting for decision.

The Supreme Court heard the oral arguments on October 8 and 9, 1956, immediately after it reconvened. The next and final word was to be its decision. Then began the game called "Supreme Court Mondays," although we really did not begin to play it before the court's winter holiday, and even afterward we played it only casually at first. By spring we were playing the game in nerve-jangling earnest, as time for decision was running out.

Mondays were then the court's decision days. No matter how we spent the weekends we thought of Monday. Weekdays were not so bad, they came after Monday; the weekends were the worst. The really bad tension began after Easter. As Mondays were crossed off and the number of them left before the court's probable adjournment in June diminished, the law of probability progressively increased the chance that the next Monday would be it. By May the Mondays remaining approximated the number of bullet chambers in a revolver, and each weekend the game became Monday roulette, only someone else was to pull the trigger. The difference in time between the Pacific Coast and the Atlantic Seaboard made it nine A.M. in San Francisco when the court convened at noon in Washington, which gave me an advantage over those who had to play the Monday game in the East. I could take my deep breath before lunch time.

The game went on and on until the penultimate Monday of the term, June 17, 1957. "Ah, Victory" said the caption over a front page photo in the *People's World* of Lima and me, our faces one big, uninhibited smile. It could have read "Oh, Joy!"

In a very unusual assumption of what is ordinarily a trial court's function, the justices voted six to one to direct an acquittal of five defendants, including me, because "we find no adequate evidence in the record which would permit a jury to find that they were members of such a conspiracy." The others acquitted were Connelly, Mrs. Chernin Kusnitz, Spector, and Steinberg. As to the remaining nine defendants, their convictions and sentences were also voided, but their cases were remanded to the lower court, giving the government the option to try them again. (All the contempt sentences against Oleta O'Connor Yates, by the way, were set aside on appeal. Mathes must have set some sort of record for reversible error by one judge in one case; if I remember right, he was reversed nine times by higher courts.)

The Supreme Court's reversal of all the convictions was dangled most securely on a semantic peg: the meaning of "organize" as used in the Smith Act. There was another peg, but it resembled the sort you sometimes encounter in restaurants, from which your hat keeps slipping off. The court found Judge Mathes erred in failing to instruct the jury explicitly that in establishing the criminality of advocacy under the Smith Act "the essential distinction is that those to whom the advocacy is addressed must be urged to *do* something, now or in the future, rather than merely to *believe* in something."

As to "organize," our counsel contended that in the Smith Act it meant to "establish," "found," or "bring into existence," that it described the formative act. The government (and Judge Mathes) insisted the word also embraced ongoing administrative and organizational functions. The court upheld our interpretation and since, in this sense, the Communist party was last "organized" in 1945 the three-year statute of limitations had long since expired when we were indicted in 1951.

It was a small legal peg for a big political decision. The government chose not to retry my nine codefendants. Subse-

quently Smith Act prosecutions were also dropped against
eighty-one other persons throughout the country, most in the
appellate mill, a few still awaiting trial.

I will not read all the signs and portents in the political
cosmos that augured this decision. Only the most obvious.
Slowly, uncertainly, jerkily, an international detente appeared
to be in the making; it might have begun with the Korean armis-
tice in 1953, it reached a climax two years after our decision
with Nikita Khrushchev's visit to the United States and what
was then called "the spirit of Camp David," which attended the
Soviet leader's meeting with President Eisenhower. On the domestic scene Senator McCarthy had been censured by the Senate in December 1954. Afterward even timorous souls, discreetly silent when the senator swaggered across the national
stage, were emboldened to excoriate McCarthyism. A kind of
national revulsion against the sordid terrors and fears that had
humiliated the country was still gathering momentum in 1957.
That same year was also the first in the Eisenhower administration's second term. No one revived Harding's slogan of "back
to normalcy"; it would have sounded anachronistic, it had been
a different country in another world in 1920. Yet Eisenhower's
avuncular smile, reassuring and ubiquitous like a Norman
Rockwell magazine cover in another era, was a graphic evocation of Harding's nostrum for the nation's nerves. With due respect to legal gamesmanship all this was more pertinent in
spiking the Smith Act than a semantic quibble about the usage
of "organize."

We were very lucky in our timing. But was it pure luck?
Having spent some nights at the poker table to relieve the tedium of army life I have misgivings about the purity of luck.
Luck, like God, is inclined to be more generous to those who
help themselves. I believe we helped. Although we would not
have given much for our chances in the political climate of
1951–1952, we did not succumb to a political fatalism that envisioned the inexorable march of reaction in hobnailed boots to
fascism or something akin to it. At the very least, as I indicated
before, we prolonged the contest until the circumstances for its
resolution were most favorable for us. We did more; we cre-

ated an atmosphere around the case in which a Supreme Court reversal could achieve plausibility. We managed to have our chips in the right square when the wheel of political fortune took a lucky spin.

The Supreme Court decision came six years after my arrest; it could not restore the half year in jail and the half year in court, or obliterate marks of the suspense that ebbed and flowed but was always around somewhere for five years. Still the decision brought a feeling of release that was a delirious explosion. Let philosophers quarrel about freedom, but whatever its true nature, that day I experienced it in its untrammeled beauty. Today, I exulted, I am the freest man on earth. When the news reached our office, although it was early in the day some staff member procured a bottle to toast the victory. I drank, but in my euphoria alcohol was nothing. Our switchboard buzzed with congratulatory messages. I, in turn, finally talked with my counsel, via phone, to extend my congratulations. People dropped in to share in the celebration. Through all this joyous bedlam I floated in a cloud of ecstasy. Then it was home for a more intimate celebration, with the children, with Nancy, who had shared in the ordeals of all those years. It's real, I said. That was the difficult thing to grasp that day: it's real.

How many contradictions can human emotion encompass? I have tried to relate my sense of triumph as truly as I could. It was like that, and not quite like that, because it was not an unmarred triumph, personally or politically.

My mother was not alive to celebrate. She died in November 1954, two years after the trial, still hoping against hope, hoping as people who do not believe in miracles hope for a miracle. She died of intestinal cancer, a bad way to die. At the time of her death I wrote:

"I do not know what causes cancer. The medical men and the research scientists say they do not know, and I do not pretend to greater knowledge than they.

"This I do know: the first overt symptoms of the disease appeared shortly after the year of jail and trial, the first pain, the first disorders in the lower abdomen. Then came the more

acute pains, the surgical operations, the periods of convalescence, the terribly short respites before the malignant disease
asserted itself once again, and then finally the last weeks when
the body visibly wasted away, and the thread of life grew thin
and snapped in a last agony.

"Maybe J. Edgar Hoover and the politicians and the investigators who fashion Smith Act prosecutions did not bring on the
fatal disease. Maybe, at worst, they only accelerated a malignant growth that was there. I don't know. But I can't help
thinking about it . . ."

The embers of that bitterness flared up again on that happy
day in June.

Political blemishes. My final story about our case appeared
in a weekly paper; the *Daily People's World* had gone under in
February after nineteen years of publication, in June we were
still clinging to the wreckage, fighting desperately to keep the
weekly successor from sinking. The paper's difficulties related
to the condition in the party, which was a shambles.

Those questions about our political course that arose so circumspectly in the first meetings of our trial committee, when
we were in the Los Angeles county jail, had by then erupted
with explosive force. At the end of April 1956 the party's national committee held an enlarged meeting, the first such gathering in five years, a reassembly of the national cadre; a majority of those convicted in the first New York Smith Act trial,
having served their prison sentences, were back, so were those
who did their time in the "underground." Eugene Dennis, the
party's general secretary, fresh out of Atlanta Penitentiary,
staggered this reunion with a devastating critique of party estimates and policies.

"While we repeatedly asserted that World War III is not inevitable, the fact is that we frequently tended to evaluate certain war preparations and threats of Washington as if a new
world war was not only possible — but almost imminent . . .
More than once the party overestimated the scope, level, and
tempo of development of the process of fascization underway
. . . And some of the organizational steps the party took at
the time [1951] were bound to disorient many, as indeed they

did . . . During 1945 and again in 1949, our party — basing itself on a one-sided estimate of economic data and factors, and applying the Marxist theory on economic crisis dogmatically — wrongly concluded that a major economic crisis was then imminent. In connection with the 1953–1954 decline, we again erroneously evaluated the course of the economic development . . . considered that the decline would inevitably give rise to a major economic depression in 1955–1956."

From these erroneous estimates, he went on, flowed a series of tactical blunders. He also referred to the party's "basic, deep-seated and long-standing weaknesses," among them "the strong and persistent tendency in the party to apply the experiences of other parties and the science of Marxism in a mechanical and doctrinaire fashion — all of which inadvertently gave aid and comfort to the slander that we are 'foreign agents.' "

Just as the party was still trying to absorb the shock of the Dennis report, was just beginning to grapple with its self-critical analysis, Khrushchev's "secret report" on the crimes of the Stalin era, delivered at the 20th Soviet Communist Party Congress in February, became public in June. The impact was shattering. The American party, persecuted, isolated, depleted, having suffered great losses in membership and graver losses in influence, and possessing, to begin with, the historic defects cited by Dennis, was poorly positioned to sustain two such jolts in quick succession. The Khrushchev revelations subsumed what in any case would have been very difficult: an independent, systematic, searching, unequivocal self-examination. What ensued was disorientation, division, defection, faction, political chaos, ideological disarray.

By June 1957 the crisis was unabated, its toll was cumulative. I remember speaking at a public gathering sponsored by the *People's World*. The court's decision, I said, gives us greater legal freedom to speak; now we confront the problem of what to say. This fairly presented the dilemma of a paper, which was the voice of a movement, when the movement itself was rent by disagreement as to what needs to be said.

I will revert to these matters in a later context. They had to be mentioned here because these were the perversities of fate that attended our luck in the Supreme Court, blunting the edge of our success, thwarting any initiative it might have triggered. Just the same I take pride in that battle. It was not among the least of the engagements with McCarthyism, and it helps to illuminate that era. It and its outcome have a place in the history of those times.

XII. Reappraisal

HAVING SAVORED THE MOMENT of victory in 1957 I revert now to joyless agonies of 1956.

With Dennis' political reckoning came a cost item: national party membership had declined by two-thirds in less than a decade. But in California the loss was only half the national rate. These statistics, it seemed to me, showed that during the McCarthyite season some losses were inevitable but their extent was appreciably affected by what we did.

I thought Dennis posed more problems than he solved, for to say we misjudged major political and economic phenomena was not yet a precise judgment of these phenomena or a comprehensive analysis of the post-World War II development. Beyond the specific was his general reference to historical weaknesses: dogmatism and mechanical application of foreign experience. Inevitably confrontation with error and weakness also posed questions about the quality and methodology of leadership. As I saw it Dennis' candor augured a free, vigorous inquiry and discussion, out of which would come a much sounder relationship between the party and its environment. Into such cerebrations burst the Khrushchev thunderbolt.

Words for reactions in Communist ranks were used by very political men: "shock . . . pain" (Dennis), and "surprise . . . grief . . . bewilderment . . . perturbation . . ." (Palmiro Togliatti in Italy). It might appear odd to invoke their descriptions of such intimate feelings and yet I quote them to stress the universality of these responses. To tell how searing one man's pain was, how anguished his perturbation, may be trivial in itself; the difficult remembrance has its true validity only as evocation of what went on within millions of Communists the world over when they were suddenly confronted with the nightmare of terror, suspicion, fear, megalomania, and cruel caprice that Khrushchev unveiled. Their trauma reflected the political and ethical impulses that motivated them, for to speak of pain and bewilderment is also to speak of confrontation with things abhorrent and alien. Not that the reactions were uniform but the chords above were widespread.

Khrushchev's report, some said, was too subjective, too emotional, lacking the dispassionate balance of a political assessment. I had an opportunity to observe him briefly a few years later as a reporter covering his visit to the San Francisco Bay area. I watched this bouncy little man, constructed in the round like a Russian wooden doll or an onion in the old Russian church architecture; he was extraordinarily vital, shrewd, quick, impulsive, earthy, and all this with a spontaneity that destroyed my own stereotype of a Soviet leader. Watching him I wondered how much effort it took for him to make that report, to probe those wounds, which were also personal wounds for, as he related, he was close enough to the apex of the Soviet regime to have endured knowingly what he now condemned. Although the report was a product of collective decision it bore the stamp of his personality, which was its strength and its weakness: strength in that its bluntness and emotion, its citation of specific detail rather than total reliance on political generalization magnified the force of its impact; weakness in that it did not explain how or why such things occurred.

Khrushchev's revelations did not simply concern a particular policy or tactic that was momentarily perplexing. It was no good now to say they knew what they were doing, for Stalin, who was exalted above all others as knowing best what he did, had done some horrible things. Such disclosures posed questions about the Soviet regime and to the extent your fundamental beliefs were intertwined with this regime, these, too, were placed in question. When you get to this core of what you live by it requires a personal reckoning, for first of all you must settle accounts with yourself.

Even in so highly personal a quest there can be a certain sustenance in the structured collectivity of a Communist party, which embraces your immediate associates and the leadership.

Collectivity was at a low ebb, as was leadership authority (and by this I do not mean the authority that is a trapping of office, but the sort that is voluntarily granted and recognized). It made the quest more solitary. Not that there was a lack of talk; there was much talk, long, often emotional conversations that went round and round, and in the end the choices were still there to be made.

That was a general condition. My circumstances were also specific. I was editor of a paper. With the Khrushchev report all the accumulated frustrations, discontents, doubts, grievances in and around the Communist party erupted with an elemental force, and much of it was directed at the paper. The paper was there, tangible, visible, bearer of the printed word, durable and recorded, reacting (on rare occasions by silence) to events as they occurred, projecting each day of publication a view of the world, and in this process constantly defining its own character. Boards and committees, these relatively sheltered repositories of political leadership, had low and infrequent visibility in the best of times, and it reached zero during the underground period when the general Communist membership had no idea of which leader was doing what. Moreover, these collectives and individuals dealt mostly in the ephemeral currency of the spoken word, and they were under no compulsion, of course, to supply a daily, public record of their reactions to events, personalities, movements. In this latter respect the paper served as their surrogate.

For all these reasons the paper was a natural focus of the angry eruption. It is very difficult to keep a steady helm when a ship is buffeted by stormy waves; it is impossible to do so when the man at the wheel is not sure of what point of the compass to steer by. This was my predicament. The ship swayed and swerved. Doggedly I held on to one deep conviction: the ship had to be kept afloat. With all the centrifugal forces at work on the Left, it seemed to me the paper could serve as a channel for communication, an instrument for cohesion on the Pacific Coast, pending conclusions reached in the debate then raging. Now and then I tried to suggest the restraints of rationality in the debate as it was waged in the paper's expanded letters section, and more specifically in the flagellation of the paper, pointing to the fine line between criticism and abuse, remonstrating that even Jesus did not say one should turn a third cheek. The paper and the times would have been better served, I suppose, by a bold leader, rather than a temperate moderator; I only suppose this because all would have then depended on where the leader led. To have essayed such a role would have required much more self-assurance than I had at the time. Situated in the eye of the storm I was trying to put my own inner house in order.

This effort was attended by another personal circumstance, not altogether unique, but no less personal on that account. The appeal from my conviction and prison sentence under the Smith Act was then before the Supreme Court, and a final decision was virtually certain in the term beginning October 1956. I still thought the odds were better than even that the decision would be unfavorable. Despite the stupidities one hears occasionally about an innate Communist craving for martyrdom the prospect of prison is depressing at any time. For the political person, convicted in a political case, the prospect is absolutely tragic if it is clouded by ambiguity or uncertainty about what he is going to prison for. And this involves not only his own convictions, which are primary, of course, but also their embodiment in a movement. When there are symptoms of disintegration in the community of shared vision, of comradeship and solidarity, that was his, then the integrity of his own credo is the more urgent as the source of inner strength. Such considerations were often in my mind during the year between June 1956 and June 1957 when the Supreme Court decision dispelled the shadow of prison. They constituted a powerful psychological influence in my reappraisal, an added compulsion for settling accounts with myself.

I went back to beginnings, to foundations, in the quest for a coherent position. What I arrived at was briefly as follows:

In their essence, the Marxian analytical critique and indictment of capitalist society were valid. So, too, for me, was the Marxian conception of socialist revolution as the historically necessary and possible resolution of the execrable problems that are insoluble under capitalism, and as the threshold to a rational society that would create the conditions for the unprecedented realization of the human potential. In its sum Marxist theory represented the most rational comprehension of the world and the most cogent guide for confronting reality and defining one's relationship to it in action. To paraphrase Marx, his labors produced an explanation of the world in order to change it. These reaffirmations came quickly and without difficulty.

In contrast a reappraisal of the Soviet Union as historical fruition of Marxist thought and action entailed more time and complications. The epochal nature of the revolution as a popular conquest, as confirmation of working-class capacity to reconstruct society, as a decisive turning point in history — this, for me, was ineradicable. Undimmed were the heroism, the boldness, the vision of this people and its leaders through the early years of civil war, foreign intervention, economic collapse, famine, epidemic; I had glimpsed something of all this as a child, imperfectly and peripherally, embellished perhaps by childhood imagination and the whims of memory later on, and yet those early impressions served as sensory authentication of what I later read and heard. The stimulus and inspiration of the Soviet example for revolutionary forces everywhere was a momentous fact; the world was forever altered, another alternative had been presented to mankind, 1917 was the natal year of a new historical era. In the contemporary setting the Soviet Union served as workshop and arsenal and bastion of world socialism and colonial revolution. (This was before Vietnam and Cuba called forth these services in fuller measure but even then, rendered less conspicuously, their availability was a paramount fact of world politics.)

Furthermore, nothing detracted from the Soviet epic in World War II. Attempts to attribute it all to an innate Russian patriotism (akin to the Dostoevskian mystique of the Russian soul) struck me as meretricious. One needed only to contrast the performance of the Russians (and other peoples who now constituted the Soviet Union) in the First and Second World Wars. In the First War patriotism was not enough to prevent demoralization and disintegration of the armies once the troops lost faith in their military commanders and political governors, once the society demonstrated its incompetence to provide the material and moral sustenance for continued combat. Patriotism was, of course, a powerful motivation in the Second War, but not as an abstraction; it was rooted in a social order, it was conditioned by the relationship between the people and their society.

In the same light, as witness to the relationship between the people and their society, I saw the incredible labors and feats of industrialization that transformed the country's economy. The catalogue of impressive achievement could be augmented from other spheres of life (education, health, science, and more).

As against all this, which attested to the timber of the society, to its viability and potential, and in maddening contradiction with all this was the revelation of monstrous evil. (Stalin, it seemed to me, was this contradiction incarnate.) This was the incongruous, contradictory reality, and not the picture postcard we had been given and accepted. A near-Rotarian deference to the power of positive thinking was illustrated by an anecdote told at this time (June 1956) by Togliatti, the Italian Communist leader. He related that at a Communist school in the Soviet Union, attended by some Italian students in the early 1930s, a months-long polemic was directed against those who had praised the sacrifices made by the Russian workers for the success of the first Five-Year Plan. It was not permissible to mention sacrifices, for if there was talk of them, what would the workers of the West think? Togliatti saw two consequences of this approach. A stagnation of popular initiative and action, for masses of people would not respond to appeals based on a rendition of reality that did not correspond to their own experience and knowledge. Worse yet, since difficulties and contradictions were supposedly eliminated from the society, when these did arise, and in forms that could not be ignored, increasingly only one explanation could be offered for them: sabotage by hostile conspirators. (These did, indeed, exist, Togliatti noted, but in the distorted picture of Soviet life their true proportions were also distorted.)

What had to be comprehended now was the complex actuality, the contrast between the malignant manifestations of Stalin's reign and the Socialist economic foundations and the Socialist ethical impulses, which were affirmed by the advances of Soviet society. Like others, I recalled Lenin's forthright description of the Soviet regime in 1920, "A workers' state . . . with bureaucratic distortions," and recalled, too, his preoccupation in the final years of his life with these distortions, his manifest anxiety, his persistent search for the means to overcome them. (Incidentally, in offering that description of the regime Lenin acknowledged with a natural candor that he had been mistaken previously in using the characterization "workers' and peasants' state," and that his adversary in that debate, Bukharin, had been right in challenging him. Such natural admission of human error went out of style once Stalin donned the mantle of infallibility.) Stalin's regime represented an incalculable magnification of those "bureaucratic distortions." I agreed with the many expressions in world Communist ranks that Khrushchev offered no explanation for the evils he revealed, that placing the total burden of them upon Stalin's personal defects was no more valid than prior attribution of all Soviet successes to Stalin's personal genius, that it was still necessary to explore what it was in Soviet society that permitted these evils to develop and to achieve the magnitude they did. Such questions were not dispelled by a lengthy explanatory declaration issued subsequently by the Soviet party's Central Committee. Inextricably bound to the roots of the phenomenon was the measure of its consequences, not only in the Soviet Union but throughout the world movement.

Amid these questions and differences about roots and consequences one paramount factor intruded. The Soviet leaders, experienced political men at the helm of a great state, patently did not embark upon an exposure of Stalinist evils in the spirit of a confessional. It was a political act. Moreover, one had to assume they were aware this act would have disturbing and negative repercussions, not only in general, but also for themselves; as Togliatti phrased it, "in this criticism they are losing without a doubt a little of their own prestige." Nonetheless, they displayed the courage to do it. As a political act its primary meaning seemed twofold: a recognition that Stalinist methods and their residue represented so intolerable a brake on the forward movement of Soviet society that a cataclysmic shock was warranted to remove this impediment, and a guarantee to themselves and to their people against a regression to terrorist practices and personal power.

In the dynamic of social development one cannot simply say one will not go back, one also has to move forward, and Soviet society was moving along new paths, not only in rectifying past injustices and reforming the security apparatus, but in economic innovations, in a certain relaxation of rigid cultural norms, in its relations with the external world. These phenomena were sufficiently numerous to produce such popular catchwords as "the thaw" or "de-Stalinization." A profound process was set in motion, it seemed to me, and whatever its tempo, its detours, its relapses, it was impelled by a basic need of the society to achieve an equilibrium between its economic structure and defined goals, on the one hand, and the norms of political rule and civil life, on the other.

Simultaneously a great discussion had been touched off in world Communist ranks, unprecedented in scope and depth since the early years of the Communist International, and in an important sense more genuine than those earlier debates, which too often mirrored personal rivalries and factional antagonisms in the Soviet party. Demolition of the Stalin cult removed the theoretical binders he had imposed with his uniquely dogmatic and didactic style, which had arrested the development of Marxist thought in the three decades after Lenin's death. (His style was one of his strengths as a political leader, for Stalin was easier to read, understand, and even to memorize than either Marx or Lenin, whose scrupulous regard for the complexities of reality and its reflections in ideology restrained them from reducing all things to categorical formulae as Stalin tended to do.) The emphasis at the 20th Congress on different roads to socialism, corresponding to diverse national circumstances, reinforced the exercise of autonomy by the individual parties and new patterns in their relations, allowing a freer exchange of opinion and fraternal criticism.

The setting for the intense worldwide discussion was thus distinguished by these factors: a convulsive jolt that upset complacency and inertia, a crumbling of calcified dogmatic impositions, a new sense of autonomy, which increased the possibility for independent initiatives and explorations. And this discussion was unfolding in a movement that was a titanic revolutionary force. This movement commanded state power in a constellation of countries covering one third of the globe. It included several nongoverning mass parties that were a formidable political presence in their respective lands. It extended to every corner of the earth. This movement represented an unmatched accumulation of revolutionary experience, a vast assembly of cadre tested in the most varied and difficult trials: in the protracted, arduous, tactically diversified warfare that was the Chinese revolution; in the partisan detachments and anti-Nazi underground of Europe; in the gallant liberation war of the Vietnamese; in the crucible traversed by the Soviet Union; and these were only highlights.

Though the discussion revealed significant differences it was begun within a common framework of theoretical references and principles, a framework I accepted. In this discussion I saw the seeds of renewal and growth, of a new, more penetrating confrontation with world reality that had changed so profoundly since Lenin's time, of a cleansing release from the revealed abnormalities and their consequences. Comprehending the world movement as I did, the ferment within it was a fact of paramount historical importance. I recognized other revolutionary forces, notably in the colonial liberation movements, and yet for all their specific significance they impressed me as peripheral and subsidiary in the world balance. World communism, with its ideological, human, and material resources, was the principal arena for resolving the problems of revolutionary theory and strategy. The internal development of this movement would exert a determining influence upon the destiny of mankind.

Despite the compass of these thoughts and speculations, I was essentially trying to define a position for myself, and first of all to delineate the world matrix for such a position. My effective orbit was far more modest than the sweeping panoramas I could sketch in my mind. I functioned politically in the American Communist party. What I related to directly then was this party, with its history, characteristics, personnel, and methodology, with its immense difficulties in trying to create a viable revolutionary movement in the wealthiest and most powerful capitalist society, whose rulers, under the sign of the dollar and the bomb, were the vigilantes of counterrevolution throughout the world.

Although the revelations by Khrushchev overwhelmed the criticisms by Dennis the two were intertwined in the untrammeled debate that now shook the party. The debate soon centered on what was required in the way of theory, program, tactics, style, inner life to fashion an effective revolutionary party in the American environment, and inseparable from all this were issues of relationship with the Socialist camp and the world movement. For me the American debate gained in importance because it was part of a worldwide ferment, which seemed to me so decisive for the human future. I resolved to join in the struggle for the renewal of the American party, recognizing that its potency and credibility as an autonomous force depended, in the first instance, on its independent capacity to cope with the problems in American society. For that matter, this was its reason for existence.

Such, in substance, were the positions I defined for myself. There was so much to be reexamined. But events kept exerting their own pressures, especially on a newspaper. In the autumn came the Hungarian eruptions.

Soviet troops intervened in force on November 4, a Sunday. On Monday morning my associate editor, Lapin, and I, conferred with two party leaders from the San Francisco area; we also consulted by telephone with Los Angeles party leaders. There was disagreement (the Los Angeles leaders taking the firmest position that the intervention was justified) and no consensus was possible. But we were publishing a daily paper, which had to deal with these events in its next edition. We finally agreed I would write a signed article that would present a factual résumé of the Hungarian events, would frankly acknowledge the existence of disagreement, would state my own opinion, making clear it was a personal opinion, and would also summarize the contrary view.

Reading that piece now the sketch of the situation in Hungary is bolder and more persuasive than the conclusion reached. Once the "popular upheaval against the misdeeds and blunders of the previous regime . . . carried the issue of political power into streets . . . where it was being resolved with guns," I wrote, "there was inherent in the situation the peril of counter-revolution." An initial, brief show of Soviet military power "only fanned nationalist sentiment . . . turned it ever more vehemently against all those in Hungarian life who stood for cooperation with the Soviet Union . . . helped feed the burgeoning forces of counter-revolution."

"In the chaotic situation a government with authority resting on popular support and with a clearcut program of action to rally the people might have established the conditions for a peaceful and democratic resolution of the crisis."

The "makeshift Nagy regime . . . proved its incapacity" to constitute such a government. As a result, "the counter-revolutionary forces were on the ascendant. A white terror was in the making. The mass murder of Communists was begun . . ."

This capsule of internal developments was followed by a chronology of foreign relations.

TUESDAY (Oct. 30): The Soviet government made its declaration, acknowledging it had committed "violations and mistakes which infringed upon the principles of equality in relations between socialist states," and offering to negotiate withdrawal of its troops not only from Hungary, but from Poland and Rumania as well. The Soviet declaration, the *New York Times* reported, "had a delirious reception in the streets of Budapest."

WEDNESDAY: "Withdrawal of Soviet forces from Budapest was completed."

THURSDAY: "Premier Nagy announced the unilateral renunciation of the Warsaw Treaty. This was an act of provocation . . . hardly designed to improve the atmosphere for fruitful negotiations . . . Such abrupt renunciation of the Warsaw Pact was pressed upon Nagy by the forces who were not interested in a peaceful settlement of differences between Hungary and the Soviet Union . . . while the Nagy regime continued to protest that it desired friendship with the Soviet Union, it simultaneously began to broadcast frantic appeals for assistance and intervention by the capitalist states of the West.

". . . From the facts it would appear that the Soviet Government decided upon the second and large-scale military intervention in the belief that by so doing it would thwart the threat of a clerical-fascist regime in Hungary and the peril of a hostile salient in Eastern Europe that would be allied with the most bellicose anti-Soviet elements throughout the world.

"It would be shortsighted to minimize either peril. Such catchwords as 'free elections' have a hollow ring in the face of the incipient white terror that was bent on resolving the issues of political power by blood and murder. Nor is it permissible to dismiss the elaborate U.S. apparatus for intervention in Hungary and all of Eastern Europe."

Thus was the reality perceived. Now came the question. "Recognizing all those facts . . . should Soviet troops have intervened?" The answer was constructed on two pillars:

Because of the large share of Soviet responsibility for the crisis in Hungary, because of the revelations at the 20th Congress, "the position of the Soviet Union is compromised" and "there is a grave question, therefore, whether what it lost in the political arena it can now recoup by military force."

Can "the Kadar government . . . installed by Soviet military power . . . gain the confidence of the Hungarian people in the wake of what had gone on before? I personally doubt it." The prospect then was for an indefinite Soviet occupation, and this "will only further discredit socialism in Hungary and . . .

diminish its prestige (and effectiveness) on a worldwide scale."

All this was written in the charged atmosphere the morning after the Soviet intervention, under the pressure of a deadline only a few hours away, and against the convulsive background of the months between June and November. It is easier now, years later, to pinpoint the defect in the argument: it offers no alternative and thus there was an element of contradiction between the placement of the situation and the conclusion. The article also presented contrary views of "people whose judgment and integrity I respect." Our response to the events reflected a political stalemate that produced the national party's official position of neither condemning nor condoning the Soviet military action.

The Hungarian episode typified the party situation in the two years, 1956–1958, marked by divisions, factions — and a political stalemate. A venture into all the details and personalities would be of interest to the specialized student, or would be appropriate in a history of the party, which is not my undertaking. In the rough, three major alignments emerged and these, in turn, embraced shadings, divisions, offshoots.

When Dennis delivered his broadside in April William Z. Foster immediately rose to the challenge, for he had been the principal author of the policies under fire. Then in his late seventies (he turned seventy-six in 1956) and in poor health, Foster was a remarkably tough and tenacious man, wise and practiced in the skills of intraparty struggle, and commanding formidable advantages over his adversaries: he knew much more clearly what he wanted (the status quo, or even a modified approximation of it, is more tangible and more sharply defined than a new departure, which involves the untried and unknown); he struck the deep chords of party tradition and habit, and he enjoyed considerable personal prestige. In contrast was an alignment thrown together by the impulse for profound changes that motivated the inchoate upheaval in the ranks; this alignment was distinguished by a lack of political cohesion and coherence, and although John Gates, editor of the *Daily*

Worker, was billed in the press as its spokesman neither he nor anyone else could speak for this mixed array. Dennis and his associates occupied a middle ground. The actual diversity was greater than those neat categories.

One by-product of the crisis in the party was my election to the national committee at the party's 16th National Convention in February 1957 (a post I was to retain until the 20th Convention in February 1972). All the conflicting crosscurrents had the freest play at the 1957 Convention and the outcome was an apparent reconciliation of irreconcilables.

I was associated with the heterogeneous mix for renovation. Some people in it, from the outset of the debate, had one foot out of the party ideologically. But to fight effectively on the party terrain you must have both feet firmly planted on it. This is not simply a matter of balance. To contest seriously for the leadership of a party that is, after all, a voluntary association, composed primarily of devoted adherents, you must possess and convey a strong conviction that the party is worth leading. Without this indispensable foundation, programmatic issues, polemical skills, or tactical expertise are of little use in an intra-party battle. The other people in the heterogeneous mix, who were not hobbled by this disability although they were affected by it in the loose aggregation, lacked precision and clarity in program and boldness in leadership.

Like others I was motivated principally by three aims: a sharp break with bureaucratic patterns, an effective exercise of autonomy in a fraternal relationship with the world movement and the Socialist camp, and an independent confrontation with American reality in the spirit of Marx and Lenin, without borrowed spectacles or dogmatic preconceptions. The last objective was much the most difficult and, in the long view, the most fundamental, for it entailed a profound analysis of American society, its economy, politics (domestic and foreign), culture, tradition, regional diversity, class structure, oppressive ethnic patterns, and pervasive chauvinism. Out of such analytical research one would have to evolve strategy, tactics, organizational forms for a viable American Socialist movement. So inclusive an enterprise, requiring a high order of ability (which is not produced by resolutions or decrees), would have to assimilate critically prior researches, experiences, insights and reach beyond the sum of this accumulation. This labor, it seemed to me, would be hopelessly encumbered by a bureaucratic regime and by the premise that fraternity precludes rational (i.e., critical) examination of phenomena in the Soviet Union and allied Socialist countries. One could not exclude a vast chunk of the human experience from the exacting standards of the Marxist method without vitiating the method itself.

Early in 1958 the heterogeneous alignment was decisively beaten and there was yet another sizable exodus of party cadre and membership. These were people who had gone through the worst McCarthyite years; some had been in the underground with its odd tensions and abnormalities, others had endured prosecution and imprisonment. Among those who left were five of my codefendants in the Smith Act trial, including Oleta O'Connor Yates. For some the exit represented a fundamental ideological rupture; others simply lost confidence in the viability of the American party as constituted and left even as they asserted adherence to the general principles of communism; still others were imbued with enough skepticism to preclude membership but not amicable relations and active cooperation in specific projects. In this instance, too, neat categories are a poor approximation of a more complex actuality.

The people who left then or shortly before were, in the main, of my generation, among them old friends and co-workers. Old bonds were loosened or dissolved, and even where associations and friendships were maintained there was a subtle difference. This was not the same as the tales told in the "old gang" or "you can't go home again" literature. This was not about people who had shared in the wonderful comaraderie of youth, then drifted apart and became estranged and could not recapture what they once had. There were elements of that human experience, and yet this was different. Here the camaraderie of youth, animated by the exalted vision of a common odyssey to remake the world, braced by shared convictions and values, had grown more intimate with the passage of time. These were not the transient associations of youth; these had been enduring parts of one's life and hence of one's self. And now there was a feeling of ineffable loss.

I did not join the exodus. Underlying my decision was the position I defined for myself in the months after the 20th Congress, and there were also corollary circumstances. In the California party there was an openness that permitted grappling with the unsolved problems of creating a viable Socialist movement. And there was the paper. At its nadir circulation was 6000, and to cite this figure is already to guard against any exaggeration of its effect; nonetheless, given the general condition of the California Left in the late 1950s the paper was the most potent single factor on the scene. Such things are relative. Moreover, within the boundaries generally defined by its primary Communist base the paper enjoyed a considerable autonomy, enhanced by a consensus, which included party leaders in the state, that it should strive to reflect (not merely reach) a constituency broader than the party. In its tone, its range, in its treatment of events and of social and cultural phenomena, in its relation to existing movements, in the discussion it stimulated, the paper could, I believed, contribute to a revival of the Left. Editing it struck me as useful work that could be done with integrity.

The paper was a weekly now. Its base of support had shrunk during the McCarthy era and the progressive Communist isolation so that its existence as a daily was already precarious at the beginning of 1956; the post-20th Congress atomization administered the coup de grâce. In the transition to a weekly about half the staff left and this was a special parting, for these were people with whom I had worked day to day for many years under severe pressure, for the most part with a high morale and a fine camaraderie. Now goodbys were said in the dispiriting turmoil that embraced us.

Against the stream of farewells there was one brave hello. For Mike Gold, prophet of "the red decade of proletarian literature" when he, a few years older than the century, was also in his thirties. In that time he was the most beloved of Communist writers. His was an incandescent light then, luminous and intense. His column, "Change the World," was a popular fea-

ture in the *Daily Worker*. By the mid-1950s his column was a
fading memory. Even in better times Communist solicitude for
cultural figures was not great; in the McCarthyite time Mike
was left pretty much on his own, continuing to write but sub-
mitting very little for publication, and trying to eke out a living
at a variety of odd jobs. He even tried a Venetian blinds factory
— and lasted less than a day. Some friends of his talked of
setting him up in business as a laundromat operator but nothing came of it.

In 1956 Mike moved to San Francisco. It was Lapin's idea
that Mike, who had been a literary tribune of the Left for four
decades, should be encouraged to revive his column. With his
agreement we organized a modest syndicate that also included
the *Worker* and the Jewish *Morning Freiheit* in New York. The
three-paper pool produced fifty dollars a week.

The most distinctive vein in Mike's writing was a fierce, occasionally abrasive, partisan passion. Past sixty and ill, he no
longer commanded passion as he once did. And for maximum
effect journalistic passion must flow from an intimate engagement with one's time; the 1950s and '60s were not Mike's time.
When he brought in his weekly column it bore the marks of his
difficult labor. By the mid-1960s his eyesight failed and the
column was too much for him. His final one, a brief farewell,
appeared on July 30, 1966. Ten months later he died. The first
of that last cycle of columns had coincided with the death of the
daily *People's World*. It had appeared in our first weekly edition, February 9, 1957.

Left with twelve tabloid pages a week we still tried to maintain a journalistic balance and not lapse into the propagandis-
tic, inner-dialogue patterns of sect publications. A two-page
spread on culture and entertainment was presided over for
some years by Alvah Bessie, one of the Hollywood Ten; idio-
syncratic, opinionated, sensitive, he was part romantic, part
curmudgeon, and an able professional (he had been a literary
critic on the Brooklyn *Eagle* and a drama critic on the *New
Masses*, as well as a novelist, screenwriter, and personal historian in *Men in Battle*, the best narrative of the Spanish Civil
War produced by any veteran of the International Brigade).

All these attributes were combined to create a lively, provocative, and competent section. We even had a sports page, knowledgeably produced by Steve Murdock, our expert on state politics (and also expert on Western lore, ghost towns, railroads, and Western labor history). We strove for a decent level of professional and popular journalism, not only for its intrinsic virtue and as an expression of craft pride, but also in part, I suspect, as compensation for the low ebb of Left politics.

The two years of acute internal crisis, coming after the attrition and retreat of the McCarthy era, left the Communist party and its periphery in a state of exhaustion, permeated with the psychology of a holding operation. Convalescence was not helped by the social climate; in those waning years of the decade and the Eisenhower era the country's protracted withdrawal from McCarthyism exhibited symptoms of torpor and false optimism. Elephantine research studies were appearing on the "silent generation." The "end of ideology" was being proclaimed, meaning, of course, the presumed end of ideology that challenged the reigning ideological assumptions that imparted legitimacy to the existing social order.

The merger of the AFL and CIO in 1955 had turned into a tragicomedy titled *Waiting for Walter*. Biennially some of the hosts of the old CIO, mumbling incantations for a return to the "Spirit of '37," lamenting their captivity in George Meany's bureaucratic compound, trooped to the conventions of the merged federation. I observed them as a correspondent at the 1959 Convention in San Francisco. Their lamentations were discreetly uttered in corridors or barrooms, not on the convention floor. When asked what they intended to do they replied they were waiting for Walter, for Reuther the militant redhead, to come forth as Moses to lead them out of their bondage. They waited in vain for too long, and some years later when the chieftain of the United Auto Workers finally spoke, more as Jeremiah than as Moses, it was too late, they heeded him not.

Coincident with the social lethargy was the optimism, which peaked with Khrushchev's spectacular tour of the United States in September 1959, his conference with Eisenhower, and the consequent "spirit of Camp David," apparent herald of a détente that could lead to a stable era of peaceful coexistence. This particular balloon was shot down early in the next year with the U–2 spy plane deep over Soviet territory, and was further tattered in the acrimonious collapse of the Big Four summit conference in Paris. But the U–2 incident was an omen of the 1960s, not the emblem of the prior decade's exit.

It is useful to distinguish between the reality and the illusion of Khrushchev's tour. Indicative of the paper's short staff (and also indicative, perhaps, of how I exercised my bureaucratic prerogatives as editor), I covered simultaneously his visit to the San Francisco area and the AFL-CIO Convention, which overlapped. I witnessed his reception atop Nob Hill.

I am fascinated by crowds and believe a true comprehension of them is a very important and difficult exercise of the reportorial art. I studied that waiting crowd of 10,000 on Nob Hill, trying to adapt Eisenstein's film technique of the close-up to divine the mood and soul of this mass, picking out individual faces for scrutiny, walking through the crowd to overhear snatches of conversation. The faces were impassive, the people were still. I checked my impressions with seasoned reporters who had trailed the Soviet leader across the country, and we all agreed we could find no clues as to how this crowd would respond to him. There had been manifestations of rudeness and hostility on his westward journey.

As the Khrushchev motorcade emerged from the dazzling brilliance of a setting sun and came up the western slope to the crest of Nob Hill there was a scattering of applause. Then, when Khrushchev stepped out of his car there was a spontaneous roar of warm welcome, which grew and grew as with incredible swiftness he broke away from bodyguards to traverse the semicircle inside the parapet of the carriage entrance to the Mark Hopkins Hotel, so that he could face each section of the crowd and respond to it with his hands clasped overhead.

The people had come individually or in pairs or at most in tiny groups, and each unit was uncertain about its neighbors. But when each realized the others shared its feelings the crowd let itself go. There was a moment of self-recognition. As the roar grew I sensed the crowd was cheering itself as well as the visitor. Nothing afterward was quite like that, but the receptions ranged from friendly to courteous as I followed Khrushchev from an impromptu visit to the longshoremen's hiring hall on San Francisco's waterfront to the ultramodern IBM plant south of San Jose and on an unannounced, absolutely wild invasion of a supermarket in a quiet middle-class neighborhood. When 300 newspapermen, photographers, and security guards (Soviet, federal, state, and municipal) suddenly swarm into a supermarket on a weekday afternoon, and their ranks are soon swelled by every kid in the neighborhood and no small number of adults, it is wild.

I thought the remarkable encounter on Nob Hill reflected a deep popular yearning for an end to the Cold War, no small thing in the politics of our time, and it was easy to be carried away by that spontaneous enthusiasm. But the people who came to this San Francisco hill were not at the summits of power in the United States. An important reality was revealed in the "spirit of Nob Hill"; the illusions were attached to the "spirit of Camp David."

For me the 1960s began with the spirit of Havana. At the end of April 1960, I went to Cuba as a reporter for two weeks that spanned the May Day demonstration. This was sixteen months after Fidel Castro and the Rebel army made their triumphant entrance into Havana. Sixteen months can be a long time in the life of a revolution but this revolution was still young, still in the first stage of transition, epitomized by a diplomatic paradox: the United States Embassy was big and busy; there was no Soviet Embassy. The Cuban Revolutionary government, exercising its sovereign right, had concluded a trade agreement with the Soviets, and there were threats of economic reprisals from Washington. But there still were no formal diplomatic relations between Havana and Moscow.

The feeling of transition was everywhere. So was "the euphoria of revolution," in C. Wright Mills's phrase. This euphoria is a most pleasant contagion. Ordinary people, who ordinarily regard politics as an external intrusion into their lives, are suddenly possessed of the consciousness that they are, indeed, makers of history, that in the revolution they have discovered a sense of human community, of human destiny that transcends narrow, enervating preoccupations of what so often passes for private life. It is enough to make euphoria, and if it momentarily obscures the true difficulties that lie ahead this is a tax levied by history, but the impulses that create this unique social elation are indispensable in a popular revolution.

I met veterans of the Rebel army, schoolchildren, agricultural laborers, teachers, dock workers, members of the middle classes, government employees, and a few political leaders. Revolutionary socioeconomic reconstruction was in its beginnings, much of it improvised, and in this "Year of the Agrarian Reform" it was more visible in the countryside than in Havana. Among the people I met there was a very uneven comprehension of the fundamental transformations under way but there were two common denominators: an enormous sense of liberation from the Batista tyranny and a glowing pride in Cuba, in the assertion of its independence, political and economic.

I met an employee in the Ministry of Justice, a mother whose only child, a boy of fifteen, had been tortured and murdered by Batista's police. "This is why I took a job in the Ministry of Justice," she explained, "because there has never been justice before in Cuba and now there is justice. I believe in the justice today."

I met a couple who had operated a small retail poultry and egg business. They were also members of a small underground group in Havana that procured medical supplies for the Rebel army, ministered to sick or wounded soldiers who were smuggled into the city from the distant battle zone, and helped volunteers find their way to a rebel base. The wife had been arrested by Batista's secret police and tortured for three days and nights. She was, as I described her at the time, "a large and ample woman, looking very much like the image one might have of a chicken monger's wife . . . who surely could hold her own in a market argument." I asked her how she held up for those three days and nights of torture and she said, "It was faith in our country and in the ideals of our apostle, José

Martí." Then she volunteered: "I am proud of the revolution."
Normally people are hesitant or embarrassed to use such words
as "ideals" in conversation; they seem pretentious, like ornate
platitudes in the politician's oratory. It is a miracle of revolution that large numbers of people use these words with absolute
sincerity, without any self-consciousness. The choice of words
— justice, ideals — and of symbol — José Martí — also denoted the revolution's self-image at that moment as humanist
and Cubanist, in the rhetoric of the July 26th Movement.

Not that revolutionary élan was universal. Walking in the
evening along streets of the old city the North American was
accosted by furtive solicitors of the old order, the runners, hustlers, and other whispering ambassadors of the industry called
tourism, which in Havana particularly had been a euphemism
for gambling, prostitution, pornography, and other exotic
pleasures, catering mostly to the moral leaders of the world
who came from only ninety miles away. I allowed myself only
one entertainment, a visit to a baseball game.

To illustrate the transition the revolution was in, Havana's
professional ball club was still in the International League.
The night I saw the Cuban Sugar Kings they played the
Buffalo Bisons. I suppose visiting clubs from Jersey City, To-
ronto, and other North American cities in that league may have
been startled by the sign on the broadcasting booth high
behind home plate at Havana's Gran Stadium, a spacious,
wooden, barnlike structure of the type that has mostly vanished
from the United States scene. The sign read: *"Union radio —
la voz de los trabajadores al servicio de la revolucion."*

More startling was another revolutionary innovation in the
professional baseball business. All official league baseballs had
to be imported, requiring the expenditure of dollars, for which
the revolution had more important uses; the government therefore appealed to the fans not to keep baseballs hit into the
stands, but to throw them back onto the playing field so they
could be used again, thus conserving Cuba's precious dollar reserves.

My first witness of this ritual came when a line drive went
into the left-field stands. A white-shirted citizen retrieved the

ball and promptly tossed it back into the playing arena with cheers from the crowd. In the third inning a foul tip soared into the stands to the right of the net behind home plate, and then something happened that illustrates the difficulties a revolution can encounter. A little boy (he looked to be about ten) grabbed the ball — and he kept it. There were cries of disapproval and reproach, most conspicuously from three little girls several rows below him, but the little boy was stubborn. He buried his face in his arms on the railing in front of him — and he kept the ball in his pocket.

The next ball into the seats was grabbed by an elderly man behind first base, and now there was suspense, but only for a moment; without hesitation he threw the ball well and true toward the green grass. The cheers from the crowd were of a volume normally reserved for a home run by the home team. In the easy democratic manner of baseball crowds the moral incentive of an offering to the revolution was a clear favorite over the economic incentive to pocket a baseball

I enjoyed writing about the baseball revolution. But May Day was the revolutionary spectacle on the grand scale and its axis was the relationship between Fidel Castro and the people in the plaza, numbering somewhere between a half million and a million. Many agricultural workers had been on the move since long before dawn, some coming from as far away as 150 miles to get to their Havana assembly points by eight A.M. Later, for seven hours they paraded or stood under the hot Havana sun. And then Castro spoke for more than three hours. It sounds unnatural, but listening to him and observing his audience it was not unnatural at all. I do not minimize the man's gifts as an agitator but what awed me was his genius as a teacher, in the classical or Biblical sense. Arrayed before him was this vast, vivid, colorful, manifold human power that the revolution embodied, and he was imparting to it a heightened consciousness of the meaning and the content of the revolution, its problems and hazards, its needs at the moment.

I do not know Spanish but I could understand long passages of his address, particularly when he fell into a repetitive rhythm that is a pedagogical skill. He did it at the outset in reviewing the parade that had gone by. "The soldiers alone constitute a force, but only one force . . . the peasants alone constitute only one force . . . the workers constitute a force, but only one force . . ." So he went on with the students, the delegations from other Latin American countries, finally exclaiming, "What a formidable education!" The crowd chanted, "Unidad! Unidad!"

He fell into the rhythm again in a passage on the nature of revolutionary democracy. Democracy is that which provides jobs for the workers . . . democracy is that which provides land for the peasants . . . democracy is that which provides schools for the children . . . and the recitation went on. It must be remembered that in prerevolutionary Cuba, masses of workers had no jobs, masses of peasants had no land, masses of children had no schools, to understand why his description of democracy was interrupted by a sixteen-minute acclamation.

I have observed more than my share of orators and audiences but never in the encounter between the two have I had the same feeling of dialogue as I did in that plaza. This was overt when the crowd shouted or chanted, as it often did, but even when the people were still, there was the feeling, almost uncanny, that he was not just talking to them, that there was an exchange of communication. In the hours he spoke there were many manifestations by the crowd of affection, admiration, utter confidence, but there was no awe, not a trace of formalized reverence. His own manner, blending with the easy fraternity of his audience, precluded any stiff obeisance.

What I have related thus far touches mostly on the style of the revolution, its spirit, its profoundly popular character, but just where was it in its swift transition? The best answer I could get to this question was a brief sentence, which I heard more than once, the first time from a member of the Central Committee of the old Cuban Communist party (called the Popular Socialist party). He wore a beard and a big revolver in his holster, these being the distinctive insignia of men who had fought with the Rebel army.

"Every day," he said, "the revolution is becoming revolutionary . . ." So it was in the brief fortnight I was there. Each day produced its own revolutionary milestone . . . The Revolutionary Government takes possession of 270,000 acres of United Fruit Company sugar land in Oriente province . . . The Revolutionary Government announces that 2,640,000 acres of sugar land have been turned over to 200,000 peasants and agricultural workers, organized in 1000 cooperatives . . . Castro appeals over television for 1000 young volunteers, possessing at least minimum qualifications for teaching, to go to the remote mountain regions for an assault on illiteracy; within three days more than 1500 volunteer . . .

The popular militia was still new but it already comprised 500,000 workers, peasants, students, professionals. In the first days of my visit I saw its units everywhere in Havana, training and also preparing for May Day when 120,000 of the militia, bearing guns or machetes, paraded through the plaza. This was the people in arms. And its motto, constant and omnipresent, was "Pátria o Muerte!" Everyone in Cuba understood very well to whom this message was addressed. This defiance of United States threats, this active preparation to resist any assault (which even then was taking shape in what was to be the Bay of Pigs expedition a year later), were also making the revolution more revolutionary. Washington thought it was putting its heavy foot on the brake; instead it was pressing down on the revolution's accelerator.

By its assault on the possessions and privileges of great wealth, foreign and domestic, coming into irreconcilable conflict thereby with the hemispheric custodian of capitalist and feudal property, the United States government, the revolution was shedding the ambiguity of its class character, more sharply defining itself as the power of the propertyless and dispossessed, the workers in agriculture and industry, the landless peasants. This made it more revolutionary.

I came away from Cuba deeply skeptical of a common assumption among my political associates in the States that this revolution would pause on a plateau that was essentially bourgeois democratic, even though I did not truly gauge the swiftness of the pace that in a year's time would lead to public proclamation of the revolution's precise objective: socialism. The word actually followed the deed, for by then revolutionary agrarian reform had been accompanied by extensive nationalization of enterprises in all branches of the economy.

After the shocks and disturbances of the preceding decade the liberating, energizing reality of revolution in Cuba was an inspiriting reaffirmation. This revolution also reinforced the conviction about the diversity of revolutionary paths in different countries, for in its development and method it conformed to no dogmatic blueprint or model. Indeed, the old Cuban Communist party candidly acknowledged that Castro had displayed the bold initiative and perception to seize the historical moment for effective guerrilla warfare, whereas it had failed to do so; even after the armed combat began the party was slow to appreciate its import. Undoubtedly it was retarded by the rigidity of its own conceptions, which may have been correct in general, but a narrow, canonical adherence to them in the specific circumstances proved to be an obstruction. Having conceded their grievous default, however, the Communists threw all their force behind the Castro leadership unreservedly and with a selflessness that is rare in any kind of politics. They did this despite attacks against them by important sectors of Castro's July 26th Movement. And they did it without abandoning their own basic principles, a consistency that was to prove of inestimable value in the future course of the revolution.

Something of all this entered into my conversation with the man from the Communist Central Committee. He outlined his party's policy and it boiled down to the mobilization of all the party's resources to secure understanding and support, particularly in the working class, of the program enunciated by the non-Communist Revolutionary government. How, I asked, does this position relate to the vanguard role of the party as defined in Marxist-Leninist theory? We had a young interpreter who was inexperienced, in Communist terminology as well as translation. It took some time before my question got through to the man with the beard and the gun. When it did he roared with laughter.

"We are not the vanguard now," he said, "Fidel and his people, they are the vanguard." He paused and reflected for a while. "At any rate," he added, quoting Lenin, "the future belongs to us." If the afterthought is understood, not in narrow partisan terms, but as a reference to fundamental theory and principle, it has since proved an apt prophecy.

Returning from Cuba I was met at the San Francisco airport by my wife and a message from my associates. Don't go home or to your office, the message said, the House Un-American Activities Committee is serving subpoenas around town; if there is one for you it is best that you be unavailable because the committee may try to use you as a foil, not only to get at the paper but to mess with Cuba. You can't go home — and so I knew I was home again.

So I missed the HUAC hearing, the impressive student protests, and "Bloody Friday," the day San Francisco police swept the students with fire hoses and then mopped up with clubs. In the HUAC-FBI film version of the incident, "Operation Abolition," Communists are the heavies, engaged in a plot to subvert America's youth.

I knew too well that Communists had very little to do with the student upheaval. I did not know then that the HUAC encounter was the major debut of a force that was to be so potent and spectacular on the American scene throughout the 1960s. But I did recognize that here was a new social phenomenon of prime importance, meriting a thoughtful investigation. To indicate my approach to this journalistic project it may be helpful to refer to an attempt I once made at a schematic definition of various levels of relationship between a radical paper and social conflicts or movements.

Elementary level: you try to report sympathetically and accurately; if people say, look, this paper tells the truth about us, you already have established a consequential relationship.

Intermediate level: you also try to heighten the consciousness of the participants in the struggle or movement by supplying interpretive background, in-depth portraits of the antagonists, by relating the particular phenomenon to the general social setting and social development. For this you may need to enlist resources outside of the paper's staff.

Highest level: in addition and finally you project policies, demands, tactics, a strategic objective; you try, that is, to exercise an active leadership function, and for this the paper's own resources are totally inadequate, there has to be close liaison with activists. Without effective forces in the given field a pretension to leadership tends to become gratuitous counsel.

I set out for the Berkeley campus of the University of California on my elementary level; we had no tigers in that academic jungle, and as for intelligent influence upon consciousness it seemed wise to comprehend first the consciousness that existed, to know how this nascent movement defined itself in its own terms. Two terms were repeated most often: we are not ideologically oriented, they said, we are issues oriented; in the 1930s the issues were economic, today they are moral. Maybe I would not have been told these things quite so many times if my interlocutors did not identify me with a definite ideological orientation — and the 1930s. On both counts I met with a skeptical reserve, and I was not sure whether it was directed to my motives or my capacity to understand what they were talking about. Maybe both.

The more sophisticated student activists recognized they could not rush eternally from issue to issue, from a vigil at San Quentin against the execution of Caryl Chessman and the barbarity of capital punishment, to a confrontation with HUAC, to a civil rights or antibomb demonstration. Somewhere along the line they would have to pause and ask: where does all this lead? So they said, in the course of action we will evolve an ideological framework. Actually the Berkeley campus was teeming with ideologies and ideological grouplets; you would have been hard put to think of an ideological trend, even the most bizarre or esoteric, that was not represented in some way in the student body or faculty. I suspect it was this very ideological profusion that helped to prevent any one group from establishing hegemony, thus permitting the Berkeley movement (it had not yet acquired the capital M) to retain its nonideological inclusiveness.

Organizations proliferated on campus (notably, at that time, there was SLATE, a campus political party), but the movement itself was unstructured. Since it was issues oriented *ad hoc* forms were improvised to meet issues as they arose. There was considerable interlocking in these *ad hoc* directorates and some variation in constituencies from issue to issue. To many, perhaps most activists, the term *Establishment* embraced all that was established as organization or institution, irrespective of political labels or class and ethnic lines. Left, Right, or Center, working class or capitalist, black or white, all old organizations and institutions were tainted with failure and the compromise of morality. Some perceived the implications of this sweeping negation, and they did not shrink from them. We are the last hope of this society, one student said, and if we fail . . .

What emerged most forcefully, with depth and vehemence and the rare outbursts of eloquence because mostly the talk was cool, was a moral revulsion against the society, its hypocrisy and corruption, its spiritual emptiness, its dehumanization, its duplicities, its pervasive demand for conformity and the compromise of integrity. This anger was articulated in personal terms. One student, near graduation in the liberal arts, ticked off the ordinary vocational choices open to him: the mass media, advertising, the law perhaps, teaching, some minor bureaucracy in the corporate world or civil service. All, he said, all entail a compromise of integrity.

Such intellectual and spiritual rejection of things as they are was to find its most articulate expression in the Port Huron manifesto of Students for a Democratic Society, and on the Berkeley campus this phase of the campus rebellion was to reach its apogee in the Free Speech Movement at the end of 1964 and Mario Savio's outcry that there comes a time when "you've got to put your bodies upon the gears and upon the wheels, upon the levers, upon all the apparatus" to halt the bureaucratic machine.

A few months later President Johnson ordered the bombing of North Vietnam and beyond the abomination of the computerized campus was the atrocity of napalm and the methodical use of American technology to kill people because they would not bow to Washington's will. Students were then thrown into direct confrontation, not just with the university as the agent of society, not with a particular institution or practice of the society, but increasingly and ever more profoundly with the whole social order. The consequences were many and mixed.

Back in 1960, however, the student movement was in the first flush of its nascence. I wrote about it as accurately as I could, sympathetically and without passing judgments, well enough so that even some skeptics joined the few students friendly to the paper in suggesting publication of the series in a pamphlet as an authentic account of what they were about. I dwell upon the episode because it was a revealing introduction to the 1960s. Had I ventured to report anything comparable in the 1930s or '40s the odds are that I would have gone with the feeling of the insider, for even if the movement were not the result of Communist initiative there would have been a significant Communist involvement and influence. Now I was the outsider, the sympathetic observer, received with tolerance and regarded, in the jargon of the day, as irrelevant, an all-purpose term that blanketed anachronism and obsolescence. This attitude was common in the new movements and conflicts that exploded with such force and frequency in the 1960s.

Berkeley was an early and valuable learning experience in confronting this attitude. It was necessary, it seemed to me, to maintain an openness that did not succumb to a reflex hostility and suspicion in response to this attitude and to the objective criticism implicit in the premise of these movements that they were filling a general vacuum of Left initiative and leadership. The easiest and hence most tempting thing to do would have been to pronounce judgmental characterizations, a dubious expedient even when you possess the authority that lends weight to such pronouncements. In the prevailing circumstances they would have been ignored for the most part as self-serving captiousness from an irrelevant source. If one saw these movements, irrespective of foibles, as authentic manifestations of a radical revival after a period of retreat, attrition, and stagnation, then the first necessity was to establish communication, a relationship and atmosphere in which dialogue and debate were possible and useful. Since these movements were engaged in battle you also had to pay your dues as an active combatant to gain a hearing, they had no use for elder statesmanship or think-tank counsel.

That dialogue and debate were imperative was self-evident to me. With the spontaneous eruption of social dissent, protest, rebellion, there also came a profusion of fads and shibboleths, most of which enjoyed a fleeting if spectacular vogue, and an assortment of theories. I was convinced that the fundamental theoretical premises of the paper provided a much sounder and firmer guide for Left orientation and tactics than the intellectual potpourri of the new radicalism. The paper's embodiment of continuity and experience was a valuable attribute when so much was ephemeral and flighty. The problem was how to render the paper's resources effective in a new era when its political constituency did not have the initiative and hegemony in the American Left, how to absorb new experiences and critically assimilate new ideas, how to engage in critiques that were both valid and persuasive. Especially complicated was a primary aspect of the problem: how to project credibly the conception that without the working class all other forces for radical change are sterile or impotent, for this could not be done with abstract argument alone, it had to be validated by the authenticity and intimacy of the paper's own identification with the working class at a time when signs of challenge to the conservative labor bureaucracy were faint and few in the organized ranks.

In fertile California, movements and upheavals proliferated. Here the Black Panthers leaped upon the scene and the Watts ghetto uprising, forerunner of many to follow, dealt its shattering blow to the societal complacency being cultivated with fanfares about the war on poverty and self-congratulations on the progress of civil rights. Here the farm workers' movement, breaking out of the conventions of a union strike with its appeals to "La Raza" as the symbol of ethnic identity and destiny, served as a catalyst for a Chicano liberation movement in the barrios of the Southwest. Here the Peace and Freedom party mushroomed in 1967–1968 as a startling growth reminiscent of panacea movements in another time. Here militant resistance to the Vietnam war and the draft assumed several original forms. This is no exhaustive catalogue but it indicates a vigorous resurgence of radical action and social protest. In almost all instances the problems I recognized in Berkeley were posed anew. Difficult though these were, they were far more attractive than the problems of the 1950s.

XIII. Difficult Decisions

MY PREOCCUPATION with the problems I have mentioned as an editor in California was temporarily interrupted in 1965. Gus Hall, who succeeded Dennis as general secretary of the Communist party in 1959, asked me to work on a draft of a party program. Dennis had been at the helm during the chaotic crisis of 1956–1958. Hall was in prison in those years, so did not bear the wounds and scars of their internecine battles, which gave him a decided advantage in creating an atmosphere of stabilization. In 1961 the party faced a different sort of crisis when the United States Supreme Court upheld the constitutionality of the McCarran Act's major provision that authorized the government to require registration of the party, its officers, and members with the Attorney General. Enforcement of this provision would have rendered the party's legal existence untenable. Rejecting the demand of one "Left" faction that the party be immediately dissolved, the party leadership creditably decided to stand its ground and fight.

Despite the apparent finality of the court's decision it had a penultimate twist: the registration requirement was constitutional but whether it was enforced constitutionally was another matter that would be adjudicated if and when an appeal from the law's penalties for failure to comply reached the court. This decision, culminating in almost ten years of litigation, owed as much to Shakespeare as to Blackstone; the government could try to exact its pound of flesh and only after the attempt was made would the justices ascertain whether it could be done without constitutional bloodletting. In 1965 — four years later — the court found the government could not, in fact, compel party members to register without violating the Constitution.

Even before the inhibiting uncertainties about the party's

legal status under the McCarran Act were essentially dispelled by the court's decision, Hall tried to generate a sense of forward momentum. The program project fitted into this design. When asked to work on it I demurred, saying I had experience in agitation and propaganda but not in theoretical labors and most definitely was not a theoretician. But having been asked I was naturally reassured that my self-deprecation was excessive, that in any event I would be collaborating with Gil Green, a veteran party leader and writer who was proficient in this realm, and there would be a committee to discuss approaches and assume a working responsibility for the final draft. Some of Hall's colleagues in the national party center were unenthusiastic about the project, being apprehensive about what might emerge finally and about the discussion and debate that might be touched off. After all, the party had functioned for forty-five years without a written program, and why the rush now? But Hall pushed ahead with great determination.

For much of 1965 I worked on the draft. Green was a thoughtful, considerate collaborator with a fertile mind, probity, and much political experience. He was in the process of thinking through or rethinking certain programmatic propositions, and this became more marked as the work advanced, which meant that in his own mind he was altering or modifying conceptions of the structure and content of a program. This contributed to the excitement of exploration and also to the difficulty of arriving at precise, definitive formulations that ought to distinguish a program. Anyone engaged in this sort of venture is prone to be haunted by the specter of *The Communist Manifesto,* but this is a totally gratuitous vanity, even if one puts aside the genius of the *Manifesto*'s authors. Theirs was the seminal document, composed for a movement that was in embryo and yet to be born. All subsequent programmatic declarations of communism are, of necessity, derivative, drawing on the original insights of Marx and Engels and on the accumulated experiences and conclusions of the movement that their prescience signaled.

The American draft program, as finally published at the beginning of 1966 for public discussion, was not marked by theo-

retical originality, but it was, I believe, a systematic, comprehensive, coherent, and competent presentation of theoretical,
strategic, and tactical positions at which the party had arrived.
In this basic sense, as well as in the detailed labors of a committee on the draft before its publication, it was a collective
document. Doing most of the writing I felt this was a serious
attempt, the most advanced yet and much beyond the capacity
of any other group on the United States scene, to chart an
American path to socialism and to indicate general outlines of a
Socialist society in this country. (To go beyond general outlines is either to duplicate an existing model or to relapse into
utopianism, although a rare ingenuity sometimes manages to
combine the two.)

By the time the draft program came off the press Nancy and
I were in Europe (I received galley proofs in Rome and first
saw a bound copy in East Berlin). My journey was a by-
product of the program; in recognition of my work on it I was
designated as one of two fraternal delegates to the Italian Communist Party Congress in Rome at the end of January 1966. My
fellow delegate, Mike Zagarell, the party's youth director, was
accompanied by his bride, Laura.

We boarded the plane in New York before midnight and
when we landed the day was new, the world was novel: a capitalist country where the Communist party was a salient political power, its material presence was manifest and pervasive,
and a reckoning with it was a primary condition for all serious
politics. In the Italian news media just two political stories
rated prominence: the collapse of a Center-Left coalition government on the eve of the Communist congress and the congress itself.

To me, coming from San Francisco, which, as a city, was little
more than 100 years old, the antiquity of Rome was also enchanting. Indeed, the juxtaposition of the two, Italian communism and Italian antiquity, was a constant fascination. Posters proclaiming the party congress were plastered all over
Rome and there was something bizarre about seeing them,
modern and dominated by a field of bright red, with Saint
Peter's dome in the distant background or the brooding, mas-

sive shell of the Colosseum nearby. I had the same feeling on
being greeted by Communist mayors in city halls that were relics of the flowering days of feudalism.

Observing the Italian party on that occasion and once more
later I was struck by the remark of an Austrian journalist that
the Italian party derives its distinctive character and vitality
from a rare combination: the intellectual and political legacy of
two towering figures, Antonio Gramsci and Palmiro Togliatti,
and its strong, deep popular roots, nourished by the hundreds
of thousands of the party's militants who are resourceful and
combative. This insight impressed me and I agreed with it because by then I had seen both parts of the combination.

During the congress some of the English-speaking fraternal
delegates were taken to a reception in Albano, a small town in
the hills south of Rome, one of the Communist and Socialist
municipalities that encircle the Pope's summer residence at
Castelgandolfo, like a crown of political thorns for the papal
brow. The hills were lovely in the twilight, we passed a lake en
route, and now and then we could see Rome stretched below
us, just beginning to twinkle as it awakened for its nocturnal
life. We were greeted by the mayor at city hall and this brief
ceremony was the only bow to formality. At the reception in
what looked like an old, homespun restaurant the fare was
ordinary pasta and ordinary wine, and much of both. The
people, fewer than a hundred, were mostly agricultural and
building workers (the building trades do not enjoy the same
status in Italy as in the United States). The eminent summer
neighbor from the Vatican might have called them hewers of
wood and drawers of water; they were the masses, not in the
political cliché, but in the spirit and the flesh, and the visible
flesh, those faces and hands, stamped by weather and work, were
all the credential they needed to establish their identity.

The visiting guests spoke briefly and answered some questions. We all drank much wine and sang. As the Italians sing it
I never tired of "Bella Ciao," a romantic folk song that was
transformed into the militant hymn of the partisans during
World War II. The dimly lit room was suffused with a fraternity so natural, so warm that all the distance between San

Francisco and Albano melted away. It was an extraordinary experience and I have never had one quite like it in a group encounter, where barriers of language, culture, and much else were overcome so quickly and completely in the embrace of solidarity.

In a postcongress trip through Tuscany we had lunch at the home of a sharecropper. I hesitate to describe it as a hovel but to call it anything else would be drawing a very fine distinction. Poverty and hardship were plain in the surroundings and their occupants. At table a debate about the congress flared up. I could tell it was about the congress by the names and a few words I caught, but that's all I knew. I tugged at the sleeve of our young translator, an architectural student at the University of Florence. "Gigi, what are they saying?" But Gigi brushed me off. He was no longer the interpreter, he was the engaged political combatant. He, the local party organizer, our sharecropper host, and some neighboring Communists all joined in this intense debate. From names they mentioned I gathered the disputants identified with personalities who represented the several tendencies in the Italian party. Our truant interpreter, who was the one intellectual in the group and the only member of the younger generation, appeared to have formed a united front with the middle-aged sharecropper. Their principal adversary seemed to be the local party organizer, but clearly his was not the commanding voice of authority. I could not follow what was said and yet this political debate remains memorable. It was the setting, this habitation of the most extreme agricultural poverty in Italy, and the participants, their total involvement and lack of inhibition; it may be pure assumption on my part but I sensed the argument raged on a very high plane.

In Tuscany I was told that after Togliatti was wounded by a would-be assassin in July 1948, when Cold War tensions were on the rise, workers in many towns seized the police arsenals. They wanted to be prepared if, as they feared, the attempt on Togliatti's life signaled a reactionary offensive.

Such were glimpses of the popular roots. The pinnacle of Italian communism was on display at the congress. With a bigger than lifesize photo montage of Togliatti and Gramsci as part of the stage backdrop, the floor of the Palace of Congresses was filled with 871 delegates representing 1.6 million party members and a larger constituency of 8 million as measured with the imprecise yardstick of popular votes. In the mezzanine and two balconies were forty-three delegations from Communist parties and other revolutionary movements abroad, representatives of the news media, and thousands of visitors.

The Italian party, numerically small during the Fascist regime, began to burgeon into a mass party as the leader of the partisan detachments against the Nazis and their Italian collaborators in the final years of World War II. As a consequence much of the cadre was molded in partisan warfare. At the congress, for instance, 250 delegates had fought in the partisan ranks. A dwindling core of old party veterans dated back to the trials of Fascist terror but within the memory of a far larger number partisan combat constituted the great heroic tradition.

Togliatti had died a year and a half before and this was the first congress without his political astuteness and skill, his intellectual stature and moral authority. In some respects, I thought, the situation was comparable to that faced by the Soviet party when Lenin died. I suggested this parallel to a couple of Italian Communist leaders, and they agreed it had validity. The several tendencies in the Italian party, all articulated by strong political personalities, had contended in the precongress debates. Not that these tendencies had crystallized into political platforms; the contrasts were expressed in nuances, emphases and other subtleties. By the time of the national congress a clear majority consensus had emerged and one had to be very discerning to detect shadings and allusions that reflected the differences.

I had difficulty in following the discussion, partly because of the simultaneous translation, which was very uneven, and when some translator fell behind the speaker of the moment the frantic effort to catch up produced an incoherent jumble of phrases and words. If the translation had been perfect, however, I probably would have been perplexed; even Luigi Longo, the short, stocky successor to Togliatti as general secretary, complained he had difficulty in understanding some of the pre-congress debate, although his native tongue was Italian and he was intimately conversant with the party's inner politics.

I chided some Italian friends that it was a poor testimonial to Gramsci to imitate the elusive literary style of his *Prison Note-books* when this was clearly not his choice but the imposition of a cruel necessity. (Gramsci, guiding genius of Italian communism in its formative years, was imprisoned by the Fascist regime from 1926 to 1937. His *Prison Notebooks,* 2848 tightly covered, handwritten manuscript pages, were composed mostly between 1929 and 1934. To save these from destruction by the Fascist authorities he resorted to circumlocution, symbolism, and a code for certain names and terms. The notebooks exhibited a range of knowledge and a profundity that stamped him as one of the great thinkers of this century. Always physically frail, he was chronically and seriously ill in prison, unable to eat or sleep; this physical suffering was heaped on top of the cruelty of confinement for a man whose whole being had been immersed in conflicts and confrontations of public life. Produced in these torturous circumstances Gramsci's notebooks are a monumental affirmation of the human mind and spirit.)

Despite its subtleties the Italian debate did outline several tendencies, involving estimates of world and domestic developments, and the appropriate political responses. To what degree had the world situation deteriorated (the Vietnam war was still on its escalator), and how did this affect the prospects of struggle for peaceful coexistence? To what extent had the governing Center-Left coalition managed to integrate sections of the Italian working class into the system? These questions were in dispute and varying answers suggested varying tactics, ranging from a politics of the lowest common denominator to a far more aggressive, independent initiative by the Italian party, based on a more rigidly defined and detailed program of radical alternatives.

In the background of the debate I sensed two factors. One was the strain of being the country's second party for two decades, of having the conquest of political power so tantalizingly near, and yet always safely beyond its outstretched fingers.

The other was the enormous sense of responsibility toward its mass constituency, for this party was regarded by a majority of the working class as its political expression; it was the chosen party of a fourth of the Italian electorate. Without this party there was no realistic alternative to the Italian status quo, which had been maintained through shifting political combinations.

The party's position was comparable to that of a mountain-climbing expedition that traversed many thousands of feet and is poised for the final and most difficult assault upon the several hundred feet to the summit. How to assemble the effective political force and chart the path for the final push? — this was the urgent question.

The success of that assault can only be established in practice. But I was deeply impressed by the maturity of the debate, by its sense of responsibility, by its level, and, in the unique political vocabulary of Italian Communists, by its serenity. In these qualities, as well as in specific references, one felt the legacy of Gramsci and Togliatti, a heritage that stamped this party's character as an autonomous force, defining its relationship to the Italian and world environment.

From Rome we flew to Moscow. February is a poor month for street-strolling in Moscow or Leningrad. Even if I were more warmly dressed and more daring there would have been little point in strolling to get a feel of city life because most pedestrians, wrapped in their winter apparel, were sensibly bent on getting out of the cold as swiftly as they could. The Russian winter has its severe disadvantages for the visitor. But it also has its rare moments.

One such moment came when we went to the outskirts of Leningrad. I had seen photos of the place, resplendent with green grass and foliage and the prismatic splash of many flowers under a summer sky, but on this day it was stark, a white expanse of snow, gaunt silhouettes of barren trees, a gray sky, and not another soul; then more snow fell, further muffling our footsteps and soft music from an amplifier, the only sounds in the infinite stillness. Beneath the huge snow-covered mounds of Piskaryovskoye Cemetery lay the remains of a half a million

human beings who perished in the siege of Leningrad. We had
seen a film of this incredible ordeal that went on for 900 days.
Standing before those white mounds in that somber setting, the
images of the film still vivid, one was overwhelmed by humility
before the heroism of this people, before the land that reared
and nurtured them. This feeling returned in Stalingrad (re-
named Volgograd); one had read about it and yet was startled
to see how tiny was that patch of land on the banks of the
Volga where Soviet troops withstood the fury of the Nazi armies, how thin was the thread of history then.

Winter was most evocative in Leningrad, cradle of the revolution. Approaching the architectural grace of the Winter Palace one remembered that in this season and into this square
the people walked in humble procession to petition the Czar, the
Little Father, only to be met with a volley of gunfire and the
saber-wielding charge of mounted Cossacks. Riding through
the city one tried to imagine these streets teeming with crowds
of workers and soldiers in the cold and snow of another February, their revolutionary power and anger toppling an autocracy
of many centuries.

Other places, associated with other seasons, evoked other
scenes etched on one's consciousness for many decades: Smolny
Institute, where the Congress of Soviets waited on an October
night for word that the Winter Palace had been taken to proclaim the conquest of the Socialist revolution; Finland Station,
where Lenin was welcomed on his arrival from Switzerland to
take the helm of the revolution on an April evening in 1917.
Visiting these and other historical sites was like a retrospective
journey through one's own memories; although the original
events had been glimpsed only in books and films, in the imagination of one's youth they had acquired a tactile reality.

Our tour was affected by our status. We had been to Italy as
delegates and we did not altogether shed the delegation mantle
as guests of the Communist party in the Soviet Union. Our active hosts, workers in the apparatus of the party's central
committee, were hospitable, cordial, considerate, solicitous. Although we had no official business to discuss and were essentially enjoying a hospitality visit, still there was a thread of

official formality. It cropped up on our arrival when we were
welcomed by two of our hosts at the Moscow airport. In a car,
riding into the city, I said what was uppermost in my mind at
the moment: how impressed I was by the Italian congress.
There was a silence. The subject was changed. They chose
not to enter into a conversation that might involve judgments of
the Italian party (or, possibly, any other party except a pariah
like the Chinese party). A similar sense of propriety was manifested when one of our hosts, a very knowledgeable man, learned
I had proofs of the American party's draft program. He and his
colleagues were very eager to read it, he said, and would I leave
the proofs with him while our delegation went on its trip to
Leningrad, Stalingrad, and Tblisi. Upon our return I asked him
if he had read the program. He had. What did he think of it?
Well, it has just been translated and was being duplicated, the
other people didn't have a chance to read it . . . On something so important as a party program he would not offer a personal opinion, it would have to wait for collective consideration
and assessment at the appropriate level.

Our young interpreter-guide was very bright, informed, personable, efficient, and a superb translator. Traveling together
we had much opportunity to talk and I was impressed by his
consummate tact in drawing the line between personal conversation and topics that came within the purview of official position; the same line marked the impassable boundary between
cordiality and intimacy. I say this not in reproach; it might
indeed be a tribute to our individual hosts in the performance
of their duties. On a nonpolicy-making level these men represented the governing party of a mighty state and were obliged
to present its official positions. Most often, as a consequence,
what one got was the official position without any insight into
the political dynamic, the process that led to this decision and
none other. This, of course, is an element of Soviet style.

We were treated to a round of entertainment (several bal-
lets, the circus, a fabulous puppet theater, a young woman pop
singer, a Strauss operetta in Stalingrad, a variety show in
Tblisi), tours of museums, visits to factories, schools, institutions, and a prize state vineyard and winery in Georgia that

produced excellent wines which intoxicate you pleasantly, as I can happily testify, when you drink enough of them. Out of all this (even without the service of the fine Georgian wines) emerged a picture of a strong, viable, self-assured society, proud of its achievements, confident in its progress and its goals. With people encountered on these rounds there was the special communication of shared values; aside from world peace, the goals mentioned most often — economic progress and improvement in living standards — were couched in terms of the Socialist ethic, which considers the advance of the collective, of the whole society, as the primary condition of individual fulfillment.

After a farewell party with toasts, expressions of mutual esteem and friendship, and gifts, we went to Poland, the German Democratic Republic, Czechoslovakia, France, and England — five countries in little more than three weeks, a jumbled montage in which some pictures are clear, and because of events to come I pause before the one I got of Czechoslovakia.

In the preceding several years Czechoslovakia's economic road had been bumpy and potholed. Indices for industrial production, national income, and real wages declined in 1962–1963. The dips were small enough so that in a capitalist economy they would have signified a mild recession at worst. In the growth dynamics of a planned Socialist economy they represented crisis symptoms. They also meant disappointment of popular expectations. In 1964 the long-term upward trend of these indices reasserted itself, but the general conviction persisted that the economy was not performing as it should. Then came 1965, a bad year in agriculture, the potato crop off by more than half, the pick of fruits and grapes by almost half.

These economic phenomena were the more perplexing because the Socialist regime took power in Czechoslovakia in the most favored circumstances: a high level of industrial development and culture, relatively moderate war destruction (one needed only to compare Prague with Warsaw or Berlin). Alone among the new Socialist countries Czechoslovakia had not been governed by fascism before the Second World War, but by a fairly advanced bourgeois democratic regime; in the relative freedom for propaganda, agitation, organization, and diverse forms of class confrontation, the working class had acquired much political experience. The Communist party was a mass party, indisputable representative of the working class and premier political force in the country. Indeed, the party's assumption of unqualified hegemony in February 1948 was effected with mass mobilization of the working class and its armed militia, so that to the workers who participated in those events the Socialist regime was their conquest. Because Czechoslovakia had been oppressed by the Austrian Empire an affinity with the Russians as potential liberators was a strong strain in national tradition, reinforced by more recent history: betrayal by the Western democracies at Munich in 1939, liberation by Soviet armies in 1945. Not imbedded in national consciousness were historical grievances (as there were in Poland, for instance) that could be manipulated for the metamorphosis from anti-Russian into anti-Soviet into anti-Socialist. The weight of national tradition was in the opposite scale.

Why then was Czechoslovakia beset by such difficulties?

I got varied answers from people in Prague. Sudden cancellation of large Chinese orders had thrown out of kilter the delicate balance of a planned and integrated economy. Rigid imitation of the Soviet model had distorted the Czechoslovak economy, vitiating strengths, magnifying weaknesses. An excessively centralized and top-heavy bureaucracy in economic management stifled local initiative and tended to entrench yes men who compensated for incompetence with sycophancy. Czechoslovakia had more nearly exhausted its potential for extensive growth and therefore faced problems of intensive growth in a more acute form than the other Socialist countries. Popular morale had been damaged by Stalinist repression, which claimed more victims in Czechoslovakia than in any other new Socialist country, and subsequently by the excruciating slowness and grudging reluctance of the regime to acknowledge injustices and to make such amends as were possible. On this score, as well as in effecting other changes, Czechoslovakia lagged behind other Socialist countries. This curious lethargy in the Czechoslovak leadership's responses to the 20th Congress created a psychological pall over the country.

I had come prepared to explore economic problems. I did not anticipate the symptoms of social malaise. The feeling was widespread that big changes had to be made but people did not know how such changes could be brought about. A consequent sense of frustration bred social passivity, often counterbalanced by complacency and inertia, emanating from old Hradcany Castle, across the Vltava River and high on a hill, official residence of the President of the republic, Antonin Novotny. He also was First Secretary of the Communist party and chief of the National Front, combining in his person a concentration of bureaucratic power that placed him at the helm of the country's three major political institutions. I walked the streets of Old Prague in the chill winds of March, past the maze of scaffolds erected to repair the crumbling façades of old buildings, and maybe it was the things I heard, or the wane of winter before the appearance of spring, but the city seemed to be brooding.

Remembrance of those things kindled my reaction to the startling news from Prague early in 1968. The changes, which seemed so imperative and so uncertain two years earlier, were actually taking place. The barrier of frustration was broken. And it was all proceeding through the institutional framework of the Socialist republic. There had not been the violent explosion of repressed discontent and the resultant bloodshed that served as catalysts for changes in the regimes of Poland and Hungary in 1956 (as they were to serve once again in Poland in 1970). A dramatic renewal was in progress and from all reports the initiative and leadership came from the Communists and the legitimate organs of their party.

The *People's World* had two infrequent volunteer correspondents in Prague, George and Eleanor Wheeler, veteran American Communists who had settled in Czechoslovakia after World War II. He was a highly regarded economist, honored with election to the Czechoslovak Academy of Sciences, a rare distinction for a person in his discipline. When I met them in

1966 they expressed the general discontent and frustration, except that he had more intimate insights than most into bureaucratic mismanagement. They had both stopped writing by 1968, but with the changes that began in January they resumed their correspondence. Over the years the paper had received many dispatches from the Socialist countries but none ever pulsated with the enthusiasm that Eleanor Wheeler now exhibited. Her report of May Day in Prague was ecstatic, depicting it as a torrential outpouring of popular support for the new course, a festival of affection between the people and the country's new leaders, Alexander Dubcek, First Secretary of the Communist party, and Ludvik Svoboda, President of the republic.

From the golden city of Prague the correspondence glittered, from Czechoslovakia's Socialist neighbors early rumors were followed by hard reports of somber uneasiness. By mid-July the divergence was formal with the published exchange of sharp letters between the Czechoslovak Communist party and the parties in the Soviet Union and four other Warsaw Treaty countries, Bulgaria, the German Democratic Republic, Hungary, and Poland. (Later I learned that at about the same time, in private advices to other Communist parties the Soviet party was much grimmer and more apprehensive than in the public letter. Indeed, so implicit was the logic of military intervention in the tenor of the Soviet communication that the most influential Western European parties, the French and Italian, each in its own way interceded to head off such a dénouement. They were rebuffed, told this was an internal affair of the Socialist camp. Enduring the resultant suspense in private, their public sigh of relief was the more heartfelt in the first days of August when an apparent agreement was reached between Czechoslovak and Soviet leaders in an emergency meeting at the border town of Cierna and was subsequently co-signed by representatives from the four other Warsaw Treaty states . . .)

As the summer wore on the suggestion of a friend hardened into a personal resolve to go to Czechoslovakia. A climactic event was in the offing, the 14th Congress of the Czechoslovak Communist party, then scheduled for September 9, and this was an appropriate target date; the congress would be the summation and culmination of the extraordinary developments since January, as well as the authoritative mapping and marshaling assembly for Czechoslovak socialism's future course. I made arrangements: a visa, contacts in Prague, collection of a special fund so as not to impose an added strain on the paper's meager financial resources. Drawing on family savings (derived from Nancy's salary as legal secretary, not from mine as *People's World* editor) and throwing in the vacation pay due her it was financially possible for Nancy to join me. We planned to leave right after Labor Day, which fell on September 2 that year. I had never prepared for a journalistic mission with as much anticipation. But I was not prepared for what happened. On August 21 Soviet troops, joined by contingents from the four Warsaw Pact allies, moved into Czechoslovakia . . .

The *People's World* reaction was sharply critical in its coverage and comment. The *Daily World*, successor to the *Worker* and voice of the national Communist center in New York, defended the intervention. This contrast was made possible in part because the United States party, unlike its major Western European counterparts, had evolved no official attitude toward the Czechoslovak developments; indeed, its most authoritative policy-making committees had not even discussed them. Only after the troop movement was the party's national committee summoned to an emergency session on the Labor Day weekend. By a margin of better than five to one that meeting approved a report by Gus Hall, which was an unequivocal, comprehensive argument for the Soviet action as essential to thwart counterrevolution. Two days later Nancy and I left for Europe.

Our first stop was Rome. Here I had made friends and acquaintances in 1966 who might be helpful, I thought, in gaining entrance into Czechoslovakia, for my pre-August 21 visa was an incidental casualty of the military intrusion. We were received courteously and sympathetically at the Czechoslovak Embassy, which had a funereal air; its personnel was undiplomatically candid in expressing distress at the turn of events back home. A query to Prague brought an unsympathetic response. A young embassy secretary told me the gist of it: no visas for Western correspondents in general, for Western Communist correspondents in particular, and no visa for me.

During the days it took to arrive at this diplomatic impasse I talked with an Austrian Communist journalist who advised me to go to Vienna if I could not make it to Prague from Rome. "In Vienna," he said, "many things are possible." With several introductions from him we set out for Vienna, stopping en route at Bologna to attend the national festival for *L'Unita,* the Italian Communist newspaper, which I admired for its professional and political competence.

Huge strips of red with white lettering were splashed against the still lush, late summer green of Montagnola Park, the festival site in the center of this Communist-governed city, bearing such messages as "For a Youthful Socialism Open to New Ideas" and "Unity in Diversity to Reinforce Proletarian Internationalism." On the climactic day 200,000 thronged to the festival, coming by the trainload and in special buses and trucks from all over the region of Emilia Romagna, from Lombardy to the north and Tuscany to the south, from Padova and Verona, from Ferrara and Florence, from dozens of cities and towns, coming in a festive procession of red bandanas, red balloons, red sombrero-shaped hats. On this day there was a parade, an endless stream of red banners flowing through the ancient streets, flowing at one time toward the two twelfth-century towers, graceful relics of feudalism that are the incongruous emblems of red Bologna. The Italian contingents had bodies enough, so this free-lance American marched with a small band of Greek refugees, serving as anchor man for a big streamer that said, "Greek Colonels + USA + NATO = Fascism." The good feeling of the festival was marred by one encounter.

The Rome correspondent for Ceteka, the official Czechoslovak news agency, laughed when I told him I was going to Prague. "You are not going to Prague," he said. "You only think you are going to Prague. The only way you can get into Czechoslovakia now, my friend, is if you have a medical certificate that says you will die if you cannot get to the mineral waters at Karlovy Vary, or if you are a bona-fide businessman with something to sell or buy at the Brno industrial fair."

His heartiness deepened my depression. I was not at death's door, nor on the threshold of any big business deals at Brno, and I had to assume the man knew what he was talking about. Perversely his confidence also chafed my professional pride, I had come all this way, spent all this money, and it would be lame to go back home and say I did not even get to the locale of the story. Doggedly next morning at six A.M. we caught the train for Vienna. If you do not know Italian do not try to catch a six A.M. train out of Bologna. Polylingual people are not about at that hour and the railroad depot is not quite awake; unless your instincts and resources, physical and orientational, are better than mine you will have much trouble running up and down the platform with heavy luggage, trying vainly to find the car assigned to you. Your troubles will be greater if you are an American and say you are going to Vienna (instead of Wien) because this will sound like Venezia to the Italian ear, and before you can establish that it's Vienna you want, not Venice, the train will tremble with the anticipation of forward motion. You will leap aboard the nearest car, ineluctably at the opposite end of the train from the car you want, a fact you will confirm if you are very lucky and find a helpful train crewman. Then, trying to maneuver your luggage through the narrow passageways of hushed and darkened sleeping cars you will stumble over sleeping porters, and although you do not understand what they mutter, you know it is not complimentary. You must also assume that a train stopping at Bologna at six A.M. is prone to make many more stops. It was a slow train to Vienna. I might have relaxed and enjoyed the scenery, specially through the Alps where the passage from Italy into Austria traverses a corner of Yugoslavia, if it were not for my impatience and the laughing assurance of the Ceteka man that my trip was in vain.

By the time the train arrived in Vienna late that evening I was all but convinced that the jovial Czechoslovak pessimist in Bologna was right. It turned out that the Austrian optimist in Rome was the better prophet. In the city of Freud and Strauss many things are possible. The big possibility was the Brno International Trade Fair, that and a telephone call from a staff member of *Volksstimme,* the Austrian Communist newspaper, to an old acquaintance at the Czechoslovak Embassy. The opening of the annual Brno fair, one of the world's major industrial exhibits, originally set for September 8 had been canceled "due to recent events," as a press release put it. But much capital had been invested by many enterprises, in Socialist as well as capitalist countries, to assemble and ship exhibits. Moreover, after Soviet and Czechoslovak representatives signed the "Moscow Protocol," the interim postintervention agreement concluded on August 26, the watchword in Czechoslovakia was "normalization." ("Agreement was reached," said the protocol, "on measures aimed at the quickest normalization of the situation in the Czechoslovak Socialist Republic.") Cancelation of the fair would hardly have harmonized with the image of a country returning to normalcy. Thus political as well as economic considerations dictated the decision that the fair must go on — one week late. It would not be normal to have a world fair without the world press. So special Brno fair visas were issued to journalists. Later in Prague I ran into a correspondent for *L'Humanité,* the French Communist newspaper, who also came in on a Brno fair visa. He did not even bother to stop at Brno. Nancy and I came to the fair.

We came, so did 50,000 other visitors that day, and except for special interest groups they came as people come to fairs, in the spirit of an outing or a holiday, families together, young people in couples or larger bunches, the occasional loners, crowding refreshment stands or looking at wonders of modern technology. A fair-going crowd exudes normalcy, and yet the mood of the country, the politics of it, was discernible.

Buttons with portraits of Dubcek and Svoboda were everywhere, worn particularly by the young (we had seen their names scrawled on walls and fences all through the Moravian countryside on the bus trip from Vienna, and their portraits were all over Brno, sometimes with the legend, "We are with you. Be with us."). In the huge fair building for display of machine tools and farm equipment viewers were conspicuously few at the Soviet exhibit, and there were none at the Polish exhibit where two men in white smocks sat in solitude at a small table, sipping tea and conversing with each other.

Buttons, shunned exhibits, casual conversations at the hotel, begun with a request for directions or some such information — all conveyed two recurrent motifs in the popular temper: a deep feeling of affront and injury to national integrity and a gathering of the people around their leaders. On the latter score Brno bore witness to what President Svoboda said a few days earlier: "We are rightly proud of the unity with which our people stood these days by their leading representatives, by the leadership of the State and the Communist Party of Czechoslovakia."

Arriving in Prague from Brno I tried to telephone a man to whom I had an introduction. A feminine voice in his office said, "He is dead." This telephonic confrontation with death was impersonal; I did not know the man, the voice volunteered no more information and I asked for none. Later I saw a letter this man wrote to a mutual friend shortly before his death. "As you know," he wrote, "I'm generally inclined to be pessimistic but now for the first time I feel a true optimism." The letter was dated August 20. That night the troops moved in. His two teen-aged children were abroad and like many Czechoslovak youngsters similarly situated they were uncertain about returning home. He decided to go to them, to tell them that in this difficult time of their country's history they should come back to be with their people, to share in their destiny. While on this mission he was killed in an automobile accident in France. These details I learned later. The day after my arrival in Prague all I knew about him was what a disembodied voice conveyed over a wire: he is dead.

Simultaneously I ascertained I would not be extended official recognition by the central apparatus of the Czechoslovak Communist party. Lacking the appropriate credentials, I did not expect it, did not ask for it, but just the same was advised I would not get it. Such recognition conferred many perquisites; this I knew from my previous visit to Prague and it was confirmed by dropping in at the party's hotel to scan foreign periodicals and compare notes with Communist correspondents who had official status. The hospitality they enjoyed went beyond lodging and food. They had cars and drivers at their disposal, guides and translators, authoritative phone calls that set up interviews with important personages and opened doors to varied institutions and enterprises, not only in Prague but throughout the republic. Their peers had complained that Czechoslovak Communists were denigrating the leading role of their party in society; chatting with the correspondents I had a wry feeling about that accusation. From their very practical benefits my journalistic colleagues did not doubt that their host exercised preeminent authority within Czechoslovak society.

Bourgeois correspondents, of course, did not receive the same red carpet. But they could compensate for this lack. Compared with me they commanded the advantage of the celebrated difference between the rich and the poor: they had more money. They also had their diplomatic establishments with the services and contacts these provided. I was told the British Embassy, for example, issued an excellent daily digest in English of what appeared in the Czechoslovak press. To a correspondent not knowing the language of a country, such a digest is invaluable. But I would not go to the British Embassy, and certainly not to the United States Embassy; it would have done me little good to say all I went for was a press digest if someone made something sinister out of my visit.

Denied the privileges of both worlds, Communist and capitalist, I was thrown back on my own resources. I got my digest of the Czechoslovak media on the run, a bit here, a bit there, from people I met. For several translating chores I picked up a lad of nineteen who was eager and felt self-important in the role of interpreter but lacked the experience that makes for quickness and precision. Everything had to be done the hard way, which was partly to the good, as my communication with people was more informal and I probably met a greater variety of them. Because much of the operation was haphazard there had to be a more painstaking double-check on facts, impressions, interpretations.

I managed to visit two large industrial enterprises in Prague

tary guests, for the leading organs of the party and the government had not formally repudiated their initial reaction to the intrusion as unsolicited and unwarranted. The country's leaders referred to the Moscow Protocol, which said: "The Allied troops . . . have temporarily entered the territory of Czechoslovakia . . . Agreement was reached on conditions of the withdrawal of these troops . . . depending on the normalization of the situation in the Czechoslovak Socialist Republic." Referring to this proviso the leaders appealed to their people for "normalization," urging them to recognize the military presence as a hard reality, at the same time tacitly holding to their view that it was also an undesirable reality. Many people realized that in the circumstance this position was untenable, that the Soviet Union and its allies could not be reconciled to a continuing Czechoslovak ambiguity about the legitimacy of their action. (A full year was to pass before the Communist central committee formally annulled the position taken by the committee's presidium on August 21.)

The country's leaders were also an anomaly. The military action was a forcible expression of nonconfidence in Dubcek and his associates, the Socialist allies voting overwhelmingly with their troops and armor. And yet, after being spirited away to Moscow in the early morning hours of August 21, Dubcek returned to Prague as leader of the party and the premier political spokesman in the country. Most people understood this could not last, and not just politically sophisticated people. An eighteen-year-old economics student told me with the categorical certainty of youth, "Dubcek will have to go." This young man, like many others of his generation, said he was uninterested in politics before the January reforms, but in the months that followed he developed sufficient interest so that now he spoke with assurance not only about Dubcek's exit but also about his successor. It will be Dr. Gustav Husak, the young man said. Other people were saying it, for the veteran Communist leader from Slovakia had emerged as the credible alternative.

Husak's false arrest in 1951, his unjust imprisonment for nine years, his public identification as a proponent of the post-

January course, his disassociation in the public mind from leaders who were believed to have asked for the troops, endowed him with unique political credentials. After August 21 the line between his position and Dubcek's was more sharply drawn; he laid greater emphasis on "negative tendencies" that had cropped up, although he affirmed "the determining political factor was the healthy core in the post-January developments." An articulate man with a clear, methodical mind, he was a public figure with a history to attract public support, and simultaneously he had defined a political position that invited the confidence of the other Warsaw Pact powers, making him an efficacious instrument for reconciliation with them. By mid-September he was widely regarded as the coming man in Czechoslovakia.

Dubcek's days were numbered, only no one knew the exact number. That he managed to hang on for eight months more until April 1969 attests to the amazing contradictions in the politics of the transition, and certainly at the beginning, in the autumn, the most credible explanation for his survival was the unity of the country behind him.

Life in Prague had an ephemeral quality; people regarded the present as tragic, the future as uncertain. These feelings about present and future, as I encountered them, were universal, shared by people who differed about the past, although about the past, too, there was a preponderant majority sentiment, described by Husak. "The August events," he said, "brought a bitter awakening from the euphoria that existed here." All I could learn confirmed Husak on both counts: the bitterness of the awakening and the euphoria that preceded it. In the subsequent judgment of Husak and his colleagues in the reconstructed Czechoslovak Communist leadership the euphoria blossomed, not in a Socialist dream, but in a nightmare of counterrevolution. This, of course, has been the issue of profound controversy within the world Communist movement and beyond it.

I came to Prague in the aftermath, after the euphoria and the awakening. People who were there during both phases, either as firsthand observers or participants in the events, have written millions of words, reflecting the most varied shades of political opinion. In the brief time I was there, during the tentative beginnings of a still vaguely defined transition, I do not pretend to have obtained reportorial insights and revelations that have not been recorded.

To recapitulate in detail the five-part newspaper series I wrote at the time would be repetitive. To enter into polemics against observations and interpretations that differ from mine would be redundant, for seriously to transcend the familiar arguments would entail the elaboration, the additional research, and critical analysis to make another and different book. I record here my impressions and reactions as essential ingredients of a personal history, and in this context my perception of events may be more conducive to a judgment of me than of the events. I have pored through the notebooks I filled, through the collection of documents and clippings, but memory itself is revealing as a sensitive selector; the most affecting impressions did not require a search of the files. What I remembered most vividly were conversations with older Communists, men and women of my generation with whom I shared a community of language (even through an interpreter) and experience (although the detail of it was vastly different).

There was the Czech who marked off on his life's calendar his three moments of supreme exaltation as a Communist. May 1945: rifle in hand he participated in the anti-Nazi uprising in Prague that was synchronized with the approach of the Soviet army. February 1948: he was with the armed workers who massed in the streets as the guarantors of the Socialist revolution. January-August 1968: to him it seemed like the renascent fulfillment of the hopes that animated him in 1945 and 1948. Another Czech, the worker for the Communist organizational journal who accompanied me on the visit to Prague factories, said with great pride, "For six months we had more democracy than any country on earth." (He was talking about *socialist* democracy.)

One Communist conveyed what he felt by reference to a comrade of his who had fought in Spain, had worked in the anti-Nazi underground, had been imprisoned in Mauthausen concentration camp. This veteran Communist said of the pre-

August period, "Those six months — they are the real meaning
of my life."

To these people it was ineffably tragic that anyone would not
understand that they and the duly constituted Communist
leadership they followed were bent on eliminating deforma-
tions and obstructions that thwarted fulfillment of the Socialist
potential in their country, on recapturing for their party, as the
leading and energizing force in society, the moral and political
authority that had been eroded by repressive and bureaucratic
excesses. To them the expressions, public manifestations, and
groups hostile to socialism, which had surfaced after January,
were minor excrescences with little effect on a profound process
of Socialist renewal, petty irritants that could be coped with
easily by the Socialist regime commanding the instruments of
state power, buttressed by the confidence and allegiance of the
people. What they thought and felt was not atypical, whether
measured tangibly by the alignment in their party or reflected
atmospherically in the euphoria to which Husak referred.

Among Czechoslovaks the complex of political attitudes and
motives was often laced with national feeling, but such national
involvement did not affect foreign Communists on the scene,
and there were many of them, attached to the profusion of
international institutions, either explicitly Communist or initiated by Communists, which had their headquarters in Prague.
Among some of these, as among correspondents and foreigners
employed in Czechoslovak institutions, there was deep empathy with the post-January development, but even among the
most dispassionate, including men whose international outlook
was molded by long years of service in international agencies of
the Communist movement, I found disagreement with the
judgment that a threat of counterrevolution necessitated the
military expedient.

Czechoslovak Communists, who believed arrival of the troops
was necessary, have since said that at the time they were si-
lenced by political blackmail and moral terror. Pejorative
terms aside I can understand that. It would have required extraordinary moral courage to buck the surge of national feeling
that engulfed the country (existence of this feeling is not denied

by anyone, only its meaning and significance are in dispute).
Some weeks after I left Communist opponents of the Dubcek
course began to make their public appearance in Prague.
While I was there they were neither seen nor heard. And I had
no reason to believe that if I succeeded in seeking them out
they would confide to a foreign journalist with my credentials
what they would not openly say to their own people.

What I had then was the Communist testimony I cited and
what I could independently ascertain of the political situation
by interviews with workers, students, intellectuals, and by the
cannibalism of my profession in which journalists feed off each
other. I have argued too many times with journalistic colleagues about the fallacy of pure objectivity to claim it for myself. Undoubtedly prior attitudes and sympathies were also in
the scales when I weighed the testimony of my Communist witnesses in Prague from half a dozen countries, when I honored
the integrity of their commitment to socialism.

I read all the documents then available that justified the August 21 action. I studied them carefully for I believed the Soviet Union and its allies were motivated by the desire to safeguard the interests and security of the Socialist camp, and for
me the paramount necessity of doing that was not in question.
The dilemma was that the reality, as I comprehended it in
Prague, was at variance with the documents I read.

Pre-1956 I would have asked: who the hell are you to pit
your judgment against theirs? This still was a good question,
only now it was truly a question and just to ask it was not to
answer it. The protective and comforting psychological shell of
someone else's infallibility had been shattered and one had to
assume the burden of one's own comprehension, specially in
matters of great moment, vulnerable to the hazards of a fallibil-
ity which was one's own.

I left Prague totally enveloped by the permeative sense of
tragedy I encountered, and by the residual glow evoked among
people I met in their remembrances of what they so fervently
believed was a Socialist renewal in the months after January.

En route home we stopped in Vienna and London. In these
cities I charted a series and wrote the first two installments.

The Austrian and British Communist parties, like the Italian, French, and almost all the Western European parties were critical of the August 21 action. (In the rest of the world the party alignment went the other way.) Conversations with Communists in Vienna and London, as earlier in Rome, meshed with my observations in Prague.

From all those conversations the point that sticks most sharply in my memory was made by an Italian Communist. As Italians are prone to do he quoted Togliatti. The passage was contained in the Yalta memorandum, written at a Crimean vacation resort for presentation to Soviet leaders just before Togliatti's death in August 1964, and published posthumously by the Italian party as "a precise expression" of its position. The military action of the Warsaw allies coincided with the fourth anniversary of Togliatti's death and yet what he wrote at that time, the Italian said, illumines the events that concern us now.

"A fact worrying us, and one we do not succeed in explaining fully," Togliatti wrote, "is the manifestation among the socialist countries of a centrifugal tendency. In this lies an evident and serious danger with which the Soviet comrades should concern themselves. Without doubt there is a revival of nationalism. However, we know that the national sentiment remains a permanent factor in the working class and socialist movement for a long period, also after the conquest of power. Economic progress does not dispel this, it nurtures it. Also in the socialist camp perhaps (I underline this 'perhaps' because many concrete facts are unknown to us) one needs to be on one's guard against the forced exterior uniformity and one must consider that the unity one ought to establish and maintain lies in the diversity and full autonomy of the individual countries."

The Italian thought the Soviet action was prompted not by the threat of imminent counterrevolution but by deeper anxieties about the centrifugal tendency. The problem is real, he emphasized; he did not belabor the contrast between the military expedient and the political lines suggested by Togliatti for coping with the problem.

Aside from this memorable specific point one general concern was paramount in the conversations: how to contain the differences on the Czechoslovak events within a framework of fraternal solidarity in the world Communist movement. In itself complex, the problem was complicated by attendant factors. The Soviet Union, with its great authority and enormous resources for publication and dissemination of printed matter, waged an energetic campaign in Western Europe (and the rest of the world) to win sympathy and support for what it did. Understandable as this was, objectively it encouraged and reinforced an opposition within the several parties to the incumbent leadership. The leaders were obliged to defend their position in intraparty debate and yet do it in such a way as would least exacerbate relations with the Soviet party. At the same time all these parties were also obliged to resist and rebuff the constant pressure from other political quarters and the mass media for a hostile confrontation with the Soviet Union. The axiom of unity in diversity was being put to a severe test. The Italians and British were trying to meet it. The Austrians were too rent by internal division to try much of anything; because of their proximity to Czechoslovakia and their historical ties with it, they suffered the most shattering blow of all on August 21.

Rome, Prague, Vienna, London — and then Santa Monica. True, my airline ticket said San Francisco and I did pause there for a day and a half. But if fate wrote out tickets the destination would have been Santa Monica. I was to speak there on Sunday, October 13, at the twelfth annual banquet for the *People's World* in the Los Angeles area.

I have not had the practice to take all of me across oceans and continents as swiftly as the jet flies. I came to Santa Monica, but my heart was still in Prague and my mind was scattered over Europe, from Rome to London. I had not yet been exposed again to the frenetic undercurrent in American life that cuts across political lines. I had made no effort to ascertain what happened to the temper of American Communists and their close associates, the people who came to *People's World* banquets, in the five weeks I was gone. I had spent the brief time in San Francisco totally insulated, opening mail, adjusting to the time change, and preparing the talk for Santa Monica, which was billed as a report on my trip to Czechoslovakia.

The first installment of my series had just appeared (splashed sensationally by my editorial colleagues), so with respect to the topic of the day the 950 persons who filled the banquet hall at the Miramar Hotel, a faded elegance amid the palms, knew more about me than I did about them. I was immersed in the thoughts, impressions, emotions of my journey. I did not strike the low key of calm reason, did not reach for the carefully formulated phrase of prudent political analysis. I came on strong, talking with passion, trying to transmit mood and atmosphere, to make vivid the euphoria before and the bitter awakening after August 21; mostly the talk was narrative and anecdote, rather than exposition, focusing on significant details of human expectation and response, on those representative expressions of individual consciousness and feeling, which in their sum make up a political canvas. Lesson A, learned in almost forty years of public speaking, was forgotten. I was so preoccupied with what I wanted to say I was oblivious of the audience. Passion begets passion. Toward the very end I wanted to read a quotation. While I fumbled for it among the papers on the lectern the flow of speech stopped. The brief silence was broken by a chorus of boos and scattered heckling. I found the quotation, did not lose my composure, and went on to finish my talk. The audience stood, some to cheer and applaud, others to boo and shout their disapproval. There was no division of the house but if I were chairman I would have ruled the ayes clearly had it. Then a few angry faces came to the speakers' table, voicing hostility, bitterness, indignation.

All of a sudden all of me was back in the U.S.A. I was home again. It was a kind of awakening. My initial reaction to the vocal hostility was shock and disbelief, then came pain and anger. I had been heckled before and in principle I believe there is much to be said for heckling. There is no inherent logic in a rule that says audience reaction must be limited to applause or silence. I have my own ideas about the atmosphere and circumstance in which heckling is useful, but to go into that would not be useful here. I mention these generalizations about heckling only because they entered into my reflections on the Santa Monica incident. Why did I react as I did? It was the quality of the heckling, it was so unexpected in that setting and from that audience with which I had been joined for many years in a common endeavor that fashioned bonds of mutual respect and affection. In my reflections the feeling grew that I had outlived my usefulness as *People's World* editor. To me a prime value of the paper always was its service as a medium of cohesion in its Left constituency and even in times of controversy, irrespective of my opinions on points at issue, I had tried as a rule to retain this cohesive quality. The Santa Monica scene rendered this role dubious.

The doubts about my editorial function were reinforced a month later when Gus Hall and two colleagues from the national Communist center came to San Francisco to meet with a small group of party representatives from California, South and North, and the Pacific Northwest. Hall's castigation of my series on Czechoslovakia embraced its journalistic competence along with its politics. But Czechoslovakia, he said, was only the final straw. Many other things that had appeared in the paper came under his flail. The burden of his indictment was that the paper was waging guerrilla war against party policies in a number of areas. I jotted down a few notes of what he and some others said, but I could not take notes of what I said, and I cannot even begin to reconstruct what it was. Quite likely, if it were not for the notes I would not be able to recall the remarks of others; this could be memory exercising its protective function. No one who has not participated in this sort of meeting can truly understand the unique tensions it generates. Although some strong exceptions were taken to Hall's characterizations and their sweep, to his tone and placement of the problem, the minutes of the meeting would not particularly affect the relationship of what he said to the paper's autonomy and my performance as editor.

I had always recognized the defined limits of the paper's autonomy. The political radius of the paper varied from time to time but one thing remained constant: the center from which

the radius extended to the periphery of the circle was always
the Communist hub. If it ever came to a clash over a fundamental issue between the paper and the Communist hub, at
that point the outer limits of autonomy would be breached.
The same principle applied to my authority as editor. This I
always knew and I never quarreled with it, for this was the
essential nature of the paper. Anyone who accepted the post of
editor without this understanding would have to be either incredibly naive or dishonest. As Hall posed the issue, the critical clash had come and the outer limits of autonomy had been
breached.

In retrospect I should have resigned as editor at that point.
The consideration that deterred me seems ill-advised now.
This consideration was a party convention scheduled for the
spring, only a few months away. During a preconvention period — extending over three or four months — all issues and
policies are open for discussion and debate. Despite Hall's
sweeping condemnation my critical points of difference with
official party policy were those epitomized by the Czechoslovak
events and the responses to them. These points included relations within the world Communist movement, particularly as
they involved the Soviet Union and the Socialist camp, the exercise of autonomy by the individual parties, the qualities of
socialism. Not sanguine about it, still I thought perhaps the
preconvention discussion would afford the opportunity to re-
consider these issues; as it turned out they were submerged between two strong currents. Among older Communists, whose
entire political evolution prompted a visceral response to anything directly concerning the Soviet Union, a preponderant majority had solidified behind the party's official policy. Among
the best of the younger Communists, men and women of the
1960s with a different political history, Czechoslovakia and all
that was a diversionary issue, an attitude shared by some others
in the party active. Foremost among the best were the young
black militants and they said: How come you older people get
more worked up about Czechoslovakia than you do about anything that happens in the ghetto? They were preoccupied with
the difficult and touchy problems of the black liberation

struggle and I would not quarrel with their priorities. By the time of the convention the issues that touched me so deeply were quiescent, the official policies were reaffirmed with only token dissent.

My position as editor was untenable: either I did all the things that had to be done at this post (write, select, display, edit) to project attitudes with which I disagreed, or I pursued, in effect, a course of evasion and opposition. Neither alternative, it seemed to me, was compatible with integrity.

At about this time another irritation of the paper's staff was occasioned by a decision that the paper incorporate a magazine section published by the *Daily World* in New York. The staff was reluctant to include something over which it had little control in a paper for which it was accountable, and this reluctance was aggravated by reservations about the style and content of the magazine. Steve Murdock, political reporter and stand-in editor when I was away, chose the magazine as his point of departure, although he acknowledged in a farewell column that his decision to leave was also influenced by other policy differences. (An old newspaperman, who had worked for Associated Press and several papers before he came to the *People's World,* he said in his farewell, "The fact I can write this column in this vein is, I think, the greatest tribute I can give to this paper for the opportunity it has provided me to practice my profession in singular freedom . . .")

Acquisition of the magazine, which ran cultural features, also meant abandonment of the paper's own two-page spread on culture and entertainment. The magistrate of these precincts, Nancy Scott, left. She had succeeded Alvah Bessie and introduced a quality different from his. Alvah was the critical man for the mass media and what is called the cultural mainstream; her primary critical interest was in the youth culture, the underground culture, the dissident and dissonant cultures that flourished in the San Francisco area. Despite my personal tastes, which were closer to Alvah's, I appreciated the value of the dimension she added to the paper.

Steve, twenty-two years on the paper, was, aside from myself, the last of the editorial staff veterans. After he left for a spell I, who had come on at twenty-three, was a solitary old man of fifty-five presiding over an assembly in its twenties or barely thirty. It was the changing of the generational guard, which can be hastened or even delayed, but not for too long. Now at least there were guardsmen of the new generation to make the change, which would not have been the case only a few years before. My sensibility to the generational dialectic of Ecclesiastes was the greater because by then I had privately submitted my resignation.

"I have serious differences about some very important problems with the national party leadership," I wrote to the appropriate party committee. "These differences are of a nature that make it impossible for me to convey party policy on these issues in any sustained and credible way through the uniquely sensitive post of editor, which entails writing and editing, and places, therefore, a special premium on the element of conviction . . .

"An atmosphere of mutual distrust has developed between national party leaders and myself . . . I am persuaded that the paper and my work are subjected to constant, hostile, suspicious scrutiny, which is coupled with a questioning of motives. The consequence is a destructive pressure, an unseen censorship, which inhibits the kind of vitality that imparts life to journalism. And lifeless journalism has little political value.

"I have been in a leadership post at the *People's World* for more than thirty-one years. I am proud of those years, but they do represent a long, long time. Even in the best of circumstances, after so long a time it is not easy to escape the pitfalls of routinism, to retain some freshness and creative imagination. As noted above the present circumstances are far from the best. To descend to hackdom would be a disservice to the paper, to the party, to myself.

". . . Having been with the paper . . . almost all of my adult life, it ought to be clear that my decision was reached only after the most serious consideration of the factors involved."

It took time to have the resignation considered and formally accepted, and still more time to agree on a successor, a young, black, talented staff member named Carl Bloice. All of it difficult time and finally it, too, passed. Free from the despotism of deadlines, from the frenetic pursuit of salami slices of human events, cut up by the day or by the week, there was time now for a more comprehensive, more contemplative look at the span of my years. I have taken that look, not always content with what I saw, not always certain about it, and yet this retrospection sustained the pride affirmed in a farewell to readers of the *People's World*.

"By this [pride] I do not suggest," I added then, "that the paper's past (and mine with it) was one triumphal procession, a glorious parade in which dazzling successes were followed by brilliant victories.

"No, the principal merit of those years is that they were years . . . of the most profound struggle . . . to supplant an evil and dying social order with one in which man, through collective mastery of his destiny, can realize the human potential made possible by the fruits of human genius and labor.

"By now it ought to be clear that this struggle for the revolutionary transformation of our world is even more complex and difficult, is beset by more pitfalls and marred by more blemishes, than was envisioned by the great thinkers and leaders who originally illuminated its course.

"The main thing is, however, that the paper engaged in this struggle, that it fought so many battles honorably and well for objectives that in the span of history will be mileposts along the road to its ultimate goal, that it ever was animated by the conviction that it represented the best aspirations of man in our time. This, in a profound sense, was true and so it remains."

. . . And so it remains.

Index

Index